TOWARD OREGON 2050

Toward Oregon 2050
Planning a Better Future

EDITED BY MEGAN HORST

Oregon State University Press   Corvallis

Cataloging in publication data is available from the Library of Congress.

ISBN 978-1-962645-16-4 paperback; ISBN 978-1-962645-17-1 ebook

♾ This paper meets the requirements of ANSI/NISO Z39.48-1992 (Permanence of Paper).

© 2024 Megan Horst
All rights reserved.
First published in 2024 by Oregon State University Press
Printed in the United States of America

Oregon State University Press
121 The Valley Library
Corvallis OR 97331-4501
541-737-3166 • fax 541-737-3170
www.osupress.oregonstate.edu

Oregon State University Press in Corvallis, Oregon, is located within the traditional homelands of the Mary's River or Ampinefu Band of Kalapuya. Following the Willamette Valley Treaty of 1855, Kalapuya people were forcibly removed to reservations in Western Oregon. Today, living descendants of these people are a part of the Confederated Tribes of Grand Ronde Community of Oregon (grandronde.org) and the Confederated Tribes of the Siletz Indians (ctsi.nsn.us).

Contents

Foreword vii
BRIAN CAMPBELL, GIL KELLEY, DAVE SIEGEL, & PADDY TILLETT

1 Why Oregon 2050? *Foresight for a Better Future* 1
MEGAN HORST, SY ADLER, & ARTHUR C. NELSON

2 Population: *The Changing Face of Oregon toward 2050* 31
ETHAN SHARYGIN & ARTHUR C. NELSON

PART I. NATURAL ENVIRONMENT 57

3 Climate Change, Environmental Hazards, and Resilience 59
CONNIE P. OZAWA

4 Environmental Quality and Health: *An Overview* 88
DANA HELLMAN & VIVEK SHANDAS

5 Natural Resource Management in Oregon 115
SHANE DAY, TYLER WOLFE, & CARLOS ARIAS

PART II. BUILT ENVIRONMENT 143

6 Housing 145
MATTHEW GEBHARDT

7 Land Use 175
MEGAN HORST & MELIA CHASE

8 Transportation 209
JOHN MACARTHUR

PART III. SOCIAL FOUNDATIONS 241

9 Arts and Culture 243
RICHARD A. CLUCAS

10 Economy, Wages, and Other Economic Factors 275
    EMMA BROPHY & JENNY H. LIU

11 Homelessness. 307
    JACEN GREENE & MARISA A. ZAPATA

12 Reinvesting in Rehabilitation: *Sites of Incarceration,
    Mental Health Care, and Substance Use Disorder Treatment* 339
    MORIAH MCSHARRY MCGRATH & MELIA CHASE

    PART IV. GOVERNANCE 371

13 State Revenue and Spending 373
    PETER HULSEMAN & JENNY H. LIU

14 Voting and Representation 398
    RICHARD A. CLUCAS

    Conclusion 429
    MEGAN HORST

    Contributors 435

    Index. 441

Foreword

Oregon stands out as a livable place with a strong tradition of innovation, public participation in decision-making, and highly intentional planning for its future. Although these attributes go far back in its history, one watershed moment occurred in 1972 with the publication of *The Willamette Valley Choices for the Future*, commissioned by then governor Tom McCall and prepared by landscape architect Lawrence Halprin. This study took stock of trends that indicated substantial growth in the state's most populous areas over the coming decades and posited options for managing that growth in ways that would protect Oregon's treasured landscape, livability, and sense of community while providing the capacity for substantial economic growth and a new and more diverse population. This forward looking study ultimately led to political action, including the passage in 1973 of Senate Bill 100, which ushered the nation's first statewide comprehensive planning system and shaped the growth and character of Oregon over the succeeding decades.

Now, fifty years on, Oregon faces daunting new trends and realities in a dynamic global and local environment unlike any time before. The climate crisis, growing economic disparities, threats to public health, the soaring cost of housing, substantial growth and changes in population, and the accelerating pace of technological and economic change are major challenges to be faced over the coming decades. Oregon clearly needs and deserves another watershed moment in its thoughtful and deliberate shaping of its future. With eyes wide open and hearts and minds engaged, it is time for Oregon to take the next thirty- to fifty-year look ahead to plan—and act—deliberately to realize its desired future. This will unquestionably be a major effort, requiring political, industry, and community champions to carry it through. It will also require the able assistance of technical and subject matter experts to help articulate choices and illuminate the implication of those choices for discussion by communities, interest groups, and leaders across the state. It's an exciting, opportune, and important moment for all Oregonians to once again take stock of the state's traditional strengths of future-casting and articulate how to best go about creating that future.

To be successful, any such undertaking needs a clear sense of current trends and unfolding social, economic, and environmental dynamics, including potential conflicts, tensions, and possible surprises. Such foresight will allow this process to be well informed, meaningful, and implementable, based in both science and the values expressed by participants in the process going forward. As a group of senior professionals in various disciplines and initiators of the Oregon 2050 concept, we approached then governor Kate Brown, who, near the end of her term, asked Portland State University to produce an interdisciplinary foresight report to articulate those likely trends and issues that Oregon will face over the coming decades, to inform the future-making process. This undertaking by PSU faculty, led by Megan Horst, has resulted in *Toward Oregon 2050*, and we are thankful for her tremendous effort and those of all participating faculty.

As this book notes, a foresight report is just that—it is not a specific point forecast nor a prediction. Instead, it is a picture of unfolding and dynamic trends and issues that should be considered in any meaningful strategic planning exercise. Outcomes of these trends and issues can and should be manipulated by thoughtful efforts and consideration of options in the process to follow. Oregonians need not be, nor want to be, passive recipients of forecasted trends; rather, we desire to shape the outcomes we want for our desired future using the lessons learned in this foresight information. With this book in hand, leaders, advocates, and interested parties throughout Oregon can begin to shape the next stages of the process of shaping our future—beginning with articulating future scenarios and choices, engaging as many people as possible in making those choices, and then working with a broad reach of potential implementers to take these choices into action.

This work by Portland State University colleagues will elevate the issues and possibilities and spark the interest among many Oregonians across the state to seize the moment and help determine our desired future.

BRIAN CAMPBELL
Fellow of the American Institute of Certified Planners
GIL KELLEY
Fellow of the American Institute of Certified Planners
DAVE SIEGEL
Fellow of the American Institute of Certified Planners
PADDY TILLETT
Fellow of the American Institute of Architects,
Fellow of the American Institute of Certified Planners

TOWARD OREGON 2050

1
Why Oregon 2050?
Foresight for a Better Future
MEGAN HORST, SY ADLER, AND ARTHUR C. NELSON

How do we plan for a better Oregon in 2050? This is the main question considered by leading urban planning and public administration scholars at Portland State University in this book. The authors seek to (1) tie into Oregon's policy innovation and planning legacy, (2) broaden the concept of planning to go beyond physical space to analyze other social determinants of the quality of life, (3) follow up on the vision of the original Oregon 2050 initiative, and (4) utilize the expertise of Portland State University faculty to develop a trusted vision for how Oregon could become more livable, equitable, and sustainable by 2050.

This book's publication comes as the state planning program reaches fifty years in existence, and thus it serves in some ways as a reflection. Our comments expand into directions not included in 1972, however, and are intended to be more focused on strategic foresight rather than on assessment of past practice. Throughout the book and in many ways, the editors and authors collectively urge that land use planning in Oregon move beyond the current foci of preserving working landscapes and promoting dense development to include deeper, integrated attention to environmental stewardship and the social foundations of a healthy society. Said differently, we push for integrated attention to the natural, built, and social environments as part of democratic and fiscally sound governance.

This edited collection grows out of the broader Oregon 2050 project. The project also intends to engage youth, state legislators, public agency staff, elected officials, community leaders, and leaders of statewide institutions, funders, businesses, and nonprofit organizations on the key issues raised, wicked problems, big ideas, and alternative futures envisioned. This engagement will ideally lead to the development of, and collective support for, specific policy proposals and other actions to bring about a more positive 2050.

We invite readers to envision the future of Oregon with us, and to contribute their ideas toward a better future for the state. We pose to our readers and professional colleagues the same challenge that Lewis Mumford—a proponent of regional planning and ecological stewardship with long-lasting influence on the field of planning and on the subsequent development of the Pacific Northwest—presented to local leaders in 1938 at the Portland City Club.[1] Mumford asked them about their willingness and capacity to protect the region's unique and special environment: "Have you enough intelligence, imagination, and cooperation among you to make the best use of these opportunities?" We pose a similar challenge to Oregon planning leaders today.

Inspirations for the Year 2050

While we use 2050 as an anchor point for our discussions, there is nothing magical about that particular year. One value of thinking that far ahead is that it requires a shift in perspective that we appreciate—a shift beyond the normal planning horizon and the short-term thinking of capitalism, productivity, and so-called progress culture. Planning for thirty years ahead is more akin, though still limited in comparison, to seventh-generation thinking practiced in many Native American traditions.[2] The longer time horizon also enables us to feel less constrained as we imagine what is possible.

As we look ahead, many Oregonians are worried about the future of our state and our communities. In recent surveys by the Oregon Values and Beliefs Center, top concerns by residents across the political spectrum and identities include homelessness, housing affordability, crime and public safety, the economy, environmental issues, and climate change.[3] Many express concern that the State of Oregon is headed in the wrong direction. The authors of this book, informed by deep context expertise, are also concerned. But we refuse to accept that current trends must prevail. Changing course won't be easy, and it will take significant effort to make the needed course corrections. We hope this book contributes to these course corrections.

Another inspiration for this book is the lack of an existing effort by government or another statewide actor for comprehensive foresight regarding the future of Oregon. In response to that vacuum, a group of visionary Oregonians, including members from the Oregon chapters of the American Planning Association, the American Institute of Architects, and the American Society of Landscape Architects, along with key state leaders, initiated in 2014 the Oregon 2050: Healthy, Vibrant, Resilient Project. They proposed a vision and set of goals, principles, and strategies for action at the state, landscape, and community levels. They had the idea (not implemented) that other organizations and individuals would participate in developing the vision, endorse it, and join the Oregon 2050 Alliance to push action, communications, and possible legislative engagement. This effort in some ways follows up on that one, although it takes a different approach.

We see this book as contributing to a shared vision of Oregon, something that is especially important in these times when political, class, racial, geographic and other divides seem insurmountable. We hope our established identities as scholars from state public universities will help readers navigate, in an era of "fake news," a shared reality. A main goal of the book is that readers from across urban, suburban, and rural Oregon as well as from different cultural communities, professions, and political leanings will gain new perspectives on statewide problems. We anticipate potential readers to include state legislators, staff at public-serving organizations and agencies, planners, high school and university students, and anyone interested in the "Oregon experience" or the interdisciplinary effort to engage in strategic foresight.

It is important to clarify what this book is and what it is not. First, this is a book about futures, about planning in a broad sense, and about scenarios—but it is not a scenario planning process. We hope these chapters inform future scenario planning processes, but we do not see the book itself as doing the scenario planning. Instead, we aim to set the stage for future deliberations and decision-making. This book is also not an indicators project. By that we mean this book is not an attempt to report on a set of data points about the state of our state, like Oregon Benchmarks was (more on that later). Our primary focus is on offering our scholarly perspectives in narrative form, using data, on key statewide issues now and looking into the future.

While we often use the word *plan* in this book, we are actually engaging in *foresight*, and it is worthwhile to explain what we mean by the term. The American Planning Association describes *strategic foresight* as "an approach that aims at making sense of the future, understanding drivers of change that are outside of one's control, and preparing for what may lead to success or failure in the future. Applying foresight in cycles creates agility and enhances one's preparedness for disruption before it happens. In today's quickly changing world, it is important for planners to integrate foresight into their work to make their communities more resilient."[4]

More context for our intentional use of foresight comes from *Foresight As a Strategic Long-Term Planning Tool for Developing Countries*, by the United Nations (UN) Development Programme's Global Centre for Public Service Excellence.[5] In it, the authors distinguish foresight (from, e.g., forecasting) because it "cultivates the capacity to anticipate alternative futures and an ability to visualize multiple possible outcomes and their consequences." The authors suggest that foresight thinkers and practitioners are not guessing; they are concerned with developing and testing methodologies that contribute to sound, forward looking decision-making. The authors also note some potential critiques of foresight, including that it is often too theoretical, abstract, and not connected with the short-term needs of policymakers. Critics also warn that futures thinkers bring biases to all phases of generating foresight, from the relevance of information collected (prioritizing recent happenings over older events), to how information is filtered (situational bias), and eventually to the identification of strategies congruent with prevailing mindsets of the time (zeitgeist bias). In this book and the Oregon 2050 project, we are aware of these critiques and at the very least clarify our biases and communicate in a straightforward way without jargon. Even then, foresight is not capable of telling the future, and we remain humble to that limitation. We intend, as encouraged by the UN authors, "to confront people with alternative worldviews and to make them consider possibilities that they would not otherwise think of."

The chapters in this book make use of a range of foresight tools. For example, chapter 2 uses population forecasts, and chapter 7 reflects on a set of three different land use and transportation scenarios. Yet our aim is not to get lost in showing off our technical capabilities. We are inspired by Hopkins and Zapata,[6] who in the book *Engaging the Future: Forecasts, Scenarios, Plans, and Projects* urged planners that "we can and should move beyond the notion of distinct areas of expertise to create forecasts, scenarios, plans, or projects. Instead, we should frame expertise in shaping the future through utilizing forecasts, scenarios, plans, and projects in our efforts to influence others and make choices."

Oregon's Policy Innovation and Planning Legacy: Historical Context

As we write about Oregon, we start by noting that there are some things unique to the state: diverse landscapes, high amount of public lands, and reputation as an environmental and social leader (only partially deserved, as discussed in this book). Another uniquely Oregonian trait is a spirit of policy and planning innovation. Many past Oregon leaders have, over decades, fostered a particular Oregon progressivism that is centered on environmental values and more recently on social equity values. Some historical examples of such include the Beach Bill of 1967, which ensured public access to Oregon's beaches from the first dune to the sea. Another is the Bottle Bill of 1971, which made Oregon the first state in the nation to establish a deposit/refund requirement for glass bottles.

Another focus of this book is Oregon's statewide planning program. It's unique in the country if not the world for its comprehensive approach and consistency among all levels of government statewide. In fact, Oregon is the only state that "forecasts" (though it may be more accurate to say "projects") future populations and attempts to plan to accommodate their housing needs—a fairly basic premise of long-range planning, but one not commonly practiced anywhere else in the United States. The Oregon land use planning program is closely watched by residents and advocates at all points along the political spectrum, and by spatial/environmental/land use planning scholars, practitioners, and students around the world.

State legislators adopted the statewide land use planning program in 1973 by passing Senate Bill 100.[7] An unlikely coalition of farmers, real estate developers, environmentalists, and urbanists, who shared concerns about the negative impacts of unrestrained sprawl, particularly in the Willamette Valley, advocated for the bill.[8] Its chief sponsor, Senator

Hector McPherson, was a Republican farmer from Linn County. Many readers today, in an era marked by political divisiveness, find it remarkable that the bill had strong bipartisan support. In the decade leading up to passage of the bill, development was spilling into Willamette Valley farmlands, home to some of the most fertile soil in the world. According to the Census of Agriculture, between 1964 and 1969, the valley lost nearly half a million acres, or nearly a fifth of its farmland base, to development. Republican Governor Tom McCall famously worried about "sagebrush subdivisions and coastal condo-mania" and warned that "unlimited and unregulated growth leads inexorably to a lowered quality of life."

At the time, Project Foresight was one of many efforts that underscored the need for SB 100. The project gathered state agency staff, elected state officials, commission members, and local elected officials to draft a first phase of a Willamette Valley Environmental Protection Plan, and to refine and sustain a process for resolving intergovernmental, interregional, and interagency conflicts in the Willamette Valley region.[9] Through that process, participants gained a deeper appreciation for the possible role of the state in regulating land use—an appreciation we share today for other motivations.

SB 100 affects all nonfederal and nontribal land in Oregon. It consists of nineteen legally binding statewide goals (five of them apply only to specific parts of the state), as shown in table 1.1. Some scholars characterize the program as a contract.[10] From the beginning, though, it has been a political compromise. For example, developers said they'd support urban growth boundaries (UGBs) and resource land preservation if development within UGBs was made easier than the current process, which often featured opposition by NIMBY (not in my backyard) interests. The bargain included requiring zoning land up-front to meet market needs during the planning horizon (twenty years), thereby reducing much of the need for zone changes. It also included "clear and objective" standards so developers knew what was expected through a kind of checklist. Those were breakthroughs in the late 1970s, followed in the early 1980s by the Land Use Board of Appeals (LUBA)—the nation's only land use appeals tribunal with authority to review and overrule land use decisions made by local governments— and new laws that required local government land use decisions within

Table 1.1. A Summary of Oregon Planning Goals

Goal	Focus	Short Summary
Goal 1	Citizen Involvement	Goal 1 calls for "the opportunity for citizens to be involved in all phases of the planning process." It requires each city and county to have a citizen involvement program containing six components specified in the goal. It also requires local governments to have a committee for citizen involvement (CCI) to monitor and encourage public participation in planning.
Goal 2	Land Use Planning	Goal 2 outlines the basic procedures of Oregon's statewide planning program. It says that land use decisions are to be made in accordance with a comprehensive plan, and that suitable "implementation ordinances" to put the plan's policies into effect must be adopted. It requires that plans be based on "factual information"; that local plans and ordinances be coordinated with those of other jurisdictions and agencies; and that plans be reviewed periodically and amended as needed. Goal 2 also contains standards for taking exceptions to statewide goals. An exception may be taken when a statewide goal cannot or should not be applied to a particular area or situation.
Goal 3	Agricultural Lands	Goal 3 defines "agricultural lands." It then requires counties to inventory such lands and to "preserve and maintain" them through farm zoning. Details on the uses allowed in farm zones are found in ORS Chapter 215 and in Oregon Administrative Rules, Chapter 660, Division 33.
Goal 4	Forest Lands	This goal defines forestlands and requires counties to inventory them and adopt policies and ordinances that will "conserve forest lands for forest uses."
Goal 5	Natural Resources, Scenic and Historic Areas, and Open Spaces	Goal 5 covers more than a dozen natural and cultural resources, such as wildlife habitats and wetlands. It establishes a process for each resource to be inventoried and evaluated. If a resource or site is found to be significant, a local government has three policy choices: preserve the resource, allow proposed uses that conflict with it, or strike a balance between the resource and the uses that would conflict with it.
Goal 6	Air, Water, and Land Resources Quality	This goal requires local comprehensive plans and implementing measures to be consistent with state and federal regulations on matters such as groundwater pollution.
Goal 7	Areas Subject to Natural Hazards	Goal 7 deals with development in places subject to natural hazards such as floods or landslides. It requires that jurisdictions apply "appropriate safeguards" (e.g., floodplain zoning) when planning for development there.

(continued on next page)

Goal	Focus	Short Summary
Goal 8	Recreational Needs	This goal calls for each community to evaluate its areas and facilities for recreation and develop plans to deal with the projected demand for them. It also sets forth detailed standards for expedited siting of destination resorts.
Goal 9	Economic Development	Goal 9 calls for diversification and improvement of the economy. It asks communities to inventory commercial and industrial lands, project future needs for such lands, and plan and zone enough land to meet those needs.
Goal 10	Housing	This goal specifies that each city must plan for and accommodate needed housing types, such as multifamily and manufactured housing. It requires each city to inventory its buildable residential lands, project future needs for such lands, and plan and zone enough buildable land to meet those needs. It also prohibits local plans from discriminating against needed housing types.
Goal 11	Public Facilities and Services	Goal 11 calls for efficient planning of public services such as sewers, water, law enforcement, and fire protection. The goal's central concept is that public services should to be planned in accordance with a community's needs and capacities rather than be forced to respond to development as it occurs.
Goal 12	Transportation	This goal aims to provide "a safe, convenient and economic transportation system." It asks for communities to address the needs of the "transportation disadvantaged."
Goal 13	Energy Conservation	Goal 13 declares that "land and uses developed on the land shall be managed and controlled so as to maximize the conservation of all forms of energy, based upon sound economic principles."
Goal 14	Urbanization	This goal requires cities to estimate future growth and needs for land and then plan and zone enough land to meet those needs. It calls for each city to establish an urban growth boundary (UGB) to "identify and separate urbanizable land from rural land." It specifies seven factors that must be considered in drawing up a UGB. It also lists four criteria to be applied when undeveloped land within a UGB is to be converted to urban uses.
Goal 15	Willamette River Greenway	Goal 15 sets forth procedures for administering the 300 miles of greenway that protects the Willamette River.
Goal 16	Estuarine Resources	This goal requires local governments to classify Oregon's twenty-two major estuaries in four categories: natural, conservation, shallow-draft development, and deep-draft development. It then describes types of land uses and activities that are permissible in those "management units."

Goal	Focus	Short Summary
Goal 17	Coastal Shorelands	This goal defines a planning area bounded by the ocean beaches on the west and the coast highway (State Route 101) on the east. It specifies how certain types of land and resources there are to be managed (major marshes, e.g.) are to be protected. Sites best suited for unique coastal land uses (port facilities, e.g.) are reserved for "water-dependent" or "water-related" uses.
Goal 18	Beaches and Dunes	Goal 18 sets planning standards for development on various types of dunes. It prohibits residential development on beaches and active foredunes but allows some other types of development if they meet key criteria. The goal also deals with dune grading, groundwater drawdown in dunal aquifers, and the breaching of foredunes.
Goal 19	Ocean Resources	Goal 19 aims "to conserve the long-term values, benefits, and natural resources of the nearshore ocean and the continental shelf." It deals with matters such as dumping of dredge spoils and discharging of waste products into the open sea. Goal 19's main requirements are for state agencies rather than cities and counties.

Created by Megan Horst, adapted from figure from the Oregon Department of Land Conservation and Development, accessed January 17, 2024, https://www.oregon.gov/lcd/OP/Documents/goalssummary.pdf

120 days, appeals to LUBA to be resolved within 120 days, and appeals from LUBA to the Court of Appeal to be resolved also within 120 days. On paper, this made Oregon "open for business" inside the UGBs. As this book discusses, the so-called Oregon contract seems to have been somewhat effective in this regard, though in chapter 6 we discuss the current realities of slow development and permitting processes.

While the program has state-level goals, the goals are implemented at the local level. The primary standards are set by the legislature in statute, and the Department of Land Conservation and Development (DLCD) and the Land Conservation and Development Commission (LCDC) enforce these standards. All local comprehensive plans (from the 36 counties and 241 cities and towns) and implementing ordinances must be compliant with applicable statutory and rule requirements (except in cases where federal law supersedes). The planning decisions made by state agencies (e.g., Department of Transportation and Department of Environmental Quality), regional bodies (e.g., the Central Oregon Intergovernmental Council, Metro Regional Government, and the Rogue Valley Council of Governments), and local governments must also be compliant with state guidance (with one exception being the Forest Practices Act). Plans must be informed by data, including population forecasts and housing and economic needs analyses. Altogether, this infrastructure means that planning in Oregon is—at least relative to other states—coordinated.

Notably, statewide land use planning did not fully confront the reality that all land in Oregon was Native-occupied land, stolen or acquired via tremendous pressure from the Native Americans who stewarded it for thousands of years prior. The program only acknowledges tribes and lands that are federally recognized. The land use system does not apply to tribal lands, and tribes do their own planning, though DLCD works as an intermediary between tribes and local governments. As one example of tribal land planning, the Confederated Tribes of the Umatilla Indian Reservation (CTUIR) developed their first comprehensive plan in 1976, shortly after mandated statewide land use planning.[11] They updated the plan in 2010 and again in 2018. Their plan includes similar elements (e.g., economy, energy, community facilities, housing, natural resources, and transportation) and goals that differ from state mandates (e.g., land base restoration, cultural heritage, and treaty right protection). The CTUIR are also currently working to update their land use code, adopted in the 1980s. Unlike most codes and processes, which govern how people conduct development on the land, the tribe's code and process is focused on how to protect land when development occurs. According to their current planning director, this is a seemingly small but ultimately significant difference in land use philosophy than SB 100, which is more about ensuring there is land for development.

There were other long-range planning efforts going on the 1970s in Oregon, such as the Oregon 2000 Commission, established in 1978 by Governor Straub. In 1979, the commission produced the report *Challenges and Costs of Rapid Population Growth*. The forecast for the year 2000 was for one million additional residents compared to 1975. Like today, there were also major changes afoot in the economy and in eastern and western Oregon as people moved to urban regions for better employment. A major difference from today is that at the time, Oregon was a poor state compared to others. Noted as two main themes of unique importance to Oregon were the role of "citizen involvement" and the emphasis on the "natural environment," also salient issues today and central goals in the land use program. Many of the concerns raised, like the environmental and social costs of sprawl, lack of affordable housing, and uneven economic opportunities, sound familiar today. So do the recommendations of the commission, which called for a stronger state role in promoting and regulating growth management tools, creation of affordable housing and alternative housing types, promotion of alternative growth areas outside of the Willamette Valley, and innovative taxation (e.g., regional tax sharing within UGBs). Ultimately, while Governor Straub was not reelected and the commission's work ended, the issues persist. Many of the recommendations are echoed in this book.

More local examples of experimentation with innovative planning in recent decades come from the Metro region and the City of Portland. Metro, the regional government (the only directly elected multi-county government in the United States) for the metropolitan area including Clackamas County, Multnomah County (Portland), and Washington County, was established in a statewide ballot measure in 1979. Historian Carl Abbott identifies two major pressures that led to the vote: the desire for effective regional coordination and comprehensive long-range regional planning, and the desire to deliver regional services like compost, waste, and recycling and to place parks and venues under regional management. Compared to other regional governments, Metro has been successful. It produces regional population and employment forecasts and manages the forecasts with other entities within the region's urban growth boundary. Metro has grown slowly since its inception, with increased planning and service responsibilities as well as new programs like Metropolitan Greenspace.[12]

Oregon's largest city and its major economic hub, Portland, is also unique relative to its counterparts across the country. In the 1970s, its character was exemplified by the city's Downtown Portland Plan, which envisioned a Portland inspired by principles like mixing a diversity of uses and transportation options, such as those advocated by Jane Jacobs (activist and author of the *Death and Life of Great American Cities*).[13] More recently, concepts like complete neighborhoods, racial equity, and climate resilience have become pillars of Portland planning. Portland is an important laboratory for the state and the nation, an economic driver with outsized contributions in terms of tax revenue.

The successes and challenges of the city and Metro also have major influences on the state. Today, fifty years after the adoption of the downtown plan, city leaders are reconsidering the future of downtown. They are confronted with vacant office and retail space, a decrease in foot and other traffic following the COVID-19 pandemic, an exacerbated housing crisis, and a rise in the number of people experiencing homelessness, substance use disorders, and mental health crises. In the context of these challenges, Portland's leaders see opportunities to strengthen the identity of the riverfront and to increase the numbers of residences and other services to make the downtown a more vibrant, safe, and "complete" neighborhood.

Oregon's history with planning is important context as we look to 2050. The land use planning program has survived several political attacks and attempts to weaken the program, but it has survived largely intact. Oregonians across the state and from a range of political and social identities and backgrounds value land use planning. In repeated surveys of state residents by the Oregon Values and Beliefs Center, the majority of state residents considered protecting productive farm- and forestland from development very or somewhat important, and preferred the strategy of directing population growth toward existing cities and towns and away from natural areas and farmlands.[14] But some respondents also placed a high priority on private property rights, a tension that has regularly surfaced in public conversations about the land use system and can sometimes be at odds with the public interest. Even if most Oregonians prefer strong land use planning, powerful interests with minority viewpoints—such as lobbyists for the single-family home construction industry and vocal property rights activists—can have great influence.

Oregon's land use program was endorsed by 57 percent of voters in 1976, 61 percent of voters in 1978, and 55 percent of voters in 1982.[15] In the twenty-first century, however, some aspects have been contested on the premise of economic harms done to landowners. In 2004, 61 percent of voters passed Ballot Measure 37, which required state and local governments to either waive land use regulations or compensate landowners when a regulation reduces a property's fair market value. Measure 37 was subsequently modified by Measure 49, which reduced the number of properties eligible for Measure 37 claims. Nonetheless, a number of Measure 37 and 49 claims have been approved, notably along the I-5 corridor and in central and northeastern Oregon.[16] Despite the land use program's many successes, it also has limits, and as we look to 2050, it will be critical for leaders to both build on its strengths and address its shortcomings.

The Incompleteness of Oregon Progressivism to Date

While Oregon's approach to land use planning reflects the state's progressive identity, there are some limitations to that identity. One is that there is not political consensus about values and approaches. Oregon has many political differences, the most notable perhaps being the so-called urban and rural divide. This rift is increasingly evident in elections, with Portland and other metropolitan regions voting Democratic and the rural areas voting largely Republican. At the root of the divide are cultural and economic differences.[17] There are major disagreements about issues like taxation, the role of government in regulation, and the promotion of private versus public interests. Even while the more urban regions of the state and their Democratic legislators have gained greater control over the legislature, it has not led to greater political consensus (see chap. 14).

Another reality of the limits of Oregon's progressivism is that much of the state's past and current policies have caused, exacerbated, or failed to address racial, class-based, and other inequalities. The land use planning program itself has not explicitly or thoroughly addressed equity—an oversight in the views of this book's authors. Here we briefly discuss this complicated context, and future chapters build on this point.

Oregon is not alone among US states in having a history rife with colonialism and white supremacy, though Walidah Imarisha and other scholars point out that Oregon is unique for having been founded as a white utopia. For at least 14,000 years prior to the 1800s, when European settlers began arriving, numerous Indigenous tribes lived in Oregon. They used both temporary and permanent structures for housing, moving through the region to access food and resources based on seasonal availability. When the Oregon Trail was established in the 1840s, much changed. The settler population in Oregon exploded to nearly 12,000 by 1850. Colonists often laid claim to land without legal title, declaring areas used for communal purposes but not occupied by permanent structures as "unoccupied" and available for settlement.[18] The Donation Land Claim Act of 1850 legalized existing claims and further encouraged settlement. It afforded white settlers and "half-breed Indians" the opportunity to claim and settle 320 acres per individual or 640 acres for married couples and established a system of legal title and private, individual ownership of land—despite the history of communally stewarded land by Indigenous peoples. Negotiated and forced agreements coupled with plagues and violent conflicts with settlers led to most tribes eventually accepting treaties that abrogated their claims to most of the land in the Willamette Valley.

Between 1850 and 1855, approximately 30,000 settlers made their way to Oregon, and 2.5 million acres were redistributed through nearly 7,000 claims. Most settled in the Willamette and Rogue River Valleys, establishing farms and founding many of Oregon's cities, creating a settlement pattern and system of property ownership and rights that continues to shape Oregon today.[19] Most Oregon reservations were dissolved and the land sold, and many Indigenous people moved to urban areas in search of economic opportunity. Today, Portland has the ninth-largest population of urban Indigenous people. The culmination of this history is that Indigenous people of Oregon experience some of the worst outcomes and greatest disparities of any group across all measures, including environmental quality and housing (further discussed in chaps. 4 and 6).

Another part of Oregon's history is that of racial exclusion. As one example, an 1849 Black exclusion law made it illegal for any Black or mixed-race person to "enter into, or reside" in Oregon. The initial 1859 Oregon State Constitution incorporated this ban, excluding free Blacks and mixed-race persons not currently living in the state (at the time, a total of 124) from residing, voting, holding real estate, entering contracts, or using the legal system in Oregon. Chinese immigrants were also banned from holding real estate.[20] The state also rescinded its ratification of the 14th Amendment (which granted citizenship and equal rights to Black Americans) in 1868 (it was not reratified until 1973) and refused to ratify the 15th Amendment (the right to vote for all people) until 1959.

In the mid-to-late 1800s, Oregon experienced an influx of migrants from Mexico and China. Laborers, primarily single men, were brought to Oregon primarily to perform hard labor, including building railroads and working in agriculture and canneries. These migrants were often limited in where they were allowed to live, either in specific neighborhoods within cities, such as Chinatown in Portland, or in rural areas. Starting in 1882, Congress passed a series of Chinese Exclusion Acts/Laws, nearly eliminating new immigration from China.[21] Conversely, Mexican laborers were regularly recruited to come to Oregon to work, particularly in strenuous agricultural jobs that were unable to attract other workers. Some programs, such as the Mexican Farm Labor Program or Bracero Program, recruited large numbers of Mexican agricultural workers to address shortages during World War II. While the program largely ended in 1947, many Mexican farmworkers continued to be recruited to come to Oregon. A large number of these workers were undocumented, faced regular threats of deportation, were unable to utilize public aid programs, and lived in precarious housing situations. Many lived in farmworker housing, which was often overcrowded, poorly constructed, and lacked basic services. More recently, Latino immigration has come from a wider range of countries in Central and South America, with immigrants preferring cities to rural areas. Latinos now represent the largest community of color in Oregon. Many Latinos working in forests, on farms, and in retail experience precarious economic conditions.[22]

Oregon's Black population grew significantly in the 1940s as Black workers were recruited to support World War II production efforts. Most moved to Vanport, a city created in north Portland by Henry Kaiser to support his shipbuilding operations. The city housed nearly 40,000 residents, around 40 percent of them Black. Vanport was built quickly (in 110 days) with poor-quality construction. In 1948, a levy protecting Vanport from the Columbia River collapsed, killing 15 people and leaving the remaining 18,500 residents homeless. For the city's displaced Black residents, the only neighborhood available to them was Albina, which was not large enough to accommodate all people, resulting in overcrowding.[23] Ironically, the overcrowding provided justification for urban renewal projects that cleared large swaths of Albina to allow the construction of Veteran's Memorial Coliseum and the expansion of Emanuel Hospital. Black residents have subsequently experienced the negative impacts of gentrification, including economic displacement to lower-cost parts of the Metro region or outside of Oregon.

These racial inequities are especially important considerations when looking ahead to 2050. Demographers forecast that Oregon's population will, like many other states in the U.S., become more diverse and include a larger percentage of Latino, Black, Asian, and Native American residents (chap. 2). But Oregon's social inequities are not solely racial. While Oregon's economy has been booming in recent years, there is plenty of evidence, from data on income inequities to the visible amount of homeless people on our streets, that the boom is benefitting some far more than others. The chapters in this book elaborate on the relevant history of the structures that perpetuate ongoing racial, class, and other inequalities. Collectively, the authors identify a suite of actions to address some of the gaps in the state's social foundation. Oregon has already been innovating in the areas of racial and social equity in recent years (e.g., in housing policy, discussed in chap. 6), though this book describes some of the additional, sustained, and interdisciplinary actions needed to deeply address the inequities of the past.

Evaluating Oregon's Land Use Program

Over the years, there have been efforts to reflect on the statewide planning program. Scholars have initiated a range of reflections and evaluations. For example, in 1994, Carl Abbot, Deborah Howe, and Sy Adler published the book *Planning the Oregon Way: A Twenty-Year Evaluation*.[24] In that book, a number of practitioners and academics commented on many of the same strengths, limitations, and challenges that this book does. The editors urged Oregonians to continue reflecting and improving upon the program, noting, "The extent to which Oregon can foster a culture of learning will determine the relevance of the statewide planning program as a framework for meeting the needs of the twenty-first century. It is a commendable system and well worth efforts to adjust, refine, and improve."

As we approach the fiftieth anniversary of the program, we have heard and participated in many reflections. State agency staff, advocates and watchdogs, and planners across the state consistently claim as general program successes agency collaboration on goals, commitment to community engagement, and the public prominence of planning-related issues. Some of the measurable indications of success in the built environment include less sprawl and more protected resource lands, a greater mix of transportation mode options and fewer vehicle miles traveled by residents, and a wider range of housing choices is available than in comparable states. These are discussed in the relevant chapters in the book. Meanwhile, commonly identified priority areas include engagement strategies that focus on Oregonians who are typically left out of decision-making, attention to reparations and other concrete efforts to reduce inequities, more actions to address housing crises, and a need to integrate resource land protection with goals like environmental stewardship and community benefits.

While scholars have engaged in reflection, the state itself has only done somewhat limited assessments over the years. For example, Governor Atiyeh appointed a task force to study the statewide land use program in 1981. More recently, the Big Look Task Force, created in 2005 by the Oregon Legislature and Governor Ted Kulongoski, was charged with making recommendations to the 2009 legislature on issues like the effectiveness of the land use planning program, the respective roles and responsibilities of state and local governments, and land use issues specific to areas inside and outside urban growth boundaries. After three years of extensive input from experts and residents across the state, the task force published some recommendations, including that Oregon should respond to regional variations rather than providing "one-size-fits-all" standards; foster greater regional cooperation among cities and counties to resolve land use planning issues collaboratively and efficiently; coordinate planning for land use, economic development, and transportation and clearly articulate desired outcomes; develop systems to monitor progress in achieving those outcomes, along with asking for feedback about what is and what is not working; and simplifying the land use system to remove the complexity that has built up after thirty-five years. In the face of those broad and far-reaching conclusions, however, only minor modifications to the program were implemented.

There also has not been a comprehensive revision or update of the state land use planning program since it was enacted, though there have been ad hoc reforms, voter measures, administrative processes, and legislation.[25] In terms of ballot measures, in 2004 voters sided with private property interests and passed Measure 37, which required state and local governments to either waive land use regulations or compensate landowners when a regulation reduces a property's fair market value. Voters subsequently modified that measure by passing Measure 49, which reduced the number of properties that qualify for regulatory waivers or payment and restricted allowed uses.[26] Some of the other more incremental reforms that the state has made include expanding the allowed uses on exclusive farm use and forest-zoned land and allowing more housing options in residentially zoned areas. In recent years, there have been significant administrative updates. One important one is House Bill 2001, passed in 2019, which made significant changes to residential zoning statewide (chap. 6). Also in 2020, Governor Brown issued Executive Order 20-04, which directed state agencies to reduce climate pollution (chap. 3). These recent changes to the planning program again put Oregon in front of many states as a policy innovator (though it is too early to assess their actual impacts) in statewide planning.

An example of attempted statewide strategic planning—broader than physical planning—is the Oregon Shines State Strategic Plan and associated benchmarks. Oregon Shines was originally written in the late 1980s, as the state was emerging from a deep recession, and was focused mainly on economic initiatives meant to make Oregon "a uniquely wonderful place to live" with "a prosperous economy amid a rewarding quality of life." From 1989 to 2009, the state Progress Board (with members appointed by the governor) measured the state's progress toward goals established in Oregon Shines by using a set of social, economic, and environmental indicators. As time went on, the Progress Board became highly politicized, with disagreement about which indicators (particularly which environmental indicators) to include and the purpose of the indicators. Some legislators expressed concern that the indicator efforts were going beyond simply measuring progress to "social engineering," especially indicators related to social services.[27] After the 2009 report was completed, the state decided not to continue funding the Progress Board. Going forward, some possible lessons learned about politically shared indicators are the need for clear goals, a good leader, culturally conscious communication, discipline with data, and a sense of caution about attempting to drive policy through the context of an indicators project. This book is not an explicit effort to establish indicators, though we do comment on a broad range of data points that we think are useful in reflecting on where we have been and where we are headed.

As we consider the future of Oregon in 2050, it is helpful to note that there has not been a cross-cutting statewide vision or plan since the end of Oregon Shines. In addition to the state land use program, there are examples of specific state departments embarking on long-range planning efforts. For example, the governor's Natural Resources Office and state agencies have established a 100-Year Water Vision for Oregon, which includes an examination of key challenges and the articulation of goals and strategies. Governor Brown subsequently appointed a Water Vision Advisory Board, which is tasked with making recommendations. There is some potential relevance to Oregon 2050, in that both have long-term time frames (though the Water Vision has an even longer time frame, to 2100). Oregon 2050, however, seeks to be intentionally interdisciplinary, and it is not directly tied to electoral politics.

This book focuses on planning at a state level, which we believe merits more attention than it usually receives in the United States. The increased push for state-level planning in the late twentieth and early twenty-first century has mainly subsided, with most of the attention currently on local planning and, to a much lesser degree, regional planning. In terms of past efforts, the Lincoln Institute of Land Policy supported the development of the book *Planning for States and Nation States*,[28] which examined past cases of state and national planning in the United States and Europe.

Other past state-level planning efforts were led by the American Planning Association and focused mainly on the state's role in promoting "smart growth," including the publication of the *Growing Smart Legislative Guidebook* (2004).[29] That involved an effort to draft the next generation of model planning and zoning legislation for the United States. Part of the broader Smart Growth movement, which tried to convince states that fragmented local land use regulation was inadequate to address environmental and social problems, it stopped short of advocating for state-level planning and instead encouraged local innovation. The focus on state-level efforts seems to have waned for now at least, though perhaps future social organizing and federal policy and funding will redirect attention to state efforts.

We also did not find contemporary state-level foresight or visioning efforts as relevant models or inspirations. Perhaps the closest is Florida 2070, a scenario comparison exercise (rather than a foresight exercise) and joint project of the Florida Department of Agriculture and Consumer Services, University of Florida Geoplan Center, and 1000 Friends of Florida. It looks ahead to 2070, when the state is expected to have 15 million additional residents, or a population of nearly 34 million (and a much higher population and growth rate than Oregon). Florida 2070 examines three alternative land use scenarios to accommodate these new residents, along with their impacts on resource lands, water consumption, and more. Florida 2070, and its accompanying project Water 2070, is a land use scenario exercise and influences the discussion in chapter 7. It is not an attempted comprehensive foresight effort, however.

Environ Utah's Your Utah, Your Future project is another case that is not quite a model for this effort. Five scenarios were built based on input from experts and a survey of 53,000 Utahns to identify common concerns and shared preferences among the scenarios. Over half of Utah residents preferred one of the five scenarios, called "Quaking Aspen," which called for strong state investment and strategic prioritization in a suite of areas. The resulting statewide vision includes four key strategies: a network of quality communities; homes, buildings, landscaping, and cars of the future; a thriving rural Utah; and people prepared for the future. The organization Environ Utah does not have sufficient authority to implement the vision alone, but it hopes to make the vision a reality with the involvement of hundreds of stakeholders and thousands of residents. Considering the dearth of models, we consider the Oregon 2050 project as an effort at innovation, more than the continuation of something tried and true.

Utilizing the Expertise of Portland State University Scholars

This book's primary authors are leading scholars across a range of disciplines from the community-engaged, urban-serving Portland State University (PSU) and specifically from the College of Urban and Public Affairs. This book focuses on topics that have connections to the built environment and are traditionally addressed by planning in Oregon, such as transportation, environment, and land use. There also are chapters on topics not fully addressed by Oregon's planning practices (though of increasing attention by planning practice and scholarship more broadly), such as arts and culture and incarceration and rehabilitation. The topics were chosen for their salience today and tomorrow, their connection to environmental stewardship and social equity, and because we, scholars within PSU's College of Urban and Public Affairs, have expertise on them. Our list of chosen topics is non-exhaustive, as any book necessarily is. For example, it does not include education or health care, which arguably fall in the domain of social public policy rather than built environment issues and long-range planning.

The main authors are based in Portland, and we recognize this as a possible limitation in the context of a state with a significant urban-rural as well as political divide. We made efforts to overcome this limitation by involving community partners and experts from across the state and from various political perspectives, including elected officials, public employees from various levels of government, leaders of community-based and nonprofit organizations, and those of various political perspectives as thought partners and reviewers. Notably, all of the authors are involved, in one way or another, on issues that transcend Portland and that are experienced across Oregon.

One of the goals of this book and the broader Oregon 2050 project is to get people out of their siloes or their "spheres of excellence" and think about the interconnections among topics and the entirety of the future, not just in one specific domain. There is no one right way to organize a book that is intentionally trying to be interdisciplinary, and we recognize that topical boundaries frequently change. We organized the book in a way that would be accessible to most readers and to build interdisciplinary connections, for example, among housing, land use, and transportation. Another aspect of a book with chapters written from different academic and disciplinary perspectives is that each author draws on their own theoretical and professional training to a degree, and each has their own writing style. While this means a little less consistency at times, we see the multidisciplinarity as a strength of the book.

This book is mainly a practical exercise in foresight, drawing on our collective, deep academic knowledge. To that end, we do not delve into theoretical discussions or comparisons of different values bases and approaches. One general inspiration for our shared approach, which includes a broad range of environmental and social issues, comes from a visual framework for the concept of just and sustainable development. The framework—called the doughnut model for the shape of the visual—was developed by University of Oxford economist Kate Raworth,[30] though we see her ideas as drawing on conceptions of sustainability by Native and Indigenous thinkers and practitioners, among others. The model proposes that at any scale, from household up to global, as we engage in foresight, we should be aiming to stay within our ecological boundaries or ecological ceiling and to strengthen and address gaps in the social foundations. Figure 1.1 is a visual of the model.

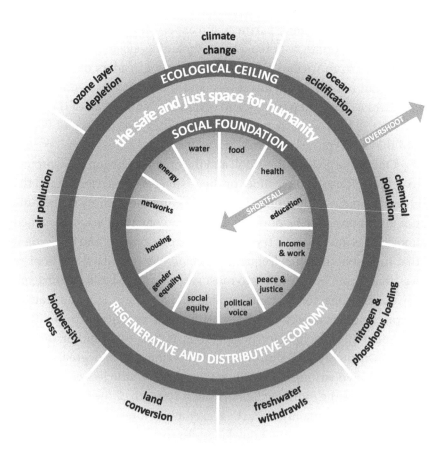

Figure 1.1. The doughnut economic model. *Source*: Doughnut Economics Action Lab, https://doughnuteconomics.org/tools/50

We do not address all of the doughnut model's topics, but we similarly think about aiming for a state in 2050 that has balance, without environmental overshoot or major gaps in social foundations. The chapters collectively discuss shortcomings in Oregon's current social foundations, like inequities in housing, jobs, and income, and areas of ecological overshoot, like in biodiversity loss, climate change, and unhealthy environments. Cumulatively, we suggest a key point: our approach to statewide planning, based mainly on preserving working lands and encouraging population growth in cities, has had some positive environmental and social impacts. We should be proud of and continue this uniquely Oregon program. The approach is necessary but insufficient, however. As we look to 2050, there is a need for more holistic, deeper attention to ecological stewardship to reduce our overshoot, especially as we try to halt and adapt to the worst of human-caused climate change and accommodate a growing population. It is also time to focus more attention on the social foundations of our state—to more secure housing, income, and mental health care for Oregonians of all socioeconomic and racial/ethnic backgrounds.

About the Book: Preview of the Chapters

In chapter 2, Ethan Sharygin, the director of the Population Research Center at PSU, identifies some of the major trends in Oregon's population that inform what other authors go on to address in subsequent chapters. One important highlight is that Oregon is expected to grow to about 5.4 million residents by 2050 (up from about 4.2 million in 2021). Other important trends include an increasing population of older people, declining household size, and increasing percentages of racial and ethnic minorities. Each of the subsequent chapters uses these forecasts as a key consideration when offering foresight to 2050. For example, as the authors engage in foresight about natural resources, housing, and land use in Oregon in 2050, they grapple with who is likely to live here; what kinds of housing they will need, prefer, and can afford; how they will get around in terms of regular activities; and how to meet those housing and transportation needs while stewarding natural resources and advancing social equity.

The remaining chapters each focus on a specific topic or issue area. Each chapter addresses a similar set of points, including: contextualization of the issue, including a reflection on statewide governance regarding the land use planning program; history and factors that make Oregon unique or similar to other states; identification of key bright spots and concerns as related to broader values of ecological stewardship and social foundations; a look at differences and similarities across regions, counties, and urban, suburban, and rural communities; and anticipation of likely and possible futures. In their discussion, authors discuss the wicked problems (problems that lack simple solutions)[31] at the root of each issue. The chapters culminate with authors recommending both practical actions and big ideas, aimed at addressing the roots of problems and producing a state that has balance, without environmental overshoot or major gaps in social foundations, in 2050. The big ideas are intended to bring both the head (research-based interventions) and heart (values) to the forefront and to be a political stretch, but they will be viable as a continuation of Oregon's past as a policy innovator. The chapters are organized into four parts: part I, Natural Environment; part II, Built Environment; part III, Social Foundations; and part IV, Governance.

Part I: Natural Environment

Chapter 3, "Climate Change, Environmental Hazards, and Resilience," by Connie P. Ozawa, discusses the risks posed to Oregon communities by two significant hazards: climate change and earthquakes. She reviews what is being done today across the state and local levels in preparation. Then, Ozawa presents key elements to consider regarding the concepts of risk, resilience, vulnerability, and equity. The chapter concludes by discussing potential pathways to best position the state for the future with regard to hazards, including drawing on lessons learned from the COVID-19 pandemic.

In chapter 4, "Environmental Quality and Health: An Overview," Dana Hellman and Vivek Shandas consider how to advance statewide environmental planning efforts. They review the relationship between environmental health and quality and summarize available statewide data and trends. Using three case studies from across the state, they illustrate shortcomings in environmental health data and understanding. Finally, they argue for improvements in data collection and analysis, community engagement and planning efforts, and regulation of polluters.

Chapter 5, "Natural Resource Management in Oregon," by Shane Day, Tyler Wolfe, and Carlos Arias, highlights various trends in some of the more politically salient natural resource "stocks of concern" to Oregonians, including forestry, protected lands, species health and diversity, renewable resources, and water issues. The chapter concludes with ideas for better stewardship of our natural resources, such as expanding payment for ecosystem services and aiming for ambitious 100 percent renewable energy goals.

Part II: Built Environment

In chapter 6, "Housing," Matthew Gebhardt discusses a topic of top concern. Despite statewide policies that have resulted in more diverse housing types than in most other states, and recent interventions at state and local levels aimed at increasing supply, many aspects of housing in Oregon—home prices, homelessness, and overall housing supply— have worsened in recent years, especially during the pandemic. The benefits and burdens are inequitably distributed: some homeowners profit while renters, households of color, and low-income households experience harm. Gebhardt identifies some big ideas, like confronting racism, a statewide rental housing registration system, increasing shared-equity and shared-ownership housing options, and massively expanding state participation in housing markets and development.

Megan Horst and Melia Chase in chapter 7, "Land Use," discuss the positive impacts and limits of Oregon's land use program. The program has had remarkable success in preserving farmland and reducing the amount of sprawling development. But it is not comprehensive enough to address some of the structural inequities and problems in the broader systems of capitalist land markets and racist policies and actions, private land ownership, and resource exploitation. The authors explore the likely impacts of three different land use futures, including sprawl, business as usual, and smart growth. The chapter concludes with big ideas about how to address social and racial equity, communal over individual or corporate-owned benefits, and include fiscal responsibility as a long-term land use planning goal.

In chapter 8, "Transportation," John MacArthur of the Transportation Research and Education Center discusses some of the main statewide transportation issues, including the status of transportation infrastructure like roads and bridges, state funding for transit, and rates per capita of driving compared to other modes like transit, walking, and biking. He reflects on some of the connections with land use, housing, and climate change. The chapter concludes with some big ideas for a more environmentally sustainable and equitable twenty-first-century transportation system for Oregon.

Part III: Social Foundations

Chapter 9, "Arts and Culture," by Richard A. Clucas, discusses how the arts have come to define the state and makes the case that the arts amount of attention as has been given to other innovative policy domains in Oregon. The chapter is divided into five parts. The first section provides a definition of terms and some additional explanation of the material covered in the report. The second provides an overview of why the arts matter. The third and fourth sections provide a brief history of the state's cultural policies and a snapshot of the state of the arts in Oregon today, respectively. The final section offers some thoughts on planning for the future of arts and culture in the state.

Chapter 10, "Economy, Wages, and Other Economic Factors," by economists Emma Brophy and Jenny H. Liu from the Northwest Economic Research Center, starts with a broad look at the state economy and then focuses on the differing economic realities for disadvantaged groups within the state. It also explores the impact of the recent COVID-19 pandemic. The chapter concludes with some ideas for addressing the wicked problems of inequities, including universal income, negative income tax, access programs, safety net programs, and tax reform.

Chapter 11, "Homelessness," by Jacen Greene and Marisa A. Zapata from the Homelessness Research and Action Collaborative, examines statewide trends and patterns by different classifications of homelessness. They look at inequities in who is experiencing homelessness and the root causes of the recent rising rates, as well as the myriad negative impacts. They reflect on the current response and offer big ideas for a more coordinated statewide response.

Moriah McSharry McGrath and Melia Chase discuss some alarming trends in Oregon's levels of incarceration and addiction in chapter 12, "Reinvesting in Rehabilitation: Sites of Incarceration, Mental Health Care, and Substance Use Disorder Treatment." They describe some wicked problems, including rapid deinstitutionalization without the creation of a community-based mental health system, the view of prisons as economic development tools, workforce issues, lack of public support, challenges with reentry, and the lack of shared political will for restorative approaches. Finally, the chapter concludes with big ideas to help Oregon become a place where wealth is no longer a predictor of incarceration, people can access care, rural residents have economic opportunities, and smart "decarceration" continues.

Part IV: Governance

In chapter 13, "State Revenue and Spending," economists Peter Hulseman and Jenny H. Liu from the Northwest Economic Research Center examine the state government's financial system, looking first at the state's sources of revenue and then the state budget. In seeking to improve Oregon's government by 2050, policymakers and the public have to hold a serious conversation on what can be done to adequately fund programs and reduce the deep swings in revenue from year to year.

Richard A. Clucas in chapter 14, "Voting and Representation," discusses some aspects of the state's political history and culture that may affect the state's ability to address current problems and improve the performance of Oregon's government by 2050. He also examines the ability of Oregonians to have a voice in policymaking.

Altogether, the chapters in *Toward Oregon 2050* document the successes and shortcomings of programs in place—with the consistent focus of reflection on the statewide and use planning program. They also identify the kinds of initiatives that might be developed to shape a warmer, more welcoming state to benefit its urban and rural populations, industries, and ecological health. As examples of recent progress, the authors identify enhanced protection of natural resources, the cleaning up of toxic communities, high voter participation, and increased involvement in arts and culture. Authors also describe some of Oregon's strengths as a policy innovator, for example, in funding and using trustworthy population projections to plan for housing, and in accommodating population growth in urban areas without the extent of land-extensive suburban expansion seen in other states. The chapters also illuminate that all parts of the state face interconnected challenges, including the lack of affordable housing, increased need for mental health and substance abuse services, and threats posed by climate change.

This book envisions the various possible futures of Oregon in 2050. Some of those futures, with worsening effects of climate change, environmental harms, and social inequities, are not bright for many Oregonians. We also imagine other futures, such as those with enhanced resiliency after forest fires and flooding, more Oregonians in high-paying jobs and in secure housing, and more children walking and biking to school. But those positive futures are not guaranteed, and getting there won't be easy. In this book, we offer honest and unflinching assessments and big ideas for a better Oregon in 2050. We believe that all actors—state and local government, members of all political parties, private businesses, nonprofit organizations, and individual residents—have responsibilities and roles to play in leaving our state better for future generations.

Notes

In the spirit of trying to represent all of Oregon, bringing many perspectives into this book, the authors solicited the participation of people from across the state, with their own angles of expertise, to serve as community reviewers. The reviewers shared ideas on data sources, offered differing perspectives, gave constructive feedback, and served as a reality check and encouraged visionary thinking, not just critique. The authors are grateful to all of the community reviewers for their contributions to this effort.

Thank you to Ethan Seltzer (retired Portland State University professor), who contributed to this chapter. Thank you to Sadie Carney, Joshua Lehner, and Gerard Sandoval, who each offered constructive feedback on a draft of the whole book. Other reviewers are acknowledged at the end of each chapter as relevant.

1. Stephyn Quirke, "Lewis Mumford's legacy in Portland," *Southeast Examiner*, January 1, 2016, www.southeastexaminer.com/2016/01/lewis-mumfords-legacy-in-portland.
2. Robin Wall Kimmerer, *Braiding Sweetgrass: Indigenous Wisdom, Scientific Knowledge and the Teachings of Plants* (Minneapolis: Milkweed Editions, 2013).
3. "Concerns about the Future and the Most Important Issue," Oregon Values and Beliefs Center, January 4, 2022, oregonvbc.org/future-and-most-important-issue.
4. Petra Hurtado, "Planning with Foresight," *PAS QuickNotes* 94 (July 2021): www.planning.org/publications/document/9217988.
5. United Nations Development Program, *Foresight as a Strategic Long-Term Planning Tool for Developing Countries* (Singapore: Global Centre for Public

Service Excellence, 2014), www.undp.org/publications/foresight-strategic-long-term-planning-tool-developing-countries.
6. Marisa A. Zapata and Lewis D. Hopkins, eds., *Engaging the Future: Forecasts, Scenarios, Plans, and Projects* (Cambridge, MA: Lincoln Institute of Land Policy and New York: Columbia University Press, 2007).
7. "People and the Land: An Oral History of Oregon's Statewide Land Use Planning Program," PDXScholar, Portland State University, accessed March 27, 2023, pdxscholar.library.pdx.edu/planoregon_interviews.
8. Sy Adler, *Oregon Plans: The Making of an Unquiet Land Use Revolution* (Corvallis: Oregon State University Press, 2016).
9. "Project 'Foresight': First Phase," *Portland Regional Planning History* 22 (1971): pdxscholar.library.pdx.edu/oscdl_planning/22; "40 Years of Planning in Oregon," *Oregon Planner's Journal* (June 2013): 13, www.oregonapa.org/wp-content/uploads/2014/09/17221_2.2013MayJuneOPJ.pdf.
10. Adler, *Oregon Plans: The Making of an Unquiet Land Use Revolution* (Corvallis: Oregon State University Press, 2016 (2012).
11. J. D. Tovey, "Tribal Planning," presentation to the Oregon Chapter of the American Planning Association, 2019.
12. Carl Abbott and Margery Post Abbott, "A History of Metro," *Urban Studies and Planning Faculty Publications and Presentations* 109 (1991): pdxscholar.library.pdx.edu/usp_fac/109.
13. Portland Bureau of Transportation, *Elements of Vitality: Results of the Downtown Plan* (Portland, OR: Portland Bureau of Transportation, 1995).
14. "Oregon Department of Transportation: 2006 Transportation Plan Survey," Oregon Values and Beliefs Center, accessed February 28, 2024, https://oregonvbc.org/study-topic/community-planning/. Note the survey is among the most comprehensive attempts to understand the values of Oregonians, but it has limits. According to the project itself, "the goal is not to offer an ultimate statement of Oregon values but rather a baseline of information from which to draw inferences and a platform for more detail as circumstances permit."
15. John Ame, "History of Land Use Planning," Oregon Explorer, accessed December 14, 2023, oregonexplorer.info/content/history-land-use-planning?topic=4123&ptopic=62.
16. "Measure 49 Analyzer," Oregon Explorer, accessed December 14, 2023, tools.oregonexplorer.info/OE_HtmlViewer/Index.html?viewer=m49.
17. Michael Hibbard, Ethan Seltzer, Bruce Weber, and Beth Emshoff, eds., *Toward One Oregon: Rural-Urban Interdependence and the Evolution of a State* (Corvallis: Oregon State University Press, 2011).
18. Kenneth R. Coleman, "'We'll All Start Even': White Egalitarianism and the Oregon Donation Land Claim Act," *Oregon Historical Quarterly* 120, no. 4 (Winter 2019): 414-37.
19. William G. Robbins, *Landscapes of Promise: The Oregon Story, 1800-1940* (Seattle: University of Washington Press, 1997).
20. Philip Thoennes and Jack Landau, "Constitutionalizing Racism: George H. Williams's Appeal for a White Utopia," *Oregon Historical Quarterly* 120, no. 4 (Winter 2019): 414-37.
21. Douglas Lee, "Chinese Americans in Oregon," Oregon Encyclopedia, updated September 21, 2022, www.oregonencyclopedia.org/articles/chinese_americans_in_oregon/#.YkWgk-hBzIV.
22. Mario Jimenez Sifuentez, *Of Forests and Fields: Mexican Labor in the Pacific Northwest* (New Brunswick, NJ: Rutgers University Press, 2016).

23 Karen J. Gibson, "Bleeding Albina: A History of Community Disinvestment, 1940–2000," *Transforming Anthropology* 15, no. 1 (2007): 3-25.
24 Carl Abbott, Deborah A. Howe, and Sy Adler, eds., *Planning the Oregon Way: A Twenty-Year Evaluation* (Corvallis: Oregon State University Press, 1994).
25 Oregon Task Force on Land Use Planning, *Final Report to the 2009 Oregon Legislature* (Portland: Oregon Task Force on Land Use Planning, January 2009), www.oregon.gov/lcd/OP/Documents/Big_Look_Report.pdf.
26 "Measure 49 Analyzer."
27 Karmen Fore, personal communication, November 12, 2019.
28 Gerrit-Jan Knaap, Zorica Nedović-Budić, and Armando Carbonell, eds., *Planning for States and Nation-States in the US and Europe* (Cambridge, MA: Lincoln Institute of Land Policy and New York: Columbia University Press, 2015).
29 Stuart Meck, *Growing Smart Legislative Guidebook: Model Statutes for Planning and the Management of Change* (Chicago: American Planning Association, 2002).
30 Kate Raworth, *Doughnut Economics: Seven Ways to Think Like a 21st-Century Economist* (New York: Random House, 2017).
31 Horst W. Rittel and Melvin M. Webber, "Wicked Problems," *Man-Made Futures* 26, no. 1 (1974): 272-80.

2
Population
The Changing Face of Oregon toward 2050
ETHAN SHARYGIN AND ARTHUR C. NELSON

The Population Research Center (PRC) at Portland State University projects that Oregon will grow to 5.2 million residents in 2050, or 1 million more than in 2020. Occupying 400,000 additional households, these new Oregonians will be more socially diverse than ever, with record-high numbers of people 65 years of age and older, and unprecedented racial and ethnic diversity. They will have different housing needs going forward to 2050, as demand for smaller homes on smaller lots and attached homes in walkable communities will eclipse demand for large homes on large lots. Nonetheless, despite growth combined with what will likely be monumental technological changes to come, we expect that Oregonians will live in a social, economic, political, and demographic world not so far removed from today.

This chapter tells the story of Oregon's future based on forecasts. To be sure, the future is a mixture of trends—things that are foreseeable but hard to shape—along with alternative scenarios—things that are difficult to foresee but malleable. Thinking about the futures that are best for Oregon is a strategy that has served the state well since the statewide land use planning program, Senate Bill 100 (SB 100), was adopted. The challenge is to envision a future that advances the well-being of the next 1 million Oregonians.

First, a look back. What a difference half a century makes! In 1970, just a few years before SB 100 was signed into law (in 1973), Oregon was home to about 2.1 million people. Its population doubled to 4.2 million in 2020, averaging more than 400,000 new residents each decade. Oregon's growth is expected to continue, reaching about 5.4 million

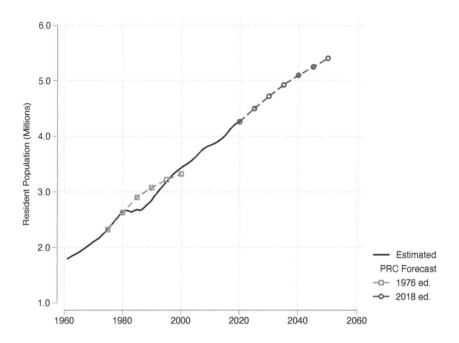

Figure 2.1. Oregon's total population estimates and forecasts, 1960-2060. PRC, Population Research Center.

by 2050 (fig. 2.1).[1] When SB 100 was adopted, Oregon was among the least diverse states in terms of race and ethnicity, with nearly 97 percent of residents identifying as white. Yet nearly all new growth from 2020 forward to 2050 will occur among what has been called the "New Majority," composed of persons of color or Hispanic ethnicity.[2]

In four sections, this chapter focuses on how Oregon's demographic profile has changed from 1970 and is likely to evolve by 2050. The first section summarizes what Oregon does better than any other state: forecast population and require coordinated local, regional, and state planning to meet forecasted needs. The next section offers the big picture of how Oregon's population has grown and changed since the 1960s. Forecasts show that the white non-Hispanic population will decline by 2050. The third section focuses on implications of an aging population and growing income disparities, with special reference to housing (see also chap. 6). The chapter concludes with our worry that without immediate policy interventions to reduce income disparities by race and increase wealth among lower-economic households, Oregon may be headed for decades of declining economic and social well-being with attendant political instability. Adding to this dynamic is the aging of baby boomers, which we posit could further compound economic and social inequality and may fuel political instability. Many of these concerns are echoed in the chapters on housing (chap. 6), homelessness (chap. 10), and employment, wages, and other economic concerns (chap. 11).

Forecasts as a Foundation of Oregon's Planning

Chapter 1 provides the overall context for Oregon's statewide land use planning program. But first a word about what Oregon does that no other state does as rigorously: forecast growth and change, and integrate those forecasts into local housing needs analyses (HNAs).

Planning is all about making desired futures happen. Without planning, billions of dollars in infrastructure investments may be misallocated, leading to over- and underserved areas. Without planning, landscapes important for economic and environmental sustainability could be lost. Without planning, issues related to housing, employment, and social changes may go unaddressed, with the consequence of jobs and housing misallocations with attendant economic inefficiencies that rob the economy and people of stability and even income. Oregon is unique in the nation in requiring plans that meet the needs of a growing population, expand the economy, and preserve or enhance land resources. These and other statewide planning goals were codified after the passage of SB 100 (1973). Chapter 7, on land use, reviews the key statewide planning goals in greater detail. Here we summarize the kinds of forecasts Oregon requires and their role in the Oregon land use and growth management program.

As reviewed in chapter 1, Oregon's planning system is driven by nineteen statewide goals. Goal 14 addresses urbanization, which in turn guides nearly all of the state's development patterns. That goal requires all planning jurisdictions to contain urban development within urban growth boundaries (UGBs) based on long-range (twenty-year) forecasts of population and housing (detailed in Goal 10, housing) and employment (detailed in Goal 9, economic development). It also requires a determination of the need for public infrastructure, which is addressed in more detail in Goals 11 (public facilities and services) and 12 (transportation). While many states require forecasts, Oregon arguably imposes the strongest mandates for the use of forecasts to guide planning and public infrastructure investment. To ensure consistency in methodologies and objectivity in their use, the state designated the Population Research Center, based at Portland State University, as the official source for forecasts. We rely on those forecasts in this chapter.

The Big Picture: How the Face of Oregon Has Changed since SB 100

In this section, we trace how Oregon's population has changed from the decade before SB 100, through decades of planning transition to maturity, and how it might further change approaching 2050.

- Before SB 100: The 1960s were a time of social and economic turbulence in America. As noted in chapter 1, Oregonians at the time were also concerned about rapid growth occurring especially in a narrow band of land that also happens to be the state's most productive farmland, the Willamette Valley. We will add to that context by showing the nature of the growth pressures during the 1960s.
- Transition Planning: SB 100 required all general-purpose local governments to make plans consistent with statewide planning goals, and once deemed such, they were to be approved by the state Land Conservation and Development Commission (LCDC). This process lasted into the mid-1980s. We thus report how the state's demographics changed during the "transition planning" decades of the 1970s and 1980s.
- Mature Planning: This period extends from 1990 to 2020, during which time the entire state was implementing land use plans to achieve state and local goals. This was also a period of continued refinement of planning rules and procedures, several statewide ballot measures, court cases, and legislative attempts to roll back elements of SB 100.
- Oregon toward 2050: Whether the "mature planning" period is sustained in Oregon toward 2050 or a new epoch emerges is unknown. Chapter 1 calls for a new epoch focusing on people-centric planning, a theme echoed especially in the chapters on housing

(chap. 6), homelessness (chap. 11), and employment (chap. 12). Lacking legislative guidance to frame such a new planning epoch in Oregon, one could assume that the mature planning epoch continues. Whether it does or not, we assign a separate epoch to the future of Oregon toward 2050.

Because of the vast differences in geography and growth, for purposes of discussion, we divide the state into nine regions: five are west of the Cascade divide, and the other four lie east of it (fig. 2.2).[3]

Tables 2.1A and 2.1B report total and New Majority population trends across the epochs and forecast them for 2050. Our analysis shows that metropolitan Portland and the Willamette Valley clearly dominated growth during the 1960s, accounting for nearly 90 percent of the state's population change. Its share fell substantially during the Transition Planning period to about 70 percent of the state's growth before rising to account for about 75 percent of the state's growth between 1990 and 2020, the epoch during which statewide planning had matured.

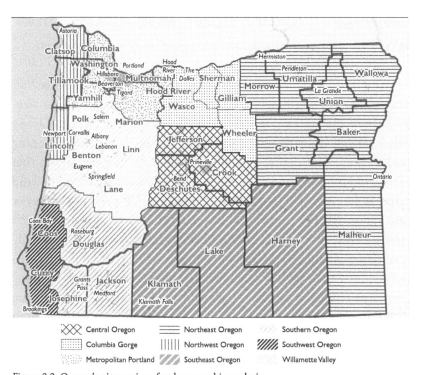

Figure 2.2. Oregon's nine regions for demographic analysis.

Table 2.1A. Past, Present, and Future Population in Oregon

Region	Population 1960	Population 1970	Population 1990	Population 2020	Population 2050
Oregon	*1,768,687*	*2,091,385*	*2,842,321*	*4,237,256*	*5,293,907*
Metropolitan Portland	796,340	962,865	1,294,302	2,021,489	2,645,077
Willamette Valley	408,333	525,706	722,974	1,040,118	1,282,736
Metro PDX + Valley[a]	*1,204,673*	*1,488,571*	*2,017,276*	*3,061,607*	*3,927,813*
Northwest Oregon	70,970	72,158	93,760	118,857	128,639
Southwest Oregon	68,938	69,521	79,600	88,375	81,958
Southern Oregon	172,337	202,022	303,687	422,550	465,860
Columbia Gorge	28,442	26,453	26,714	31,986	34,663
Central Oregon	39,660	48,975	102,745	247,493	372,035
Northeast Oregon	122,290	120,096	146,591	181,320	198,782
Southeast Oregon	61,377	63,579	71,948	85,068	84,147
Balance of Oregon	*564,014*	*602,814*	*825,045*	*1,169,336*	*1,433,903*

[a]PDX is the Federal Aviation Administration abbreviation for Portland. "Valley" means Willamette Valley.

During the 1960s, much of Oregon outside of the Willamette Valley saw stagnant growth, with only southern Oregon attracting a sizeable share of the state's population change (about 10 percent). These trends changed dramatically at the start of the Transition Planning period through the Mature Planning period. Our analysis shows that the share of Oregon's growth occurring outside metropolitan Portland and the Willamette Value doubled (from 13 to 26 percent) from the decade before SB 100 (the 1960s) through the fifty years during which SB 100 was mostly in effect (1970-2020). While we know anecdotally that some public officials in these regions worried that land use planning restricted their growth, the evidence shows that growth in many regions was has been far more robust following SB 100 than in the years before. Nearly three-quarters of the growth outside metropolitan Portland and the Willamette Valley occurred in central and southern Oregon, however.

Table 2.1B. Oregon's Population Trends over Time

Region	Population Change	Share of State Change (%)	New Majority Change	Share of State Change (%)	New Majority Share of Regional Change[a] (%)
PRE-PLANNING DECADE, 1960-70					
Oregon	*334,279*		*34,237*		*10*
Metropolitan Portland	167,893	50	15,147	44	9
Willamette Valley	122,686	37	10,405	30	8
Metro PDX + Valley	*290,579*	*87*	*25,552*	*75*	*9*
Northwest Oregon	1,725	1	1,399	4	81
Southwest Oregon	1,124	0	1,035	3	92
Southern Oregon	31,765	10	3,308	10	10
Columbia Gorge	-1,989	-1	83	0	100
Central Oregon	9,976	3	1,177	3	12
Northeast Oregon	-1,983	-1	997	3	100
Southeast Oregon	3,082	1	686	2	22
Balance of Oregon	*43,700*	*13*	*8,685*	*25*	*20*
PLANNING TRANSITION DECADES, 1970-90					
Oregon	*739,355*		*134,647*		*18*
Metropolitan Portland	330,069	45	77,815	58	24
Willamette Valley	191,955	26	30,911	23	16
Metro PDX + Valley	*522,024*	*71*	*108,726*	*81*	*21*
Northwest Oregon	21,065	3	1,044	1	5
Southwest Oregon	9,538	1	1,734	1	18
Southern Oregon	99,585	13	6,973	5	7
Columbia Gorge	261	0	1,180	1	100
Central Oregon	53,109	7	3,241	2	6
Northeast Oregon	23,010	3	6,078	5	26
Southeast Oregon	10,763	1	5,671	4	53
Balance of Oregon	*217,331*	*29*	*25,921*	*19*	*12*

Region	Population Change	Share of State Change (%)	New Majority Change	Share of State Change (%)	New Majority Share of Regional Change[a] (%)
MATURE PLANNING DECADES, 1990-2020					
Oregon	*1,394,935*		*729,550*		*52*
Metropolitan Portland	727,187	52	414,647	57	57
Willamette Valley	317,144	23	175,763	24	55
Metro PDX + Valley	*1,044,331*	*75*	*590,410*	*81*	*57*
Northwest Oregon	25,097	2	13,277	2	53
Southwest Oregon	8,775	1	5,840	1	67
Southern Oregon	118,863	9	46,300	6	39
Columbia Gorge	5,272	0	4,943	1	94
Central Oregon	144,748	10	27,868	4	19
Northeast Oregon	34,729	2	32,415	4	93
Southeast Oregon	13,120	1	8,497	2	65
Balance of Oregon	*350,604*	*25*	*139,140*	*19*	*40*
OREGON TOWARD 2050, 2020-50					
Oregon	*1,056,651*		*883,021*		*84*
Metropolitan Portland	623,588	59	496,999	56	80
Willamette Valley	242,618	23	223,436	25	92
Metro PDX + Valley	*866,206*	*82*	*720,435*	*82*	*83*
Northwest Oregon	9,782	1	16,474	2	100
Southwest Oregon	-6,417	0	7,155	1	100
Southern Oregon	43,310	4	48,882	6	100
Columbia Gorge	2,677	0	6,220	1	100
Central Oregon	124,542	2	33,735	4	27
Northeast Oregon	17,462	2	39,307	4	100
Southeast Oregon	-921	0	10,813	1	100
Balance of Oregon	*190,435*	*18*	*162,586*	*18*	*85*

[a]Where New Majority growth accounted for all the region's growth, we assigned a 100% share for ease of interpretation.

Sources: US Censuses of 1960 and 1970 for total population, less white as defined by those censuses; US Censuses 1990 and 2020 for total population, less white non-Hispanic as defined by those censuses; and Population Research Center, Portland State University, for overall population and population forecast by race/ethnicity.

Also, during the 1960s, whites (including white Hispanics) accounted for about 90 percent of net population growth. In contrast, New Majority persons (including all people identifying as nonwhite or Hispanic) accounted for all or nearly all the change in residents in northwest and southwest Oregon, the Columbia Gorge, and northeast Oregon during this decade. Except for the Columbia Gorge, the New Majority share of growth moderated toward the state average during the Transition Planning epoch. Following national trends, most of the state's growth between 1990 and 2020 (the Mature Planning epoch) was attributable to the New Majority persons. This was seen in all regions except southern and central Oregon.

Growth through the Mature Planning epoch has occurred where intended by SB 100—in urban areas. Notably, Oregonians living in urban areas grew from about 71 percent of the state's population in 1990 to about 79 percent in 2000 and then to 81 percent in 2010, where it remained in 2020 (80.5 percent).[4]

By 2050, Oregon's population will change even more dramatically than during SB 100's first fifty years. The forecasts in table 2.1B show that 80 percent of the growth in metropolitan Portland will be New Majority persons, as well as 92 percent of the change in the Willamette Valley. Only in central Oregon will the New Majority account for a small share of race/ethnicity change, at 27 percent. In the rest of the state, the New Majority will account for 85 percent population change. The next section explores racial/ethnic, migration and household trends.

We exclude analysis of the Washington state portion of the Portland-Vancouver-Hillsboro metropolitan area as it is under a different governance system and would require a separate discussion of Washington's Growth Management Act approach and its differences from the Oregon system, which is outside the scope of *Toward Oregon 2050*.

Emerging Demographic, Race/Ethnicity, and Household Trends

The 2020 Census counted more than 4.2 million residents in Oregon, representing an annualized growth rate of 1.1 percent since 2000, or approximately 40,000 new Oregonians each year since the start of the twenty-first century. This rate of growth exceeds the US average (0.8 percent) and implies a doubling of the population about every sixty-five years. Yet as Oregon adds 1 million new residents and 400,000 new households by 2050, its rate of growth will fall by more than half. Moreover, but for in-migration, Oregon's growth would stagnate. Of great interest for planning, Oregon's growth among aging residents will have profound implications for housing, transportation, and services to 2050. This section focuses on emerging demographic, race/ethnicity, migration, and household trends in Oregon toward 2050.

Trends represent things that are foreseeable but hard to influence, whereas futures are those things that are difficult to foresee but malleable. Thinking about the futures that are best for Oregon is a strategy that has served the state well, especially since SB 100. Will past policies like SB 100 be enough to maximize the well-being of the next one million Oregonians? That is a question we cannot answer, but we can supply fodder for discussion in the form of a summary of demographic trends.

Oregon's growth toward 2050 will be driven by births, deaths, and in-migration. Based on anticipated changes in these factors, the state's annual average population growth rate is expected to hover around 0.5 percent toward 2050—about a quarter of the rate seen in the 1990s (fig. 2.3). Lower growth is largely attributable to fewer births each year: during 2020, deaths outnumbered births for the first time. This was projected to occur by the mid-2020s, before the COVID-19 pandemic accelerated the timeline of this grim milestone. The dynamics behind slower growth are likely to persist in coming decades.

Life expectancy at birth in Oregon has increased steadily over time, to a high of 79.7 years in 2018. As in most of the United States, there has been little change since 2010, though there has been a decline in 2020 and 2021 from COVID-19, accidents/unintentional injuries (including drug overdose deaths), heart disease, chronic liver disease, and suicide.[5] There are radical differences in health and life expectancy across the state, however. There is a large gap between how long a newborn can expect to live in central Medford (66.2 years) and northwest Portland (89.1 years). Statewide, we expect life expectancy to improve after Oregon emerges from the COVID-19 pandemic—but we expect the national trends toward an increasing burden of noncommunicable diseases such as heart disease, chronic obstructive pulmonary disease (COPD), and stroke to continue. Uncertainty remains as improvements in life expectancy have stalled at the national level owing to higher

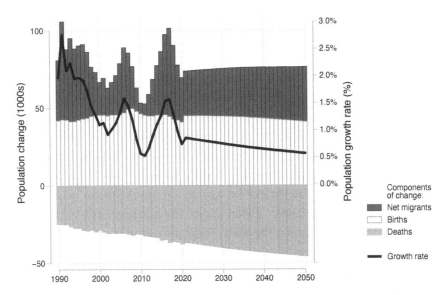

Figure 2.3. Oregon's population growth and components of change, 1990-2050. *Source*: "2017 National Population Projections Datasets," US Census Bureau, retrieved November 23, 2021, https://www.census.gov/data/datasets/2017/demo/popproj/2017-popproj.html; "Current Forecast Summary for all Areas," Portland State University Population Research Center, retrieved November 23, 2021, https://www.pdx.edu/population-research/population-forecasts

burdens of disease and injury from drug overdoses, alcohol, suicide, and violent causes of death, which continue to be points of concern. Drinking and suicide deaths are higher per capita in Oregon than the nation, and while drug overdoses are lower, they generally follow the same persistent trend. To the extent that they occur, improvements in life expectancy will have a modest effect on Oregon's demographic future. They may magnify the effects of population aging and slow the growth in the annual count of deaths, which will continue to steadily grow through 2050 and drive population declines in some parts of the state. Indeed, chapter 1 calls for a new state initiative, dubbed SB 1000, to address these very concerns, among others.

In-migration faces a higher degree of uncertainty in the coming decades. Research has occasionally spotlighted the possibility that the Pacific Northwest could become a destination for populations displaced by climate change in the rest of the United States and abroad. There is insufficient knowledge to make predictions about the effect of climate change on migration to or from Oregon, however.[6] The region itself faces significant risks—including wildfire, ocean acidification, sea level rise, and water shortages—that may exert pressures the other direction. Economic uncertainty and exposure to risk could be a further contributor to declining birth rates. In contrast, mitigation efforts could have a stimulus effect, creating new jobs and enhancing regional competitiveness in ways that increase population growth. On balance, it is not yet possible to anticipate whether climate-driven migration will significantly alter patterns of residential settlement in Oregon; economic, technological, political, and institutional considerations are likely to be more important than climactic factors alone.

Migration will nonetheless be key to Oregon's future population growth. During the 2010s, 78 percent of Oregon's growth was attributable to net migration to the state. Migration requires resources and motivation, and movers tend to be younger and to colocate with jobs, friends, relatives, or educational opportunities—factors that often favor urban areas. Census data for the period 2015-19 show that migrants tend to be clustered between ages 20 and 30 years old, and that migrants from within the United States account for 80 percent of net migration. Overall, a quarter of in-migrants to Oregon came from California, with another quarter coming from other states in the region (Alaska, Hawaii, Idaho, Nevada, and Washington). The remaining in-migrants came from the rest of the states. Census data for 2015-19 also show that southwest Oregon predominantly sees migration to and from Northern California, while eastern Oregon and the North Coast tend to exchange people with their neighboring states, Washington and Idaho. In contrast, migration from nonadjacent states accounts for more of the movement to Portland and other metropolitan areas in the Willamette Valley.[7]

International migrants contributed less than 15 percent of new arrivals in the latter 2010s. Only 11 percent of Oregonians are foreign born, compared to nearly 14 percent on average across the United States (and 27 percent of Californians). Notably, migration from Mexico and Latin America tapered off during the 2010s, mostly a result of an aging immigrant population and public policies. Oregon currently receives 1.1 percent of the nation's total foreign arrivals, so if the status quo continues, it may therefore welcome between 6,000 and 20,000 immigrants each year by 2050.[8] Oregon's share of immigrants to the United States has never exceeded its share of the US overall population (currently, about 1.3 percent). Immigration is more sensitive than domestic migration to national policies and global affairs, and therefore it is impossible to forecast into the distant future.

In table 2.2, we show how Oregon's race and ethnicity has changed dramatically during the decade between the Great Recession (lasting from 2007 to 2009) and the years leading up to the COVID-19 pandemic (2010 to 2020). The 2020 Census shows a state population that is undergoing transformative change with double-digit growth posted for Asian, Black, Native Hawaiian or Pacific Islander, and Hispanic or Latino ethnicities and doubling of the multiracial population. At the same time, there has been little change in the population that is American Indian or Alaska Native or white alone. The multiracial population exceeds 10 percent of the state total (443,000 out of 4.2 million). Nearly half of these persons identify as white and "other race" (of whom a large share also identified as Hispanic); another one-fifth are persons who are white and American Indian or Alaska Native, and one-tenth are persons who are white and Asian. To put this into perspective, whites accounted for about 90 percent of the population growth in 1960 (see table 2.2). while nonwhites will account for close to 90 percent of growth to 2050. Approaching 2050, persons of two or more racial/ethnic groups may become a plurality in the United States as well as Oregon, necessitating changes in the way that race/ethnicity is conceived of and quantified.

Table 2.2. Change in Oregon's Race and Ethnicity, 2010-20

	2020 Population	% Share	Change 2010-2020 Number	% Change
Total population	4,237,256	100%	406,182	11%
American Indian or Alaska Native	42,042	1%	-664	-2%
Asian	191,797	5%	52,361	38%
Black or African American	78,658	2%	13,674	21%
Native Hawaiian or Pacific Islander	18,197	0%	5,500	43%
Some other race	22,962	1%	17,460	317%
White	3,036,158	72%	30,310	1%
Two or more races	258,685	6%	148,846	136%
Hispanic or Latino (any race)	588,757	14%	138,695	31%

Source: "2020 Census: Redistricting File (Public Law 94-171) Dataset," US Census Bureau, August 12, 2021, https://www.census.gov/data/datasets/2020/dec/2020-census-redistricting-summary-file-dataset.html.

One of the most significant demographic changes since SB 100 took effect is falling household size. In 1960, the average household size in Oregon was 3.1 for about 1.7 million Oregonians who occupied about 560,000 housing units. By 2020, the state's average household size had shrunk to 2.5 persons for 4.1 million residents. As a result, more housing units are required today than in the past. Put differently, Oregon had to add about 400,000 new housing units between 1960 and 2020 just to meet the needs of falling household size *on top of* meeting the needs of a growing population. But forecasts toward 2050 show that the trend toward smaller households has waned; average household in Oregon is expected to hover around 2.4, close to where it was in 2020.

One reason that household sizes fell so quickly between 1960 and 2020 is that birth rates fell precipitously. Where 2.1 live births per female between the ages of 15 and 49 are needed to sustain population, in 2020 the nation's fertility rate was just 1.6, down by more than half from 3.4 in 1960. The reasons for falling birth rates are numerous but are ultimately tied to decisions by partners as to when to have children—or whether to have children at all.

Another reason for declining average household size is population aging. Whereas persons over 55 accounted for about 20 percent of the population in 1970, by 2020 they accounted for more than 30 percent. As the population ages but remains in their homes, the share of households without children increases, as does the share of single-person households. Going forward to 2050, however, the share of those over 55 in Oregon will grow to about 37 percent, which is a much slower pace than between 1970 and 2020. The reason is that baby boomers who were born between 1946 and 1964 and accounted for the largest change in the nation's population historically will have mostly passed away before 2050, yielding to smaller cohorts of future elderly.

In the beginning, we noted that Oregon may add about 400,000 households during 2020-50. More important than this number is the distribution of demand based on households at different life stages. Consider what American households were like in 1960, at the height of the baby boom, which extended from the end of World War II to 1964. The nation's population exploded from 141 million persons in 1946 to 191 million in 1964—the largest percentage increase in the nation's history in such a short period. More than 76 million babies were born during the baby boom. Largely to meet the needs of unprecedented growth, America became a "suburban nation" as cities simply could not house millions of new households. On top of land availability, generous federal subsidies, and a national shift in social attitudes favoring suburbs over cities, baby boomer households created suburban America. A popular television program in the 1950s and early 1960s, *I Love Lucy*, started with the couple living in New York City and ended with a move to the suburbs. As boomers grew up, they raised their children in the suburban landscape they knew. America into the 1980s was a decidedly suburban-oriented nation for practical reasons: suburbia had the space and resources to meet the needs of households with children, and families had the resources to purchase newly constructed homes thanks in part to the expansion of the thirty-year mortgage during the 1950s.

Given how boomers changed America's and Oregon's housing markets when they were growing up and raising their own families, their influence approaching 2050 will be no less monumental. Table 2.3 shows the change in householders by age cohort between equal thirty-year periods, 1990-2020 (the mature planning epoch) and 2020-50 (the epoch toward 2050). There are three age cohorts:

- Under 35 years of age, which are households usually seeking starter homes such as smaller homes on smaller lots and attached homes.
- Between 35 and 64 years of age, where households are in their peak housing demand cycle of their lives, supporting the highest range of average household sizes with the most need for housing services.
- Adults 65 years of age and older, where households are typically downsizing because they become empty nesters or lose their partners, and whose housing needs become more like those of starter households, although usually with higher housing budgets.

Toward 2050, downsizing households will dominate housing demand while starter home demand will be about half of what it was 1990-2020. The change in demand for homes meeting the peak housing needs will be on the order of two-thirds less toward 2050 than during 1990-2020. For many of Oregon's regions, however, meeting the needs of downsizing households will account for *all* the change in housing demand.

There is another consideration that warrants future exploration: the change in households with and without children, and single-person households. In the 1960s, more than half of American households had children, but in 2050 only about a quarter will.[9] In Oregon, more than 70 percent of the change in households will be without children, while

Table 2.3. Change in Householders by Age Cohort, 1990-2020 and 2020-50

Region	Householder Change, 1990-2020	Starter (Age <35) (%)	Peak (Age 35-64) (%)	Downsize (Age 65+) (%)	Householder Change, 2020-50	Starter (Age <35) (%)	Peak (Age 35-64) (%)	Downsize (Age 65+) (%)
Oregon	*585,614*	*9*	*52*	*39*	*402,398*	*5*	*32*	*64*
Metropolitan Portland	305,734	10	59	31	209,714	7	32	61
Willamette Valley	134,064	11	44	45	83,890	1	42	57
Metro PDX + Valley	*439,798*	*10*	*54*	*36*	*293,604*	*6*	*35*	*60*
Northwest Oregon	12,970	-10	39	71	7,011	14	27	60
Southwest Oregon	6,774	-24	18	106	1,833	-19	61	180
Southern Oregon	62,038	7	36	57	36,563	4	16	80
Columbia Gorge	2,363	0	40	60	1,004	4	9	86
Central Oregon	58,655	11	50	40	55,737	4	29	67
Northeast Oregon	12,496	1	38	61	4,492	-11	21	90
Southeast Oregon	-9,480	-2	-27	128	2,154	-38	30	108
Balance of Oregon	*145,816*	*6*	*45*	*49*	*108,794*	*3*	*23*	*75*

Sources: Adapted from Population Research Center, Portland State University, and Woods & Poole Economics.

in some regions the number of households with children will be less in 2050 than in 2020. Single-person households will also increase as a share, from less than a fifth in 1960 to about a quarter in 2020 and then to about a third in 2050, mostly as people live longer and lose their partners. The implication is that demographic-based housing needs of Oregon in the mid-twenty-first century will be vastly different than those of the previous century.

What kind of housing will Oregonians need toward 2050? Although this is addressed in chapter 6, we frame the demographic implications here. The historic demand for large homes on large lots to meet the needs of households with children will give way to smaller homes on smaller lots, apartments and condominiums, and conversions of some single-family homes into multiplex units such as two-, three- and four-plexes, or the addition of accessory dwelling units (ADUs). According to the National Association of Realtors' *Community Preference Survey*,[10] buyers prefer homes that are close to shopping, restaurants, parks/greenspace, and transit, even if that means accepting smaller homes on smaller lots. Indeed, during the period between the Great Recession and the start of the COVID-19 pandemic, single-family detached homes had already become less than half of all new housing produced (fig. 2.4). The implications of these demographic drivers on housing demand are addressed more fully in chapter 6, which addresses housing.

Emerging Regional Demographic and Socioeconomic Disparities

In the thirty years between 2020 and 2050, Oregon can look forward to gaining 1 million new residents and 400,000 new households. This is illustrated in fig 2.5. Despite technological changes that may appear, from driverless cars to fully sustainable isolation in one's home, Oregonians will still live in a social, economic, political, and demographic world recognizable to us today. It is in this vein that in the next section we introduce regional and socioeconomic disparities that will need to be addressed toward 2050. Above, we introduced Oregon's regions and differences in their expected demographic futures. In this section we focus on more details of these regional differences, addressing aging and race/ethnicity as well as growing socioeconomic disparities.

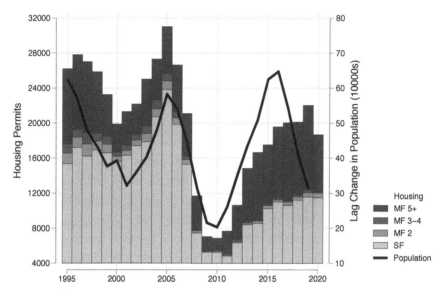

Figure 2.4. Housing production and population growth in Oregon by type, 1995-2020. MF, multifamily; SF, single family. *Source*: "Building Permits Survey," US Census Bureau, retrieved November 23, 2021, https://www.census.gov/construction/bps/index.html; "2020 Annual Population Report Tables," Portland State University Population Research Center, retrieved November 23, 2021, https://www.pdx.edu/population-research/population-estimate-reports

The 2020 Census showed that despite its growth over the past decade, Oregon saw virtually no change in the size of the population under age 18 (866,000 in both 2010 and 2020). Nationally, the population under age 18 declined in absolute terms (from 74.2 to 73.1 million). Forecasts for Oregon have the working-age population (defined here as 20-65 years old) declining from 58 to 51 percent of the population, while the share of the population age 65 and older is expected to increase from 19 to 24 percent between 2020 and 2050.

The share of persons under 25 years of age will decline, from 29 percent to 23 percent. But the variation between regions is substantial, as seen in table 2.4 for those persons 65 years of age and over. In those regions dominated by an aging population with little or any, or even negative, change in younger persons, there will be less demand for primary and secondary schools as well as other youth-serving social, medical, and related support systems. Can society prosper in the face of aging, or even population decline? The nature of these changes and how they affect the future has not really been addressed in the literature.

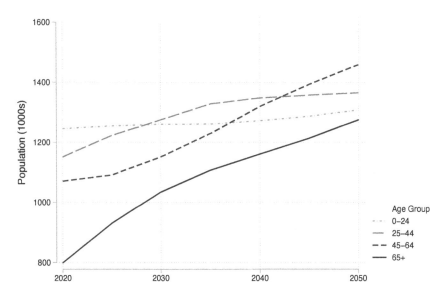

Figure 2.5. Oregon population forecast by age group, 2020-50.

The economic and social fabric of the state will change as an ever-larger share of the population is at traditional post-work ages. Retirement will change as health and income entitlements face new eligibility criteria. New cohorts reaching retirement age are healthier than their predecessors (owing largely to the greatly reduced rates of smoking), though as mentioned above, there is a worrisome increase in lifestyle-related deaths and deaths of despair. These aside, the population age 65-74 will likely be more economically active than past generations, engaging in part-time or volunteer work after retirement, traveling, and consuming goods and services. The current populations reaching retirement age are preferring to remain in their homes and rely on in-home support services for their increasing care needs, which may continue alongside growing demand for independent and assisted-living housing (but not institutional settings—despite the growing old-age population, little growth should be expected in the demand for nursing home beds).

In 2050, the population age 60 and older will be more diverse by race, ethnicity, and nationality than ever in the state's history, leading to greater demand for culturally and linguistically responsive services. The baby boom generation (born 1946-64) will depend on a smaller pool of workers to sustain social security benefits, and at the end of their lives, they will have drawn down an unprecedented amount of stored wealth and redistributed it through a combination of inheritance, philanthropy, or taxation and spending—the details of which will have important repercussions for economic inequality and opportunity. The distribution of older persons may lead to increased economic, social, and political stresses throughout the state, especially outside metropolitan Portland and the Willamette Valley.

Table 2.4 shows that between 2020 and 2050, persons 65 years of age and older are forecasted to account for an equivalent of 46 percent of the state's population change ("equivalent" because most people of that age then were already living in the state in 2020, so they are not adding to the population). For metropolitan Portland and the Willamette Valley, they will be equivalent to 41 percent of the population change, while for the balance of Oregon, that figure is more than half, 68 percent. In southwest

Table 2.4. Change in Population 65 Years and Older by Region, 2020-50

Region	2020 Total Population	2020 Population 65+	2020 Population Share 65+ (%)	2050 Population	2050 Population 65+	2050 Population Share 65+ (%)	2020-50 Population Share of Change 65+, (%)
Oregon	4,244,736	789,378	19	5,407,002	1,277,798	24	42
Metro Portland	2,029,563	333,304	16	2,675,099	589,963	22	40
Valley	1,044,723	178,022	17	1,298,000	259,305	20	32
Metro + Valley	3,074,286	511,326	17	3,973,099	849,268	21	38
Northwest	117,699	32,231	27	122,815	34,755	28	49
Southwest	87,556	25,741	29	86,968	29,985	34	-722[a]
Southern	421,691	105,160	25	517,531	159,498	31	57
Columbia Gorge	31,794	7,261	23	34,957	8,811	25	49
Central	250,299	53,788	21	395,847	127,751	32	51
Northeast	177,789	34,725	20	190,999	43,186	23	64
Southeast	83,622	19,146	23	84,786	21,586	25	210
Balance	1,170,450	278,052	24	1,433,903	425,572	30	56

[a] The forecast for southwest Oregon shows it will lose population overall but will have more persons 65 years of age and older in 2050 than in 2020, thus accounting for the large negative percentage change.

Source: Allocated proportionately for age change by Woods & Poole Economics (2021).

and southeast Oregon, the population is projected to fall, but the number of persons 65 years of age and older is projected to increase. In all other regions, the equivalent share of population change attributable to those persons 65 years of age and older will be larger and in many cases much larger than seen in metropolitan Portland and the Willamette Valley. Figure 2.5 illustrates these trends for the state as a whole.

Unfortunately for land use planners, these are trends largely beyond their influence. One approach to improving prospects for Oregon's stressed regions is to create incentives or other support systems to encourage population redistribution, especially among younger persons from metropolitan Portland and the Willamette Valley to them. Another is to encourage international migration into stressed regions, though that may require federal coordination. Although population dynamics are predictable, policies designed to change trends are difficult, can be expensive, and may have unpredictable outcomes.

Short of reversing trends in these regions, more dramatic policy approaches may be needed, with some of them falling within the purview of land use planning and related fields. "Right-sizing" housing markets might be needed in especially stressed counties or areas.[11] This could include public acquisition of excess housing stock in targeted areas. Excess housing would be easy to determine based on vacancies, underinvestment, and other indicators. Targeted areas would include those with lagging sales, rents, and occupancy that are distant from population or employment centers. Once acquired, excess housing would be removed from the inventory and the land merged with other properties to increase the supply of working landscapes, watersheds, carbon sinks, or other socially productive uses. Oregon's policymakers need to consider these and other ways in which to elevate the well-being of stressed regions.

Oregon has transformed over the past fifty years from one of the least socially diverse states to one with a rapidly diversifying population. Table 2.5 reports demographic trends approaching 2050. For the state as a whole, the vast majority of new growth will be attributable to the New Majority. The largest numerical changes will occur in metropolitan Portland and the Willamette Valley, where three quarters of a million new residents will be New Majority, while the White population will grow by just one fifth of that amount.

Table 2.5. Distribution of Population by Race and Ethnicity by Region, 2020-50

Region	Population Change	White Change	Black Change	Native American Change	Asian and Pacific Islander Change	Hispanic Change	Total New Majority Change	New Majority Share of Change (%)
Oregon	1,052,403	168,522	69,354	14,324	216,779	583,421	883,878	84
Metropolitan Portland	620,501	120,410	41,917	5,588	169,538	283,047	500,090	81
Willamette Valley	238,510	15,728	13,754	4,483	32,682	171,861	222,780	93
Metro PDX + Valley	859,011	136,138	55,671	10,071	202,220	454,908	722,870	84
Northwest Oregon	10,195	-6,226	1,452	648	1,459	12,859	16,418	161
Southwest Oregon	-6,048	-12,242	693	150	659	4,690	6,192	-102
Southern Oregon	44,602	-4,464	4,315	1,319	5,060	38,371	49,065	110
Columbia Gorge	3,098	-3,039	335	-105	376	5,532	6,138	198
Central Oregon	120,311	87,160	2,723	1,299	4,347	24,783	33,152	28
Northeast Oregon	21,151	-19,144	3,136	1,129	1,880	34,151	40,296	191
Southeast Oregon	83	-9,661	1,029	-187	778	8,127	9,747	>1000
Balance of Oregon	193,392	32,384	13,683	4,253	14,559	128,513	161,008	83

Note: All races are exclusive of Hispanic/Latino persons.
Source: Portland State University Population Research Center projections by race/ethnicity for 2020 and 2050.

The rest of the state will also change. Nearly 75 percent of the population change in central Oregon will be white non-Hispanics. Southwest Oregon will see declining population overall and among all minority groups, although its New Majority population will increase. Most regions of the state will see declining numbers of white non-Hispanic residents.

The Hispanic/Latino population of the state is expected to account for the lion's share of growth in the state—nearly 500,000 people, representing half of the state's growth to 2050. This is followed by the addition of more than 200,000 non-Hispanic Asians and Pacific Islanders, comprising another 20 percent of the state's growth. Other groups are expected to grow as well, although they remain less significant as a share of the state total.

Oregon toward 2050

In review, the PRC forecast for 2050 shows Oregon adding 1 million new residents, equivalent to 400,000 new households. Most of the state's new residents will be New Majority persons. One in four Oregonians will be 65 or older; in some regions, all or nearly all the change in households will be those with householders over 65 years of age. Statewide, more than 70 percent of the change in households will be without children, while in some regions the number of households with children will be less in 2050 than in 2020. Is Oregon prepared for a state in 2050 that is vastly different in demographic composition than when SB 100 was adopted eighty years earlier? We think not.

How can Oregon prepare itself for a vastly different society in 2050? For one, it can increase its analytic foundations. SB 100 catapulted Oregon into a national leadership position by using state forecasts to drive coordinated local-regional-state planning. It may be time for another leap forward when it comes to integrating forecasts into planning. Some enhancements can include but are not limited to the following.

- More local detail is needed for historical data as well as forecasts to planning horizons. These data would include persons by age, race/ethnicity, and gender in five-year age cohorts historically by decade (perhaps starting with 1970, just before SB 100 was adopted) with forecasts to the horizon year.
- Household detail is needed in forecasts, such as householder age, gender, race/ethnicity, and disability status. Households could be broken down similarly by type, such as those with and without children, as well as single-parent, single-person, and multigenerational households composed of two or more generations.
- Housing supply and demand forecasts would be generated. Supply figures would be matched to population and household forecasts for the horizon year, providing a set of possible scenarios

that could accommodate envisioned growth, including mixtures of single-family detached homes; townhouses; two-, three-, and four-plexes reflected in Oregon's "Middle Housing" efforts launched in 2019; and apartments/condominiums. Demand by type and location of housing would certainly be challenging and may require consultation with local housing market experts.
- Historical under- and overproduction of housing could be incorporated and would be highly original and pioneering. These estimates could help lead to housing supply "right-sizing" efforts focused on meeting the needs of undersupplied demand.
- Forecasts could be expanded to include employment by major economic sector. Private and public sector options exist for employment forecasts down to the county level. These could be incorporated into integrated employment and population forecasts.
- Forecasts should address the state's various geographic levels, including counties, cities, areas on both sides of UGBs, and tribal nations.
- Forecasts should incorporate ranges that capture not just a central scenario, but a range of likely outcomes that planners can prepare for.

Oregon toward 2050 will need to confront the implications of social changes to improve the well-being of the state's current and future residents, before it is too late. In our view, this requires the production of more detailed forecasts of people, housing, jobs, infrastructure, and land with a social and equity lens. We refer the reader to other discussions in this book that identify policies needed to move Oregon toward 2050, notably the chapters on housing (chap. 6), homelessness (chap. 10), and employment, wages, and economic concerns (chap. 11).

Notes

1. Oregon has had three years of negative growth about every forty years since 1900: in 1941, 1983, and 2021. Growth was robust after each of these short-term downturns and is expected to remain so toward 2050, although the average rate of growth is expected to decline as the state's total population increases.
2. Arthur C. Nelson, *Reshaping Metropolitan America* (Washington, DC: Island Press, 2013).
3. Defining regions is equally art and science. Hood River County could be considered a part of the central Oregon region instead of metropolitan Portland, but in our view the economic and commuting linkages put it firmly within the extended Portland metropolitan region. Wheeler County could have been assigned to either northeastern Oregon or central Oregon; because Fossil, its principal city, is connected directly to Arlington via the Columbia River, we assign it to the Columbia Gorge region. Malheur County is assigned to northeastern Oregon because of the location of Ontario, its principal city.
4. The annual growth rate of 0.49 percent in urban areas significantly exceeded the 0.24 percent national annual average increase during the period. The US Census Bureau defines urban areas after each decennial census, making exact comparisons between decades impossible. Alternative definitions of urban/rural reflect similar trends; e.g., urban areas under the US Department of Agriculture RUCA (Rural-Urban Commuting Area code scheme indicate the percentage of Oregon's population in urban census tracts increased from 65.6 percent in 1990 to 70.9 percent in 2000 and 75.7 percent in 2010.
5. "Life Expectancy in the U.S. Dropped for the Second Year in a Row in 2021," National Center for Health Statistics, Centers for Disease Control and Prevention, August 31, 2022, www.cdc.gov/nchs/pressroom/nchs_press_releases/2022/20220831.htm.
6. L. C. Whitely Binder and J. Jurjevich, *The Winds of Change? Exploring Climate Change-Driven Migration and Related Impacts in the Pacific Northwest: Symposium Summary* (Portland, OR: Portland State University Population Research Center; Seattle: University of Washington Climate Impacts Group, 2016), cig.uw.edu/publications/the-winds-of-change-exploring-climate-change-driven-migration-and-related-impacts-in-the-pacific-northwest-symposium-summary/.
7. Specifically, 2 percent from Mexico or Central America, 5 percent from south or East Asia, and 7 percent from elsewhere.
8. This is the midpoint of low and high scenarios, respectively, with 12,000 being the median, according to the latest national projections from 2017.
9. Arthur C. Nelson, "The Great Senior Short-Sale or Why Policy Inertia Will Short Change Millions of America's Seniors," Journal of Comparative Urban Law and Policy 4, no. 1 (2020): 473-528, readingroom.law.gsu.edu/jculp/vol4/iss1/28.
10. These surveys are produced about every two to four years and provide a scientifically based assessment of market demand for homes by type and key demographic features for metropolitan areas. For details and access to the surveys, see "NAR 2023 Community and Transportation Preferences Survey," National Association of Realtors, accessed December 15, 2023, https://www.nar.realtor/reports/nar-community-and-transportation-preference-surveys.
11. Nelson, "The Great Senior Short-Sale."

PART I

Natural Environment

Oregon contains a diverse array of landscapes and ecological regions, many of them unique to the state, and environmental concerns are of top concern to residents. Collectively, these chapters comment on the extent to which Oregon stays within or overshoots it ecological ceiling and identify strategies for better environmental stewardship by 2050.

These chapters celebrate some positive trends that are at least partly a result of proactive state policy. For example, in chapter 3, Connie Ozawa discusses how Oregon is better poised to reduce greenhouse gas emissions and address climate change than many other states. In chapter 4, Dana Hellman and Vivek Shandas note that in most counties across the state, air and water pollution levels have been trending downward in recent years. Meanwhile, Oregonians are faring better in terms of some environmental-health related outcomes. Finally, in chapter 5, Shane Day, Tyler Wolfe, and Carlos Arias highlight how Oregon has maintained a consistently generally healthy forestland base that is one of the country's top producers of renewable energy.

But the chapters in part I also offer some cause for concern. In terms of climate change and other hazards, we anticipate a more volatile climate, including more extreme summer heat waves and forest fires as well as changing precipitation, impacts to agriculture, and flooding and rising sea levels. The state is underprepared to address these changes or other hazards like earthquakes. As for environmental quality, some communities—including West Eugene, the Warms Springs reservation, and certain parts of Portland—already disproportionately experience worse environmental quality, such as more polluted air and water or more extreme summer heat. Without interventions, those disproportionate burdens will worsen. In terms of natural resources, alarming trends include the ongoing declines in salmon and other important species, intensifying drought and water quantity concerns, and the destructive impacts and high costs of managing invasive species.

The authors collectively identify some big ideas about planning for greater ecological balance and resilience and a healthier environment for all, now and in the future. To prepare for climate change and other disasters, Ozawa argues that we must move beyond data collection and planning and begin actual readiness implementation. For example, the state must make capital investments in public facilities (including infrastructure) to address both current and future business-as-usual needs, at standards likely to withstand the anticipated hazards, despite a higher price tag. To promote healthier environments for all, Hellman and Shandas suggest we apply environmental determinants of health thinking (rather than individual behavioral models) and include affected communities in data collection and decision-making. Finally, Day, Wolfe, and Arias suggest that Oregon can deepen its involvement with the Oregon Water Trust, innovate in incentivizing the stewardship of ecosystem services, and foster more landscape-scale ecosystem management.

3
Climate Change, Environmental Hazards, and Resilience

CONNIE P. OZAWA

Climate change is already affecting Oregon in significant ways. In 2020, the state experienced weeks of some of the worst air quality in the world from nearby forest fires. In the summer of 2021, the state suffered an unprecedented "heat dome," with temperatures well above 110°F for days on end, causing at least ninety-six deaths.[1] As we look to 2050, we must plan for increasingly dry summers, lower snowpack levels, and less precipitation in general. Wildfires, flooding, habitat loss, and lower ground water levels are additional effects.

With less certainty of when but certain to occur in Oregon's future is a powerful earthquake. Accompanying the earth's shaking could be a towering tsunami that washes away whole communities up and down the Oregon coast. Further inland, landslides could bury structures, roads, and bridges. What once seemed like solid ground may drop beneath our feet. Increasing numbers of persons who once felt safe could be suddenly rendered houseless, losing their valuables, memories, and sense of security. Others already living without reliable access to shelter, food, or a bank account would sink even lower into despair.

How prepared are we for the anticipated impacts of climate change and environmental hazards that may occur over the next thirty years? How can we build resilience in our state? This chapter focuses on two illustrative and major hazards—climate change and a massive 9.0-magnitude earthquake—and their societal impacts. After a summary of the likely impacts of these hazards, we provide a review of what is being done today across Oregon at the state and local levels to improve resilience. We make clear that Oregon is not prepared. Low-income populations and certain geographic areas of the state are most vulnerable. We conclude with clear recommendations for preparing Oregon for climate change and earthquakes.

Who Will Be Affected? Risk and Equity

While this chapter discusses statewide hazards, not all residents face the same level of vulnerability or risk. As the authors of chapter 4 note, vulnerability is a product of intersecting variables: the likelihood of exposure to an event, the magnitude of the impact and the sensitivity or vulnerability of the people exposed, and the adaptive capacity. Poverty is a core factor that affects a population's vulnerability to risks and capacity to recover from tragic events. More than 9 percent of Oregonians live below the federal poverty level and others are just above, according to past statewide risk assessment analysis by the US Department of Agriculture (chap. 11 suggests that state poverty rates are even higher, above 12 percent, in 2022). Table 3.1 lists other important vulnerability factors, including physical disabilities, age, difficulty with English, lack of access to a car, and residing in mobile home.[2]

It is not difficult to imagine why poverty, age, disabilities, and other factors may cause persons to suffer disproportionately from tragic events. Families living near the poverty line have fewer resources to help them adapt to crises. For example, they may have less access to cash or little food stored in their pantries to weather a period of

Table 3.1. Oregon's Population by Vulnerable Groups

	Number of People	Percentage of Population
Families in poverty	92,438	9.2
People with disabilities	584,576	14.5
People over 65 years	682,546	16.7
Difficulty with English	114,956	3.0
Lack of car transportation	119,031	7.5
Mobile home residents	125,306	7.9

Note: The values above are estimates, with a small margin of error.

Source: "Wildfire Risks to Communities," US Department of Agriculture, accessed February 12, 2021, https://wildfirerisk.org/explore/3/41.

restricted travel and employment. Persons with disabilities and households without a car may be less able to evacuate dangerous conditions such as wildfires. Persons with difficulty with English may not understand urgent public advisories. Additionally, immigrant communities may harbor a distrust of government, either here in the United States because of their immigration status or because of past hardships with governments in their home countries. Finally, the vulnerability of persons over 65 years would vary in their capacity to respond, depending largely on their socioeconomic status and the extent to which they also fall into any of these other categories.

Many other traits noted above have cascading and compounding effects. As the Oregon Health Authority notes, environmental hazards are "cross-cutting and will disproportionately affect communities of color, tribal communities, farmworkers, and underinvested rural communities. Disruptions in local economies, social safety net systems, and housing will further affect Oregonians already experiencing financial and social stressors."[3]

As we look to 2050, it is critical to examine how to better help vulnerable Oregonians, especially the homeless or those living in mobile homes destroyed by the 2020 wildfires (further discussed in chaps. 6 and 10), be resilient in the context of multiple big risks. We can learn from one recent crisis, the COVID-19 pandemic, which highlighted the fact that vulnerability is not just a personal characteristic but a consequence of exposure together with socioeconomic status and personal health conditions. We can make parallels between the COVID-19 pandemic and the cases of climate change and environmental hazards as discussed here. While we can predict the geographic boundaries of various hazards and even the frequency (e.g., flooding compared to a Cascadia earthquake) and while we can identify especially sensitive populations, how these factors will collide is uncertain. Ultimately, we will need to make a choice about which factors to prioritize, but in the course of doing so, remembering to search for "and" (or actions that will address multiple problems) rather than "or" pathways (that address solitary problems) remains critical.

Another lesson learned from the pandemic is that the loss of trust in government and institutions may prevent us from adapting to, mitigating, or overcoming a calamitous event. Massive environmental hazards rapidly turn into widespread "disasters" when our social fabric fails to address the initial destruction, leading to secondary impacts and beyond. We can act today to build stronger social relationships among community members. These connections will go a long way toward ensuring our survivability. But until the state can restore a sense of legitimacy, credibility, and trust in government and advisory institutions, factions will continue to compete for limited resources, render us individually impotent, and weaken our collective ability to respond to the challenges ahead.

Climate Change

For many years now, scientists at the International Panel on Climate Change (IPCC) have been warning about the catastrophic results if the world reaches average temperatures of 1.5°C above preindustrial levels. Above that temperature rise, the planet will pass tipping points. As of 2022, global temperatures have already risen by 1.1°C, and already we are seeing an increase in effects from disasters such as flooding and hurricanes. Temperatures in Oregon have been climbing over the past century, with accelerating increases (depending on emissions levels) predicted by 2050 and beyond.

A second major impact of climate change on Oregon is the timing and form of precipitation. While the total amount of precipitation and its geographic distribution across the state are not expected to change dramatically, increasing rain and less snowfall are expected. Lower snowfall means less water available as snowmelt, intensifying seasonal drought conditions. This is already occurring. In 2015, the Oregon Global Warming Commission noted that lower snowpack across the state resulted in "official drought declarations for 25 of Oregon's 36 counties," and "for each 1.8 degrees F of warming, peak snow water equivalent in the Cascade Range can be expected to decline 22%–30%."[4]

Wildfires are increasingly common across Oregon. In August 2018, air quality in all counties except Coos and Curry was deemed unhealthy due to blazes in Oregon, Northern California, and Washington.[5] As Oregon experiences warmer and drier summers, acres of forest and grasslands are expected to flare up more frequently and for longer fire seasons. Meanwhile, current development patterns in the wildfire-urban interface (the band of land separating wildfire-prone areas from urban settlements) mean that more homes and businesses will be at risk of fire damage.

Changes in heat and precipitation will disrupt not only human health, but also agricultural growing seasons, stream flows and water temperatures, wildlife habitat, pest populations, and the human economies that rely on these natural resources as well as groundwater in the drier southeastern areas of the state. Along the coastlines, rising sea levels will aggravate coastal erosion and flooding.[6]

Another area of concern is the impact of climate change on flooding. Paired with rising sea levels, flooding in coastal deltas is likely to increase. The rate and level of sea level rise appears to be accelerating and is believed to have increased from 3.2 millimeters per year since 1993 (as compared with a 1.2-mm rise between 1901 and 1990).[7] A change in sea level will affect Oregon's 363 miles (583 km) of coastline, intensifying coastal erosion and with negative impacts to marine life.

Farther inland, increased flooding from intense rainfall events will affect urban and suburban areas, like the Portland metropolitan region, that have mainly been built on level land close to rivers. Heavier rainfalls combined with early snowmelt will also likely increase flow surges. The devastation in the town of Vernonia in the Coast Range Mountains in 2007, and the flooding of the coastal highway in Tillamook and other coastal communities in 2015, are reminders of the magnitude of damage that flooding can impose.

The Oregon Global Warming Commission (OGWC) has published an eye-opening summary of the financial impacts of climate change on Oregon's economy.

- Ecosystem services provided by forests threatened by fires and drought:
    - $3.2 million per year in water purification
    - $5.5 million in erosion control (in the Willamette Valley alone)
    - $144 per household per year in cultural and aesthetic benefits (e.g., hiking, camping, and viewing)
- Tourism impacts:
    - Nearly $51 million in tourism revenue was lost in Oregon in 2017 because of wildfires

- The Shakespeare Company in Ashland experienced a 10 percent loss in revenues ($2 million) because of wildfire smoke in 2018
- Ski resorts have experienced losses due to shorter skiing seasons.
• Agriculture and seafood industry impacts:
    - Crop losses due to heat, insect predation, weed growth, reduced precipitation and irrigation water during summer months, and excessive precipitation in winter months
    - Seafood industries (including scallops, oysters, mussels, and crabs) as well as commercial and recreational fishing (a $9.5 billion industry in Oregon and Washington, with 84,000 jobs at stake) are likely to be affected by climate change
    - Ocean salmon, herring, mackerel, and other commercial finfish, dependent on food chain base species, are also likely to be adversely affected.[8]

The list above focuses on direct financial and economic impacts. Beyond those are the effects on inland wildlife and biodiversity, the loss of ecosystem services, and the impact on public health, as increased summer heat and poor air quality stress our most vulnerable residents, including older populations; those with heart disease, asthma, and other respiratory diseases; and homeless people and those who otherwise lack access to adequate shelter. Wildfires burn homes and aggravate the housing crisis. Moreover, this "snapshot" doesn't account for the cumulative effects of climate change. Multiple years of a depressed tourism industry due to wildfires or shorter skiing seasons can cause business closures and the loss of jobs. Increasing blackouts and brownouts from overstressed electricity grids negatively affect businesses and the residences. The likely interconnected consequences of climate change are enormous.

Finally, these data give only a "30,000-foot view" of the effects of climate change. Some clusters of populations will suffer earlier and more critically from climate change. Residents in poorer urban neighborhoods like East Portland, where there are fewer trees and air conditioners, already suffer from rising temperatures through what is known as the "urban heat island" effect (discussed in chap. 4). During the heat dome in summer 2021, dozens of people in Multnomah

County—mainly low income, elderly—died. As another example, residents in parts of southeastern Oregon may suffer disproportionately from the impacts to water resources from climate change. Drought has already caused water tables to drop, forcing residents to either dig their private wells more deeply, or to drive tens of miles to the nearest town to fill water tanks to meet their daily domestic needs.[9] These "silent" impacts will worsen in years ahead.

Other Environmental Hazards

Besides climate change, another significant environmental hazard to people and built structures in Oregon is earthquakes. Numerous faults run across the state, especially in the central Cascades and Portland metropolitan regions. State policy to increase the stringency of statewide seismic building standards was implemented in 1993, after a 7.1-magnitude quake damaged the state capitol. In 2013, the state issued the *Oregon Resilience Plan*, a report by the Oregon Seismic Safety Policy Advisory Commission, which brought in expert perspectives.

In 2015, an article in the *New Yorker* brought increased awareness to the public about the threat of a potentially devastating earthquake.[10] The "Big One," considered in the article is an earthquake triggered in the Cascadia Subduction Zone. As shown in figure 3.1, much of Oregon—especially western Oregon—is classified as part of the highest hazard category for earthquakes, compared to much of the rest of the country. State geologists have determined that, historically, an earthquake has occurred along this plate roughly every three hundred to six hundred years, with the last occurring in 1700. They estimate that there is a 37 percent chance of an earthquake of 7.1 magnitude or higher occurring in the next fifty years. Most of the western part of the state would experience the impacts of such a quake. Waves up to a hundred feet high would inundate the Oregon coast, and severe earth shaking and liquefaction would affect inland areas.[11]

The damage from a severe earthquake will be direct, indirect, or both. Direct impacts are the physical effects of buildings collapsing, water supplies becoming contaminated, and utilities being interrupted. Indirect effects are disruptions to transportation routes, communication lines and financial services, medical care for chronic ailments, supply chain failures, and business closures. The interdependent nature of

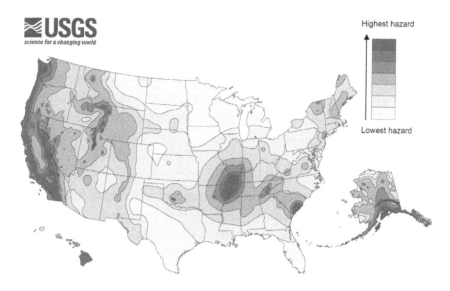

Figure 3.1. Long-term national seismic hazard map, 2018. *Source*: US Geological Society, https://www.usgs.gov/media/images/2018-long-term-national-seismic-hazard-map

our systems suggests that regardless of physical proximity, the whole state would feel the disruption of a 9.0-magnitude earthquake for an extended amount of time. An earthquake that large would devastate coastal areas with ground shaking, landslides, and a tsunami. The Willamette Valley would experience severe shaking, liquefaction, and potentially horrendous damage to oil storage facilities, triggering lethal fires and toxic smoke. Landslides and fallen bridges would paralyze transportation along the I-5 corridor and across to the coast.

Besides climate change and earthquakes, there are other hazards. Altogether, the state faces a lot of risks, though those vary by geography. Figure 3.2 illustrates the areas at risk from drought, according to state and federal sources. During the past twenty years, more than half the state has experienced some level of drought, and during the period 2014-16, about half the state was recorded at the "severe drought" or higher level. Crop losses are highly likely at this level.

Many environmental hazards are aggravated to varying degrees by changes in the global climate, thus highlighting the linkages between and among changes in our biophysical environment.

The state faces additional hazards that are not illustrated here, such as coastal erosion, landslides, volcanoes, windstorms, and tornadoes.

CLIMATE CHANGE, ENVIRONMENTAL HAZARDS, AND RESILIENCE 67

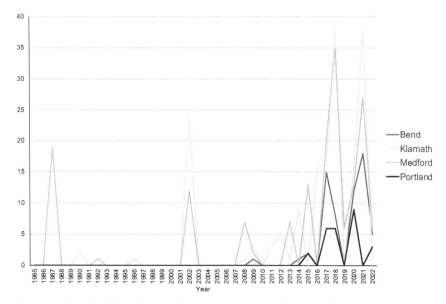

Figure 3.2. Drought-affected areas in Oregon in 2023. *Source*: "US Drought Monitor: Oregon," National Drought Mitigation Center, University of Nebraska-Lincoln, accessed January 17, 2024, https://droughtmonitor.unl.edu/CurrentMap/StateDroughtMonitor.aspx?OR

A cumulative look across the risks, and at the maps on HazVu, suggests that virtually no part of the state is safe from potentially devastating hazards, and many parts of the state face intersecting hazards. Drought will intensify water shortages in southeastern Oregon, parching rangelands and agriculture and likely forcing up the price of food for all Oregonians. Residents in the Cascades and coastal mountain ranges are subject to wildfires, aggravated by drought conditions and lower precipitation as weather patterns shift due to global climate change. And climate change will intensify many of these conditions in severity and frequency.[12] The next sections discuss more about who is most at risk and identify some promising interventions and big ideas.

Current Actions to Address Hazards

It is not a lack of public interest that is keeping Oregon from better preparing. In a 2020 random survey of two thousand Oregonians, 82 percent acknowledged climate change, and 62 percent of survey respondents replied that it was "very important" or "extremely important" to them personally. Nearly 70 percent of respondents replied that they believe climate change is harming people now or will in the future.[13] Meanwhile, respondents indicated low satisfaction with the action taken by federal, state, or local public agencies about climate change. In the next pages, we take a look to 2050 and consider, What are we in Oregon doing to prepare for the impacts of climate change and other hazards?

The International Panel on Climate Change emphasizes that there is no one intervention, and local actors like the State of Oregon must pursue a range of strategies, including reducing the use of fossil fuels for electricity dramatically and quickly, changing food production and eating habits, and adapting our land use and transportation systems. In addition to reducing greenhouse gasses as quickly as possible, the IPCC stresses that states and local entities must prepare for and adapt to the changing climate conditions described above. State- and local-led activity to decarbonize and address on-the-ground impacts from climate changes has increased in recent years, though it is not nearly enough. As we look to 2050, Oregon must ramp up the pace of its climate action.

Two important existing organizations in the state are the Oregon Climate Change Research Institute (OCCRI) and the Oregon Global Warming Commission, both established in 2007. The OCCRI is a network of researchers. Its charge is to report to the state legislature information that will contribute to "building climate-informed communities" and "advance the understanding of regional climate, impacts and adaptations."[14] It has issued reports on the state of Oregon's climate in 2010, 2013, 2017, 2019, and 2021. The OGWC is composed of agency heads, legislators, and at-large representatives from academic or state agencies. The OGWC is required to issue a report to the legislature every two years.

One piece of groundwork the state has had in place for a while is the statewide land use planning program, which already includes some elements that help the state prepare for, mitigate, and adapt to climate change and other hazards. For example, Goal 7 identifies some known environmental hazards (wildfire, tsunami, earthquake, landslide, flooding, volcano, etc.) and requires local governments to adopt a natural hazards inventory and to plan in ways that mitigate harm to people and the built environment. While this is more proactive than many other states, the requirements are not stringent, and a lot of infrastructure and housing has already been constructed in high-risk areas, like along the coasts and near rivers, as shown in state hazards maps. Another limitation is that the land use planning program was adopted before widespread knowledge of the risks of earthquake and climate change, and therefore it has not adjusted to current and predicted future incidents related to these (e.g., the increased risk of forest fires due to climate change).

Another related state effort on climate change is its Climate Change Adaptation Framework, first issued in 2010. In 2021, the DLCD updated the framework,[15] a coordinated effort with twenty-four state agencies (called the Workgroup). In response to the more-rapid-than-expected climate changes, they identified five administrative goals in their report:

1. Establish a multiagency leadership structure.
2. Ensure use of best practices in diversity, equity, and inclusion (DEI).
3. Complete a comprehensive climate change vulnerability assessment.
4. Improve interagency coordination and information sharing.
5. Integrate responses to climate change throughout agency operations.

Finally, the report identified climate adaptation strategies organized around six themes: the economy, the natural world, the build environment and infrastructure, public health, cultural heritage, and social relationships and systems. The 2021 framework also emphasized equity, as committee members acknowledged the history of under-engagement of many subpopulations owing to racial, ethnic, and socioeconomic bias. The framework pointed out the need to assist state agency staff with more leadership, communication, training, and tools to advance equity-informed climate action planning. The Climate Adaptation Framework was integrated into the state's Natural Hazards Mitigation Plan in March 2021.

Meanwhile, responding to the Climate Change Framework writers' observation that more rapid actions are needed, Governor Kate Brown issued Executive Order 20-4 in 2020. This executive order instructs sixteen state agencies and commissions to better align their policies and practices to meet goals to reduce greenhouse gas (GHG) emissions to 45 percent below 1990 levels by 2035 and 80 percent below by 2050. State agencies and commissions are directed to strengthen regulatory standards, modify their own operations, and conduct studies to explore more climate-friendly options. For example, the Commission of Environmental Quality and Department of Environmental Quality (DEQ) are instructed to revise fuel standards, emissions standards from stationary sources, methane emissions from landfills, and food waste reduction.

Despite the described efforts, more action is needed. The Department of Land Conservation and Development publicly acknowledges on its website that "Oregon is off track in its work to meet statutory goals and policy to reduce climate pollution, particularly pollution from transportation." As one effort to course correct, the Land Conservation and Development Commission updated Oregon's Transportation Planning Rules and related administrative rules. After two years of extensive community engagement, the commission adopted Climate-Friendly and Equitable Communities rules on July 21, 2022. The rules strengthen Oregon's transportation and housing planning in regions with populations over 50,000 people (Albany, Bend, Corvallis, Eugene/Springfield, Grants Pass, Medford/Ashland, Portland Metro, and Salem/Keizer), intentionally reduce parking requirements, and encourage or require denser development and multimodal transportation and transit planning. While the rules seem poised to advance improved land use and transportation planning, they are being legally contested by up to fourteen local jurisdictions.[16] Meanwhile, it is not clear the new rules are strong enough, or that development interest is high enough, to have a significant impact in terms of reducing GHGs.

Besides state-level efforts, federal efforts will be necessary, though they have been slow in coming. In 2021, the Federal Emergency Management Agency (FEMA) announced a proposal to reassign up to $10 billion in grants for states to adapt to climate change, though this has not moved forward.[17] The Inflation Reduction Act (a slimmed down version of President Biden's Build Back Better Act), passed in 2022, is expected to bring funds to Oregon to accelerate clean energy investment, repair roads and bridges, and increase economic activity and job growth.

In summary, while considerable data have been collected and reports issued about the impending impacts of climate change, much state-level effort remains at the stage of planning and policy development rather than implementation. State agencies have begun to investigate issues concerning equity, but the work is still immature. DLCD's recent efforts may have impacts, but it will take years. Altogether, the state is not acting with the same urgency or comprehensiveness as stressed by the IPCC. With the potential availability of funds from the federal government in coming years, the state is better poised than in the past to undertake concrete actions, but to date the action is still less than what is needed.

While state leadership has been slow, some local governments have made efforts to take climate action. Portland made headlines by becoming the first US city to create a local action plan to address global climate change. The city renewed its efforts in collaboration with Multnomah County and issued the 2015 Climate Action Plan. It has now been joined by several other Oregon cities, including Eugene, Bend, Salem, and Jackson County. These initial efforts focused singularly on greenhouse mitigation efforts, specifically by reducing carbon emissions rather than addressing impacts on the population.

Portland's 2015 Climate Action Plan was innovative among its peers in that it emphasized climate change adaptation and issues of equity and prioritizing vulnerable groups. The 2015 Climate Action Plan integrated a Climate Change Preparation Strategy and a Risk and Vulnerability Assessment, with the latter focusing specifically on the likely impacts on the most sensitive populations. While the city has been forward thinking in planning, it has been slower to actualize concrete projects.

The 2015 plan expired in 2020 and has been replaced by the Climate Emergency Workplan. It is intended to be more actionable and is oriented around the two main strategies of decarbonization and building resiliency, with a continued focus on social equity, including the identification of "resilience actions that respond to the reality that Black, Indigenous and communities of color are being hit first and hardest by these events."

The workplan is only a general blueprint, and now city bureaus and departments must approach their local councils with specific requests over the next three years (2022-25). It remains to be seen if the plan has adequate resources and whether it will result in significant decarbonization and resilience.

Perhaps most promising in Portland has been the passage by voters of a referendum to tax local businesses to fund the Portland Clean Energy Community Benefits Fund (PCEF). Since its start, PCEF has awarded over $120 million in grants to nonprofit organizations to advance energy efficiency, green infrastructure, regenerative agriculture, renewable energy, and/or workforce development projects, and as support for planning and capacity-building efforts. With climate justice as a key goal for the fund, all funded projects must demonstrate leadership by and benefits to the identified priority communities, including people of color and low-income residents. This is an important priority, since a lot of research shows how disaster aid by FEMA and other organization often favors rich communities and white people, rather than those who need it most.[18] The fund has generated more revenue than anticipated, and the Portland City Council recently passed changes to enable the fund to be spent in support of five-year Climate Investment Plans, with some of the funds being channeled through city agencies. In part because of its scope, PCEF seems poised to advance climate justice and resilience in meaningful and concrete ways. It also attracts national attention, as well as critics, and it will be important in terms of statewide efforts to build upon what proves to be effective.

We turn now to how prepared the state is for other environmental hazards, especially earthquakes. In areas prone to such hazards, states and communities historically have looked to FEMA for assistance, which has come largely in the form of after-the-fact recovery aid rather than in planning for mitigation and adaptation. In Oregon, much of federal assistance has come in the form of free workshops and CERT (Community Emergency Response Team) training. Recognizing the challenges of responding quickly to large-scale catastrophic events, FEMA encourages local and state governments *not* to rely on being rescued by the federal government but on their own capabilities and resources.

Meanwhile, at the state level, there are similarities to the state's action regarding climate change. Oregon legislators have elected to provide information and guidelines to local communities, but they have largely shied away from mandating actions or, more importantly, providing material resources to fund mitigation actions.

We can trace Oregon's tepid preparation for hazards back to Goal 7 of Oregon's Statewide Planning Goals, which is to "protect people and property from environmental hazards" by adopting "comprehensive plans (inventories, policies and implementing measures) to reduce harm to people and property from environmental hazards." But much of Goal 7 is narrowly focused on the community participation in the National Flood Insurance Program (NFIP). Generally, the Land Use Commission does not reject comprehensive plans if they fail to address Goal 7 to the level of "best practices." The implication is that communities have planned rather thinly for Goal 7 until recently.

There may be some change afoot with the recent passage of SB 762, Oregon's Wildfire Omnibus Legislation. The bill allocates $220 million to "modernize and improve wildfire preparedness through three key strategies: creating fire-adapted communities, developing safe and effective response, and increasing the resiliency of Oregon's landscapes." Specific projects under the bill like updated wildfire risk maps are underway and are seeking public feedback.

In April 2015, DLCD issued a document titled "Preparing for a Cascadia Subduction Zone Tsunami: A Land Use Guide for Oregon Coastal Communities." This document lays out a strategy for coastal communities to involve residents in creating a plan to prepare for and avoid making land use decisions that will continue to put human lives and property at risk. It provides a useful starting point for a community with adequate resources to carry out such a process.

Following the Loma Linda Earthquake in the Bay Area of California in 1989, the Oregon Senate passed Senate Bill 96 in 1991, establishing the Oregon Seismic Safety Policy Advisory Commission (OSSPAC), also known as the Earthquake Commission. The Earthquake Commission was charged with promoting earthquake awareness and preparedness in Oregon and developing design policies regarding pre-disaster mitigation of earthquake and tsunami hazards.

An indication of the state's awareness of earthquake risk is apparent by the history of seismic building codes. The first statewide building codes in Oregon were passed in 1974. In this action, the entire state was designated as lying in a "zone 2" risk category. The code underwent minor amendments three times until 1988, when a third risk zone was created, acknowledging additional risk to structures closer to faults. In 1998, a fourth risk zone was added, in which most of the Oregon coast was included. Finally, the eleventh code revision in 2010 brought the state's building codes up to international standards.[19] While this is a step forward for resiliency, builders often point to regulations like these as increasing the cost of new housing and office buildings.

In 2013, OSSPAC produced the Oregon Resilience Plan (as instructed by a resolution of the Oregon House in 2011) to propose "recommendations on policy direction to protect lives and keep commerce flowing during and after a Cascadia (megathrust) earthquake and tsunami."[20] The plan is divided into seven topical areas and contains hundreds of recommendations for action. In 2018, the state resilience officer (a position created in response to a recommendation in the plan) issued an assessment of the plan's accomplishments to date. In summary, with the exception of the creation of the state resilience officer in 2016, most recommendations are "in progress" at best. A notable exception to this lack of support are grants for seismic upgrading that have been allocated to many (not all) school districts.

The Oregon Department of Geology and Mineral Industry (DOGAMI) has been the primary source of technical information on earthquakes and tsunami in the state (though it is plagued by funding challenges). The agency has provided hundreds of maps and other forms of consultation for communities delineating tsunami inundation zones, landslide-prone mountainsides, and other hazardous areas, including the HazVu online map viewer. It has also set up a grant program to subsidize seismic upgrading of critical public facilities and schools. The Seismic Rehabilitation Grant Program provides up to $2.5 million per project for upgrading. Its efforts depend heavily on federal grants and local contracts to fill out its budget (other than mining oversight activities, which are conducted on a fee basis), a limitation to its efforts.

DOGAMI recently issued revised tsunami inundation maps that brought more land into the high-risk zone, which was highly unpopular among coastal state legislators who blocked their release. In June 2020, a high-level engineer who provided essential information on earthquakes, tsunamis, and the state's resilience plan was just one of several essential experts who were laid off.[21] The downsizing of DOGAMI and the loss of expertise there pose a serious threat to public safety.

DLCD continues to have authority under Goal 7 to "trigger Goal 7 review" by a local government, but it has chosen to use an incentive approach instead. While "triggering" Goal 7 does not necessarily mean that a local government needs to respond with best practices, it would force them to consider and make plan adjustments to respond to the data they found compelling. If this process does happen in the future, it would ideally involve public engagement (Goal 1) and bring community voices and experts in hazard management to the discussion.

Perhaps the most telling statement about preparedness efforts at the state level, however, was the Oregon state legislators' 2019 repeal of a law prohibiting the siting of new schools, hospitals, jails, and police and fire stations in the tsunami inundation zone. Legislators noted the importance of providing such community amenities to coastal residents in obtaining property insurance, and in overall economic development in their communities.[22]

In summary, the state has sponsored commendable efforts to increase the information and knowledge base for hazard mitigation. As with climate change impacts, however, until recently, the state has stopped short of directing specific actions by local governments or private actors. The state has also failed to provide local governments with funds, resources, or political backup that would enable them to take more directive stances and withstand local political opposition to adaptive policies. State agencies have begun to investigate issues concerning equity, but the work is still immature. With the potential availability of funds from the federal government under the Inflation Reduction Act, remedial actions are expected.

Meanwhile, local responses across the state to the threat of a large magnitude earthquake and tsunami have been mixed. An "early responder" in 2011 of the tsunami warning, Lincoln City's voters supported a $63 million bond to move the Waldport High School out of the tsunami zone. After years of controversy and a failed bond measure in 2013, the coastal city of Seaside finally approved a $100 million bond measure to relocate three schools out of the tsunami inundation zone.[23] The affirmative vote was no doubt helped along by a donation of upland land by Weyerhaeuser.[24] Finally, reflecting both concerns about tsunami threats and the intent to create a research facility on the coast, the Hatfield Marine Science Center at the mouth of the Yaquina Bay included construction of a forty-seven-foot building to serve as a vertical evaluation site for up to nine hundred persons, and it provides regular staff training in emergency preparedness and response.

In contrast, farther south, the City of Gold Beach chose to build their new hospital four blocks off the coast. Although some seismic upgrading was included in the construction, the location is only fifty feet above sea level and squarely in the tsunami inundation zone. Town leaders cited budgetary issues and ease of access to the site (about one block off the main highway, US 101) as the reasoning behind their decision.[25]

Decisions in the state's largest city have similarly been fraught with controversy. The City of Portland has failed to enact a policy that would protect human lives in the event of a major earthquake, in part because of public opposition. Unreinforced masonry buildings (URMs), brick buildings constructed without structural reinforcements, are susceptible to earthquake damage. Portland has identified hundreds of URMs, including schools, churches, commercial establishments, and multi-family housing across the city. But despite the potential danger from collapsing structures, opposition to new regulations, including the placement of a simple placard notifying occupants of URMs, erupted. Property owners, including church organizations, organized in a group called Save Portland Buildings. Fearing the costs of retrofitting and reinforcing the largely historic structures, and the potential loss of character and identity of older neighborhoods, the group vehemently opposed policy changes. After years of public discussion and deliberations, the city repealed a requirement for notification and placarding of URM buildings in 2019, and dissolved the task force to develop URM standards in 2020.[26] Furthermore, the city's database of URMs is now available only through a public records request.[27]

Other local responses to the threat of earthquakes have centered on recovery rather than mitigation. Several of the larger communities in the Willamette Valley have organized local teams to assist in emergency response. In the City of Portland, Neighborhood Emergency Teams (NETs) are composed of resident volunteers trained by the Portland Bureau of Emergency Management (PBEM) to help their neighbors during an emergency. NETs are otherwise known as CERTs, or Community Emergency Response Teams, a FEMA program designed to promote emergency preparedness among a local population. The assumption here is that during a massive emergency, communities should not rely on "getting rescued," but they need to be ready to help themselves (and each other) because emergency responders will be limited in their ability to reach all areas in need, either due to high demand or because of physical obstacles like landslides, bridge failures, and fires.

Interestingly, despite the threat of tsunamis, not all coastal communities have mobilized around emergency response or have organized CERT teams. Cannon Beach is a notable exception, and that community has made the news by attempting to construct a community "cache" where residents can store emergency supplies. In Seaside, some elected officials are focusing efforts to generate additional city funds to fortify the town's many bridges.[28] A proposal to impose an additional lodging tax on visitors was unsuccessful. Local officials in communities heavily dependent on tourism often face an uphill battle to educate residents and motivate the hospitality industry to adequately inform visitors about disaster preparedness. That said, a survey conducted in 2014 showed that visitors were willing to add one to twenty dollars per day per person to the cost of visiting the coast if such funds were dedicated to earthquake and tsunami safety, suggesting another possible source of revenue.[29]

With respect to voluntary organizations, a rare example is the Emergency Volunteer Corp in the Manzanita/Nehalem/Wheeler area. This group has conducted surveys to establish resident awareness and provided critical information to residents regarding evacuation routes and go-bags. Another example is the North Coast Land Conservancy. This organization has worked for years to connect and increase protected lands along the Oregon coast for habitat protection. Their efforts to preserve older trees concurrently increase water-filtering functions of forestlands and contribute to improved water quantity and quality, which can be conceived as long-term strategy to overcome a water crisis due to either a massive earthquake (that ravages reservoirs) or climate change. Recently, the North Coast Land Conservancy deeded land to a local Native American tribe, acknowledging the sustainable attributes of the tribe's philosophy and approach to nature.[30]

Although voluntary efforts are admirable, they raise equity concerns since not every subcommunity can afford to expend time, energy, and resources on voluntary actions. So, while voluntary efforts by concerned citizens is a smart strategy for many reasons, the state's non-mandatory approach and lack of leadership has resulted in reinforcing a pattern in which communities with financial and human resources are able to respond, while those without cannot. Those most vulnerable to risks are often left out.

Barriers and Opportunities for Action on the Path to 2050

Unfortunately, the historical development of our state has misled us down a path of less inclusion and participation in decisions about our public spaces and collective resources. Instead, as political scientist Charles Lindblom and sociologist Harvey Moloch pointed out decades ago,[31] local (and state) governments, alongside others, have privileged the demands of business and industry over residents, reflecting their dependence on local tax revenue, employment opportunities for residents, and even personal political favors. The past decades of development in Oregon have created a path dependency, a concept in economics and the social sciences where past events or decisions constrain later events or decisions. Moreover, and perhaps more insidiously, the methods that are relied upon to assess options for public action, such as cost-benefit analysis, favor high-value land over areas of lower value. For example, the benefit-to-cost ratio of installing flood protection in a wealthy neighborhood would outweigh the same effort in a poorer neighborhood. Without consideration of nonmonetized values, investment in protecting higher-price land and properties would yield a higher "bang for the buck." Uncritically relying on cost-benefit analysis leads decision-makers to opt to prevent flood damage in the more expensive areas. Finally, as environmental justice scholars have noted for decades, racism in public decision-making disempowers communities of color and puts them at higher risk of hazards.[32]

The State of Oregon is known for its commitment to planning ahead. This review of the status of Oregon's readiness to respond and adapt to expected but unpredictable events through effective adaptation and mitigation up to now is not encouraging, however. While the state has provided valuable information and reports to Oregon's communities to clarify where threats exist, without staff resources and funding, local governments are left on their own, buffeted between the winds of economic imperatives and the local business community demands, building and development practice that is uncritical of business as usual and path dependency, human and ecosystem safety, and calls to right environmental injustices by attending to the needs of vulnerable groups that have been overlooked in the past.

When state or local officials attempt more stringent regulations in order to nudge communities to strengthen their resilience, they sometimes find resistance. After the wildfires of 2020, homebuilder groups seeking to help victims rebuild their homes and lives continued to oppose statewide fire codes requiring the use of fire-resistant materials, in part because of the higher short-term costs. SB 762 has moved the conversation some, but not dramatically. While "building back better" is an admirable goal, under- or uninsured property owners may struggle simply to build back.[33] Although the timing of introducing more stringent policies may have been a critical factor in the case of wildfires, opposition of the City of Portland's URMs policy demonstrates political challenges even in times that seem to lack urgency. The examples above illustrate the powerful role that private industry, landowners, and lobbyists hold in undertaking mitigation measures. The financial cost of mitigation is a huge deterrent to action and requires a strong commitment to action.

The choice is between investing our limited funds now to adapt to or mitigate the impacts of climate change or a massive earthquake, or to wait and patch funds together to clean up debris and respond to disasters. The FEMA estimate of six dollars of savings to every one dollar invested in mitigation is impressive, but apparently not persuasive. The slow but certain depletion of water resources, wildlife, and increasingly warmer temperatures is occurring at a pace that challenges elected leaders, given their limited terms of office and the urgency of other economic and social issues. Meanwhile, a massive 9.0-magnitude earthquake is hard to predict and tends to be out of sight, out of mind. It is hard to choose to invest the state's millions of dollars to thwart the effects of invisible forces. With current demands for equity and rectifying systemic harms, where and how much to invest first adds new complexity. The urgent needs for housing, food security, and public health today have often gotten more political attention than longer-term concerns and hazards like climate change, despite their interrelated nature.

One way to build political will to address hazards may be in getting people to consider a variety of scenarios and impacts. The state's economy is one thing; another is our own personal safety and well-being and those of friends and neighbors. Even if our homes are in an "earthquake-safe zone," for example, we (and our loved ones) won't be protected if we (or they) happen to be traveling down a coastal highway or crossing a bridge when the catastrophic quake strikes. John Rawls coined a useful phrase that is relevant here: a veil of ignorance.[34] He suggested that if we did not know what our societal position would be in the future—where we will be, what resources we will have access to, who we will be with—we would likely choose principles of governance that would protect the least well-off in society.

With a Rawlsian frame, the following ideas for moving forward emerge. First, our conversation about "what to do" must be inclusive geographically and politically. Owing to the great uncertainties surrounding these threats, we need an "all-hands-on-deck" approach to developing options, including various levels of government with an emphasis on state and local, private businesses, and community organizations that represent the diversity of racial and socioeconomic identities in our state. The overarching reality is that the biophysical impacts of climate change or a catastrophic earthquake will affect all of us, regardless of whether we are rich or poor, young or old, a fifth-generation Oregonian or a newcomer. Finding ways to work together will ensure a better future for all of us.

Second, this conversation must recognize the value of listening to and synthesizing all forms of knowledge, from the sophisticated climatologists, geologists, economists, and other experts to the knowledge of and about the people and aspects of the place that are not detailed on a map or captured in a model but are held by residents on the ground. Technical information should be designed for the receiver—both in terms of how it is communicated, by whom, and the likely impacts on the work and mission of the organizations, and with consideration of the daily lives of the individual and their close family and friends. We have learned that some people respond to numbers and statistics while other relate to stories and narratives.[35] In other words, in addition to projecting the impacts of rising global temperatures or the probability of a 9.0-magnitude earthquake, we need to create scenarios of these future (potential) changes that residents can relate to, scenarios that are as real as the wildfire smoke outside my window during the summer of

2020. We have learned that people are more likely to trust those within their established social networks, such as friends, family members, and community or religious leaders. So, returning to the importance of process—who is involved in the sharing of information and their connections to the public—is critical. Well-respected community leaders with whom the public can identify and trust must be among the first to include.

The third critical factor is leadership, including specific direction and resources. There are basically two alternatives: public leadership (through state government actions) or private initiatives (through business and nonprofit organizations, churches, and individuals). Rights and responsibilities of public agencies blend with private (individual and business) initiatives. Voluntary efforts by both residents and businesses to prepare and mitigate potential harm is essential, laudable, and to be encouraged. Indeed, the High Desert Collaborative in Eastern Oregon demonstrates how community leaders from multiple levels of government and local landowners and businesspeople can successfully develop and implement wise solutions to sticky resource management issues, ranging from wetlands conservation to wildfires.[36] While these partnerships have developed up to now without explicit attention to the impacts of climate change, the relationships and shared commitments have demonstrated their ability to meet challenges as they emerge. This collaborative has exploited well the strengths of each stakeholder group: private businesses, federal agencies, and property owners. Importantly, landowners have legal rights to make decisions about the use of their land and property. In southeastern Oregon, however, residents have learned that working together yields benefits that working alone has not and cannot.

In summary, the process must be inclusive in order to succeed. We will need to work together, recognizing that our future depends on others, asking for and offering help, cultivating a sense of shared responsibility for all Oregonians. Decisions and actions may best be made at the local level with local intelligence and information, expertise and resources from all sources. More importantly, local governments rarely have either the financial resources or the political strength to counter arguments from industry and property owners concerned about costs. Therefore state government may be in the best position to develop a system to generate and reallocate funds to assign them where they are most needed through a process that involves local communities.

Big Ideas

We now turn to some big ideas for Oregon to best prepare for the impacts of climate change and environmental hazards. Given the variations in the types of threats different parts of the state face, we cannot prescribe a single course. State leadership, however, can be demonstrated through a set of guiding principles.

First, given the uncertainties of the impacts noted in this chapter, efforts should protect and help all people in the face of hazards, especially the most vulnerable. This is not a matter of moral imperative, but it is also instrumentally rational. We simply don't know who will be in a position to help others when a calamity occurs. We have learned that technologies and services that help the most vulnerable among us often serve a wider array of groups than we may have originally considered. For example, public transit helps not only the elderly with limited mobility, but also teens not yet old enough for a driver's license and those who do not have access to a car. This sort of thinking should be applied to thinking about mitigation and adaptation strategies.

Second, capital investments in public facilities (including infrastructure) should be built at standards likely to withstand anticipated hazards—such as increased flooding risks and storm events—despite a higher price tag. This could be required under a strengthened and updated Goal 7. This is not a huge deviation from the idea of seismic standards for new building construction, but we haven't transferred this philosophy to the locations and construction of big capital projects such as hospitals, bridges, and water reservoirs. Localities are often on their own to navigate the realities of repairing historic infrastructure and preparing for natural hazards, all on tight budgets. A recent positive example of assisting local efforts was made in 2021 by US Senators Ron Wyden and Jeff Merkley, who obtained more than $13.5 million from the American Rescue Plan Act to enhance the capacity of seven regional airports to deal with evacuating residents during emergency situations.

Third, we should aim to seek "and" rather than "or" solutions. We face a long list of urgent needs today, such as affordable housing, adequate medical care, food security, and healthy air and water. When affordable housing or reservoir expansions are needed today, we should opt to invest in technologies that will afford better protection against earthquake and other extreme events. The costs may be higher than other alternatives, but a statewide agreement to allow local communities to access state funds to enable such development will save the state's mental and (likely) fiscal health. The Seaside public school relocation is an excellent example this idea—constructing newer facilities both to accommodate a growing population and to protect the lives of children in the event of an epic tsunami.

In order to afford these potentially costlier options, the state will need to generate funds that can be disbursed to communities. The City of Portland's approach with the PCEF is one model, and its justice lens is one that should be followed to avoid the otherwise likely reality that funding would disproportionately benefit the rich and white residents and more resourced organizations. Although tax increases are generally strenuously resisted by business and voters alike, there are many benefits of reducing the likelihood of deaths and injuries, the loss of homes, and business interruptions. For additional ideas for revenue generation, and some of their considerations, see chapter 14.

Fourth, we can foster pods of self-sufficiency of varying scales, depending on the functions. One way to start is to reshape the urban forms of our towns and cities to create more compact communities—a strategy also discussed in chapters 7 and 8, as it intersects the topics of land use and transportation. The City of Portland has adopted the notion of a "twenty-minute neighborhood" or "complete neighborhoods," the idea that daily services and needs should be available to all residents within a twenty-minute walk, wheelchair, or bike ride. Such changes in urban form won't happen overnight, but if we start today, we will get that much closer in thirty years' time. Such physical layouts enable residents to access amenities without driving—an important decarbonization strategy—and increase the likelihood that a collapsed bridge or a landslide will not cut people off from necessary services and resources during an emergency. The state has fostered such urban forms through the land use planning program and more recently through the Climate Friendly Equitable Communities rule changes, but there is a long way to go, particularly in neighborhoods that were built to accommodate automobiles and that face challenges like unconnected streets and busy multilane highways.

Many communities, from Portland (in East Portland to La Grande, are also creating "resilience hubs" using existing community centers or schools, often upgraded with renewable energy production and infrastructure to withstand sustained brownouts and blackouts, to serve as refuge areas for those suffering from extreme heat or long-term damage to their homes caused by flooding or wildfires. Such resilience hubs are likely to be critical infrastructure in terms of saving lives as extreme weather intensifies.

A fifth big idea is to re-localize our economy, at least to a degree, in the aims of resilience. Along these lines, "buying local," from food to other goods, not only supports our local economy today but also creates a production system of essential products and supports the cultivation of skills among local residents. When a catastrophic 9.0-magnitude earthquake occurs, the surviving population will already have skills and resources to withstand disruptions in services and supply chains, and to support recovery. While total self-sufficiency for any community may be out of reach and outside of our desires (given our dependence on imported products such as coffee and spices grown elsewhere, alongside a more diversified food supply than Oregon's climate allows year-round), a move toward "local production for local consumption" will serve us well. This will take massive investments on different fronts, for example, the matching of local farmers with appropriate infrastructure and steady markets. Even with those efforts, there will be a need to adapt during emergencies.

Finally, advances in solar and battery storage technologies increase opportunities for decentralized energy production. A massive earthquake will likely disrupt energy generation and transmission facilities; the more that dispersed sources are distributed across our landscape, the less likely extreme events are to disrupt services. Although examples of decentralized electricity grids are scarce, one can imagine that schools or community resilience centers fitted with solar panels and battery storage can serve as community cooling centers during heat waves and recharging sites for household and personal appliances when an earthquake, flood, or landslide damages infrastructure and curtails service. Along with an initiative to increase decentralized solar energy production facilities is the ongoing efforts to aim for "net zero" energy and water needs (discussed in chap. 4), which can also serve as employment generators in communities where it is needed (as noted in chap. 11). Public policies that support energy and water conservation put in place today will reduce reliance on these critical infrastructures.

These are just a few big ideas that Oregon can pursue to create greater resilience in the face of climate change and environmental hazards. A final plea for sound governance is the creation of a "watchdog" group. While the State of Oregon must show leadership, nongovernmental organizations (e.g., the American Civil Liberties Union, labor unions, environmental groups) that equitably represent the public interest and full diversity of Oregonians can play a critical role (as did 1000 Friends of Oregon in the case of land use) to keep the state on task and moving forward, enabling the state to attain true resilience.

Notes

This chapter would not have been possible without the inspiration and guidance of four community reviewers: Brenda Smith and Dan Nicholson from Harney County, Jay Wilson from Clackamas County, and Tom Horning of Seaside, Oregon.

1. "Oregon Heat Deaths, Revised," Oregon Public Broadcasting, accessed December 17, 2023, www.opb.org/pdf/OREGON_heat_deaths_revised_1628632311939.pdf.
2. "Wildfire Risks to Communities," US Department of Agriculture, accessed February 12, 2021, wildfirerisk.org/explore/3/41.
3. Oregon Health Authority, *Climate and Health in Oregon: 2020 Report* (Portland: Public Health Division, Oregon Health Authority, 2020), www.oregon.gov/oha/ph/healthyenvironments/climatechange/pages/profile-report.aspx.
4. Meghan M. Dalton, Kathie D. Dello, Linnia Hawkins, Philip W. Mote, and David E. Rupp, *The Third Oregon Climate Assessment Report* (Corvallis: Oregon Climate Change Research Institute, Oregon State University, 2017), 14.
5. P. W. Mote, J. Abatzoglou, K. D. Dello, K. Hegewisch, and D. E. Rupp, *Fourth Oregon Climate Assessment Report* (Corvallis: Oregon Climate Change Research Institute, Oregon State University, 2019).
6. Oregon Department of Land Conservation and Development, *2020 Climate Change Adaptation Framework* (review draft, August 12, 2020) (Salem: Oregon Department of Land Conservation and Development, 2020), www.oregon.gov/lcd/NH/Documents/Apx_9.1.23_DRAFT_ClimChgAdaptFmwk_08122020.pdf.
7. Oregon Global Warming Commission, *2018 Biennial Report to the Legislature* (Salem: Oregon Global Warming Commission, 2019), 31.
8. Dalton et al., *Third Oregon Climate Assessment Report*.
9. Dan Nichols and Brenda Smith, personal communication, November 2020.
10. Kathryn Schulz, "The Really Big One," *New Yorker*, July 13, 2015.

11 "Cascadia Subduction Zone," Oregon Office of Emergency Management, accessed December 23, 2020, www.oregon.gov/OEM/hazardsprep/Pages/Cascadia-Subduction-Zone.aspx.
12 Oregon Department of Emergency Management, *Oregon Natural Hazards Mitigation Plan* (Salem: Oregon Department of Emergency Management, 2020), 14.
13 Unpublished data from ongoing study by Chris Koski and Paul Manson, Reed College, Portland, OR, December 2020.
14 Website of the Oregon Climate Change Research Institute, accessed February 19, 2024, https://blogs.oregonstate.edu/occri/.
15 Oregon Department of Land Conservation and Development, *2021 State Agency Climate Adaptation Framework* (Salem: Oregon Department of Land Conservation and Development, 2021), www.oregon.gov/lcd/CL/Documents/2021_CLIMATE_CHANGE_ADAPTATION_FRAMEWORKandBlueprint.pdf.
16 Sophie Peel and Nigel Jaquiss, "Fourteen Local Governments Sue State to Block Implementation of Governor's Executive Order on Climate," *Willamette Week*, November 21, 2022, www.wweek.com/news/courts/2022/11/21/fourteen-local-governments-sue-state-to-block-implementation-of-governors-executive-order-on-climate.
17 Christopher Flavelle, "Officials Want to Free Up as Much as $10 Billion to Protect U.S. against Natural Disasters," *New York Times*, January 26, 2021, A17.
18 Christopher Flavelle, "How Disaster Aid Favors White People," *New York Times*, October 27, 2021, https://www.nytimes.com/2021/06/09/climate/nyt-climate-newsletter-fema.html.
19 "A Summary of Requirements in the State of Oregon: Earthquake Design History," Building Codes Division, State of Oregon, February 7, 2012, www.oregon.gov/bcd/codes-stand/Documents/inform-2012-oregon-sesmic-codes-history.pdf.
20 Oregon Department of Emergency Management, *Oregon Resilience Plan, 2016* (Salem: Oregon Department of Emergency Management, 2016), www.oregon.gov/OEM/emresources/Plans_Assessments/Pages/Other-Plans.aspx.
21 Kale Williams, "Loss of High-Level Engineer at State Geology Agency Is a Detriment to Public Safety in Oregon," Oregon Live, August 3, 2020, https://www.oregonlive.com/pacific-northwest-news/2020/08/loss-of-high-level-engineer-at-state-geology-agency-is-a-detriment-to-public-safety-in-oregon.html.
22 Traci Loew, "Oregon Legislature Repeals Tsunami Zone Building Law," *Statesmen Journal*, June 24, 2019, https://www.statesmanjournal.com/story/news/2019/06/24/oregon-legislature-repeals-law-prohibiting-building-tsunami-zone/1449450001/.
23 Keely Chalmers, "Seaside District Voters Approve Bond to Relocate 3 Schools," KGW, November 10, 2016, www.kgw.com/article/news/seaside-district-voters-approve-bond-to-relocate-3-schools/283-350784388.
24 Chalmers, "Seaside District Voters Approve Bond."
25 Kristian Foden-Vencil, "Why Build a Hospital in a Tsunami Zone?," Oregon Public Broadcasting, January 26, 2015, www.opb.org/news/series/unprepared/new-hospital-planned-in-tsunami-zone/.
26 "Development Services," City of Portland, accessed February 12, 2021, https://www.portlandoregon.gov/bds/70766.
27 "Unreinforced Masonry Buildings," City of Portland, accessed February 12, 2021, https://www.portland.gov/bds/unreinforced-masonry-urm-buildings.
28 Interview with Tom Horning, Seaside City councilor, June 2019.

29 C. Ozawa and P. Manson, unpublished report, 2015.
30 "NCLC Returns Ancient Cultural Site to Clatsop-Nehalem Confederated Tribes," North Coast Land Conservancy, accessed February 12, 202,1 https://nclctrust.org/nclc-returns-ancient-cultural-site/.
31 Harvey Molotch, "The City as a Growth Machine: Toward a Political Economy of Place," *American Journal of Sociology* 82, no. 2 (1976): 309-32.
32 Robert Bullard, *Dumping in Dixie: Race, Class and Environmental Quality*, 3rd ed. (Boulder, CO: Westview Press, 2000).
33 Lauren Sommer, "Rebuilding after a Wildfire? Most States Don't Require Fire-Resistant Materials," *Morning Edition*, National Public Radio, November 25, 2020, https://www.npr.org/2020/11/25/936685629/rebuilding-after-a-wildfire-most-states-dont-require-fire-resistant-materials.
34 John Rawls, *A Theory of Justice* (Cambridge, MA: Harvard University Press, 1999).
35 Iris Lok, Evan Eschelmuller, Terje Haukaas, Carlos Ventura, Armin Bebamzadeh, Paul Slovic, and Elizabeth Dunn, "Can We Apply the Psychology of Risk Perception to Increase Earthquake Preparation?," *Collaborative Psychology* 5, no. 1 (2019): 47.
36 High Desert Partnership website, accessed February 19, 2021, https://highdesertpartnership.org/.

4
Environmental Quality and Health
An Overview
DANA HELLMAN AND VIVEK SHANDAS

Individuals, cities, tribes, and counties across Oregon are confronting environmental crises such as climate change and resource degradation. In times like these, considerations of environmental quality and health have new meaning and urgency. Environmental health is rooted in a concern for human experience and quality of life, free from toxics, climate-induced disasters, and suffering as a result of environmental factors. While a high degree of environmental quality can provide social, economic, aesthetic, and health benefits, a low degree of quality can create or exacerbate socioeconomic precarity and produce health conditions that lead to distress, sickness, and mortality. All Oregonians may feel the effects of environmental change and degradation, though environmental quality and health outcomes vary significantly across counties, reservations, municipalities, neighborhoods, and demographic groups. This is often the result of historical exclusion, marginalization, and disinvestment, which have disadvantaged low-income areas and communities of color. As we consider how to advance statewide environmental planning efforts within these variable contexts, several difficult questions remain: How should environmental health be conceptualized? What would it take for every community, family, or individual to live in a healthy environment?

In this chapter, we review the relationship between environmental health and quality, and summarize available statewide data and trends. Using three case studies, we then illustrate gaps in understanding that persist owing to shortcomings in environmental health data and insufficient focus on marginal and lived experiences within diverse places.

We argue for changes to agencies like the Department of Environmental Quality (DEQ) and Oregon Health Authority (OHA) to implement improvements in data collection, analysis, engagement, and planning efforts, and to strengthen pollution regulations. These steps for Oregon are discussed in light of current conditions and institutional limitations. We recognize that these actions will be challenging to implement, but we argue that they are worthwhile and necessary if we are to fully comprehend environmental health conditions in Oregon and address ongoing injustices against disinvested communities.

An Overview

Environmental quality is often framed and assessed in terms of public health;[1] quality is a mechanism through which health goals are met or missed. This coalescence of ideas is referred to as environmental health.[2] The American Public Health Association (APHA) defines environmental health as "the branch of public health that focuses on the relationships between people and their environment; promotes human health and well-being; and fosters healthy and safe communities."[3] According to the Centers for Disease Control and Prevention (CDC), it includes any "non-infectious, non-occupational environmental and related factors" that might cause preventable death or illness.[4] For example, poor health outcomes such as asthma or cancer can and often do result from prolonged exposure to toxics such as lead, synthetic chemicals, and household or industrial waste.[5] Inadequate access to outdoor recreational space has been tied to higher rates of obesity.[6] Natural hazards such as heat waves, wildfires, or floods can cause immediate death or injury.[7]

When it comes to environmental quality and health, not all groups will experience the effects equally. The conceptual triad of vulnerability (also discussed in chap. 3), widely used in global climate change literature, explains risk according to exposure, sensitivity, and adaptive capacity.[8] Exposure is the extent to which an individual or community is in direct contact with a potential threat, while sensitivity is the extent to which an individual or community is predisposed to harm from the threat. Adaptive (or coping) capacity describes the ability of an individual or community to prepare for, respond to, and efficiently recover from a potentially harmful threat.[9] Depending on the specific nature of one's vulnerability, health outcomes tied to environmental quality may be more or less severe and require varying types of intervention. For example, some individuals face high risk of exposure to environmental hazards owing to their physical location, perhaps in a floodplain or near an industrial site.[10] Others, such as young children and those with preexisting conditions, are more sensitive to some environmental irritants like wildfire smoke.[11] Low-income individuals, people of color, and other historically marginalized groups often lack the resources to respond to or avoid negative environmental impacts.[12]

Why We Need an Environmental Justice Lens in Oregon

An environmental justice approach emphasizes the just distribution of environmental risks and benefits and may help ensure that improvements to environmental health outcomes and quality are evenly experienced, particularly by those who have been marginalized.[13] An environmental justice lens also directs planners and policymakers to consider historical factors that shape present environmental conditions and inequities, and to pursue community empowerment. The State of Oregon has expressed a general interest in environmental justice and equity across departments. For example, the state runs an Environmental Justice Taskforce and houses the Office of Diversity, Equity, and Inclusion, which has introduced an equity framework for all state agencies. When it comes to environmental health, all Oregonians deserve access to healthy air, clean water, and safe and well-supported neighborhoods. This will require that state agencies—namely, OHA, DEQ, and the Department of Land Conservation and Development (DLCD), among others—and other actors like industry proactively counter deep inequities, and specifically center those communities most affected by and least able to respond to poor environmental quality.

The harmful effects of environmental degradation often fall disproportionately upon communities who are already vulnerable owing to past planning policies, siting decisions, and systemic racism and classism.[14] Understanding environmental quality within the context of historical inequities is essential for correcting them in the future.[15] This means redressing past actions such as the siting of polluting facilities near Black, Indigenous, Latinx, Asian, Pacific Islander, Middle Eastern, mixed-race or mixed-ethnicity communities redlining and other neighborhood covenants that reduced municipal services to specific areas.[16] Despite long-standing theories addressing equity and justice through planning, past processes and programs centered racial and monetary privilege and did not engage a diverse audience in decision-making.[17]

These national trends hold within Oregon. In the Portland region, for example, low-income neighborhoods and communities of color—often relegated to disinvested neighborhoods—currently experience higher-than-normal exposure to extreme heat, are at greater risk of residential flooding, and face disproportionate exposure to air pollution.[18] Meanwhile, Latinx residents in Eugene experience high exposure to air pollution, and in Corbett, they experience rural water pollution from industrial logging.[19] Unfortunately, specific studies and reports from nonurban or less populous localities in Oregon are scarce. Given national trends, however, as well as Oregon's specific history of codified racism, colonialism, segregation, and exclusionary zoning (discussed in other chapters, notably 1, 6, 7, and 10), we can expect many additional environmental justice and health concerns throughout the state.

Situating environmental quality and health outcomes in historical context is critical, but so is fully capturing conditions in the present. We suggest first thinking in terms of environmental threats that consider what environmental threats exist, where they are occurring, and who is most affected by them. While some localities, academic institutions, and community groups within Oregon have granular, evidence-based insights in alignment with these three dimensions, there is no publicly available state repository that tracks or synthesizes data to the same extent.[20]

State Context

There are several key state agencies whose mission and work intersects with environmental health. This book mainly looks at the role of state planning. Among the state land use planning goals administered by DLCD, Goal 6 instructs local governments to consider protection of air, water, and land resources from pollutants when developing comprehensive plans. The pollutants addressed in Goal 6 include solid waste, water waste, noise and thermal pollution, air pollution, and industry-related contaminants. The goal asks cities and counties to designate areas suitable for controlling pollution and to use a variety of market, zoning, and management tools in creating these outcomes.

While it provides a decent foundation, it leaves the details flexible and up to local jurisdictions, so there is not a common, strong baseline of protection. Also, it does not come with its own regulatory authority, so it is only as strong as existing federal and state environmental laws, which (as further discussed in this chapter) are not strong enough. Meanwhile, there is no explicit attention to equity/justice in this goal, a limitation we examine in the case studies in this chapter. Finally, the goal does not contend with the issue of climate change or associated environmental health concerns like urban heat effects and the increase in air pollution from forest fires.

Meanwhile, DEQ is a regulatory agency responsible for protecting the quality of Oregon's air, water, and land. Its statutory mandate is that it administers federal (e.g., the federal Clean Air and Clean Water Acts, the Resource Conservation and Recovery Act, and the Oil Pollution Act) and state laws designed to limit pollution in order to protect public health and the environment. DEQ also works with the Environmental Protection Agency (EPA) to implement the federal Superfund program, which requires cleanup of sites with significant contamination. In addition to its responsibilities under federal law, DEQ implements state programs protecting public health and the environment, including the Cleaner Air Oregon air toxics program, waste management and recycling, groundwater protection, greenhouse gas reduction programs, and environmental cleanup activities for smaller contaminated sites. While DEQ is an important actor, it is both limited in its regulatory scope and authority and not well resourced to do a comprehensive job of monitoring, enforcing, and supporting clearer practices.

While DLCD and DEQ play these roles, pollution and poor environmental health is still a problem in Oregon. The OHA is the central entity responsible for tracking environmental health and quality conditions across Oregon. OHA often collaborates with federal agencies such as the CDC and receives grants to advance specific dimensions of environmental health. For example, the Oregon Data Tracking program is one of twenty-six state-based programs funded by the CDC. As a part of this program, OHA tracks data across four broad categories: environmental quality, health outcomes, people, and community design. This program aims to standardize data across the participating states, but it has some limitations, including overreliance on quantitative methods and coarse data. Still, funding from federal partners like the CDC offers an opportunity to expand statewide data collection.

Environmental health data are housed within OHA's Environmental Public Health division. Some of the issues under the purview of this division include drinking water, food safety, healthy homes and neighborhoods, radiation protection, and workplace health—a more comprehensive list compared to state agencies in California and Washington. Although Environmental Public Health provides general information on all these topics, specific data are more limited. Currently, the division maintains a data portal under the header "environmental quality." This includes information on various facets of water quality, air quality, and health outcomes across the state, typically at the county level.[21]

Water quality data sets include public water use and concentrations of four common contaminants: arsenic, nitrate, haloacetic acids five (HAA5), and trihalomethanes (TTHM). Prolonged exposure to these contaminants may cause cancer, organ damage, and reproductive harm, among other conditions, and they are regulated by the EPA.[22] Air quality data include average annual concentration of PM 2.5 (particulate matter less than 2.5 μm in size), percentage of days with PM 2.5 rates over the national safety standard, and number of days with ozone levels above the national standard. Both PM 2.5 and ozone can cause a range of heart and respiratory problems, including heart attack, difficulty breathing, aggravation of existing heart or lung conditions, and premature death, and they are also federally regulated.[23]

Water and air quality data are available for most Oregon counties for the periods of 2002-17 and 2001-14. There are gaps in the data, however, indicating that measurements have not been consistently taken, particularly apparent in rural, central Oregon counties east of the Cascades, suggesting a data collection bias that favors more populous areas. OHA also provides data on various health conditions, including asthma hospitalizations, birth anomalies, cancer, childhood cancer and lead poisoning, chronic obstructive pulmonary disease, heart attack hospitalizations, and reproductive outcomes.[24] At best, these health data sets cover the period of 2000-2017 at the county level (at the time of writing in 2021), though again, significant gaps exist.

Table 4.1 gives a summary of water and air quality data by the OHA. For each county, recent trends in air and water pollution are identified, broken out by the specific indicators noted above. A designation of "DOWN" indicates a downward trend and decrease in toxic conditions, while "UP" indicates an upward trend or increase in toxic conditions. Maximum recorded values for each indicator in each county are noted below the trend designation. The boldface numbers indicate when maximum values are in excess of federal thresholds;[25]

Table 4.1. Oregon County Trends in Water Contaminants, 2002-17, and Air Contaminants, 2001-14

County	Arsenic (μg/L)	HAA5 (μg/L)	Nitrate[a] (mg/L)	TTHM Concentration (μg/L)	Annual PM 2.5 (μg/m³)	Days Exceeding Safe Ozone Level
Baker	UP 3.03	UP 32.81	DOWN 0.64	UP 38.25	DOWN 8.5	DOWN 1
Benton	UP 4	DOWN 21.8	UP 0.91	DOWN 40.01	DOWN 10.9	DOWN 5
Clackamas	UP 2.58	DOWN 22.28	DOWN 0.64	DOWN **22.19**	DOWN **12.8**	DOWN 7
Clatsop	UP 4.25	DOWN 45.74	DOWN 0.84	DOWN 51.32	DOWN 8.2	DOWN 1
Columbia	UP 6.54	UP 18.88	DOWN 1.51	UP 28.56	DOWN 10.2	DOWN 2
Coos	DOWN 3.8	DOWN 30.28	UP 1.04	DOWN 51.23	DOWN 9.9	DOWN 4
Crook	DOWN 6.33	DOWN 24.7	UP 2.14	DOWN 23.2	DOWN 9.2	DOWN 5
Curry	UP 4.09	UP 24.01	DOWN 1.19	DOWN 46.8	DOWN 11.5	UP 1
Deschutes	UP 4.81	DOWN 11.92	DOWN 1.28	DOWN 7.37	DOWN 10.2	DOWN 9
Douglas	DOWN 4.76	UP 29.55	DOWN 0.26	DOWN 45.71	DOWN **12.8**	DOWN 8
Gilliam	DOWN 11.0	UP 3.43	UP 2	DOWN 26.65	DOWN 8.2	DOWN 3
Grant	UP 2.59	DOWN 21.21	UP 1.06	DOWN 26.06	DOWN 7.9	FLAT 0
Harney	UP 2.97	N/A N/A	UP 2.32	N/A N/A	DOWN 8.1	FLAT 0
Hood River	UP 1.4	DOWN 3.9	DOWN 2.27	DOWN 4.03	DOWN 9.1	DOWN 8
Jackson	UP 7.08	DOWN 16.38	UP 1.19	DOWN 16.74	DOWN **14.8**	DOWN 9
Jefferson	DOWN 7.3	N/A N/A	DOWN 1.11	N/A N/A	DOWN 9.9	DOWN 10

ENVIRONMENTAL QUALITY AND HEALTH

County	Arsenic (μg/L)	HAA5 (μg/L)	Nitrate[a] (mg/L)	TTHM Concentration (μg/L)	Annual PM 2.5 (μg/m^3)	Days Exceeding Safe Ozone Level
Josephine	UP 4.54	DOWN 41.3	UP 1.69	DOWN 41.21	DOWN **12.9**	UP 2
Klamath	UP 5.83	DOWN 3.84	DOWN 0.75	DOWN 2.11	DOWN **16.6**	DOWN 3
Lake	UP **22.38**	UP 4.52	DOWN 1.06	UP 28.6	DOWN 9.1	UP 1
Lane	DOWN 6.03	DOWN 27.74	DOWN 1.27	UP 25.56	DOWN **15.1**	DOWN 12
Lincoln	DOWN 4.65	DOWN 31.31	DOWN 1.1	UP 37.05	DOWN 9.4	DOWN 3
Linn	UP 3.47	DOWN 25.83	DOWN 2.04	DOWN 22.51	DOWN 11.2	DOWN 14
Malheur	UP **11.82**	DOWN 19.83	DOWN 3.32	DOWN 47.48	DOWN 9.9	DOWN 6
Marion	UP 5.84	DOWN 25.42	UP 1.12	DOWN 34.52	DOWN 12	DOWN 7
Morrow	DOWN 8.4	DOWN 7.27	DOWN 3.55	DOWN 19.25	DOWN 8.7	DOWN 4
Multnomah	DOWN 5.41	DOWN 29.17	DOWN 0.65	UP 26.18	DOWN **12.3**	DOWN 2
Polk	UP 4.68	DOWN 25.73	UP 1.78	DOWN 52.53	DOWN 11.2	DOWN 6
Sherman	DOWN 2.85	DOWN 2.4	UP 2.64	UP 27.9	DOWN 8.2	DOWN 3
Tillamook	UP 3.67	DOWN 26.86	UP 1.25	DOWN 41.05	DOWN 8.9	DOWN 2
Umatilla	UP 3.2	DOWN 11.17	UP 1.84	UP 21.39	DOWN 9.3	DOWN 6
Union	UP 2.4	DOWN 5.01	UP 1.82	UP 5.48	N/A N/A	N/A N/A
Wallowa	UP 2.51	DOWN 8.84	UP 1.03	DOWN 17.6	DOWN 8.5	DOWN 1
Wasco	UP 4.68	DOWN 39.58	UP 1.59	DOWN 23.25	DOWN 8.7	DOWN 7
Washington	UP 3	DOWN 26.65	DOWN 0.81	UP 28.51	DOWN **12.4**	DOWN 2
Wheeler	UP 6	DOWN 8	UP 1.97	DOWN 12.45	DOWN 7.7	DOWN 2
Yamhill	UP 3.38	DOWN 25.13	DOWN 0.85	DOWN 27.41	DOWN 11.6	DOWN 2

Note: Abbreviations are as follows: HAA5, halacetic acids in drinking water; NA, not available; PM 2.5, fine particulate matter in air; TTHM, trihalomethanes, chemicals in drinking water. Values that exceed federal thresholds are boldfaced.

[a]Nitrates are often from fertilizers and runoff.

Source: Data from the Oregon Health Authority.

this applies to all indicators except for ozone, which is a count of days over the federal limit and not subject to a threshold.

These numbers tell a generally positive picture of environmental health and quality conditions in Oregon. More often than not, concentrations of aquatic contaminants and air pollutants by county have been trending downward. From 2002 to 2017, maximum recorded water pollutants exceeded the federal threshold in only 3 of 144 instances (2.1 percent)—notably, arsenic levels in Gilliam, Lake, and Malheur Counties. Among maximum recorded air contaminants in 2001-14, annual PM 2.5 exceeded federal limits in 8 of 35 counties (23 percent). Many of those are in the Portland metropolitan region and along the I-5 corridor, though PM 2.5 levels are trending downward in all 35 counties reporting. High-ozone days are either trending downward, or flat at zero days, in 32 of 35 counties (91.4 percent) reporting. OHA data, not included in this table, further indicate stable or improving conditions with regard to several health outcomes. Statewide, rates of breast and lung cancer are down slightly, while occurrences of all other cancers have remained relatively stable, neither increasing nor decreasing significantly from 2001 to 2015. Heart attack and asthma hospitalizations have also been trending downward for all age groups in the state from 2000 to 2017. Rates of infant mortality, preterm birth, and low birth weight have been nearly stable or trending slightly downward from 2000 to 2015. Childhood lead poisoning has declined considerably in the past twenty years. Positive outcomes like these are likely attributable to state policies and initiatives such as the Oregon Indoor Clean Air Act and Oregon Drinking Water Quality Act, as well as compliance with federal policies including the Clean Air Act, Clean Water Act, and Lead-Safe Housing Rule. Although these data are encouraging, they do not provide a complete picture of environmental health across the state.

Gaps in Understanding: Available Data versus Lived Experience

OHA generally provides the only data set that offers comparable information by county and across the state. Most counties have their own public health departments (e.g., the Multnomah County Health Department) that may contribute data or staff expertise toward the pursuit of local environmental health, but these smaller agencies work under different protocols and are not organized statewide. OHA data, meanwhile, are narrow in scope and lack important dimensions that could support more effective decision-making. Here, we offer three case studies from across the state that illustrate gaps in understanding and opportunities for improvement. The purpose of these cases is to demonstrate the localized experiences of two marginalized communities and contrast them against the picture of environmental health evident in OHA data. The third case offers some insights into an environmental stressor, urban heat, for which Oregon does not yet have comprehensive data.

Case Study 1: Air Pollution in West Eugene

Eugene is an urban area in western Oregon and the seat of Lane County, home to the only local air quality agency in the state. Its residents account for 45 percent of the county population.[26] As a populous municipality encompassing industrial sites, major roadways, and other polluting enterprises, Eugene contributes a significant portion of air pollution countywide. At the same time, because Lane County is so large, covering many microclimates from the Pacific Ocean to the Cascades, the true extent of pollution in Eugene's industrial corridor is not reflected in countywide data. It may be expected that some urban populations in Eugene will be disproportionately exposed to air pollution and more likely to suffer adverse health effects, specifically those who live nearest to point sources of pollution (highways, railroads, factories, etc.) and/or have limited access to medical care.[27]

In 2013, two nonprofit groups, Beyond Toxics and Centro Latino Americano, released a report on environmental justice in West Eugene. This area is home to a large proportion (50 percent) of the city's Latinx residents and also faces disproportionately high exposure to air pollution.[28] The participating organizations identified this area as an environmental justice community according to the following criteria: (1) disproportionate exposure to air toxics; (2) higher percentage of poverty/low-income; (3) higher percentage of minority residents; (4) unacceptably high rates of self-reported childhood asthma, often an indicator of an environmental justice community; and (5) less access to educational materials and public decision-making processes.[29]

More than 99 percent of toxic emissions were concentrated in West Eugene, originating from railroads, highways, and industrial

Figure 4.1. Composite images of pollution sources in Eugene. Photos by Dana Hellman.

sites, and disproportionately affected low-income and Latinx communities. This situation was exacerbated by factors such as xenophobia, lack of access to health care, limited English speaking ability, and limited access to information. In addition to particulate matter and ozone, West Eugene's residents were exposed to carbon monoxide, sulfur oxides, and nitrogen oxides.

These data were collected in 2011 and reflect the findings of Beyond Toxics, Centro Latino Americano, and the Bethel School District serving children of West Eugene. If we look at the OHA data for Lane County in the same year, it is not clear that the county (or any locality within it) had a serious problem with air quality. Annual PM 2.5 was below the federal limit of 12 micrograms per cubic meter, and the county experienced only one day of ozone concentration beyond safe limits.[30] Countywide asthma hospitalizations for both children (ages 5-14) and all others decreased from 2010 to 2011 and again from 2011 to 2012, and were below the statewide rate in 2012.[31] Not only did these OHA data fail to draw attention to an air pollution problem in Eugene, they told decision-makers nothing about respiratory illnesses for those most affected communities in West Eugene. These data cannot tell us that the Latinx population faced greater exposure as well as greater difficulty in accessing care, or that childhood asthma rates in West Eugene were higher than the city or county norm. Available OHA data do not account for those airborne toxics beyond PM 2.5 and ground-level ozone, although these were also making residents sick.[32] If local groups had not investigated this situation, it could easily have gone undetected, particularly at the level of state governance.

A recent follow-up survey conducted by Beyond Toxics in 2019-20 shows that little has changed for the residents of West Eugene. Many continue to face high exposure to air toxics and report disproportionately high rates of respiratory illness, though these experiences still are not reflected in OHA's aggregate health data.[33] This case clearly illustrates the importance of granular data, personal narratives, and other qualitative or quantitative data that might challenge mainstream perceptions and encourage action.

Case Study 2: Water Pollution on the Warm Springs Reservation

The Warm Springs Indian Reservation is located in central Oregon, primarily occupying Wasco and Jefferson Counties. It is home to the Confederated Tribes of Warm Springs (CTWS), population 4,296 in 2018,[34] who rely on the Deschutes River for drinking water.

OHA data from the most recent available years show two counties in relatively good standing with regard to water quality. Though HAA5 and TTHM data are unavailable for Jefferson County, arsenic and nitrate levels have been trending downward, far below the federal limits. In Wasco County, arsenic and nitrate are trending upward, HAA5 and TTHM trending downward. Again, federal limits on contamination have not been approached recently.[35] Based on this information alone, there is no indication that either county is suffering poor environmental quality due to water pollution. It is worth noting here that the data do not go past 2017 (at the time of writing in 2021), meaning that any current problems would not be obvious among those relying on OHA datasets. Furthermore, the water quality data sets for Jefferson County are incomplete, missing information for two of the four key aquatic contaminants.

The data limitations become clear when we recognize that residents of the Warm Springs Reservation have experienced chronic water problems, including the need for boil water advisories, for the past three years.[36] Damage to the local water delivery system (mainly cracked pipes) has made tap water unsafe for consumption and limited daily activities such as showering and doing laundry.[37] Because the Confederated Tribes have been consistently disinvested over the centuries and possess limited financial resources to overhaul the system, structural problems persist.[38] Furthermore, the CTWS's emergency manager notes that water coming into the area is already heavily polluted by runoff from farms, parks, and dams. Besides the four contaminants tracked by OHA, water coming to the reservation is reportedly polluted with glass, plastic, and other debris, as well as herbicides, insecticides, medicines, and algae. Problems with water quality and availability took on new urgency during the COVID-19 pandemic as tribal members confronted parallel threats of COVID-19 infection and wildfires.[39]

The reservation's water infrastructure has received considerable media attention, and the State of Oregon recently approved over $3.5 million in funds to address the issue.[40] Structural issues are only part of the problem, however. Even if the water pollution experienced by the CTWS was reflected in OHA data, which it is not, numerical measurements would be lacking the significant complexity appropriate to this situation. Water pollution is not just about the pollutants themselves but also includes the journey the water takes from outside the reservation, and it is affected by historical and structural factors. This case study illustrates the need for more localized data as well as a data assessment that accounts for the relationships between complex health indicators, spatiality, history, and environmental justice.

Case Study 3: Urban Heat in Portland

Portland, located in Multnomah County, is the largest city in Oregon and is susceptible to the urban heat island (UHI) effect.[41] At the regional scale, a UHI occurs when built surfaces such as roads and buildings retain and release heat, producing high and often unsafe ambient temperatures in comparison to surrounding rural areas.[42] Within the city, the UHI effect is exacerbated by the presence of heat-generating activities such as driving and the relative absence of trees and other cooling features.[43] Heat exposure can cause a range of physical and psychological ailments in addition to degrading quality of life. The elderly, outdoor laborers, and those with preexisting health conditions are especially sensitive to heat and may be at increased risk of heart attack and heatstroke.[44] As climate change has progressed, Portland and all of Oregon has experienced an increase in high-temperature days; this trend is expected to continue.

We, the authors, have collaborated on various studies regarding urban heat issues in Portland. Research has shown that the relatively lower-income east side of Portland experiences markedly higher temperatures in the summer compared to the more affluent west side (fig. 4.2).[45] This corresponds with differences in vegetation, as the cooler west side features significantly higher density of trees. Our studies indicate a statistically significant relationship between sociodemographic factors and heat exposure in the city. Census block groups with high poverty, large populations of color, low levels of educational attainment, and low English-speaking ability all experience higher temperatures.[46]

Figure 4.2. Inequitable distribution of urban heat in Portland. *Source*: J. Voelkel, V. Shandas, and B. Haggerty, "Developing High-Resolution Descriptions of Urban Heat Islands: A Public Health Imperative," Preventing Chronic Disease 13 (2016): 160099, doi:http://dx.doi.org/10.5888/pcd13.160099

Another recent national study found current trends in urban heat as related to historical patterns of neighborhood segregation, also known as redlining.[47] In 94 percent of cities studied across the United States, formerly redlined areas now experience higher temperatures than those where redlining did not occur. The Portland area tops the list of 108 cities in terms of temperature differences between redlined and non-redlined counterparts.[48] Urban heat is a growing environmental threat, with demonstrated disproportionate effects on low-income communities and people of color, but it is not systematically tracked at a statewide, countywide, or local level.

These cases clearly show that statewide data are lacking critical components of scale, content, and nuance. On a case-by-case basis, local groups can identify a problem, collect data, work with impacted communities, devise solutions, or bring bigger issues to the attention of governments. But this model is not conducive to consistent or comprehensive statewide interventions, and surely many environmental health and environmental justice cases are missed along the way. Local efforts are indispensable but must be synthesized by the state in a manner that furthers a comprehensive knowledge of environmental health across communities. There is a strong case to be made for tracking environmental indicators beyond air and water quality, and for implementing a greater focus on more granular place-based experiences.

Looking Ahead to 2050: A Framework for the Future

Without major changes, we can anticipate some of the major environmental health issues in Oregon by 2050: worse air and water pollution in areas where higher numbers of Black, Indigenous, or people of color (BIPOC); low-income residents; and other historically marginalized people live. This will continue with other injustices, like housing, discussed in other chapters. If transportation emissions and industrial production emissions continue or even worsen, communities along the I-5 corridor will likely suffer poorer air quality, like higher rates of PM 2.5. This will intersect with climate change, for example, with hotter temperatures. If left unaddressed through regulation or other efforts, some rural counties may continue to suffer from poor water quality. Meanwhile, all of these issues will intersect with climate change and its impacts. For example, there may be more frequent and intense fire events in the future, which will cause prolonged poor air quality. Flooding caused by climate change could contribute to drinking water pollution. If we do not improve data collection, we will not even understand the extent or the localized nature of problems, and leaders and residents won't be able to make informed decisions.

In contrast, we can do things differently and increase environmental health, especially for those communities often overlooked. We propose a four-step framework for advancing environmental justice and health for all Oregonians moving forward. This framework moves beyond the current capacities of DLCD, DEQ, and OHA to a more data-driven, proactive, preventive approach that combines land use planning with community engages and sufficient monitoring regulation.

Step 1: Prioritize Environmental Justice and Center Marginalized Communities

State and local governments must support affected communities through protective mitigation; for example, limiting industrial development near residential areas, supporting programs which provide emergency relief, and funding environmental cleanups or ecological restoration initiatives. To achieve environmental health for all Oregonians, however, there is a need for more action, to identify and correct the underlying systems that produce vulnerability, stifle coping capacity, and disproportionately situate environmental harm in certain communities. An environmental justice approach centers and elevates marginalized communities in environmental assessments and goal-setting.[49] Furthermore, it requires the active empowerment and involvement of those communities in planning and implementation.[50] Such an approach is grounded in the principle that all individuals have the right to be protected and protect themselves from environmental hazards, regardless of social identity.

Efforts to include and empower marginalized communities in environmental planning, mitigation, and remediation have already begun in some localities. But there is a role for OHA to encourage, coordinate, and support community empowerment efforts. Planners and policymakers must make an intentional effort to center marginalized communities and develop metrics for success based on outcomes in the most affected and disadvantaged areas. This is a direct method to ensure that environmental quality interventions are benefitting all Oregonians, especially those most in need. Furthermore, those affected and marginalized communities could be engaged in environmental quality discussions, plans, data collection, and decision-making; invited to share their perspectives, experiences, and goals; and have their input operationalized. Communities know what needs they have and what obstacles they face; they should therefore be empowered to direct their own environmental futures. Planners and policymakers must be careful not to perpetuate colonial or paternalistic dynamics, which put dominant groups in charge of "protecting" those experiencing vulnerability. Instead, they can support self-determination among vulnerable groups and more readily address issues that underlie environmental vulnerability and health disparities. This approach is not just about limiting environmental harm in the short term, but elevating marginalized communities and supporting them in broad, long-term vulnerability reduction.

Data collection and evaluation systems—often at the state or county level—tend to mask inequities, favor hegemonic and simplistic ways of thinking, and do not illuminate highly localized areas of concern.[51] As illustrated in the preceding case studies, reliance solely on state- or county-level trends may paint an unrealistically positive picture of progress in environmental health while ignoring the suffering of those most impacted by environmental degradation. It is necessary to generate data at a more granular scale (individual, household, census block) to clearly see variations in environmental quality and health outcomes. Ideally, historically marginalized communities already known to be at risk will be engaged in this data generation and collection.

Step 2: Apply Environmental Determinants of Health Thinking

Oregon, and the United States generally, has at least minimally adopted a public health prevention model in preparing for and responding to environmental threats. This involves broad, population-wide risk mitigation, which can be supplemented by targeted, proactive interventions or support for high-risk communities.[52] From an environmental threats perspective, a prevention model and related solutions can take various forms, from top-down risk mitigation to community empowerment and adaptation. This often means paying particular attention to groups that face multiple layers of vulnerability and working toward education, resource reallocation, and self-determination.[53] A well-informed prevention model could

ENVIRONMENTAL QUALITY AND HEALTH

Figure 4.3. The social determinants of health. *Source*: "Healthy People 2030," US Department of Health and Human Services, Office of Disease Prevention and Health Promotion, accessed January 17, 2024, https://health.gov/healthypeople/objectives-and-data/social-determinants-health

be developed for every municipality or region within the state, reflecting the specific risks and needs of each particular area.

Practically, a useful prevention model must be accompanied in this state by a sufficiently complex conceptualization of environmental health. We propose application of the social determinants of health in situational assessment and goal setting.[54] These determinants identify environmental quality indicators across multiple levels of human experience, from the neighborhood and built environments, to social, economic, and educational opportunities that inform day-to-day well-being as well as physical and mental health. Figure 4.3 shows a simplified model. These determinants are significantly more complex than current statewide approaches to environmental health would suggest, going well beyond basic indicators of air and water quality.

It is reductive to approach environmental quality and health concerns only through high-level indicators such as county- or statewide air and water pollution. We must remember that health outcomes emerge from numerous, interacting factors down to the neighborhood and household level.[55] Quality of life is affected by climate and biodiversity, but also by housing, transportation, jobs, land use decisions, and many other factors that are within the purview of local decision-makers.[56] Environmental determinants in each tier are germane to environmental quality and health overall. Though it is certainly more challenging to collect and make sense of information on these interacting, multiscale factors, a greater depth of knowledge can only improve public health interventions and outcomes. This complexity exists regardless of whether it is acknowledged. Practitioners and policymakers must find ways to work within this messy reality as they decide how best to think about, talk about, and act for environmental health.

Step 3: Strengthen Collection and Monitoring Efforts

Available data at the state or county level offer a broad view, a starting point from which to understand trends in environmental health and quality across the state. But these data lack the detail necessary to identify areas or communities facing the greatest environmental distress, to reveal the challenges and lived experiences of those on the ground, to account for outliers, or to design and implement appropriate solutions. Only county-level data are consistently available statewide and provide an unrealistically rosy picture of environmental health within the state, obscuring pockets of real suffering that occur at a more granular scale, such as the city, reservation, neighborhood, or even household level. Furthermore, data are arguably too scant to inform holistic comprehension of environmental threats and issue areas. Air and water quality are crucial components of health, but these are hardly the only relevant factors. Although some localities have collected more granular data—particularly in populous urban areas, through the efforts of local agencies, academic institutions, and nonprofit groups—there is no state repository that documents, synthesizes, or designs policy informed by those findings.

Sole reliance on quantitative data at the county scale, as reflected in the OHA database, is problematic and limits the extent to which planners and policymakers can understand or respond to environmental health concerns. Quantitative data are arguably easier to obtain, work with, and generalize from but reveal nothing of lived experience. Numbers cannot provide a nuanced portrait of lived racism, the trauma of losing one's home or social network, or the daily reality of keeping one's family healthy in inhospitable conditions. It is important to understand these nuances, lest policymakers rely on a one-size-fits-all approach to environmental health that does not resonate with affected communities and may not even address the underlying issues they face.[57] Typically, qualitative data receive minimal attention and have been poorly integrated and operationalized in the past. Moving forward, efforts must be made not only to collect qualitative data through improved community engagement, but also to interpret findings within the context of history and environmental justice, and devise interventions accordingly.

Finally, we propose an expansion of data collection efforts that recognizes the complexity and relationality of environmental health determinants, including, for example, data on housing, walkability, access to jobs, health care, education, recreation and nutritious food (see fig. 4.3 for a conceptual model). OHA's current emphasis on air and water quality misses other natural and climate-related stressors such as extreme heat, drought, and flooding. This is to say nothing of day-to-day stressors such as blight, neighborhood safety, housing security, traffic, and noise pollution, all of which may affect mental and physical health. Currently, we lack data that might show the interrelationships among various environmental factors, some more explicitly health related than others, but all ultimately shaping human well-being.[58] For example, how does chronic exposure to air pollution affect one's lung function, work performance, and ability to recreate outdoors with children or friends? What does this mean for economic stability and quality of life? What does it mean for social stability and mental health when a person is displaced by a natural hazard such as wildfire? How does intergenerational trauma—from racism in health care and land use or repeated environmental insults—filter down to children, affecting educational outcomes, opportunities for familial wealth creation, and access to resources? These are complicated questions with no easy answers, and we are not suggesting otherwise. But there is a clear need for the state to pursue nuanced data collection efforts that begin to account for these complexities and alleviate the potentially cascading effects of poor environmental quality.

Collecting environmental health data at a local level in a consistent and comprehensive manner across the entire state is an enormous undertaking. It would require new ways of measuring environmental conditions and conceptualizing success, as well as new ways of working with organizations, governments, and citizens at various levels to access the most elusive information. Furthermore, data collection is only the first step. Effective, empowering policy begins with good data, but will also involve communication, coordination, and cooperation across sectors. It will require unprecedented attention not only to imminent environmental threats, but also to the social, political, and economic conditions, both current and historical, that have created vulnerability to them. It will mean using place-based data to put environmental problems in context, developing tailored solutions, and working toward policies and funding that support such an approach statewide.

Step 4: Shift Responsibility from Individuals to Organizational, Corporate, and Government Systems

Our interpretation of environmental risk has, at times, hinged on the culturally ingrained ideal of personal responsibility: do not work outdoors in a heat wave, keep children insulated from smoky or polluted air, evacuate your home when a storm is coming. It is easy to blame victims for their own suffering, but their options are often limited by external forces. Similarly, it has become popular to propose quick-fix interventions that gloss over underlying problems and focus on solutions for individuals, for example, giving away air conditioners to households during a heat wave. But no degree of personal action or individual-scale intervention can overcome the environmental damage caused by polluting industries, insufficient regulatory frameworks, and racist and classist zoning and land use policies and decisions.

Localities within Oregon must explicitly put responsibility for environmental health where it belongs: on the powerful actors who produce harm, amplify or accelerate the effects of climate change, and perpetuate environmental risk. Additionally, localities must honestly confront the historic policies and attitudes that have produced vulnerability and environmental injustice, including redlining, gentrification resulting from greening initiatives, siting of polluting enterprises in low-income areas, and persistent racism in the health care industry. Only through decisive government policy intervention can we correct environmental injustices across numerous sectors, from housing and transportation to air quality and green space.

This is an area in which OHA, as a powerful state entity, could have a significant impact. For example, OHA divisions could financially support policies and programs that address underlying causes of vulnerability in Oregon. In addition, OHA and DEQ could be empowered to support laws and policies that explicitly put the onus of environmental quality on the shoulders of polluting industries and corporations. This might mean increased regulations or fees for pollution, or more radical steps like environmental reparations to affected communities. Both agencies would need to be better resourced, or to reassess current activities, to take on these added activities.

Conclusion

In this chapter, we have reviewed available data on environmental health and quality maintained by the State of Oregon via the Oregon Health Authority. These include county-level accounts of air and water pollution as well as state-level data on various health conditions, including asthma and cancers. These data, although they offer a helpful starting point, are not sufficient to illuminate localized variation in environmental quality or health outcomes, do not reflect the complexity of those topics, and are unconducive to the pursuit of environmental justice. Case studies show that available data obscure pockets of local suffering and environmental concern. We see an opportunity moving forward, into 2050 and beyond, to improve environmental quality and health for all Oregonians by rethinking our approach to health assessments, planning, and data. We call for the application of an environmental justice lens in data collection, analysis, planning, and policymaking. This requires that planners and policymakers acknowledge and seek to correct historical injustices, and center, engage, and empower affected communities in their work. Furthermore, we call for an expansion both of how environmental health is conceptualized and of data collection efforts. This requires acknowledging and working with complexity, incorporating environmental indicators beyond air and water quality, and procuring and acting upon granular, qualitative data, representative of lived experience. The state can also embrace a stronger attitude of environmental pollution regulation. By working toward these goals, the State of Oregon, in collaboration with local partners, can enhance its repository of environmental health data and make significant, equitable advances toward environmental quality for all.

Notes

The authors thank Lisa Arkin (Beyond Toxics), Dan Martinez (Confederated Tribes of Warm Springs), and Julie Sifuentes (Oregon Health Authority) for feedback on drafts.

1. L. Cushing, R. Morello-Frosch, M. Wander, and M. Pastor, "The Haves, the Have-Nots, and the Health of Everyone: The Relationship between Social Inequality and Environmental Quality," *Annual Review of Public Health* 36, no. 1 (2015): 193–209, doi.org/10.1146/annurev-publhealth-031914-122646; N. Khanna, "Measuring Environmental Quality: An Index of Pollution," *Ecological Economics* 35, no. 2 (2000): 191–202, doi.org/10.1016/S0921-8009(00)00197-X; C. S. Mitchell, J. Zhang, T. Sigsgaard, M. Jantunen, P. J. Lioy, et al., "Current State of the Science: Health Effects and Indoor Environmental Quality," *Environmental Health Perspectives* 115, no. 6 (2007): 958964, doi.org/10.1289/ehp.8987; D. Ruiz, M. Becerra, J. S. Jagai, K. Ard, and R. M. Sargis, "Disparities in Environmental Exposures to Endocrine-Disrupting Chemicals and Diabetes Risk in Vulnerable Populations," *Diabetes Care* 41, no. 1 (2018): 193–205, doi.org/10.2337/dc16-2765.
2. D. W. Moeller, *Environmental Health*, 3rd ed. (Cambridge, MA: Harvard University Press, 2005); A. Yassi, ed., *Basic Environmental Health* (Oxford: Oxford University Press, 2001).
3. "Environmental Health," American Public Health Association, accessed December 19, 2023, www.apha.org/topics-and-issues/environmental-health.
4. "National Center for Environmental Health," Centers for Disease Control and Prevention, last reviewed March 28, 2023, www.cdc.gov/nceh.
5. P. J. Landrigan, C. B. Schechter, J. M. Lipton, M. C. Fahs, and J. Schwartz, "Environmental Pollutants and Disease in American Children: Estimates of Morbidity, Mortality, and Costs for Lead Poisoning, Asthma, Cancer, and Developmental Disabilities," *Environmental Health Perspectives* 110, no. 7 (2002): 721–28, https://doi.org/10.1289/ehp.02110721; E. Pukkala, and A. Pönkä, "Increased Incidence of Cancer and Asthma in Houses Built on a Former Dump Area," *Environmental Health Perspectives* 109, no. 11 (2001): 1121–25, https://doi.org/10.1289/ehp.011091121.
6. R. Ghimire, S. Ferreira, G. T. Green, N. C. Poudyal, H. K. Cordell, et al., "Green Space and Adult Obesity in the United States," *Ecological Economics* 136 (2017): 201–12, https://doi.org/10.1016/j.ecolecon.2017.02.002; P. Jia, X. Cao, H. Yang, S. Dai, P. He, et al., "Green Space Access in the Neighbourhood and Childhood Obesity," *Obesity Reviews* 22, no. S1 (2021): e13100, https://doi.org/10.1111/obr.13100.
7. Hannah Ritchie, Pablo Rosado, and Max Roser, "Natural Disasters," Our World in Data, December 7, 2022, https://ourworldindata.org/natural-disasters.

8   E.g., X. Liu, Y. Wang, J. Peng, A. K. Braimoh, and H. Yin, "Assessing Vulnerability to Drought Based on Exposure, Sensitivity and Adaptive Capacity: A Case Study in Middle Inner Mongolia of China," *Chinese Geographical Science* 23, no. 1 (2013): 13–25, https://doi.org/10.1007/s11769-012-0583-4; S. W. M. Weis, V. N. Agostini, L. M. Roth, B. Gilmer, S. R. Schill, et al., "Assessing Vulnerability: An Integrated Approach for Mapping Adaptive Capacity, Sensitivity, and Exposure," *Climatic Change* 136, no. 3–4 (2016): 615–29, https://doi.org/10.1007/s10584-016-1642-0; W. N. Adger, N. Brooks, G. Bentham, M. Agnew, and S. Eriksen, *New Indicators of Vulnerability and Adaptive Capacity*, Technical Report 7 (Norwich, UK: Tyndall Centre for Climate Change Research, 2004); J.J. McCarthy, O. F. Canziani, N. A. Leary, D. J. Dokken, and K. S. White, *Climate Change 2001: Impacts, Adaptation, and Vulnerability, Third Assessment Report of the Intergovernmental Panel on Climate Change* (Cambridge: Cambridge University Press, 2001), https://www.ipcc.ch/site/assets/uploads/2018/03/WGII_TAR_full_report-2.pdf; B. L. Turner, R. E. Kasperson, P. A. Matson, J. J. McCarthy, R. W. Corell, et al., "A Framework for Vulnerability Analysis in Sustainability Science," *Proceedings of the National Academy of Sciences* 100, no. 14 (2003): 8074–79, https://doi.org/10.1073/pnas.1231335100.

9   Adger et al., *New Indicators*; McCarthy et al., *Climate Change 2001*.

10 D. Lee and J. Jung, "The Growth of Low-Income Population in Floodplains: A Case Study of Austin, TX," *KSCE Journal of Civil Engineering* 18, no. 2 (2014): 683–93, https://doi.org/10.1007/s12205-014-0205-z; H .G. Margolis, J. K. Mann, F. W. Lurmann, K. M. Mortimer, J. R. Balmes, et al., "Altered Pulmonary Function in Children with Asthma Associated with Highway Traffic Near Residence," *International Journal of Environmental Health Research* 19, no. 2 (2009): 139–55, https://doi.org/10.1080/09603120802415792.

11 "Protect Yourself from Wildfire Smoke," Centers for Disease Control and Prevention, last reviewed November 21, 2022, www.cdc.gov/air/wildfire-smoke/default.htm.

12 W. N. Adger, "Social Aspects of Adaptive Capacity," in *Climate Change, Adaptive Capacity and Development*, edited by J. B. Smith, R. J. T. Klein, and S. Huq, 29–49 (London: Imperial College Press, 2003), https://doi.org/10.1142/9781860945816_0003.

13 D. E. Taylor, "The Rise of the Environmental Justice Paradigm: Injustice Framing and the Social Construction of Environmental Discourses," *American Behavioral Scientist* 43, no. 4 (2000): 508–80, https://doi.org/10.1177/0002764200043004003.

14 Robert Bullard, *Dumping in Dixie: Race, Class and Environmental Quality*, 3rd ed. (Boulder, CO: Westview Press, 2000); S. L. Cutter, "Race, Class and Environmental Justice," *Progress in Human Geography* 19, no. 1 (1995): 111–22, https://doi.org/10.1177/030913259501900111; P. Mohai, D. Pellow, and J. T. Roberts, "Environmental Justice," *Annual Review of Environment and Resources* 34, no. 1 (2009): 405–30, https://doi.org/10.1146/annurev-environ-082508-094348.

15 J. Mukherjee, *Blue Infrastructures: Natural History, Political Ecology and Urban Development in Kolkata* (Singapore: Springer, 2020).

16 M. Martuzzi, F. Mitis, and F. Forastiere, "Inequalities, Inequities, Environmental Justice in Waste Management and Health," *European Journal of Public Health* 20, no. 1 (2010): 21–26, https://doi.org/10.1093/eurpub/ckp216; G. Pratt, M. Vadali, D. Kvale, and K. Ellickson, "Traffic, Air Pollution, Minority and Socio-Economic Status: Addressing Inequities in Exposure and Risk," *International Journal of Environmental Research and Public Health* 12, no. 5 (2015): 5355–72, https://doi.org/10.3390/ijerph120505355; B. An, A. W. Orlando, and S. Rodnyansky, "The Physical Legacy of Racism: How Redlining Cemented the Modern Built

Environment," *Social Science Research Network* (2019): https://doi.org/10.2139/ssrn.3500612; A. Altschuler, C. P. Somkin, and N. E. Adler, "Local Services and Amenities, Neighborhood Social Capital, and Health," *Social Science and Medicine* 59, no. 6 (2004): 1219–29, https://doi.org/10.1016/j.socscimed.2004.01.008; D. H. Locke and J. M. Grove, "Doing the Hard Work Where It's Easiest? Examining the Relationships between Urban Greening Programs and Social and Ecological Characteristics," *Applied Spatial Analysis and Policy* 9, no. 1 (2016): 77–96, https://doi.org/10.1007/s12061-014-9131-1; F. Stillo and J. MacDonald Gibson, "Exposure to Contaminated Drinking Water and Health Disparities in North Carolina," *American Journal of Public Health* 107, no. 1 (2017): 180–85, https://doi.org/10.2105/AJPH.2016.303482.

17 N. Krumholz, "A Retrospective View of Equity Planning Cleveland, 1969-1979," *Journal of the American Planning Association* 48, no. 2 (1982): 163–74, https://doi.org/10.1080/01944368208976535; P. Davidoff, "Advocacy and Pluralism in Planning," *Journal of the American Institute of Planners* 31, no. 4 (1965): 331-48, https://doi.org/10.1080/01944366508978187; L. R. Barraclough, *Making the San Fernando Valley: Rural Landscapes, Urban Development, and White Privilege* (Athens: University of Georgia Press, 2001); J. Carr, "Public Input/Elite Privilege: The Use of Participatory Planning to Reinforce Urban Geographies of Power in Seattle," *Urban Geography* 33, no. 3 (2013): 420–41, https://doi.org/10.2747/0272-3638.33.3.420; K. Iveson and R. Fincher, "'Just Diversity' in the City of Difference," in *The New Blackwell Companion to the City*, edited by G. Bridge and S. Watson, 407–18 (Oxford: Wiley-Blackwell, 2011), https://doi.org/10.1002/9781444395105.ch36.

18 J. Voelkel, D. Hellman, R. Sakuma, and V. Shandas, "Assessing Vulnerability to Urban Heat: A Study of Disproportionate Heat Exposure and Access to Refuge by Socio-Demographic Status in Portland, Oregon," *International Journal of Environmental Research and Public Health* 15, no. 4 (2018): 640, https://doi.org/10.3390/ijerph15040640; B. Fahy, E. Brenneman, H. Chang, and V. Shandas, "Spatial Analysis of Urban Flooding and Extreme Heat Hazard Potential in Portland, OR," *International Journal of Disaster Risk Reduction* 39, no. 101117 (2019): https://doi.org/10.1016/j.ijdrr.2019.101117; C. C. Bae, G. Sandlin, A. Bassok, and S. Kim, "The Exposure of Disadvantaged Populations in Freeway Air-Pollution Sheds: A Case Study of the Seattle and Portland Regions," *Environment and Planning B: Planning and Design* 34, no. 1 (2007):154-70, https://doi.org/10.1068/b32124.

19 Alison Guzman and Lisa Arkin, *Environmental Justice in West Eugene: Families, Health and Air Pollution* (Eugene, OR: Beyond Toxics and Centro Latino Americano, 2013), https://www.beyondtoxics.org/wp-content/uploads/2013/07/EnvJusticeWestEugene-FamiliesHealthAirPollution_FULLreport_FINALwebres.pdf; Tony Schick and Rob Davis, "Timber Tax Cuts Cost Oregon Towns Billions. Then Polluted Water Drove Up the Price," *ProPublica*, December 30, 2020, https://www.propublica.org/article/timber-water-oregon.

20 R. D. Bullard and B. H. Wright, "Environmental Justice for All: Community Perspectives on Health and Research," *Toxicology and Industrial Health* 9, no. 5 (1993): 821–41, https://doi.org/10.1177/074823379300900508.

21 "Oregon Tracking Data Explorer," Oregon Health Authority, accessed December 19, 2023, https://www.oregon.gov/oha/PH/HEALTHYENVIRONMENTS/TRACKINGASSESSMENT/ENVIRONMENTALPUBLICHEALTHTRACKING/Pages/Data-Explorer.aspx.

22 "National Primary Drinking Water Regulations," Environmental Protection Agency, updated January 9, 2023, https://www.epa.gov/ground-water-and-drinking-water/national-primary-drinking-water-regulations.

23 "NAAQS Table," Environmental Protection Agency, updated March 15, 2023, https://www.epa.gov/criteria-air-pollutants/naaqs-table; "Air Pollution," Centers for Disease Control and Prevention, last reviewed December 21, 2020, https://www.cdc.gov/climateandhealth/effects/air_pollution.htm.
24 "Oregon Tracking Data Explorer."
25 Maximum safe levels of various contaminants are as follows: arsenic 10 micrograms per liter (μg/L); HAA5 60 μg/L; nitrate 10 milligrams per liter (mg/L); TTHM 80 μg/L; PM 2.5 12 micrograms per cubic meter (μg/m^3).
26 "Explore Census Data," US Census Bureau, accessed December 19, 2023, https://data.census.gov/cedsci/.
27 A. Makri and N. I. Stilianakis, "Vulnerability to Air Pollution Health Effects," *International Journal of Hygiene and Environmental Health* 211, no. 3–4 (2008): 326–36, https://doi.org/10.1016/j.ijheh.2007.06.005; Pratt et al., "Traffic, Air Pollution, Minority and Socio-Economic Status."
28 Guzman and Arkin, *Environmental Justice in West Eugene*.
29 Guzman and Arkin, *Environmental Justice in West Eugene*, 5.
30 "Oregon Tracking Data Explorer."
31 "Oregon Tracking Data Explorer."
32 Guzman and Arkin, *Environmental Justice in West Eugene*.
33 "Newsletter Fall 2020," Beyond Toxics, accessed December 19, 2023, https://www.beyondtoxics.org/wp-content/uploads/Fall2020_BTnewsletter_WebReady_11pp_FINAL.pdf.
34 "Explore Census Data."
35 "Oregon Tracking Data Explorer"
36 Jon Goodwin, "Support Trickling In to Help Warm Springs Reservation Deal with Crumbling Water Infrastructure," KGW8, July 16, 2020, https://www.kgw.com/article/news/local/warm-springs-reservation-oregon-water-shortage/283-932cb605-404c-4a5e-bf67-8defcdaa2e32.
37 Sarah Mowry, "Local Water Crisis Calls Us All to Action," Deschutes Land Trust, October 26, 2020, https://www.deschuteslandtrust.org/news/news-items/2020-news-items/local-water-crisis-calls-us-all-to-action.
38 Emily Cureton, "Water Crisis Returns to Warm Springs as Virus Cases Rise" Oregon Public Broadcasting, June 30, 2020, https://www.opb.org/news/article/water-crisis-returns-to-warm-springs-as-virus-cases-rise; Goodwin, "Support Trickling In."
39 Goodwin, "Support Trickling In."
40 Emily Cureton, "Oregon Lawmakers Approve $3.6 Million in Water Aid for Warm Springs Reservation," Oregon Public Broadcasting, July 14, 2020, https://www.opb.org/news/article/oregon-36-million-water-aid-confederated-tribes-warm-springs-reservation.
41 L. Howard, *The Climate of London: Deduced from Meteorological Observations Made at Different Places in the Neighbourhood of the Metropolis* (London: W. Phillips, 1820).
42 H. H. Kim, "Urban Heat Island," *International Journal of Remote Sensing* 13, no. 12 (1992): 2319–36, https://doi.org/10.1080/01431169208904271.
43 S. Peng, S. Piao, P. Ciais, P. Friedlingstein, C. Ottle, et al., "Surface Urban Heat Island across 419 Global Big Cities," *Environmental Science and Technology* 46, no. 2 (2012): 696–703, https://doi.org/10.1021/es2030438.
44 J.-F. Dhainaut, Y.-E. Claessens, C. Ginsburg, and B. Riou, "Unprecedented Heat-Related Deaths during the 2003 Heat Wave in Paris: Consequences on Emergency

Departments," *Critical Care* 8, no. 1 (2004): 1, https://doi.org/10.1186/cc2404; E. Klinenberg, *Heat Wave: A Social Autopsy of Disaster in Chicago*, 2nd ed. (Chicago: University of Chicago Press, 2015); K. Knowlton, M. Rotkin-Ellman, G. King, H. G. Margolis, D. Smith, et al., "The 2006 California Heat Wave: Impacts on Hospitalizations and Emergency Department Visits," *Environmental Health Perspectives* 117, no. 1 (2009): 61–67, https://doi.org/10.1289/ehp.11594.

45 Voelkel et al., "Assessing Vulnerability to Urban Heat."
46 Voelkel et al., "Assessing Vulnerability to Urban Heat."
47 J. S. Hoffman, V. Shandas, and N. Pendleton, "The Effects of Historical Housing Policies on Resident Exposure to Intra-Urban Heat: A Study of 108 US Urban Areas," *Climate* 8, no. 1 (2020): 12, https://doi.org/10.3390/cli8010012.
48 Hoffman et al., "Effects of Historical Housing Policies."
49 D. Schlosberg, *Defining Environmental Justice* (Oxford: Oxford University Press, 2007), https://doi.org/10.1093/acprof:oso/9780199286294.001.0001.
50 K. S. Shrader-Frechette, *Environmental Justice: Creating Equality, Reclaiming Democracy* (Oxford: Oxford University Press, 2002).
51 C. D'Ignazio and L. F. Klein, *Data Feminism* (Cambridge: Massachusetts Institute of Technology Press, 2020); O. Laurent, D. Bard, L. Filleul, and C. Segala, "Effect of Socioeconomic Status on the Relationship between Atmospheric Pollution and Mortality," *Journal of Epidemiology and Community Health* 61, no. 8 (2007): 665–75, https://doi.org/10.1136/jech.2006.053611; L. T. Smith, *Decolonizing Methodologies: Research and Indigenous Peoples*, 2nd ed. (London: Zed Books, 2012).
52 "Prevention," Centers for Disease Control and Prevention, accessed December 19, 2023, https://www.cdc.gov/pictureofamerica/pdfs/picture_of_america_prevention.pdf.
53 A. Anderson, "Climate Change Education for Mitigation and Adaptation," *Journal of Education for Sustainable Development* 6, no. 2 (2012): 191–206, https://doi.org/10.1177/0973408212475199; Shrader-Frechette, *Environmental Justice*.
54 H. Barton and M. Grant, "A Health Map for the Local Human Habitat," *Journal of the Royal Society for the Promotion of Health* 126, no. 6 (2006): 252–53, https://doi.org/10.1177/1466424006070466.
55 M. Gislason and H. Andersen, "The Interacting Axes of Environmental, Health, and Social Justice Cumulative Impacts: A Case Study of the Blueberry River First Nations," *Healthcare* 4, no. 4 (2016): 78, https://doi.org/10.3390/healthcare4040078; M. Soobader, C. Cubbin, G. C. Gee, A. Rosenbaum, and J. Laurenson, "Levels of Analysis for the Study of Environmental Health Disparities," *Environmental Research* 102, no. 2 (2006): 172–80, https://doi.org/10.1016/j.envres.2006.05.001.
56 Barton and Grant, "Health Map for the Local Human Habitat"; R. W. Marans, "Understanding Environmental Quality through Quality of Life Studies: The 2001 DAS and Its Use of Subjective and Objective Indicators," *Landscape and Urban Planning* 65, no. 1–2 (2003): 73–83, https://doi.org/10.1016/S0169-2046(02)00239-6; M. Pacione, "Urban Environmental Quality and Human Wellbeing—A Social Geographical Perspective," *Landscape and Urban Planning* 65, no. 1–2 (2003): 19–30, https://doi.org/10.1016/S0169-2046(02)00234-7; I. van Kamp, K. Leidelmeijer, G. Marsman, and A. de Hollander, "Urban Environmental Quality and Human Well-Being," *Landscape and Urban Planning* 65, no. 1–2 (2003): 5–18, https://doi.org/10.1016/S0169-2046(02)00232-3.
57 P. A. Loring and L. K. Duffy, "Managing Environmental Risks: The Benefits of a Place-Based Approach," *Rural Remote Health* 11, no. 3 (2011): 1800.
58 Barton and Grant, "Health Map for the Local Human Habitat."

5
Natural Resource Management in Oregon
SHANE DAY, TYLER WOLFE, AND CARLOS ARIAS

Natural resources are a particularly important issue to Oregonians. In one index measure of "greenest states," Oregon ranks third, while ranking first in terms of "environmentally friendly behaviors" and fourth for "environmental quality."[1] Oregonians rank issues of natural resources and environmental quality as higher-priority areas than citizens of most other states, although they often rank them still below issues like the economy, education, and health care.[2] Certain natural resource issues garner more attention and public support than others. This chapter highlights various trends in some of the more politically salient and economically significant natural resource stocks of concern to Oregonians, such as forests, energy, animal and plant species, and water. As we look to 2050, population growth and climate change will cause additional stress.

The State of Oregon in Context

Oregon is a large state, with a land area of more than 98,000 square miles, and contains a variety of ecological zones shaped by distinct geological and climate patterns. The Cascade Mountain range follows a north-south orientation that serves as both a geological and cultural line that divides the state into two broad regions. Economic activity is distinct between the two, which contributes to the different politico-philosophical orientations of its residents. While the whole state has been experiencing a transition away from a principally resource-based economy into a technology, mixed-manufacturing, and service economy (as discussed in chap. 11), the pattern differs between the two halves of the state. Western Oregon has experienced the biggest economic transition, moving away from a reliance on forestry toward the high-tech industry, concentrated in the greater Portland area. Parts of the eastern half of the state were to a lesser extent affected by the downturn in the timber industry, but agriculture and ranching continue to dominate the region's economy.[3]

This divide contributes to distinct patterns of natural resource stocks and issues that are specific to each region. Using the Trewartha climate classification scheme, the western part of the state is characterized by an oceanic climate until it meets the continental and boreal climates associated with the Cascade Range, with a small section of humid subtropical climate along the southern Pacific coast. The eastern part of the state is characterized by a more arid climate reflecting the rain shadow effect of the Cascades, with steppe and desert climates being dominant, along with interspersed smaller mountain ranges that give rise to a continental and boreal climate pattern, predominately in the northeast part of the state in the Blue and Wallowa Mountain ranges. Thus water scarcity is a more pronounced concern in the east, while the wetter climate of the west is home to most of the state's forestlands.

The land use planning program, a core focus of this book, was developed with a main goal of conserving natural resources lands from urban and suburban development. Notably, Goal 4 protects and places development restrictions on forestlands around the state. These restrictions seek to prevent activities that could conflict with forestry practices. Goal 5 is a broad statewide planning goal that is about planning for a variety of resources. It applies to natural gas, surface water, geothermal, solar, wind-generating areas, wildlife habitat, historic places, and gravel mines. It specifies the process for identifying energy sources and instructs local governments to adopt land use regulations to protect these areas from future conflicting uses. Additionally, Goal 13 addresses energy conservation efforts that should occur as part of city and county land use comprehensive planning. Goal 13 encourages communities to look within existing urban neighborhoods for areas of potential redevelopment before looking to expand, to "recycle and re-use vacant land." The goal also directs cities and counties to have systems and incentives in place for recycling programs.

The statewide planning program was written before the prominence of renewable energy and before the climate crisis was well understood. Innovation in the areas of solar and wind energy have made them increasingly popular in Oregon. Concern about climate change has resulted in an increase in public and private interest in and development of alternative energy sources. Goal 13 was not written to govern or direct where energy production like solar and wind should be located, an issue that is highly contentious currently and as we look to the future. The Department of Land Conservation and Development recently developed rules for wind and solar energy siting on agricultural land based on input from a combination of stakeholders, including energy providers and conservation groups.[4] The rules are intended to direct energy development to lands that have limited value to wildlife and farming, though local farming communities continue to express concern about the negative impacts to farmland and about the inequitable economic benefits and burdens. This chapter further discusses both the base provided by the land use program and ideas to strengthen natural resource stewardship.

Public Land Management in Oregon

More than half of land in Oregon (approximately 60.4 percent) is held by federal, state, or tribal governments. The federal government is the largest landowner in the state, with management divided among distinct federal agencies with different missions and mandates. This places Oregon fifth in the nation in terms of how much land is owned by the federal government, as shown in table 5.1.

Each of the primary federal land management agencies has a distinct mission and mandate, resulting in different approaches to natural resource management between agencies. For instance, some

Table 5.1. The Top Four Agencies with Most Federal Land Ownership in Oregon

Federal Agency	Amount of Land Owned in Oregon (acres)	Percentage
Bureau of Land Management	15,742,384	49
Forest Service	15,697,445	49
Fish and Wildlife Service	575,379	2
National Park Service	196,197	1

Source: Carol Hardy Vincent, Laura A. Hanson, and Lucas F. Bermejo, *Federal Land Ownership: Overview and Data*, CRS Report R42346 (Washington, DC: Congressional Research Service, 2020), https://sgp.fas.org/crs/misc/R42346.pdf.

agencies operate under a preservationist mandate that advantages natural resource protection over other considerations, whereas others follow a mixed-use mandate that necessitates balancing ecological health with economic and recreational considerations. First, the National Park Service (NPS) "preserves unimpaired the natural and cultural resources . . . for the enjoyment, education, and inspiration of this and future generations."[5] It thus operates under much more of a preservationist mandate than other federal agencies, with NPS lands typically accorded the highest degree of protection from human impacts. Meanwhile, the US Forest Service (USFS) operates under a mixed-use mandate that requires the agency to manage lands for the purposes of harvesting timber, providing rangeland, protecting wildlife, ensuring water quality, and offering recreational opportunities. Similarly, the purpose of the Bureau of Land Management (BLM) is "to sustain the health, diversity, and productivity of public lands for the use and enjoyment of present and future generations," and it primarily manages lands for the purpose of grazing, mining, and recreation. Finally, the US Fish and Wildlife Service (FWS) has a more specialized mission focused on conservation of plants, fish, wildlife, and their respective habitats. It has oversight and regulatory roles in endangered species protection under the Endangered Species Act, as discussed later in this chapter.

At the state and local level, the administrative structure of natural resource management in the state is somewhat unique. There is a comparatively high degree of fragmentation of authority across multiple agencies. As a result, the state's bureaucracy in terms of natural resource management has a mixed pattern of political control, with some bodies answering to the governor, legislature, or citizen commissions, or to a mix of the three.[6] State agencies and administrative bodies with significant natural resource and environmental policy responsibilities range from the Department of Agriculture and Department of Fish and Wildlife, to the Department of Geology and Mineral Industries, the Parks and Recreation Department, and the Watershed Enhancement Board. In some instances, larger metropolitan governments, such as Portland and Beaverton, also maintain standalone natural resource management agencies, operating a variety of habitat conservation programs and managing significant tracts of public parks.

Table 5.2. Oregon State Agencies with the Most Land under Public Management

State Agency	Acres Managed
Department of State Lands	774,122
Department of Forestry	711,894
Department of Fish and Wildlife	139,380
Department of Parks and Recreation (111 parks)	97,019

Source: Oregon Department of State Lands, *State of Oregon State Land Inventory System Report* (Salem: Oregon Department of State Lands, 2021), https://www.oregon.gov/dsl/Land/Documents/2bSLIStateOwnershipbyAgency.pdf.

While the proportion of state-owned lands pales in comparison to federal and private ownership, the state government owns and manages approximately 1.8 million acres (2.85 percent of the total), with oversight divided across multiple agencies.[7] Table 5.2 shows the state agencies with the most public land managed.

The Oregon Department of State Lands manages two broad categories of land, "trust lands" and "statutory lands." Trust lands are managed for the primary purpose of generating revenue for K–12 public education. These lands are maximized through recreational use (hunting, fishing, camping, hiking, etc.), and all the funds generated from these activities are later deposited into the Common School Fund to be used in the educational system. Mineral resources and unclaimed property held in trust also contribute to the fund. The Common School Fund is later invested by the State Treasure and Oregon Investment Council, with fund values ranging from $600 million to roughly $1.5 billion. Statutory lands, known as "non-trust" lands, include Swamp Act lands, lands managed for the South Slough National Estuarine Research Reserve (SSNERR), and the sale of filled lands, managed by the Land Board.[8]

Additionally, a total of 865,587 acres of land are Native American reservation lands held in trust by the federal government. Approximately 94 percent of Native American lands are held by two tribes, with the Confederated Tribes of Warm Springs holding 644,000 acres and the Confederated Tribes of the Umatilla Reservation holding 172,000 acres.[9] The Klamath Tribes of Southern Oregon formerly possessed a large land base of 762,000 acres, although they lost these lands with the passage of the Klamath Termination Act in 1953, which resulted in reservation lands being sold off to private landowners or converted into National Forestlands. The Klamath Restoration Act of 1986 reestablished federal recognition of the Klamath Tribes but did not include a restoration of reservation lands, and the tribes have been able to reestablish ownership of only 890 acres in trust.[10] In general, tribal lands are managed by the federal government on the behalf of tribes, through the Bureau of Indian Affairs. But tribes may elect to take control of a variety of land management and environmental regulatory responsibilities through "self-governance authority" or "treatment-as-state" provisions under certain statutes, such as the Clean Water Act.[11] For instance, the Confederated Tribes of Warm Springs' Branch of Natural Resources manages a wide range of programs pertaining to water and soil quality, forestry, fish and wildlife, conservation lands, and rangeland management.[12] Furthermore, both the Confederated Tribes of Warm Springs and Confederated Tribes of the Umatilla Reservation hold special reserved treaty rights to "fish in usual and accustomed places" and "in common with citizens," a right that has been upheld by the US federal court system, importantly extends beyond reservation boundaries, entitles the treaty tribes to a roughly 50 percent share of salmon harvests, and establishes these tribes as formal comanagers of the fishery alongside state and federal agencies—a responsibility that they collectively perform through the Columbia River Intertribal Fisheries Commission along with the Yakama Nation and Nez Perce Tribe.[13] These comanagement rights are extensive and have been interpreted by the court system to extend to the protection of habitat and regulation of a wide range of human activities that have a deleterious effect on salmon populations.[14]

In addition to all of the above, as of 2020, another 868,695 acres of land are held by various land trusts across the state, representing a 23 percent increase since 2010.[15] These lands are protected through a variety of mechanisms, including nonprofit-held land trusts and a variety of conservation easements. It is therefore impossible to generalize about the levels of protection accorded across all of these lands, with some of them maintaining some degree of public accessibility and others restricting all public use and access.

Most of the lands under federal control conform to the usual management and land use practices associated with their respective agencies. Yet Oregon is also unique in that a sizable portion of these lands (approximately 2.6 million acres) are "O&C lands," which were originally granted to the Oregon & California Railroad. Today, these lands are held in a unique arrangement wherein BLM (and to a lesser extent USFS) harvests timber resources on these lands on a sustained yield basis, with 50 percent of revenues going to the county governments.[16] Owing to overharvesting and its impacts on various endangered species, forest harvests were dramatically decreased under the Northwest Forest Plan in 1994. This has resulted in a significant decline in financial revenue to the eighteen affected counties and has led to a variety of proposals from these counties for exemptions and other special logging regulations specific to the O&C lands.

Because land ownership is allocated across multiple actors characterized by different land use activities and levels of protection, there is frequently a mismatch between political jurisdictions and landscape boundaries. There are also tensions between how federal lands should be used, whether for natural resource extraction, recreation, or preservation. In terms of resource management, there are conflicts in the extent to which commercial development should be allowed, with the issues of energy, grazing, and timber harvesting being the most prominent. Some agencies have relatively straightforward mandates centered on a primary goal, such as FWS and the Department of Defense (DOD) focusing on wildlife preservation and national defense, respectively. BLM and USFS land use is often more controversial, as these agencies are under a "mixed-use mandate" that often creates tensions between the various recreational, ecological, aesthetic, and commercial obligations facing the agencies.[17]

There are also debates about to what extent the federal government should expand or reduce its public land ownership in Oregon. Advocates of land acquisition and retention argue that benefits such as protection and preservation of natural resources and recreational use are key ways to protect lands from development. Many who argue for disposal question the effectiveness of the federal government's land management and that disposal can reduce deficits and balance budgets.[18] Additionally, disposal advocates argue that state, local, and private actors can be better stewards of federal lands. The disposal of federal lands typically requires an Act of Congress under the Property

Clause of the Constitution, however, and thus usually faces significant political barriers. Conversely, agencies have varying authority in the acquisition of lands: BLM has relatively broad authority, the FWS has various authorities, and the USFS authority is mostly limited to lands within or contiguous to the boundaries of a national forest.[19]

Forestry

Perhaps no other natural resource issue in Oregon is more important than forestry. Forest practices have significant consequences for adjacent natural resources such as water quality and fish and wildlife habitat, and in the context of mitigating and adapting to climate change. Historically, forestry was the largest source of economic activity in the state, and it remains important today. The forestry sector is a major employer in rural areas, with approximately 61,000 people employed statewide. The wholesale wood and paper goods industries contributed 4 percent of Oregon's $236 billion gross domestic product in 2017.[20] Oregon has consistently been the number one producer of softwood lumber in the United States, producing some 17 percent of the country's total.[21] That said, as we note a few times in this chapter and as discussed in chapter 11, the revenue to counties and jobs associated with the timber industry are nowhere near their historical levels, a real challenge for many rural Oregon counties that have not developed new economic bases.

Of the nearly 30 million acres of forestland in Oregon, the majority (61 percent) is managed by the federal government (48 percent managed by USFS), followed by private landowners (33 percent), state and local governments (4 percent), and Native American tribes (2 percent).[22] Fifteen percent of publicly owned forests are characterized as "reserved," meaning they are restricted from timber production by wilderness designations or other statutes. Approximately 10 percent of forests are additionally differentiated as "other forest land," being defined as incapable of producing substantial (more than 20 cubic feet per acre per year) timber harvests.[23]

Because of the size of federal landholdings in the state, the federal government plays a significant role in forest management. For nonfederal lands, the State of Oregon plays a big role, managing nearly 1 million acres of state-owned forests, and regulating the operations of private forestlands through the Department of Forestry and Board of Forestry.

Oregon developed the first comprehensive state forest management policy in the United States with the Forest Practices Act (FPA) in 1971, which aimed to address the various ecological impacts of private forest practices. Environmentalists especially critiqued the FPA in its earlier years for its recommendations being largely voluntary.[24] Furthermore, the composition of the Board of Forestry has long been controversial. Originally, six of the nine seats were allocated to representative of industry. After reforms, the rules are now that the seven-member board may not consist of more than three members whose incomes are derived from the forest product industry, and that at least one member must reside in each of the three major forest regions of the state, ensuring that the board consists of geographically and sectorally diverse interests.[25]

Despite the percentage of publicly owned forestland, private lands dominate harvest totals. Of all timber harvested in Oregon, measured in billions of board feet, 76 percent is harvested by private landowners, compared to 14 percent being harvested by the federal government, 10 percent by the state, and less than 1 percent by tribal governments.[26] One factor of reduced harvesting on federal lands was the Northwest Forest Plan, implemented in 1994, which prioritized biodiversity considerations over timber harvests. The plan famously protected the limited remaining old-growth and mature tracts of forest to address habitat needs for the northern spotted owl and marbled murrelet (both listed under the Endangered Species Act) and to protect riparian areas for water quality and habitat needs of salmon.[27] This led to an over 90 percent reduction in board feet of timber harvested from federal lands.[28]

Overall, the total area of forest and timberlands in Oregon has been remarkably consistent, suggesting that the resource is being sustainably managed and replenished. Timberland area diminished from a peak in the early 1960s to a low in the late 1990s, but it has largely rebounded and stabilized since the mid-2000s. The volume of overall growing stock decreased from the 1930s to the 1980s and has been steadily increasing since then, standing at 90.9 billion cubic board feet, nearly reaching 1960s totals. Harvest totals have similarly been consistent over time, despite the punctuation of a historic low coming in 2009 during the economic recession, with levels returning to 1990s volumes by 2011.[29]

The overall picture of Oregon forests is thus somewhat positive, but there are major concerns as we look to 2050. Some top considerations include the impacts of population growth and its implications for land use, with expected expansions of urban boundaries. The fragmentation of land ownership patterns is also potentially problematic for biodiversity, including for animals. As one way to mitigate that, there are talks about establishing "green corridors" of similarly managed forest tracts, though public-private land swaps for this purpose frequently generate controversy.[30] Another threat comes from climate change, notably the combination of extended draughts and increasingly intense wildfires, such as the 2020 wildfires. While over 1.2 million acres were affected by these wildfires, the number of burned acres is an oversimplified indicator in that it does not capture fire severity and can vary considerably within a given burn area.[31]

Energy Efficiency and Renewable Energy Resources

Oregon has made good progress in the conservation and efficiency of energy production and consumption in recent years. The *2020 Biennial Energy Report* notes that from 2000 to 2015, the amount of energy used in Oregon declined by 12.5 percent. At the same time, Oregon saw a steady decrease in energy consumption per capita amid steady population growth. In 2018, Oregon's per capita energy use was the lowest in the Pacific Northwest. Yet there are a number of opportunities for increased energy efficiency, including insulating homes and office buildings as well as and updating residential lighting, HVAC (heating, ventilation, and air conditioning), and water heating in all buildings. Besides the environmental motivations, energy efficiency can also help ease the percentage of household income spent on energy and transportation costs, which disproportionately affect people of color and people with low incomes. There are also opportunities for increasing efficiency in reducing the amount of miles traveled, as discussed further in chapter 8.

Besides efficiency, another aspect of the energy future is the continued transition away from fossil fuels to renewable energy, a transition that is critical to curtail the worst of climate change but comes with its own impacts that should be considered. Oregon passed the nation's first coal-to-clean law in 2016, and the Clean Electricity and Coal Transition Act eliminated imports of coal-fired electricity by 2030, while Oregon closed its last remaining coal plant in 2020. Oregon is well known for its use of renewable energy and comparatively low prices for utilities.

Oregon ranks fourth in total renewable energy production when including hydropower sources.[32] Meanwhile, as of 2021, Oregonians paid an average of 11.02 cents per kilowatt hour (kWh) for their electric utilities, ranking ninth among all states and well below the nationwide average of 13.93 cents per kWh.[33]

In 2018, Oregon was ranked eighteenth among all states in terms of the percentage of solar energy as part of all the electricity generated statewide (1.2 percent).[34] This included utility-scale, commercial, and residential solar energy. While this is a small number, it is progress, as Oregon solar increased nearly five times over between 2015 and 2019.[35] The majority of this increase comes from growing utility-scale solar. In 2018, utility scale comprised 79 percent of solar energy generated, with commercial solar representing 13 percent and residential representing 8 percent.[36] Even so, there is much more potential for expansion. The National Renewable Energy Laboratory (NREL) estimates the "annual technical potential for solar in Oregon at 1,775 terawatt-hours" compared to around 51 terawatt-hours produced in 2018.[37]

The installation and management of solar energy has potential to have a positive economic impact, providing an estimated 5,700 jobs in 2019.[38] This has been facilitated by programs like the Strategic Investment Program, which provides resources for solar projects under the guise that they can increase tax revenue and provide economic benefits to communities. Solar comes with its own impacts that must be mitigated, however, including lithium mining and land use. Scaling solar energy requires large tracts of land, which can negatively affect fragile environments. Some are concerned it can also take lands out of other productive uses, such as agriculture. The State of Oregon has implemented various rules to regulate sites for solar projects that are also supplemented by rules and regulations enforced by local jurisdictions.[39]

Wind-generated energy, both on and off shore, has been increasingly important since the first wind facility was built in 2001.[40] Onshore wind ranks behind hydropower as the second largest zero-carbon-emitting electricity source, making up 11.6 percent of the electricity generated and 4.7 percent of the electricity consumed.[41] Oregon ranks ninth in the nation in terms of overall wind capacity, with 3,415 megawatts (MW).[42] As of 2020, there are forty-six existing wind farms and four under construction, totaling 894 MW with another 550 MW under review or approved.[43] Meanwhile, a 2012 study by the NREL shows a large potential for 27 gigawatts (GW) of onshore wind power, largely in the Cascades and southeastern Oregon.[44] Development has been limited by challenges in site selection, costs, and limiting the environment and community impacts. Offshore wind is a developing resource that Oregon is poised to take advantage of, with a technical potential of 62 GW, although owing to various technical, environmental impact, and political challenges, recent rulemaking indicates that the state is only planning for the potential capacity of 3 GW.[45]

Wind generation is a zero-carbon-emitting source with minimal greenhouse gas emissions in its product life cycle.[46] Even so, it can negatively affect local plants and animals, such as birds colliding with the blades. Also, transmission lines could negatively affect surrounding environments and waterways.[47] Additionally, some nearby residents see them as an eyesore. Existing regulations help identify areas where impact on wildlife and the surrounding land would be minimal.[48] Wind energy has the potential to supplement tax revenue. Additionally, it could provide nearly a thousand high-paying jobs, with turbine technicians earning a median salary of $56,230 as of 2020.[49]

Oregon has progressed by leaps and bounds with its efforts in geothermal energy production over the years. Their first operating plant opened in 2010 at the Oregon Institute of Technology in Klamath Falls and had an electricity generating capacity of 1.75 MW. Since then, a plant at Neal Hot Springs and a 3.1-MW plant near Paisley have been developed and launched, though the Paisley plant has not generated electricity since 2017. Other sites are being scouted in Lake County near Crump Geyser and Glass Butte.[50] In addition, many local jurisdictions are using geothermal for various purposes. Klamath Falls and Lakeview are both using it to heat buildings, with Klamath Falls going further and using it to heat homes and pools, and to melt snow and ice from sidewalks and roads.[51]

Geothermal is one of the more reliable sources of renewable energy. Electricity generation is at near-zero carbon emission, with a smaller environmental footprint (in comparison to wind and solar) and lower emission of other pollutants.[52] Because geothermal requires water, it can have an impact on the water supply. Additionally, reinjecting water back into the earth can add to operating costs.[53] Environmentally, drilling, extraction, and injection can potentially contaminate water sources, though no cases have been reported.[54] Finally, geothermal wells can produce fluids that contain chemical and radioactive materials.[55]

According to Oregon Department of Energy, "hydropower has been a primary source of electricity generation in Oregon for over a century.[56] Not only is Oregon the second-largest hydropower producer in the country, but it is also home to the oldest and functioning hydropower facility, operational since 1895.[57] As of 2018, there were ninety-four hydropower plants that were generating 35 million MW of electricity.[58] This makes up approximately 55 percent of Oregon's energy generation.[59] It also represents 43 percent of its energy consumed.[60] Oregon has been focused on upgrading existing infrastructure with technological upgrades such as "micro-hydro" projects like in-pipe conduit turbines.[61] Additionally, there are efforts to use hydropower as a way to integrate wind and solar energy, by fluctuating their levels depending on the performance of other renewable energy sources.[62]

Though hydropower is a carbon-free renewable resource, the facility's life cycle generates greenhouse gas emissions through extraction, construction, and operations.[63] Hydropower has other practical uses: flood control, irrigation, water supply, even community recreational opportunities.[64] Additionally, there are economic benefits through increased tax revenue and employment. That said, hydropower facilities and dams can negatively affect the surrounding environment, water levels, water temperature, and fish migration patterns, and they are a major source of mortality for juvenile salmonids, which are frequently killed as they run through the energy-generating turbines on their migration from freshwater to the ocean.[65]

Species Diversity

A hallmark of Oregon is its incredible diversity of ecosystems and of plant and animal species. But as we reflect upon past trends and look to the future, we have concerns about our state's overall species health, including some of the state's federally listed endangered species. The Endangered Species Act (ESA), enacted in 1973, provides the FWS and National Marine Fisheries Service (NMFS) the lawful means to protect species considered at risk of extinction. Listing of endangered species depends on five criteria: threat of destruction or damage to habitat, overuse of the species, natural population decline through disease and predation, lack of usage regulation, and any other reason that may drive population decline.[66] Within these three categories, about forty native species, or species with territory in the State of Oregon, are listed. Notable among these species is the marbled murrelet, northern spotted owl, and Pacific salmon. These species are of particular interest owing to their policy and political histories.

The marbled murrelet was originally listed as Endangered at the state level in 1987 and at the federal level in 1992. Since then, there has been an ongoing effort to develop an adequate habitat conservation plan, which has been difficult in part because of lack of access to private lands for good data collection. Additionally, the forestry industry has opposed conservation efforts because the species' habitat spans large areas coastal forests of the western United States.[67]

Efforts to preserve both the habitat and the population of the northern spotted owl have been mired in political strife for nearly fifty years. Timber companies have contested efforts to set aside areas of forested land for the protection of the owl's natural habitat. Despite legal challenges, federal courts have ruled that the plan can be applied to private property. Conservation efforts remain contentious to date.[68]

Salmon are an iconic species of the Northwest and Oregon, and of cultural significance to Native Americans of the region. Their future in Oregon is uncertain, however, owing to the impacts of urban development, mining, forestry, and hydroelectric development practices, which have straightened rivers, decimated salmon habitat, polluted water, and contributed to rising temperatures in streams. Various species of salmon were listed as Threatened or Endangered in the 1990s, though their current statuses vary. The Oregon Coast coho is perhaps the closest to recovery, while Snake River sockeye populations remain significantly depressed.[69] Upper Columbia spring-run chinook, while showing slight positive population trajectories, are still deemed to be "well below viable thresholds."[70] While there have been some efforts to repair or mitigate damage to salmon habitat, it is not clear if those efforts will be enough. Some environmentalists call for the removal or major modification of dams along major rivers in or upstream from Oregon, like the Snake River. The future of Oregon in 2050 may be one with very few salmon.

Notably, a few species in Oregon have been delisted from the ESA. In best-case scenarios, the delisting of a species is due to reliable data on population and habitat health. But delisting a species can be political more than data driven. The bald eagle and the gray wolf are two delisted species with range in Oregon. The bald eagle was included on the Endangered Species List from its inception in 1973 and subsequently removed from the list in 2007 following a successful population rebound.[71] The bald eagle is now considered a Species of Least Concern with an increasing population, and the species stands as an example of a delisting that has been attributed to a successful recovery effort. Conversely, the proposed and subsequent removal of the gray wolf from the Endangered Species List in 2020 is steeped in political controversy.[72] Within Oregon, ranching proponents have led calls to remove the gray wolf from the Endangered Species List. Population numbers for gray wolves have indeed met benchmarks set out in the ESA. But conservationists as well as biologists have noted that despite population recovery, the gray wolf only occupies approximately 10-20 percent of its original habitat.[73] The gray wolf delisting serves as a contemporary and ever-evolving example of the political nature of both listing and delisting endangered species.

While some native species are declining, another related challenge is the rise of invasive non-native species, which have had many negative consequences throughout Oregon. Invasive plants and animal species can affect food chain dynamics; forest-, farm-, and rangelands; and soil quality. They can also affect humans through parasites and bacteria.[74] Invasive species are the second-largest contributing factor to native species being at risk of extinction.

The list of invasive animal species in Oregon is long and growing, with some notable species, including the American bullfrog, Asian carp or silver carp, feral swine, and zebra mussel. Perhaps the most concerning invasive species in Oregon has been the mountain pine beetle. According to the Oregon Department of Forestry, "the mountain pine beetle is the most destructive forest pest in the west and has contributed to more tree mortality than any other bark beetle in Oregon."[75] From 2007 to 2016, the mountain pine beetle affected more than 380,000 acres per year in the state. While these beetles will often destroy distressed or weak trees—sometimes playing a useful role to overall forest maintenance—during full-blown outbreaks, they also attack and kill otherwise healthy pine hosts, especially during droughts.[76]

Phylloxera are aphidlike insects that infect and eventually kill grapevines in vineyards.[77] Phylloxera was first discovered in 1955 but not identified on commercial sites until 1990.[78] Various strains have, at different stages, torn through millions of acres of wine country on different sides of the planet.[79] There is no way to eradicate phylloxera from vineyards. The only way to minimize impact is to consistently manage the infestation by ultimately replanting the vineyard to vines that are grafted to resistant rootstock.[80]

While the Oregon Department of Agriculture highlights twenty-five different species of noxious weeds as being present in Oregon, three species are particularly problematic: Armenian blackberry, Scotch broom, and Rush skeletonweed.[81] Apart from displacing native plant species and damaging riverbed habitats, the Armenian blackberry also can have "significant economic impacts on right-of-way maintenance, agriculture, park, and forest production."[82] Scotch broom also displaces native plants and kills tree transplants, which increases tree death and slows tree growth.[83] Lastly, Rush skeletonweed is "an aggressive plant in both rangeland and cropland, particularly in lower elevation, light-textured soils."[84] The most affected areas are cereal grain and potato production areas.[85] The weed affects both the yield owing to competition for nutrients/land and the harvesting period, with its "latex sap" proving to be a nuisance.[86] Extensive efforts have been implemented to eradicate or contain outbreaks, but new sites emerge each year.[87] The existing Noxious Weed Control Program has experienced significant funding shortfalls, which has limited their ability to control and combat the various noxious weeds that plague the state.

The cumulative impacts of the above discussed trends suggests that Oregon in 2050 may be a very different place, in terms of animal and plant species, than pre-European arrival and even than today, with likely fewer native species and many more non-native ones. The decline of some of the species of importance to native peoples and to the state's cultural identity is upsetting to many.

Water

The final issue we examine in this chapter is water. Historically, the United States is a "water-rich" nation, but there is great variation within the country. In Oregon, the western half of the state is relatively water abundant, and most of the eastern portion of the state is water scarce. Oregon's water future in 2050 is shaped by a variety of factors, including federal policy and local actions. Both climate change and population growth are key drivers that have an impact on the supply and demand of water, which in turn affects a wide variety of social-economic dynamics that affect agriculture, energy supplies, forests, fish and wildlife, and other issues.

Water policy in the United States is characterized by a high degree of fragmented and dispersed authority between federal, state, and local regulators. At the federal level, the Clean Water Act (CWA) and Safe Drinking Water Act (SDWA) set baseline standards for a variety of water issues, such as point source pollution into navigable waters, wastewater treatment standards, permitting for allowable discharge of pollutants, and drinking water safety standards.[88] States typically have a greater role over regulation of nonpoint sources of pollution, have devolved authority to determine surface and groundwater allocations, and can elect to directly set higher water quality standards and implementation authority under the CWA.

Another key issue surrounding water supply relates to the differentiated system of water rights in Oregon, rather unique in the United States. Here, water rights are governed under the principle of "prior appropriation," meaning that water rights were established on a first-come basis, with first users holding "senior rights," followed by a hierarchy of "junior rights" allocated to those who came later. Water rights in this system are to a volume of water sufficient to meet a rightsholder's stated "beneficial use" and operate on a "use-it-or-lose-it" basis before "excess" water is allocated to more junior rightsholders. This system sets up a set of perverse incentives whereby not using one's allocated water is considered a "waste of water," leading to inefficient use. Various attempts have been made to address water allocation issues associated with this system, including the accommodation of a "public interest" for specific uses of water, protection of fish habitat, and sufficient provision of recreational opportunities. Yet any attempt to get allocations for such purposes invariably is met with pushback from senior rightsholders.[89]

Oregon has been at the forefront of policy experimentation to address the collective access to water in such a system. The federal government has stepped in as the primary buyer of water from rightsholders to maintain instream flows for a variety of public purposes, most significantly to maintain fish habitats for fish species listed under the ESA. The State of Oregon also engages in such purchases of water quantities, ranking fourth among all states in terms of instream flow acquisitions. In parallel with these efforts, the nongovernmental sector, taking lessons from the successful implementation of land trusts by such nongovernmental organizations as The Nature Conservancy and the Sierra Club, has developed a similar model of "water trusts" to purchase water rights to maintain instream flows. The Oregon Water Trust was the first example of this model, established in 1993, and has served as the prototype for other water trusts in other areas. While funding limitations and unwillingness by some water rightsholders pose limits to the scope of such activities, such water trusts have been at the forefront of policy experimentation to identify flexible mechanisms for ensuring instream flows, such as collaborative water conservation projects, split-season leasing, rotational pooling arrangements, modified land management practices, and more.[90]

There are many ways to assess water quantity and quality issues, and the sheer number and scope of various indicators are beyond the reach of this chapter. Issues of water quality are taken up in more depth in chapter 4. But in a general sense, the state of water in Oregon can be characterized by enormous variability between the eastern and western portions of the state; highly variable patterns of generally good water quality with localized pockets of significantly polluted water bodies; and generalized concerns about the implications of continuing drought, population growth, and effects of climate change on future water supply and quantity. As of this writing in 2022, 95.8 percent of the state is under the drought category of D0, "Abnormally Dry," with 45.6 percent under D3, "Extreme Drought," and 16.2 percent, concentrated in the central part of the state, under category D4, "Exceptional Drought."[91] This is also discussed in chapter 3, as it is likely to get worse with climate change. The ongoing drought has the potential to generate significant political conflict between various water users, as evidenced by the decision by the US Bureau of Reclamation to not allocate *any* water from the Klamath Water Project.[92] These issues have been further exacerbated by the emergent problem of "water theft" by illegal marijuana growing operations, particularly in the southern part of the state.[93]

Nationwide, aggregate freshwater withdrawals increased significantly from 1950 to the early 1980s, peaking at more than 363 billion gallons per day before falling to approximately 280.3 billion gallons per day by 2015, despite a population increase of approximately 95.4 million people between 1980 and 2015. Much of this success can be attributed to various federal, state, and local policies that have incentivized water and energy efficiency improvements, such as the National Energy Policy Act and EPA WaterSense program. Total water withdrawals in Oregon in 2015 were approximately 6,580 million gallons per day, representing 2.34 percent of the national total, with the vast majority (5,160 million gallons per day) being used for irrigation purposes.[94] In terms of daily domestic use of water, Oregonians used 107 gallons per day in 2015, higher than the national average. As we look to 2050, there are opportunities for Oregon to lower water use, for example, in agriculture and industry sectors, and at the individual household consumption level, though this will take strong policy leadership.

Synthesis and Recommendations

This chapter highlights some important trends in key natural resource topics, including forestry, energy, species diversity, and water. While there are some bright spots, there also are key shared concerns about the unsustainable management and exploitation of resources for private gains. We also commented on the lack of governance and financial resources to address the problems, as well as the lack of cultural expectations, robust policy, and pricing schemes to promote efficient and accountable resource use behavior by many scales of actors. As we look to 2050, population growth and climate change are likely to worsen existing natural resource problems. For Oregon to more sustainably steward its natural resources, it needs to change past practices.

First, Oregon should ramp up efforts to decarbonize energy use, by both reducing consumption and transitioning to energy production from renewable energy sources. Most of that would almost entirely have to come from wind and solar sources. It is difficult to calculate what the land use requirements would be of such wind and solar generation, but 1 MW is roughly equivalent to 3.4 million British thermal units (Btu). Replacing the approximately 302 trillion Btu generated by natural gas alone would thus require over 888,000 MW of capacity. With direct land use requirements for solar generation ranging from 2.2 to 12.2 acres per megawatt, this would necessitate the conversion of between 72,854 and 404,010 acres of land to be converted in order to achieve strict statewide energy independence.[95] The push toward carbon neutrality and energy independence in power generation is a laudable goal that will entail significant adjustment costs and time to achieve. The state currently subsidizes conversion to renewable sources through various tax incentives, a practice that should continue and be scaled up as market demand and financial capacity warrants.

Perhaps the most worrying current natural resource issue is water availability and quality. As discussed, the use-it-or-lose-it system of water rights in the state creates perverse incentives to inefficiently use an increasingly scarce resource. This has led many to call for the overhaul of the water rights system in western states; however, such a move is extremely unlikely owing to adjustment costs and equity/fairness considerations. Oregon's pioneering efforts in the creation of water trusts to ensure sufficient stream flow for fisheries, habitat, and water quality protections should thus be funded to the greatest extent possible, acknowledging the financial insufficiencies of past efforts. An expansion of the state's involvement with the Oregon Water Trust, particularly in the form of increased financing, would bolster current efforts and establish the state as a leader in such an innovative policy practice. Furthermore, policy initiatives designed to further positive trends in more efficient water usage such as regulation of optimal scheduling for certain water uses (e.g., nighttime watering of outdoor landscapes) and financial incentives for less water-intensive practices and decreased water usage should be explored to the greatest extent possible.

This brings us to a truly big idea: the need for innovation in the provision and payment for ecosystem services. While still something of a nascent field, a growing literature highlights various design principles behind successful payment of ecosystem schemes. Successful payment of ecosystem services that guarantee sufficient provision entail clear identification of the ecosystem boundaries and specific services to be provided; a clear identification of the specific buyers and sellers, with adequate identification of willingness to pay by "downstream users"; identification of the scale of the market—international, national, or local—and specification of how prices will be set (e.g., willingness to pay matched to willingness to accept, debt-for-nature swaps, and the like); specification of the governance structure to be used, identifying legal rights and responsibilities of private parties and/or any government agencies involved; establishing the baseline scenario of what would occur without the payment scheme in place, in order to develop the metrics which will be used to gauge program success; identifying both the short- and long-term costs involved, including scheme design, capacity-building, and transaction costs of measuring, reporting, and verification; and setting the requirements and data sources used for measurement and verification.[96] While each of these tasks can be accomplished solely by private actors operating on a contract basis against a backdrop of mutual trust, particularly at smaller more localized scales, clearly there is a role for government to be involved in establishing the institutional framework necessary to accomplish these tasks in situations of larger-scale schemes that have greater potential for mutual distrust among actors. Thus ample opportunities exist for state and local governments in Oregon to take the lead in identifying uncaptured opportunities for payment for ecosystem schemes, facilitate the initial trust-building between buyers and sellers that is frequently necessary, and help design the institutional arrangements necessary for implementation in order to minimize potential transaction costs. Such actions should furthermore utilize existing private or public-private frameworks, such as the Oregon Water Trust and the various established land trusts that cooperate under the umbrella of the Coalition of Oregon Land Trusts.

Another idea for improving management processes in Oregon is to expand the use of collaborative natural resource management. The phrase refers to a number of practices that seek to engage multiple stakeholders to forge consensus and solve conflict, reduce litigation, prioritize common goals, facilitate learning among participants, improve information-sharing, build social capital, develop new institutional forms of decision-making, and include the perspectives of marginalized groups. A rich literature exists on the various forms and processes of collaborative policymaking, and the subject is far too broad for this chapter. Oregon should consider employing collaborative processes to the greatest extent possible, however, with an eye toward minimizing procedural costs, mitigating conflict, avoiding lowest common denominator decisions, and encouraging balanced representation.

Finally, in order to implement ecosystem management that addresses interrelated systems (e.g., forests, fish, wildlife, water, food, energy) at a landscape scale rather than within established political jurisdiction boundaries, the state would do well to experiment with the establishment and adequate funding of regional coordination bodies such as the Oregon Watershed Councils. Establishing such bodies on the basis of watersheds is already recognized as sound from an ecosystem perspective, but it still entails limitations. As social-ecological systems thinking continues to develop, it has become widely recognized that the design principle of "nested institutions," wherein smaller, more localized systems coordinate with and are nested within successively larger units, allows for better matching between social and natural boundaries, and facilitates cross-scale coordination and cooperation that is necessary for successful natural resource management.[97] Thus the established framework of watershed councils could be embedded within larger units that aggregate different watersheds into wildlife corridor units, units based on climatological patterns, or other bases of organization. This innovation would challenge established institutions that typically jealously guard their turf and areas of regulatory authority, leaders who are often concerned with the complexity and cost of coordinating such efforts. But this recommendation holds the most promise, and Oregon's unique history of extensive alternative citizen-led organizational forms makes it particularly well situated to become a leader and innovator in natural resource management.

Notes

1 John S. Kiernan, "Greenest States," WalletHub, April 2019, https://wallethub.com/edu/greenest-states/11987/.
2 "Public's 2019 Priorities: Economy, Health Care, Education and Security All Near Top of List," Pew Research Center, January 24, 2019, https://www.pewresearch.org/politics/2019/01/24/publics-2019-priorities-economy-health-care-education-and-security-all-near-top-of-list.

3 Oregon Secretary of State, *Oregon Blue Book, 2019-2020* (Salem: Oregon Secretary of State, 2019), https://sos.oregon.gov/blue-book/Pages/default.aspx.
4 OAR 660-033-0130(37) and (38).
5 "About Us," National Park Service, updated December 30, 2022, https://www.nps.gov/aboutus/index.htm.
6 D. Morgan, J. Beatrice, and S. Haider, "The Role of Bureaucracy in Oregon State and Local Government," in *Governing Oregon*, edited by R. Clucas et al. (Corvallis: Oregon State University Press, 2018).
7 Oregon Department of State Lands, *State of Oregon State Land Inventory System Report* (Salem: Oregon Department of State Lands, 2021), https://www.oregon.gov/dsl/Land/Documents/2bSLIStateOwnershipbyAgency.pdf.
8 Vicki Walker, "Memorandum: Annual Report on Common School Fund Real Property for Fiscal Year 2020 (July 1, 2019 to June 30, 2020)," Oregon Department of State Lands, January 9, 2021, https://www.oregon.gov/dsl/Land/Documents/2021_DSL_RealProperty_AnnualReport.pdf.
9 US Forest Service, *Forest Service National Resource Guide to American Indian and Alaska Native Relations*, FS-600 (Washington, DC: US Forest Service, 1997), https://www.fs.usda.gov/spf/tribalrelations/pubs_reports/NationalResourceGuide.shtml.
10 J. Martin and M. Henkels, "Tribal Government: Maintaining and Advancing Sovereignty through Advocacy," in Clucas et al., *Governing Oregon*.
11 D. Ranco and D. Suagee, "Tribal Sovereignty and the Problem of Difference in Environmental Regulation: Observations on 'Measured Separatism' in Indian Country," *Antipode* 39, no. 4 (2007): 691-707.
12 "Natural Resources," Confederated Tribes of Warm Springs, accessed December 20, 2023, https://warmsprings-nsn.gov/tribal-programs/natural-resources/.
13 S. Singleton, *Constructing Cooperation: The Evolution of Institutions of Comanagement* (Ann Arbor: University of Michigan Press, 1998).
14 Terri Hansen, "Supreme Court Affirms Native American Treaty Rights to Harvest Salmon," *Yes! Solutions Journalism*, June 11, 2018, https://www.yesmagazine.org/social-justice/2018/06/11/supreme-court-affirms-native-american-treaty-rights-to-harvest-salmon.
15 "Gaining Ground: Oregon," Land Trust Alliance, accessed December 20, 2023, https://findalandtrust.org/land-trusts/gaining-ground/oregon.
16 J. S. Miller, *Saving Oregon's Golden Goose: Political Drama on the O&C Lands* (Portland, OR: Inkwater Press, 2006).
17 Carol Hardy Vincent, Laura A. Hanson, and Lucas F. Bermejo, *Federal Land Ownership: Overview and Data*, CRS Report R42346 (Washington, DC: Congressional Research Service, 2020), https://sgp.fas.org/crs/misc/R42346.pdf.
18 Vincent et al., *Federal Land Ownership*.
19 Vincent et al., *Federal Land Ownership*.
20 Oregon Department of Land Conservation and Development, *Oregon Farm and Forest Land Use Report 2018–2019* (Salem: Oregon Department of Land Conservation and Development, 2020), https://www.oregon.gov/lcd/Publications/2018-2019_Farm_Forest_Report.pdf.
21 Oregon Forest Resources Institute, *Oregon Forest Facts: 2021-22 Edition* (Portland: Oregon Forest Resources Institute, 2021), https://oregonforests.org/sites/default/files/2021-01/OFRI_2021ForestFacts_WEB3.pdf.
22 Oregon Department of Land Conservation and Development, *Oregon Farm and Forest Land Use Report 2018–2019*.

23 M. Palmer, C. Christensen, and O. Kuegler, *Oregon's Forest Resources, 2006–2015: Ten-Year Forest Inventory and Analysis Report*, General Technical Report PNW-GTR-971 (Portland, OR: US Department of Agriculture, Forest Service, Pacific Northwest Research Station, 2018).

24 J. Bowersox, "Environmental Policy: The Challenge of Managing Biodiversity in Oregon," in Clucas et al., *Governing Oregon*.

25 "About the Board of Forestry," Oregon Department of Forestry, accessed December 20, 2023, https://www.oregon.gov/odf/board/Pages/aboutbof.aspx.

26 Oregon Forest Resources Institute, *Oregon Forest Facts: 2021-22 Edition*.

27 T. A. Spies et al., "Twenty-Five Years of the Northwest Forest Plan: What Have We Learned?," *Frontiers in Ecology and the Environment* 17, no. 9 (2019): 511-20.

28 Oregon Forest Resources Institute, *Federal Forestland in Oregon: Coming to Terms with Active Forest Management of Federal Forestland* (Portland: Oregon Forest Resources Institute, 2010), https://oregonforests.org/sites/default/files/2017-08/Federal_Forestlands.pdf.

29 Oregon Forest Resources Institute, *Federal Forestland in Oregon*.

30 S. J. M. Brown, "David and Goliath: Reformulating the Definition of 'The Public Interest' and the Future of Land Swaps after the Interstate 90 Land Exchange," *Journal of Environmental Law and Litigation* 15, no. 2 (2000): 235-94; G. Panagia, "A Critical, Historical and Legal Analysis of the Bureau of Land Management and the United States Forest Service Policies Relative to Federal Land Exchanges" (PhD diss., Arizona State University, 2004).

31 Palmer et al., *Oregon's Forest Resources, 2006–2015*.

32 "Oregon: State Profile and Energy Estimates," US Energy Information Administration, accessed December 20, 2023, https://www.eia.gov/state/?sid=OR.

33 "Electricity Rates in the United States," Electric Choice, accessed December 20, 2023, https://www.electricchoice.com/electricity-prices-by-state.

34 Oregon Department of Energy, "Resource and Technology Reviews," in *2020 Biennial Energy Report* (Salem: Oregon Department of Energy, 2020), https://www.oregon.gov/energy/Data-and-Reports/Documents/2020-BER-Technology-Resource-Reviews.pdf.

35 "Oregon Solar Dashboard," Oregon Department of Energy, accessed December 20, 2023, https://www.oregon.gov/energy/energy-oregon/Pages/Oregon-Solar-Dashboard.aspx.

36 Oregon Department of Energy, "Resource and Technology Reviews."

37 Anthony Lopez, Billy Roberts, Donna Heimiller, Nate Blair, and Gian Porro, *U.S. Renewable Energy Technical Potentials: A GIS-Based Analysis*, Technical Report NREL/TP-6A20-51946 (Golden, CO: National Renewable Energy Laboratory, 2012), https://www.nrel.gov/docs/fy12osti/51946.pdf.

38 "Clean Jobs Oregon 2019," E2, November 20, 2019, https://e2.org/reports/clean-jobs-oregon-2019.

39 Oregon Department of Energy, "Resource and Technology Reviews."

40 Oregon Department of Energy, "Resource and Technology Reviews."

41 Oregon Department of Energy, "Energy by the Numbers," in *2020 Biennial Energy Report* (Salem: Oregon Department of Energy, 2020), https://www.oregon.gov/energy/Data-and-Reports/Documents/2020-BER-Energy-by-the-Numbers.pdf.

42 Oregon Department of Energy, "Energy by the Numbers."

43 "Facilities under EFSC," Oregon Department of Energy, accessed December 20, 2023, https://www.oregon.gov/energy/facilities-safety/facilities/Pages/Facilities-Under-EFSC.aspx.

44 Lopez et al., *U.S. Renewable Energy Technical Potentials.*
45 Walt Musial, Donna Heimiller, Philipp Beiter, George Scott, and Caroline Draxl, *2016 Offshore Wind Energy Resource Assessment for the United States*, NREL Technical Report 5000-66599 (Golden, CO: National Renewable Energy Laboratory, 2016), https://www.nrel.gov/docs/fy16osti/66599.pdf; Jason Sierman et al., *Floating Offshore Wind: Benefits and Challenges for Oregon* (Salem: Oregon Department of Energy, 2022), https://www.oregon.gov/energy/Data-and-Reports/Documents/2022-Floating-Offshore-Wind-Report.pdf.
46 S. L. Dolan and G. A. Heath, "Life Cycle Greenhouse Gas Emissions of Utility-Scale Wind Power: Systematic Review and Harmonization," *Journal of Industrial Ecology* 16, suppl. 1 (2012): S136–S154, https://doi.org/10.1111/j.1530-9290.2012.00464.x.
47 Oregon Department of Energy, "Resource and Technology Reviews."
48 Oregon Department of Energy, *Siting of Energy Facilities in Oregon: EFSC Standards in Oregon Administrative Rule* (Salem: Oregon Department of Energy, 2017), https://www.oregon.gov/energy/facilities-safety/facilities/Documents/Fact-Sheets/EFSC-Standards-in-OAR.pdf.
49 "Clean Jobs Oregon 2019"; "Occupational Outlook Handbook: Wind Turbine Technicians," US Bureau of Labor Statistics, accessed December 20, 2023, https://www.bls.gov/ooh/installation-maintenance-and-repair/wind-turbine-technicians.htm.
50 Oregon Department of Energy, "Resource and Technology Reviews."
51 "Klamath Falls Serves as Model for Geothermal Industry Nationwide," Associated Press, March 20, 2010, https://www.oregonlive.com/pdxgreen/2010/03/klamath_falls_serves_as_model.html.
52 "Water Power Technologies Office: Benefits of Hydropower," US Department of Energy, accessed December 20, 2023, https://www.energy.gov/eere/water/benefits-hydropower.
53 "How Geothermal Energy Works," Union of Concerned Scientists, updated December 22, 2014, https://www.ucsusa.org/resources/how-geothermal-energy-works.
54 "How Geothermal Energy Works."
55 "Radiation Protection: Technologically Enhanced Naturally Occurring Radioactive Materials (TENORM)," US Environmental Protection Agency, last updated February 15, 2023, https://www.epa.gov/radiation/technologically-enhanced-naturally-occurring-radioactive-materials-tenorm.
56 Oregon Department of Energy, "Resource and Technology Reviews."
57 Oregon Department of Energy, "Resource and Technology Reviews."
58 Oregon Department of Energy, "Resource and Technology Reviews."
59 "Oregon: State Profile and Energy Estimates."
60 Oregon Department of Energy, "Energy by the Numbers."
61 Oregon Department of Energy, "Resource and Technology Reviews."
62 Oregon Department of Energy, "Resource and Technology Reviews."
63 Oregon Department of Energy, "Resource and Technology Reviews."
64 "Water Power Technologies Office."
65 "Energy Technologies and Impacts—Hydropower," Energy Development, US Fish and Wildlife, updated May 2, 2018, https://fws.gov/node/265254.
66 Stanford Environmental Law Society, *The Endangered Species Act*, (Palo Alto: Stanford University Press, 2001): 39.

67 C. John Ralph Jr., George L. Hunt, Martin G. Raphael, and John F. Piatt, "Ecology and Conservation of the Marbled Murrelet in North America: An Overview," in *Ecology and Conservation of the Marbled Murrelet*, General Technical Report PSW-GTR-152, ed. C. John Ralph Jr., George L. Hunt, Martin G. Raphael, and John F. Piatt (Albany, CA: Pacific Southwest Research Station, Forest Service, US Department of Agriculture, 1995), 3-22, https://www.fs.usda.gov/research/treesearch/27923.

68 Dominick A. DellaSalla, "Blowing the Whistle on Political Interference: The Northern Spotted Owl," in *Conservation Science and Advocacy for a Planet in Peril: Speaking Truth to Power*, ed. Dominick A. DellaSalla (Amsterdam: Elsevier, 2021), 99-126.

69 "Species Directory," NOAA Fisheries, accessed February 22, 2024, https://www.fisheries.noaa.gov/species-directory; "ESA Threatened and Endangered," NOAA Fisheries, accessed February 22, 2024, https://www.fisheries.noaa.gov/species-directory/threatened-endangered.

70 "Species Directory"; "ESA Threatened and Endangered."

71 R. Heisman, "Beacon of Hope," *Bird Conservation* (Spring 2018): 13-16.

72 Christine Peterson, "Gray Wolves Taken Off US Endangered Species List in Controversial Move," *National Geographic*, October 29, 2020, https://www.nationalgeographic.com/animals/article/gray-wolves-taken-off-endangered-species-list-in-controversial-move.

73 Peterson, "Gray Wolves Taken Off US Endangered Species List."

74 "Invasive Species," Oregon Conservation Strategy, accessed December 21, 2023, https://www.oregonconservationstrategy.org/key-conservation-issue/invasive-species/.

75 "Mountain Pine Beetle: Forest Health Fact Sheet," Oregon Department of Forestry, March 2017, https://www.oregon.gov/ODF/Documents/ForestBenefits/MountainPineBeetle.pdf.

76 "Mountain Pine Beetle."

77 Patricia A. Skinkis, Vaughn M. Walton, and Clive Kaiser, *Grape Phylloxera: Biology and Management in the Pacific Northwest* (Corvallis: Oregon State University Extension Service, 2009), https://catalog.extension.oregonstate.edu/ec1463.

78 Skinkis, *Grape Phylloxera*.

79 K. S. Powell, "Grape Phylloxera: An Overview," in *Root Feeders: An Ecosystem Perspective*, ed. Scott N. Johnson and Phillip J. Murray (Wallingford, UK: CAB International, 2008), 96-114.

80 Skinkis et al., *Grape Phylloxera*.

81 Oregon Department of Agriculture, *Economic Impact from Selected Noxious Weeds in Oregon* (Salem: Oregon Department of Agriculture Noxious Weed Control Program, December 2014).

82 "Amenian Blackberry," Oregon Department of Agriculture Noxious Weed Control Program, accessed December 20, 2023, https://www.oregon.gov/ODA/shared/Documents/Publications/Weeds/ArmeniaBlackberryProfile.pdf.

83 "Scotch Broom," Oregon Department of Agriculture Noxious Weed Control Program, accessed December 20, 2023, https://www.oregon.gov/oda/shared/Documents/Publications/Weeds/ScotchBroomProfile.pdf.

84 "Rush Skeleton," Oregon Department of Agriculture Noxious Weed Control Program, accessed December 20, 2023, https://www.oregon.gov/oda/shared/Documents/Publications/Weeds/RushSkeletonweedProfile.pdf.

85 "Rush Skeleton."

86 "Rush Skeleton."
87 "Rush Skeleton."
88 D. L. Feldman, *Water Politics: Governing Our Most Precious Resource* (Boston: Polity, 2017).
89 Feldman, *Water Politics*.
90 E. Hadjigeorgalis, "Incorporating the Environment into the Market: The Case of Water Trusts and Environmental Water Transfers in the Western United States," *WIT Transactions on State-of-the-Art in Science and Engineering* 37 (2010): 107-21.
91 "Current US Drought Monitor Conditions for Oregon," National Integrated Drought Information System, accessed December 20, 2023, https://www.drought.gov/states/Oregon.
92 N. Kirkpatrick et al., "Climate Change Fuels a Water Rights Conflict Built on over a Century of Broken Promises," *Washington Post*, November 22, 2021, https://www.washingtonpost.com/nation/interactive/2021/klamath-river-basin-drought/.
93 Andrew Selsky, "In Drought-Stricken West, Farmers of Weed are Stealing Water," Associated Press, September 24, 2021, https://leads.ap.org/best-of-the-week/illegal-marijuana-farms-stealing-water-amid-drought.
94 Cheryl A. Dieter et al., "Estimated Use of Water in the United States in 2015," *US Geological Survey Circular* 1441 (2018): https://doi.org/10.3133/cir1441.
95 Sean Ong et al., *Land-Use Requirements for Solar Power Plants in the United States*, Technical Report 6A20-56290 (Golden, CO: National Renewable Energy Laboratory, 2013), https://www.nrel.gov/docs/fy13osti/56290.pdf.
96 E. Fripp, *Payments for Ecosystem Services (PES): A practical guide to assessing the feasibility of PES projects*. (Bogor, Indonesia: CIFOR, 2014).
97 E. Ostrom, *Governing the Commons: The Evolution of Institutions for Collective Action* (Cambridge: Cambridge University Press, 1990).

PART II

Built Environment

In this next section, we discuss key topics in our built environment, meaning the spaces in Oregon primarily created by people for human use. These chapters discuss how Oregon's approach to planning—directives for housing, urban and resource land use, and transportation among other issues—has had positive impacts. Oregon has more diverse housing types of various sizes and types (e.g., duplexes, apartments) than many other states, especially in areas where the population is growing. Positive land use patterns include protected forest and farmlands as well as organized development patterns, less sprawl, and vibrant urban neighborhoods and town centers. As for transportation, Oregon is different from many other states in that it has at least somewhat planned for and prioritized a wider range of modes than just drive-alone automobile use, including walking, bicycling, and transit, and has begun efforts to reduce transportation-related greenhouse gas emissions.

Housing, land use, and transportation are deeply interconnected issues, though past planning practices have erred in planning for them in siloes. Overall, the state's approach to planning in these three areas has likely mitigated worse conditions seen in other states. Nevertheless, Oregon contends today with the negative social, environmental, and financial impacts of insufficient housing supply and stock for the needs of residents; separated, segregated, and sometimes inefficient land use patterns; and an overreliance on expensive, automobile-oriented infrastructure that doesn't serve everyone and has a range of negative environmental and health consequences.

Looking to 2050, the authors identify a range of big ideas specific to their topics. In chapter 6, Matthew Gebhardt suggests that the state can better inventory existing rental housing and more actively fund affordable housing. In chapter 7, Megan Horst and Melia Chase identify specific reforms to the existing land use planning system, alongside broader changes like full cost accounting of infrastructure, tax systems that incentivize the land use patterns desired, and land ownership reforms. In chapter 8, John MacArthur calls for the state to be bold and intentional about reducing vehicle miles traveled through incentives or pricing, regulations, and infrastructure investments that disincentivize the use of single-occupant vehicles and enhance the attractiveness of active transportation. Given the interdependence of housing, land use, and transportation, the best big ideas are ones that cut across sectors, for example, incentivizing diverse housing types in existing urban areas near transit and with good walking access.

6
Housing

MATTHEW GEBHARDT

One of the biggest concerns to Oregon's residents and leaders, both now and looking ahead to 2050, is housing. Significant interventions and leadership are needed to ensure that all Oregonians have sufficient and affordable housing in the short- and longer-term future. As we anticipate population growth, changing demographics, and continued declining household size, Oregon is projected to need 584,000 new housing units statewide by 2040 (and more by 2050). This chapter explores persistent and emerging issues likely to shape our ability to meet this need over the next two decades along with potential avenues for change. The chapter starts with a brief overview, discusses inequities in housing access, and examines the problems of supply and affordability. It concludes with "big ideas" to reshape housing in Oregon between now and 2050, including a statewide rental housing registration, expanding shared-equity and shared-ownership models, enacting tenant opportunity to purchase legislation, and significantly expanded state intervention into housing markets through investments, vouchers, and regulations.

Basic Terms and Connections

The term *housing* encompasses a complex combination of attributes: type, tenure, space, quality, location, and expenditure. Each unit is a unique combination of these. As such, no unit of housing is a perfect substitute for any other. Examples of different types of Oregon housing are single detached houses, duplexes and triplexes, townhomes and rowhomes, apartment buildings, manufactured housing, cottage cluster or cohousing, accessory dwelling units (ADUs), and tiny houses. Tenure is the conditions under which a housing unit is held and occupied. Broadly, tenures fall into two categories: ownership and rental. Space refers to specific characteristics of a housing unit: square footage, number of bedrooms and bathrooms, type of kitchen facilities, yard(s) and outdoor space, garage/parking. Quality includes specific traits of a unit—age, aesthetics and architectural style, construction type and materials, internal amenities and fixtures. Location includes both its general position in the state—urban, suburban, rural—as well as its specific position—city, neighborhood, and block. Housing location encompasses its proximity to different amenities and disamenities. Examples of amenities include highly ranked schools, new parks, or employment, while disamenities include environmental hazards, pollutants, or congestion. The final attribute is cost, or how much of a household's resources they need to expend to secure housing. This is also known as affordability.

Housing represents a combination of values and benefits for a household through its use and exchange. Housing is a basic need of all Oregonians. It is a source of shelter, and a place of physical and psychological safety and comfort. It also provides access (or not) to amenities, communities, identity, services, and opportunities based on its location. For homeowners, housing is typically an investment, and for many it is their largest source of wealth. For landlords and investors, rental housing is also a significant source of income and wealth. Problematically, use values and exchange values may be, and often are, in conflict. Households and investors tend to be deeply protective of the exchange value housing provides and will defend it against real or perceived threat—which has proven to be a challenge, for example, to increasing the regional and state fair share of affordable housing that would provide use value to a larger number of households but is thought to undermine property values. In this way, housing can be a peculiar asset, and individual homeowners are often motivated by their own private interests in increasing their home value, more so than a general regional or statewide interest in increasing housing supply and affordability.

This creates challenges for the public sector. Owners often depend on housing appreciation, and housing has indeed appreciated for many Oregonian owners in the past decades (though not evenly; for example, housing value declined for Black residents in inner northeast Portland in the 1980s and 1990s, and for some rural towns since the decline in timber industry jobs). Some of the appreciation in housing value is due to investments and improvements made by owners. Much of it is the result of external factors, such as limitations on supply, quality of nearby amenities, investments by other actors, or changes to public policy. The appreciation accrues to the owners regardless of, and sometimes in spite of, their actions. The public sector plays a vital role in protecting and increasing housing values through land use and zoning decisions, transportation and infrastructure investments, public health and safety outlays, community and economic development expenditures, and tax levies and policies. Decisions about land use often determine the parts of a city, region, or state that will experience growth, conservation, stagnation, or decline. While this typically benefits current owners and investors, it creates affordability problems for renters and homebuyers seeking to enter the market by driving up costs.

Housing is intertwined with other topics covered in this book. Population trends, outlined in chapter 2, will shift need and demand for housing and vice versa. As discussed in chapter 7, policies and decisions regarding land use (such as zoning and subdivision regulations) shape land supply, governing which locations are available for housing and which are not, what types and characteristics housing will take, and what amenities are available nearby. Transportation decisions, discussed in chapter 8, often coupled with land use planning, influence the type and cost of transportation options available to households, and accessibility and affordability (housing plus transportation costs) are vital considerations for planning, investment, and development decisions. Ability to afford and access housing is linked with employment and income (see chap. 11), while inability to access housing because of factors including income, availability, and affordability can lead to homelessness (see chap. 10). Interaction with the criminal justice system can severely limit access to housing options (as explored in chap. 12). State revenue and spending decisions and limitations (see chap. 13) shape the funds available to address housing challenges. Finally, housing is closely linked with climate change, with the residential sector accounting for a significant portion of Oregon's greenhouse gas (GHG) emissions, as explained in chapter 3.

Historical Context: Inequities in Housing

The housing system in Oregon, and the United States more broadly, is deeply and harmfully inequitable. Black, Brown, Indigenous, and low-income households (there is considerable overlap among these groups) consistently have fewer choices, encounter more affordability challenges, and experience worse outcomes in the housing market. Because of high housing prices and a lack of affordable homeownership options, as well as overt and systemic discrimination, these households are more likely to have been and continue to be denied access to homeownership and the accompanying opportunity to build wealth. For many of these same reasons, they often face challenges finding, securing, and keeping rental housing. Inequities in housing contribute to or exacerbate other inequities as well, such as less desirable housing and neighborhoods with fewer choices and fewer amenities. Disadvantaged people often face impossible trade-offs between housing and other life-sustaining necessities. These inequities have long histories, which are discussed in detail elsewhere.[1]

Some of the larger history of ongoing inequity in Oregon is discussed in this book's introduction. Here we add to that history and highlight a few specifics about housing, including the dispossession, racial exclusion, redlining, and the denial of homeownership opportunities. One of the first causes of ongoing inequities is that of dispossession and colonization of the land. For at least fourteen thousand years prior to European settlement of Oregon, numerous Indigenous tribes lived throughout the region. They used both temporary and permanent structures for housing, moving through the region to access food and resources based on seasonal availability. As Europeans settlers moved to the region, they displaced Native peoples, dispossessing them of their land and homes—without just compensation—and brought new and less ecologically sustainable forms of housing and development patterns. Many Native Oregonians were forced onto reservations, while others moved to cities in search of employment opportunities. The Portland region has the ninth-largest urban Native population in the United States. The culmination of this history is that Indigenous people of Oregon experience some of the worst outcomes and greatest disparities of any group across all outcomes, including housing.[2]

Another part of the unjust history of housing in Oregon has been the denial of home ownership—and its subsequent wealth-building benefits—to residents of color. Beginning in the early 1900s, racially restrictive covenants were written into property deeds, limiting ownership and occupation of housing to "the Caucasian or White race." In 1919, the Portland Real Estate Board revised their code of ethics to require realtors to never introduce "members of any race or nationality" who would "clearly be detrimental to property values."[3] Exclusive single-family zoning was widely adopted by cities like Eugene and Portland, with the encouragement of real estate interests and the backing of the federal government, to protect "quality of life" and property values by excluding so-called undesirable uses and undesirable neighbors (meaning people of color and low-income people). This was further bolstered by the adoption of a rating system for mortgage lending and refinance by the Federal Housing Administration (FHA).[4] A low rating—assigned to areas with older housing, mixed uses, and the presence of nonwhite households—meant that an area did not qualify for government insured loans and mortgages, a practice known as "redlining." As a result, nonwhite neighborhoods received dramatically less private investment, resulting in widespread deterioration, which made it extremely difficult for nonwhite households to receive mortgages. Those that were able to purchase homes were steered to racially segregated neighborhoods, such as the Albina Neighborhood in Portland. Government-backed mortgage programs also helped finance the movement of white households to new suburban developments, reinforcing segregation across urban areas.[5] In the 1960s, the federal government underwrote an era of urban renewal. In Portland, local leaders implemented urban renewal projects that cleared large swaths of Albina, where thousands of Black households had been steered to live, to enable the construction of I-5, the Veterans Memorial Coliseum, and the expansion of Emanuel Hospital.[6]

While practices like redlining and racial steering were officially banned by the Fair Housing Act in 1968, the patterns that were established have left lasting harm. Urban renewal also has had lasting consequences in terms of destroying and segregating neighborhoods and perpetuating wealth inequities. The gap in Oregon between Black and white homeownership rates in 2018 was 32 percent, higher than the national gap of 28 percent.[7] Table 6.1 shows the differences in rates between white, non-Hispanic households and minority-led households in the Portland metropolitan region: note that homeownership for this group declined steeply during the Great Recession, and while it has since rebounded, it remains lower. In part owing to the gaps in homeownership rates, white household wealth in 2019 was 7.8 times that of Black households ($188,200 versus $24,100).[8] Neighborhoods

Table 6.1. Homeownership Rates in the Portland Metro Area by Race, 2005-17

Race	Percentage Who Own Homes
American Indian or Alaska Native	59
Asian American	66
Black or African American	39
Pacific Islanders	29
Other races	53
White	67

Source: Oregon Housing and Community Services, *Implementing a Regional Housing Needs Analysis Methodology: Approach, Results, and Initial Recommendations* (Portland, OR: EcoNorthwest, March 2021), https://www.oregon.gov/ohcs/about-us/Documents/RHNA/RHNA-Technical-Report.pdf.

that experienced disinvestment through redlining in the mid-twentieth century—such as inner northeast Portland—have more recently served as attractive opportunities for gentrification. While housing prices have skyrocketed in these neighborhoods, many Black residents with long histories in the neighborhood had little control over and did not benefit from these changes.[9]

Key Housing Policies and Programs

This section briefly summarizes a few key policies and programs that have and continue to shape housing supply, affordability, and location in Oregon.[10] Relative to other states, Oregon has been more proactive in assessing the housing needs of the population and promoting a diverse supply. As Oregon's Department of Land Conservation and Development (DLCD) describes on its website, Goal 10 of the statewide land use planning program aims "To provide for the housing needs of citizens of the state. Buildable lands for residential use shall be inventoried and plans shall encourage the availability of adequate numbers of needed housing units at price ranges and rent levels which are commensurate with the financial capabilities of Oregon households and allow for flexibility of housing location, type, and density."

Goal 10 has been updated several times in response to lawsuits, legislation, and advocacy to provide more specific guidance for local governments, including clarifying that "buildable lands" should be "suitable, available and necessary" and "needed housing units" must include "government-assisted housing units" as well as attached, multifamily, and manufactured housing.[11] Efforts in the land use system generally, and in implementing Goals 10 and 14 specifically, have created a particular housing system and market in Oregon, with somewhat higher density housing than would likely have occurred, more compact land uses, and smaller overall lot sizes, especially for new development. Notably, Oregon has a higher share of townhouses and other "middle" homes relative to other West Coast states, at 17 percent compared to 11 percent for California and 10 percent for Washington, while matching the nation's rate. Moreover, Oregon's share of new "-plex" housing in 2010-20 leads its West Coast peers and the nation. Another indicator of some success (albeit increasingly challenged, as this chapter goes on to describe) is that housing prices and home ownership have fared better in metropolitan Portland than its West Coast major metropolitan area peers, though prices and homeownership are increasingly out of reach for many.

While Oregon's approach is better than some other states, there are limits and challenges of the past approach, which must change to meet the state's housing needs today and by 2050. First, a core underpinning of the housing system in Oregon is a reliance on private market actors to build and finance most housing options. Public and nonprofit builders develop only a fraction of total housing supply. It is one thing to plan, allow for, and incentivize a range of housing types and affordability levels (as Oregon has done), but that does not always result in the actual building of that housing. The economic pressures and interests that drive private development and finance decisions have not met public goals for housing.

Second, ensuring a supply of housing "commensurate with financial capabilities of Oregon households" is based both on housing prices and rents and on household financial capabilities, but the required actions and focus on land use only address supply, not affordability. Meeting the needs of low-income households requires deep public subsidies, and developing this housing largely requires specialized developers.

Third, Goal 10 is one of nineteen goals. The system requires seeking a balance between the different goals. Progress on one goal may complicate progress on another. Fourth, there are structural problems built into the implementation of Goal 10. Basing estimates of need on existing populations reinforces existing patterns of uneven development and income segregation. Cities that historically have few low-income households, often owing to exclusionary zoning—such as Lake Oswego—have a low starting point and thus project a lower local need, even if there are unmet regional and state needs. Recent legislative changes have attempted to address these shortcomings, as discussed below, but more is needed as we look to 2050.

Recent Housing Legislation and Policy

In the past five years, several new housing policies and programs have been enacted at the state, regional, and local level. Collectively, these represent positive steps toward addressing the housing challenges facing Oregon. At the state level, Oregon has passed a suite of new laws addressing assessment of housing need, housing production, zoning controls and approval, affordable housing finance, supportive services, evictions, and rent increases. Local governments have also enacted new programs aimed at expanding housing options, helping households get and stay in housing, and increasing the supply of affordable housing. These changes are already influencing planning and development decisions across the state. They also are increasing the number of affordable housing units being built, though not nearly fast enough to meet the need. As discussed below, challenges remain.

In 2019, Oregon Housing and Community Services (OHCS) released a Statewide Housing Plan (SHP) that outlined the depth and breadth of housing disparities and issues—many of which are also discussed in this chapter—and set forth six priority areas and associated actions to guide future decision-making and policy and program implementation:

1. Affordable rental housing: Set a target of 25,000 new affordable housing units in the development pipeline by 2023.
2. Equity and racial justice: Identify systemic and institutional barriers and expand access to OHCS resources for communities of color and provide education about injustices for partners and stakeholders.
3. Homelessness: Create a coordinated approach to increasing housing for homeless people, including a particular focus on veterans and children. Sets a goal of 85 percent of individuals retaining permanent housing six months after engaging with homeless services.

4. Homeownership: Expand opportunities for low- and moderate-income households to move into homeownership with a particular focus on homeowners of color. Sets a specific target of 6,500 households becoming homeowners.
5. Permanent supportive housing: Invest in permanent supportive housing. Sets a specific target of funding creation of a minimum of one thousand permanent supportive housing units.
6. Rural communities: Set specific goal of increasing OHCS supported housing in rural communities.

The above goals are modest in comparison to the scale of the challenges and needs as we look to 2050, though they were intended to be realistic in terms of legislative calendars, bureaucratic realignment, and financial constraints. The plan has been used to guide legislative priorities, funding requests, and program targeting and has been an important tool for communicating and organizing.

In addition to the Statewide Housing Plan, several important pieces of legislation passed in recent years have attempted to address aspects of the housing challenge. Table 6.2 summarizes recent Oregon housing legislation and highlights key features.

In addition to state legislation and changes to policies, several local programs have expanded the resources for affordable housing development and preservation and reprioritized how funds were spent. Both the City of Portland and Metro passed bond measures to support affordable housing development in 2016 and 2018, respectively. Combined, these measures authorize over $1.3 billion. In 2020, Metro voters approved a further measure to fund supportive services for affordable housing through a tax on businesses with over $5 million in gross receipts as well as individuals earning over $125,000 and couples earning over $200,000 per year. Revenue from this tax is intended to fund activities to connect households to housing and promote stability through wraparound services. During the 2022-23 fiscal year, the tax raised $336.6 million, greatly exceeding initial estimates of $250 million per year.

The state has also significantly increased appropriations to support affordable housing, including additional capital support for new supportive housing and for the Local Initiatives Fast Track (LIFT) program to provide gap financing to facilitate new affordable projects. Oregon

Table 6.2. Key Features of Recent Oregon Housing Legislation

Year	Legislation	Key Features
2017	Senate Bill (SB) 1051	Further clarified interpretation and application of Goal 10: • Housing development proposals must be reviewed using "clear and objective standards." • Affordable housing permit application reviews should be reviewed within 100 days. • Accessory dwelling units (ADUs) must be allowed in single-dwelling zones. • Religious institutions are allowed to use their land for affordable housing development. • Municipalities are required to plan for needed housing for low-income households.
2019	House Bill (HB) 2001	Expands opportunities for "middle housing" in Oregon cities: • Certain municipalities are required to revise their zoning codes to allow duplexes and other middle housing (triplexes, quadplexes, cottage clusters, and townhomes) in single-dwelling residential zones. • Municipalities were required to consider alternatives for increasing the affordability of middle housing, including waiving system development charges or granting property tax exemptions.
2019	House Bill (HB) 2003	Promotes better data-driven planning for housing: • Municipalities with populations over 10,000 required to periodically update their housing needs analysis (HNA) to determine the housing needs of their current and projected population. • Municipalities are required to adopt a housing production strategy (HPS) with specific code changes, financial incentives, and other tools to promote development to meet needs identified through the HNA. • Development or rezoning for development of affordable housing on public property within an urban growth boundary is allowed. • A pilot regional housing needs analysis (RHNA) to assess housing needs for all income levels by region authorized with results reported back to the legislature.
2019	Senate Bill (SB) 608	Stabilizing residential tenancies through two core elements: • Landlords must give a minimum of 90 days' notice for no-cause evictions—evictions without a specified just cause, such as non-payment of rent or violation of lease terms—and in most cases pay for a tenant's relocation. • A system of statewide rent stabilization authorized by this legislation prohibits rent increases during the first year of tenancy and limits subsequent increases to 7% plus the Consumer Price Index (CPI); buildings less than 15 years old are exempted.

Year	Legislation	Key Features
2021	Senate Bill (SB) 8	Changes local zoning for affordable housing development (in this legislation, it means housing for households below 80% of annual mean income, or AMI, and with the average of all units for households below 60% of AMI): • Municipalities required to change codes to allow affordable housing in areas zoned for commercial, religious, and some industrial. • Municipalities required to adopt standard density and height bonuses for affordable housing. • Attorney's fees awarded to affordable housing developers who win a land use appeal of their development proposal, to discourage frivolous appeals.

Housing and Community Services has and continues to update the Qualified Allocation Plan (QAP) governing awarding of low-income housing tax credits (LIHTCs). These changes included a tribal set-aside and areas affected by federally declared disasters. OHCS recently announced that they are reaching caps on bonding capacity, however, which will limit the use of LIHTCs.

Altogether, these actions are likely to collectively increase desperately needed funding for affordable housing. And many of these efforts place Oregon at the forefront of system changes to support housing development, diversity, and access. Unfortunately, they are not sufficient to resolve the two main issues discussed below, housing shortages and affordability.

Housing Shortages

The most pressing housing issue facing Oregon is a shortage of housing units. Housing shortages are a national problem that has worsened in recent years. Nearly 60 percent of US states are experiencing a shortage of housing units, including most western states. The situation in Oregon is particularly acute. Oregon is estimated to have the largest housing supply deficit in the country, or approximately 9 percent of the state's housing stock.[12] The number of homes for sale in Oregon in 2022 hit a record low,[13] and rental vacancy rates are also very low.

The 2021 Regional Housing Needs Analysis (RHNA) presented a stark picture: Oregon requires 584,000 new housing units by 2040 to meet projected need (by 2050, we can anticipate an even higher need).

Just under one-quarter of this—140,000 units—is required to meet *existing* need. While the nature of shortages varies across the state, every region is affected. The largest needs are nearly 300,000 units in metropolitan Portland, nearly 150,000, in the Willamette Valley, and approximately 56,000 in Deschutes County. Only the southeast region is anticipated to come close to meeting projected need. Table 6.3, from the RHNA, summarizes the estimated housing need by region.

The shortage of housing is not distributed equitably. The households most affected by housing shortages are those with lower incomes. Recently developed housing across the state has largely been for households with incomes at or above the localized median income of $81,2000 for a family of four in Oregon in 2021, according to the US Department of Housing and Urban Development. Approximately 47 percent of the total projected housing need and the vast majority of underproduction is housing that is affordable for households at or below 80 percent of median income. Ninety-five percent of existing underproduction is in housing affordable to households below 120 percent of median income. The net result is an estimated need for 139,000 new affordable housing units.[14] As discussed in chapter 10, this shortage of affordable housing units directly contributes to worsening homelessness, as there are simply not enough affordable housing units, and low-income households are priced out of market rate options. To emphasize this, 42,000 of the needed 139,000

Table 6.3. Oregon's Estimated Housing Need by Region, 2020-40

Region	Projected Need	Underproduction	Housing for the Homeless	Total Units	% of Units
Portland Metro	224,683	59,488	10,683	294,853	51
North Coast	14,731	295	2,309	17,335	3
Willamette Valley	101,704	35,913	8,972	146,589	25
Southwest	34,896	10,287	4,579	49,761	9
Deschutes	49,856	4,837	1,194	55,887	10
Northeast	16,731	-	899	17,630	3
Southeast	965	-	538	1,503	0
Oregon[a]	443,566 (76)	110,819 (19)	29,174 (5)	583,559 (100)	100

[a]Numbers in parentheses show corresponding percentage.

Source: Oregon Housing and Community Services, *Building on New Ground: Meeting Oregon's Housing Need* (Salem: Oregon Housing and Community Services, 2021), https://www.oregon.gov/ohcs/about-us/Documents/RHNA/02-21-2021-ECONW-OHCS.pdf.

affordable housing units are needed for households *already* experiencing homelessness. Across the state, there has also been uneven development of rental housing units. While the Portland metropolitan region has seen an increase in rental housing units (though still insufficient), many rural communities have little rental stock—an increasing problem in places like La Grande and Sisters. In these places, households unable to access homeownership are left with extremely limited housing options. Table 6.4 illustrates the needed housing by median family income.

Demand for housing in Oregon is rising owing to population growth and smaller household sizes (discussed in chap. 2, on population). Other factors are historically low mortgage interest rates (true in 2020-21, though not in 2022, when the Federal Reserve started raising interest rates) and increasing disposable incomes for middle- and upper-class households. Higher-income actors have been increasingly purchasing second homes or investment properties, reducing supply and driving up prices.

Supply, meanwhile, has not met demand. Instead, over the past decade, fewer housing units have been built in the United States on a per capita basis than in any other post–World War II decade.[15] In Oregon, housing permits per capita reached their lowest point in seven decades in the early 2010s. This trend holds across every region of the state.[16] After a decade of stagnation, 2021 was the first year that new housing starts exceeded the estimated number of new units necessary to meet demand. It is unclear whether this growth will continue, however.

Table 6.4. Oregon's Housing Needs by Income Category

Median Family Income (%)	Projected Need	Underproduction	Housing for the Homeless	Total Units	% of Units
120	201,656	7,725	–	209,381	36
80-120	82,796	18,326	–	101,121	17
50-80	70,013	30,574	875	101,462	17
30-50	44,400	26,119	2,334	72,852	12
0-30	44,701	28,076	25,965	98,742	17
	443,566 (76)[a]	110,819 (19)	29,174 (5)	583,559 (100)	100

[a]Numbers in parentheses show corresponding percentage.

Source: Oregon Housing and Community Services, *Building on New Ground: Meeting Oregon's Housing Need* (Salem: Oregon Housing and Community Services, 2021), https://www.oregon.gov/ohcs/about-us/Documents/RHNA/02-21-2021-ECONW-OHCS.pdf.

Fewer new homes also means that the available supply of housing is increasingly older. The average age of housing in the United States has increased to forty-one years in 2019, up approximately seven years from a decade earlier.[17] Older housing is more likely to need major repairs and investment. Many older homes are also in need of upgrades to improve energy efficiency, climate resilience, or to strengthen against natural hazards. For example, the City of Portland alone has nearly 250 unreinforced masonry apartment buildings with nearly 7,000 units. Residents in these buildings face a higher risk of harm or displacement in the event of an earthquake.

Supply shortages have been further worsened by wildfires and the COVID-19 pandemic. The 2020 wildfires destroyed 4,021 homes, including a large number of affordable units, more than 1,800 of them mobile homes and RVs. The bulk of these losses were in Jackson County, where more than 2,300 homes burned.[18] As described in chapter 2, climate change will likely continue to negatively affect housing supply through future forest fires, flooding, and more. The pandemic slowed the pace of new development as workplace restrictions and supply chain problems limited work on ongoing projects and uncertainty about demand scrambled planning for new projects. While many of these issues have improved, supply chain problems and market uncertainty continue, and new problems of inflation and higher interest rates have added further complications.

Challenges and Constraints

A central challenge of housing supply is that, in economic terms, it tends to be inelastic, particularly in the short run. This means that housing supply does not readily respond to changes in price. The primary reason for this is the complicated and time-consuming nature of housing development. It relies on availability of land, legal approvals, materials, labor, and capital. Limitations on any of these can slow or stop development or increase the overall cost, and thus price, of new housing. Oregon's housing supply has been affected by all five.

Land, Infrastructure, and Public Sector Regulation

An important component of new housing development is the availability of viable sites for (re)development. One viability factor is ownership.

In order to be available for new housing, land must be owned, optioned, or available to actors prepared to, and capable of, developing or redeveloping that land. While a property may be inside the urban growth boundary (UGB), its current owner may not be interested in making it available for new housing development for any number of reasons, including another current use (e.g., parking or agriculture), extenuating issues (e.g., contamination or prior development), multiple landowners that are not in agreement, unclear or clouded ownership or title, or the owner is holding out for a higher price, whether realistic or not. Owners of properties with low property tax assessments (Oregon's inequitable property tax structure is discussed in chap. 13) are often less motivated to sell or develop. Another factor is monopoly pressures; where a single owner or small group of owners controls numerous sites or large tracts of land, they can restrict available land for new development to drive or keep prices of land or finished housing, and thus profits, higher. Assembling sites for redevelopment or infill may be further complicated by fragmented ownership, oddly shaped or too-small parcels, and existing uses.

UGBs are a common culprit of the housing shortage in Oregon. But existing scholarship suggests that Portland's growth boundaries have minimal effect on housing prices and do not significantly limit available land.[19] In part, this is because one adaptation within the Portland region has been smaller lot sizes. While UGBs do not create a significant *actual* shortage of land, they may create a significant *perception* of a shortage. Developers and investors may respond to this perception by buying up available land and bidding up prices, either to secure sites for near-term development or as speculative investments. This is one area for possible intervention, as discussed later in this chapter. Yet states and metropolitan regions without UGBs are also experiencing land price escalation and housing shortages, so the problem of housing supply needs to be addressed much more broadly than just focusing on UGBs.

Beyond ownership, several other characteristics may limit the immediate readiness of a parcel of land. The availability of adequate infrastructure, including water, sewer, roads, power, and public services, is necessary for new development. Lack of ready infrastructure or aging or inadequate infrastructure is a common problem for many jurisdictions. In reviewing land for inclusion in a UGB, jurisdictions are required to consider existing and potential of infrastructure. The actual extension or improvement of infrastructure often requires significant capital investment and cooperation of multiple layers of government, special districts, and private utility companies, however. Infrastructure provision is particularly challenging for smaller municipalities and rural communities. While infill and redevelopment sites typically have existing infrastructure, this may be inadequate to meet the requirements of more intense use of the site or current standards and code requirements. For example, more stringent stormwater management restrictions or need for larger sewer or water lines may limit the viability or intensity of a project.

Developable land is also subject to local land use and development review. Proposed developments must comply with zoning, which governs how a particular property can be used and sets design standards for density, coverage, bulk, height, orientation, parking, and access. Proposals also require a public hearing and opportunities for public participation. Developments may need to be reviewed for compliance with subdivision and lot division standards, and some may require additional reviews, such as for tree removal or for traffic impacts, or require permits from the state or federal government, for example, if a proposal might affect wetlands. Developments are then reviewed for compliance with building codes. While some parts of this process may be able to run concurrently, many are sequential, and projects often require several rounds of revision to gain final approval. Housing developers consistently complain that the review time is onerous and a disincentive.

The State of Oregon has established time limits for land use review and recently clarified the expectation that local governments apply "clear and objective standards, conditions, and procedures regulating the development of 'needed housing,'" as noted in ORS 197.307(4), to ensure that housing developments are not subject to unreasonable cost or delay due to review. Most communities have developed a two-track process for review, a clear and objective standards path and a discretionary path that allows for more flexibility and negotiation. Public sector use, health, and safety reviews are necessary, but they are time consuming and add to the cost of development.

Building vertically can offset high land costs, which is also complementary with compact development and transit-oriented land use planning, discussed in chapter 7. High-rise construction is expensive, however, requiring more expensive construction materials, mechanical elements, and specialized labor.[20] Other code conditions, including sizable parking requirements or inclusionary housing mandates, can create real or perceived barriers to building.[21] An actual or anticipated lack of demand for that type of housing—for example, condominiums or co-ops—can lead developers to deem the risk too high. As a result, developers may choose to not build at all or not to build up to the maximum densities allowed, even with bonuses and incentives. This is a particular problem in Oregon, where projections used to determine buildable land supply within UGBs, which often assume high-density development to the maximum allowed by zoning, may be overestimating the number of housing units likely to be built if market pressures and developer behavior were more fully incorporated. An example of this is along 82nd and 112nd Avenues in East Portland, which have for years been zoned for much higher density and have seen little residential development.

Construction Costs

Construction costs and capacity also constrain housing supply. Construction costs are primarily driven by labor and materials. Lack of construction labor, particularly skilled labor in specialized trades, is a constraint for builders. Estimates put the nationwide shortage of construction workers at more than two million over the next three years.[22] The number of workers has only recently returned to pre–Great Recession levels in Oregon, but it still lags far behind need.[23] Owing to prevailing wage laws, which require developments receiving public subsidies to pay higher wages, labor costs for affordable housing are typically higher. These projects also include goals for hiring minority- and women-owned businesses and workers—important goals that firms sometimes find difficult to meet. In a recent OHCS survey, only 20 percent of respondents agreed that there were sufficient numbers of these firms to meet state goals.[24] All of these factors add layers of complexity to these projects.

Materials shortages and costs—particularly of lumber, steel, and aluminum—also constrain supply. Production bottlenecks, supply chain disruptions, and import tariffs create uncertainty, longer time lines, and higher costs.[25] Developer and contractor capacity is also a challenge, particularly given the need to substantially increase development to meet supply backlogs and projected future needs. Both nationally and regionally, there has been a consolidation of construction companies, especially subcontractors that specialize in electrical, plumbing, and mechanical systems. In addition, existing companies may be working on more jobs, creating capacity and logistics challenges for projects. To build more housing that meets identified requirements, there needs to be enough developers and contractors with the specific skills and knowledge necessary for complicated projects, such as publicly subsidized affordable housing or high-rise construction, operating or prepared to operate in markets across the state.

Housing Development Financing

Financing is an enormously influential factor in housing development. Even publicly subsidized projects require the participation of private investors and lenders. The practices and demands of private investors and lenders significantly influence (perhaps control) what type of housing gets built or not, where it gets built or not, how it is designed, and how much it costs. A housing project typically requires at least two sources of financing: equity and debt. Equity investors require a return on their investment. Crucially, development costs include investor and developer profit. Demanded returns drive up development costs and the ultimate price[26] or rents required for a project to be considered viable.

Debt financing refers to loans from banks or other financial institutions. Lenders charge interest on loans. The interest rate is based on the treasury rate set by the US Federal Reserve Bank and an assessment of the risks associated with a particular project, such as location, type, developer track record, and anticipated market demand (reflected in projected sales prices or rents). This system for assessing risk and sizing loans is strongly biased toward projects aimed at high-income households.

In addition to that bias, the system for financing housing development presents several other challenges. Federal-level banking and finance reforms in response to the 2008 financial crisis placed new restrictions on loans for most new commercial housing development, including maintaining higher capital reserves and more stringent loan requirements, which collectively reduce the amount these banks can lend. The interest rate set by the Federal Reserve can also impact investment. While still low in historical terms, the Fed funds rate increased rapidly in 2022 after a decade of historically low rates, with differentiated impacts.

Lenders and investors routinely rely on data from comparable projects to verify developer or purchaser estimates of value, costs, or income. This creates a conundrum for certain projects. One example is that multiunit rental development in small cities in Oregon may not have recent projects of this type. "New" or rare housing types such as cottage clusters, co-housing, cooperative housing, or shared-equity housing also tend not to have comparable projects. Without existing, local examples with a history of recent sales or rents, appraisers struggle to determine a project's value. Further, many banks operate in certain geographic regions, with more lenders active in urban areas and larger cities. Bank consolidation, with smaller regional banks bought out by or merged with larger national banks, has reduced the number of lenders and shifted many decisions to nonlocal actors, who tend to lend conservatively, often resulting in a smaller loan amount or rejection of a loan application for nonconventional housing.

The assessments used by lenders mean that affordable housing projects do not qualify for the same amount of debt financing as market rate projects, and LIHTCs rarely generate sufficient equity to make a project viable. The resulting gap must be filled by other, largely public, sources. Most new units serving households below 80 percent and 50 percent of median family income (MFI) need to be partially or completely funded by public subsidy, respectively.[27] Further complicating the situation, affordable housing funding regularly comes with specific reporting requirements or legal agreements, which increases the complexity of affordable housing projects and increases costs from legal and accounting fees. Recent public initiatives, including both the Portland and Metro Affordable Housing Bond measures and an expansion of state LIFT Program, have increased funding to cover these gaps. Affordable housing developers routinely face much more complicated financing arrangements than market rate developers, often juggling five to eight or more different sources of funding. This stunts the development of affordable housing.

Many of the issues discussed above apply across the state, but challenges vary by location. For example, coastal communities must consider coastal, tsunami, and environmental restrictions. Individual cities and areas may have other pressures specific to their locality. For example, Deschutes County is experiencing higher population growth than other parts of the state, many communities on the coast and in the Gorge contend with second homes and vacation rentals, and Corvallis and Eugene have large state universities and face town-gown pressures. These locational differences make it much more challenging to craft policies to address supply and mean that some areas require substantially more resources.

Housing Affordability

The second core issue related to housing in Oregon is affordability. Housing affordability refers to whether housing is available to rent or purchase at a price that a household can pay, given their income and wealth. Housing affordability is typically measured by comparing housing costs—prices, rents, or mortgage payments—to income—wages, benefits, supplemental earnings. The good news is that Oregon real median household income, adjusted for inflation, has been growing in Oregon since 2011, and since 2018, it has been outpacing national numbers. Median household incomes in Oregon in 2020 were $65,667, approximately $500 above the US median, and the nineteenth highest out of fifty states plus Washington, DC.[28] Much of these income increases have been offset by inflation both for housing and other goods, however. Additionally, by definition, half of Oregon households make below the median income, many of them substantially below, as discussed in chapter 11.

The long-used standard for measuring affordability is that a household should pay no more than 30 percent of their income for housing. For example, if a household earns $25,000 per year, or about the current minimum wage, that household should pay no more than $7,500 per year, or $625 per month, for housing—far above what prevailing housing costs are in the state. If a household pays more than 30 percent of their income for housing, they are considered housing "cost burdened"; paying more than 50 percent is considered "severely cost burdened." Overall, 131,710 households, 22 percent of all households in Oregon, are severely cost burdened, with low-income households being most affected. Of extremely low-income households, 77 percent are severely cost burdened. Cost burdens also vary significantly by race, with households of color, in particular Black and Indigenous households, more likely to be rent burdened and severely rent burdened.[29]

One factor causing this price burden is that home purchase prices and rental rates have been climbing. Home prices rose 19.7 percent in Oregon during 2021, higher than the national increase.[30] Oregon's median home value in 2021 was $429,600, nearly three times that in 2000. These increases are pricing low-income (and many middle-income) households out of the homebuying market, a phenomenon likely to have ripple effects for building wealth and intergenerational wealth transfer. Rental price increases are also a problem in Oregon. While capped under SB 608, the maximum increase allowed under that cap was 9.2 percent in 2021 and 9.9 percent in 2022 (given inflation, it is likely to be substantially higher in 2023). In 2021, fair market rents (FMRs) in Oregon rose to $1,185, nearly double the rate in 2000. A household would need to earn more than $52,000 per year in order to afford a two-bedroom apartment at FMR. FMR in the Portland metropolitan region is $1,495, more expensive than 98 percent of other areas nationally. The effects of the pandemic have been felt more significantly by rental households. While eviction moratoria have allowed many rental households to stay in their homes, a significant number of households remain behind on rent and in precarious circumstances. A report from the Portland State University (PSU) Homelessness Research and Action Collaborative (HRAC) estimated the number of households at risk of eviction post-pandemic at 125,400.[31]

There are a few important nuances of affordability to note that are important for intervening in the market. First, affordability is a function of both household (income) and housing unit (cost). While lower-income households are more likely to be burdened by housing costs, higher-income households may also be cost burdened if housing costs are sufficiently high. Second, housing affordability may vary by location. For example, what constitutes housing affordability in Portland is different than what constitutes housing affordability in La Grande. It can also be true within regions. Within the Portland metropolitan region, housing costs, and therefore affordability, are different in Gresham compared with Lake Oswego. Historically, affordability has been higher in small cities and rural communities, with lower median incomes offset by lower housing prices, but that is no longer true in Oregon, where housing prices in small towns and rural areas have climbed, too. Third, simply because a unit is affordable to a household does not mean that the unit is desirable or meets their needs. A housing unit that is affordable may be in an area that is far from work or transportation options; lack access to desired amenities such as schools, services, or cultural communities; or lack adequate size or maintenance. Finally, households may rent or buy down, not spending the maximum they can afford on housing, either by choice or because there are not units available in the higher price range they can afford. That may reduce the supply of housing affordable to a household with a lower income.

Challenges and Constraints

One challenge associated with addressing affordability is that many economic models continue to assume that a primary source of affordable housing for lower-income households will come through so-called filtering. The concept of filtering is that new housing is built at or near the top end of the housing market to appeal to the highest-income households. Higher-income households theoretically move to these newer and more expensive units, freeing up their previous units. Being older and used, these units are available at a lower cost and therefore available to households with less income. This process continues, with older and more deteriorated housing filtering down through the housing market, eventually reaching the lowest-income households as "naturally occurring affordable housing." This assumption is inherent in many arguments that connect affordability with increasing housebuilding, for example, through expanding or removing the urban growth boundary.

But filtering is much more complicated than the simplified economic model. First, it can take a *very* long time, possibly decades, for units to filter down to low-income households, those at or below 80 percent of AMI, and many units never get there. They get locked in stable residential neighborhoods (such as Laurelhurst, a close-in neighborhood in Portland) or are diverted or demolished. Those that do filter tend to be in less desirable locations and in poor shape by the time they do. Housing available to very and extremely low-income households, below 50 percent and below 30 percent of AMI, respectively, often exhibit serious dilapidation and health and safety issues. Second, the concept of filtering assumes a constant, or at least regular, growth in housing units that meets or exceeds demand. As noted above, however, that has not been the case for decades in Oregon. Finally, the filtering process is not monodirectional. Rather than old, deteriorated housing getting torn down and replaced, some older housing actually filters *up* through upgrading and rehabilitation. This upgrading is often accompanied on a neighborhood scale by the displacement of existing, low-income residents and the influx of new, high-income households, a process known as gentrification. Gentrification reduces the number of affordable housing units in affected neighborhoods and pushes low-income households out.

Another significant challenge for addressing affordability: Oregon property owners financially benefit from constrained supply and increasing housing prices. As such, they often resist any attempts to alter this system. Further, even nonowners sometimes oppose changes that threaten their possibility of joining and benefiting from this system at some point in the future (however unrealistic). Actions to address specific housing issues, such as increasing subsidized affordable housing, also tend to meet resistance from homeowners owing to the perceived negative impact on surrounding property values.

A related issue is that there is not necessarily a direct link between housing costs and housing prices. Put another way, the price a household pays for housing is not only the amount necessary to cover the cost of developing that housing. Prices for new development include investor returns and developer fees and profits in addition to the cost of development and construction. Prices for new and existing housing are based on what a seller thinks they can charge and what a buyer is willing to pay. In addition to development costs and limited supply, prices may be distorted by a variety of things, including local regulations, tax policies, interest rates, societal norms, asymmetrical information, and speculation.

Looking to 2050: Big Ideas to Address Housing Challenges

This section suggests several big ideas for addressing the housing challenges facing Oregon. This is not a comprehensive list of ideas; other ideas include those proposed in OHCS's Statewide Housing Plan, such as improving technology and streamlining processes for distributing funding, developing recycling and gap financing streams, expanding programs for affordable housing preservation and stabilization, and improving communication and resources for homeownership programs.[32] Given the focus of this book, the bias is toward big ideas and state-level actions. Changes to federal policies and programs are also necessary, particularly to provide resources for affordable housing, remove limitations on new public housing development, expand federal backing for diverse financing options, reconcile problematic tax incentives, and affirmatively promote fair housing. In 2021, Oregon Senators Ron Wyden and Jeff Merkley introduced two bills—the Decent, Affordable, Safe Housing (DASH) for All Act and Affordable HOME (Housing Opportunities Made Equitable) Act—and US Representative Earl Blumenauer in 2022 issued a report (*Locked Out 2.0*, updated from 2019) that outlined and addressed multiple changes to address specific aspects of the housing crisis. These provide an excellent list of federal changes.

Statewide Rental Housing Registration

A second idea is to create a statewide annual rental housing registration system, to collect basic information from property owners on units they intend to rent for all or part of the year. Several cities across the state already require registration of rental properties, including Gresham, Portland, and Medford, though each collects different data. In addition to greatly expanding reach, a statewide program could standardize data collection. Information collected would ideally include location, type, size, number of bedrooms, kitchen and bathroom facilities, year built, ownership or property management contact, and rent. Local governments could use this data to better track and remedy safety issues and legal or code violations. It would also allow for better outreach to landlords and tenants by public agencies, for example, to distribute rental relief or communicate regarding available programs. Rental unit registration could also be a source of revenue, either through registration fees or improved collection of tax revenue, which could be reinvested in improving housing conditions or expanding housing supply. Registering rental units would also vastly improve the available data, allowing for better understanding of existing conditions and trends and for more accurate and nuanced analyses of housing needs and production strategies.

Increase Shared-Equity and Shared-Ownership Housing Options

A third idea is to develop a state-underwritten system of shared equity and/or shared ownership. First, as some background, there are several models of shared equity in the United States, including shared-equity cooperatives and community land trusts (CLTs). Shared-equity cooperatives are residential buildings or developments that are collectively owned by residents, who purchase shares in a corporation that owns the entire project. Limited-equity co-ops are typically developed using initial public subsidies and have low-interest, long-term blanket mortgages, with cost savings passed on to residents and maintained through resale restrictions. In a CLT model, residences are sold to homebuyers while the CLT retains ownership of the land, reducing the price of the home for the buyer through long-term, low-cost ground lease. Options for the CLT to repurchase, restricted resale prices, and/or shared equity agreements are all common methods of maintaining affordability. Examples of CLTs in Oregon include Proud Ground in Portland and Kôr in Bend. Initial affordability is often achieved by land grants and subsidies from government. A separate model, known as shared ownership, exists in other countries like the United Kingdom, but shared ownership not been used in the United States. With shared ownership, income-qualified buyers purchase a percentage stake of a unit based on the amount of mortgage they can afford. They then pay a below-market rent on the remaining percentage of their unit, typically set based on cost of operation and maintenance. Over time, residents can "staircase" their ownership stake in the unit, incrementally increasing the percentage they own. As with the shared-equity models, initial affordability is typically achieved through government subsidy.

These programs primarily address affordability. They can also expand the range of options and potentially locations available to low- and middle-income households, offering the opportunity to build equity and wealth that is not available through renting. Such programs generally do not reach the lowest-income households, however. In addition, implementation typically requires donations, grants, or subsidies to support and local capacity to guide their initial creation. Widespread adoption of these models would require allocating public funding toward ownership and potentially away from rental. It would also be necessary to overcome a dearth of financing options and hesitancy of lenders. One possible avenue for expanding these options could be for state or local governments to work with community development financial institutions (CDFIs), specialized lenders that focus on underserved markets, to back the creation of financing for both organizations pursuing these models and households seeking to participate. For example, the Network for Oregon Affordable Housing (NOAH), a statewide CDFI, has developed a loan for the acquisition and preservation of mobile home parks serving low-income communities. Public funding to seed and backstop financing could start this market and help prove it to facilitate new private financing options.

Tenant Opportunity to Purchase

Tenant opportunity to purchase (TOP) refers to legislation that affords tenants in rental housing units the right to purchase the housing they are renting from landlords who are seeking to sell. The exact structure varies, but the core of TOP is that tenants must be informed of an impending sale and given the right, collectively or working with an affordable housing provider, to secure funding and make an offer to purchase.[33] Opportunity to purchase is often discussed in conjunction with one of the above limited-equity ownership structures and may include affordability requirements if public funds are used in the purchase. In addition to opposition from landlords, challenges include determining whether to limit to only multiunit rentals or include single-unit housing, how much time tenants should be afforded to assemble financing and make an offer (which could be extremely challenging for larger properties with many tenants), and how to ensure or encourage landlords to accept good faith offers from tenants. Washington, DC, has had TOP in place since the 1980s, and versions of this legislation are currently being considered in New York and California. Oregon already has a similar program, enacted through HB 4038 in 2014, in place for manufactured dwelling parks, which could be a starting point.

Land Value Tax

The existing property tax system in Oregon is broken. It generates insufficient revenue to support public services and is arbitrary and inequitable. But the aspect particularly relevant to this chapter is that the current system incentivizes underutilization of land and disincentivizes new residential development. By basing property taxes largely on improvements (e.g., housing) and locking in historic assessments, property owners continue to pay low taxes unless and until they develop or improve that property. A big idea is to switch to a land value tax, or a property tax based on the total value of land without improvements, which could spur more intense housing development on residential properties, helping address the supply challenge. This recommendation is echoed in chapter 7, as it is salient to land use as well, and further elaborated as a big idea in chapter 13.

State Housing Voucher Program

Only a small number of public programs focus on the demand side of the problem, including federal housing choice vouchers and down payment assistance. Oregon has already undertaken one step to make these more effective in banning source of income discrimination in housing. Demand-side programs supplement household income or savings, increasing their ability to afford housing along with access and stability. Existing programs serve only a small fraction (30 percent) of those eligible, however.[34] Barring an increase in federal funding, the state could institute a housing voucher program. There are a number of variants that could be considered, including a broad entitlement with a sliding scale depending on income and the ability to use for rental or homeownership options. At a minimum, vouchers could be made available for targeted groups, such as those eligible for federal vouchers or households facing eviction, and administered through existing institutional channels, such as public housing authorities.

State-Funded Affordable Housing Program

While it is possible that private actors may be able to meet the need for market rate housing, structural and institutional pressures built into the private development system described above mean that they are fundamentally unable to address shortages of units affordable to households at or below 80 percent of MFI, a reality acknowledged in the RHNA. These broad structural issues built into the way housing is provided in the United States are unlikely to dramatically change in the next decade. Public subsidies, often deep public subsidies, will be necessary to increase supply of housing for these groups. Recent increases in affordable housing funding have spurred new development in recent years, but to meet the demand, it is estimated that three times the current amount is needed. While an ideal solution might be for changes at the federal level to restart, expand, and fund the public housing program, waiting for this may mean waiting indefinitely.

A big idea is to develop a state-funded affordable housing program to build housing for households below 80 percent of MFI. A number of different strategies exist, such as working through an expanded network of nonprofit housing developers, using existing public housing authorities, or creating new statewide or regional quasi-governmental development agencies. Beyond funding, there are a number of challenges to exploring a program like this, including likely opposition from those who believe that this is not the role of government and represents unfair competition with the private market. Opinions may shift as housing challenges continue to worsen, however.

Conclusion

Housing is a basic need that provides access to many other amenities and services, benefits and opportunities. In Oregon, there is currently not enough safe, available, accessible, and affordable housing to satisfy need, much less demand. Drastic action, such as the big ideas described above, must be taken to address the two most immediate and acute issues: supply and affordability. But drastic action is insufficient unless it is also sustained. The challenges are complex, and none of the solutions simple. All will take time to implement. Development time lines are long in the best of circumstances, legislation takes time to pass and enact, and capacity takes time to build. Larger systemic and institutional changes—which must be on the table and not discarded as too radical or hard to imagine—are even more difficult and time consuming. But the benefits and ripple effects of persisting are far reaching.

Notes

1. Richard Rothstein, *The Color of Law: A Forgotten History of How Our Government Segregated America* (New York: W. W. Norton, 2017).
2. Ann Curry-Stevens, Amanda Cross-Hemmer, and Coalition of Communities of Color, *The Native American Community in Multnomah County: An Unsettling Profile* (Portland, OR: Portland State University, 2011), https://pdxscholar.library.pdx.edu/socwork_fac/91/.

HOUSING

3   Quoted in Greta Smith, "'Congenial Neighbors': Restrictive Covenants and Residential Segregation in Portland, Oregon," *Oregon Historical Society Quarterly* 199, no. 3 (2018): 358-94.
4   The definition of "white" has changed significantly over time. When the Homeowners Loan Corporation (HOLC) maps were drafted in the 1930s, individuals from eastern and southern Europe—e.g., Finland, Greece, Italy, Russia, and as well as anyone of Jewish descent—were not considered white. Their presence in a neighborhood was deemed a threat to home values and neighborhood stability.
5   Walidah Imarisha, "A Hidden History: The Stories and Struggles of Oregon's African American Communities," *Oregon Humanities Magazine* (Summer 2013).
6   Karen Gibson, "Bleeding Albina: A History of Community Disinvestment, 1940-2000," *Transforming Anthropology* 15, no. 1 (2007): 3–25.
7   Oregon Housing and Community Services, *Breaking New Ground: Oregon's Statewide Housing Plan* (Salem: Oregon Housing and Community Services, 2019), https://www.oregon.gov/ohcs/Documents/swhp/swhp-full-plan.pdf.
8   Ariel Gelrud Shiro, Christopher Pulliam, John Sablehaus, and Ember Smith, Stuck on the Ladder: Intergenerational Wealth Mobility in the United States (Washington, DC: Brookings Institution, 2022), https://www.brookings.edu/research/stuck-on-the-ladder-intragenerational-wealth-mobility-in-the-united-states/.
9   Gibson, "Bleeding Albina."
10 These are Oregon-specific policies and programs, though federal actions also shape circumstances here. Examples include financial regulations and lending guidelines, public housing and voucher funding levels, tax and tax credit policies, and fair housing laws and enforcement. For an excellent survey of relevant federal policies, see Paul A. Diller and Edward J. Sullivan, "The Challenge of Housing Affordability in Oregon: Facts, Tools, and Outcomes," *Journal of Affordable Housing and Community Development Law* 27, no. 1 (2018).
11 Diller and Sullivan, "Challenge of Housing Affordability in Oregon."
12 "The Housing Supply Shortage: State of the States," Economic and Housing Research Insight, Freddie Mac, February 27, 2020, http://www.freddiemac.com/research/insight/20200227-the-housing-supply-shortage.page.
13 Josh Lehner, "You Can't Buy What Isn't for Sale," *Oregon Economic News, Analysis, and Outlook,* January 27, 2022, https://oregoneconomicanalysis.com/2022/01/27/you-cant-buy-what-isnt-for-sale/.
14 Oregon Housing and Community Services, *Building on New Ground: Meeting Oregon's Housing Need* (Salem: Oregon Housing and Community Services, 2021), https://www.oregon.gov/ohcs/about-us/Documents/RHNA/02-21-2021-ECONW-OHCS.pdf.
15 Jared Bernstein, Jeffrey Zhang, Ryan Cummings, and Matthew Maury, "Alleviating Supply Constraints in the Housing Market," The White House, September 1, 2021, https://www.whitehouse.gov/cea/written-materials/2021/09/01/alleviating-supply-constraints-in-the-housing-market/.
16 Josh Lehner, "Oregon's Housing Supply," *Oregon Economic News, Analysis and Outlook,* January 29, 2019, https://oregoneconomicanalysis.com/2019/01/29/oregons-housing-supply/.
17 Joint Center for Housing Studies of Harvard University, *The State of the Nation's Housing 2021* (Cambridge, MA: Joint Center for Housing Studies of Harvard University, 2021), https://www.jchs.harvard.edu/sites/default/files/reports/files/Harvard_JCHS_State_Nations_Housing_2021.pdf.
18 Matthew Garrett and Ariane Le Chevallier, *Recovering and Rebuilding from Oregon's 2020 Wildfires: Key Findings and Recommendations* (Salem, OR: Governor's Wildfire Economic Recovery Council, 2021).

19 Arthur C. Nelson, Rolf Pendall, Casey J. Dawkins, and Gerrit J. Knaap, *The Link between Growth Management and Housing Affordability: The Academic Evidence* (Washington, DC: Brookings Institute, 2002); Justin Phillips and Eban Goodstein, "Growth Management and Housing Prices: The Case of Portland, Oregon," *Contemporary Economic Policy* 18, no. 3 (2000): 334-44; Anthony Downs, "Have Housing Prices Risen Faster in Portland Than Elsewhere?," *Housing Policy Debate* 13, no. 1 (2002): 7–31; Myung-Jin Jun, "The Effects of Portland's Urban Growth Boundary on Housing Prices," *Journal of the American Planning Association* 72, no. 2 (2008): 239–43.

20 This is the primary reason there has been a noticeable increase in the number of multiunit buildings with a 5 over 1 design. This design, wood construction (International Building Code Construction Type 5, combustible materials) over a concrete podium (IBC Type 1, noncombustible materials), is the least expensive construction method for multistory mixed-use residential buildings.

21 Notably, some cities like Portland have reduced parking requirements in recent years. And in response to Executive Order 20-04, issued by Governor Kate Brown prompting state agencies to take action to reduce greenhouse gas emissions, the Land Conservation and Development Commission (LCDC) voted in 2022 to require many municipalities to reduce parking requirements near transit and for smaller homes and affordable housing in 2023 (though this is likely to be the subject of a lawsuit brought by local governments).

22 "Material Costs Affect Housing Affordability," National Association of Home Builders, accessed January 7, 2021, nahb.org/advocacy/top-priorities/material-costs.

23 Robert Dietz, "Keynote Speech," Oregon Housing Economic Summit, January 13, 2022.

24 "Affordable Housing Rental Housing Program Policy and Planning Survey Report," PowerPoint presentation, Oregon Housing and Community Services, September 2, 2021, https://www.oregon.gov/ohcs/development/Documents/admin/09-02-2021-detailed-survey-report.pdf.

25 "Material Costs Affect Housing Affordability."

26 Sales prices for rental properties are typically determined on the basis of capitalization of net operating income (potential rental income less vacancies and losses less normal operating income).

27 Oregon Housing and Community Services, *Building on New Ground*.

28 "Median Income in the Last 12 Months," American Community Survey, US Census Bureau, accessed February 28, 2024, https://data.census.gov/table/ACSST5Y2020.S1903?q=median%20income.

29 National Low Income Housing Coalition, *2021 Oregon Housing Profile* (Washington, DC: National Low Income Housing Coalition, 2021), nlihc.org/sites/default/files/SHP_OR.pdf.

30 Joint Center for Housing Studies of Harvard University, *State of the Nation's Housing 2021*.

31 Lisa Bates, Marisa Zapata, Jacen Greene, and Stephanie Knowlton, *Report on Cost of Oregon Evictions* (Portland, OR: Homelessness Action and Research Collaborative, 2021).

32 Oregon Housing and Community Services, *Breaking New Ground*.

33 Julie Gilgoff, "Giving Tenants the First Opportunity to Purchase Their Homes," *Shelterforce*, July 24, 2020, https://shelterforce.org/2020/07/24/giving-tenants-the-first-opportunity-to-purchase-their-homes/.

34 Center on Budget and Policy Priorities, *United States Housing Choice Vouchers Fact Sheet* (Washington, DC: Center on Budget and Policy Priorities, 2017), https://www.cbpp.org/sites/default/files/atoms/files/3-10-14hous-factsheets_us.pdf.

7
Land Use

MEGAN HORST AND MELIA CHASE

Oregon's unique land use planning program has generated many positive impacts, including conserving farm- and forestlands as well as promoting compact and vibrant neighborhoods and town centers. There are limits to the program's effectiveness, however, and its benefits and burdens are inequitably experienced. Looking to 2050, we have an opportunity to evolve our land use planning to thoughtfully accommodate an expected one million-plus new residents, address ongoing social inequities, better steward the environment, promote community benefits, and build resilience to climate change.

Overall Context

Oregon is a large state, and land use issues vary across it. As discussed in chapter 1, land use planning is guided by the state program, but much responsibility is left to metropolitan entities, counties and cities, and tribal entities. As discussed in greater detail in chapter 4, nearly 50 percent of Oregon land is federally owned. The federal government exercises national authority over other lands through mechanisms such as the National Flood Insurance Program (NFIP) and the Columbia River Gorge National Scenic Area. This chapter focuses on land use on privately owned land. While this book overall grapples with many aspects of land use planning, this chapter specifically focuses on working land conservation and compact development/smart growth and to a lesser degree on public infrastructure.

Oregon is distinctive for the high amounts of forests and farmland, or "working lands" as they are called by the state's Department of Land Conservation and Development (DLCD).[1] In addition to their significance to Oregon's identity, working lands also are also important in terms of the economy, employment, and to rural communities. Nearly half of the state is forestland, and half of that is managed by federal or state government. The rest is privately owned. Meanwhile, about one-quarter of Oregon's privately owned land was in agricultural use in 2015. About 20 percent of this agricultural land is designated by the American Farmland Trust as nationally significant land, or the country's best land for long-term production of food and other crops.

About 70 percent of Oregon's population, or roughly 3 million people, live concentrated in the 5,800 square miles comprising the Willamette Valley. The Willamette Valley's population density already exceeds that of most European countries (notably, Denmark, France, Italy, and Poland) and by 2050 will likely exceed the density of Germany and the United Kingdom.[2] Yet much of the rest of the state has few residents and low population density, with the exception of small cities along the Pacific Coast, along the Columbia River Gorge, in central Oregon's Cascade Mountains, and along the I-5 corridor.

Like the rest of the United States, Oregon's current land use patterns extend upon histories of settler colonialism and exclusionary land practices. Some of this context was already discussed in chapter 1. Before the arrival of European-descended settlers to Oregon, various Native American communities, including the Salish (coastal) and Sahaptin (plateau) people maintained lands through controlled fires, weeding, fertilization, and other sophisticated land stewardship practices and collective ownership and management models that enabled them to thrive over many generations.[3] But colonialist government policies (like the Donation Land Act 1850-55 and the Dawes Act of 1887) and a system of private land tenure have destroyed and altered Native American land use and ownership systems and ultimately contributed to significant land loss for Native Americans.[4] As one example, on the Grande Ronde Indian Reservation, the federal government divided land into allotments, with half going to members of the Confederated Tribes and the remainder sold as surplus lands.[5] By 1950, the tribes only had 597 acres remaining of the original 60,000 acre reservation, and most of their much larger historical homelands have been sold to private timber companies.[6]

Today, there are seven Native American reservations in the state, totaling around 900,000 acres (1406 square miles), or 1.6 percent of

Oregon's land base.[7] Tribes that have reservations deal with the advantages and challenges of being a sovereign entity in terms of land use.

Another part of Oregon's racist land use history—which has ongoing impacts today—includes decades of exclusionary land use policies, many of which are discussed in chapter 1. Over the twentieth century, federal, state, and local governments followed a nationwide project of racial discrimination and segregation and created a system of disinvested urban neighborhoods, surrounded by more affluent and mainly white suburbs, in every metropolitan area in the United States. Policies enacted in Oregon included explicit racial zoning; segregating public housing that was previously racially integrated; subsidizing builders to create whites-only suburbs; and providing tax exemptions for institutions that enforced segregation.[8]

In the most populous city in Oregon, Portland, planning agencies were heavily involved in perpetuating racist land use practices, detailed in the report *Historical Context of Racist Planning: A History of How Planning Segregated Portland*, by the Bureau of Planning and Sustainability.[9] As consequences, there are ongoing major inequities by race in Portland and statewide in rates of home ownership, family wealth, and quality of neighborhood amenities.

Portland and other jurisdictions across Oregon have recently made efforts to address this history through strategies such as anti-displacement planning and focusing infrastructure improvements in historically disinvested parts of the city, like East Portland, where a higher proportion of residents are poor and Black, Indigenous, or people of color (BIPOC). Much work remains, however.

Another important part of the context is that Oregon's recent development has been characterized by suburban sprawl and auto-oriented land use patterns, albeit to a lesser degree than other states owing to the land use planning program. Before the rise of the automobile, cities of all sizes such as Baker City, Jacksonville, McMinnville, and Portland were mainly built in a "traditional development pattern," with relatively small building footprints, higher levels of development density, mixed land uses, and a connected street network. Suburban development—in which cities and towns grow out rather than up—was accelerated by post–World War II federal policies, including subsidized housing tract development and the Federal Highway Act of 1956, and as well as state agency planning (such as by the Oregon Department of Transportation) and local zoning codes. While historic city centers like Eugene and Portland have rebounded in terms of population and employment in recent decades, a high proportion of Oregonians today live in communities with suburban development patterns.

State Authority over Land Use Planning

While the land use planning program brings attention to a range of land use issues, this chapter focuses on issues related to a few specific goals, including:

- Goal 2: Land Use Planning
- Goal 3: Agricultural Lands
- Goal 4: Forest Lands
- Goal 11: Public Facilities and Services
- Goal 14: Urbanization

In addition to the statewide land use planning systems, other factors, such as land ownership and taxes, also influence land use in Oregon. Oregon is relatively unusual among states for having no sales tax, which means that local governments have less pressure to compete for sales tax–generating enterprises like malls, car lots, and big box retail. This is likely another factor that reduces sprawling development in Oregon. Oregon is also unique in its complex and inequitable property tax structure, in which the amount paid in property taxes is not directly connected to the assessed value of the property (discussed in chapter 13).[10] Another tax-related issue is that working lands—including exclusive farm use (EFU) and forest-zoned lands—are taxed at lower rates compared to residential and commercial lands, in an effort to support the continued use of these working lands. In contrast, there is also concern that the special tax assessment is misused, for example, by wealthy amenity owners who install small hobby farms to get a tax break.[11]

Oregonians from across the state and a range of political and social identity backgrounds value land use planning. Ongoing statewide surveys by the Oregon Values and Belief Center suggest that a majority of the state's residents, across political and other identities, consider protecting productive farm- and forestland from development to be very or somewhat important and preferred the strategy of directing population growth toward existing cities and towns and away from natural areas and farmlands.[12] But some respondents also placed a high priority on private property rights, a tension that regularly surfaces in public conversations about the land use system. Even if most Oregonians prefer strong land use planning, powerful interests with minority viewpoints—such as lobbyists for the single-family home construction industry and vocal property rights activists—can have great influence.

Oregon's land use program has been repeatedly endorsed by the public, as discussed in Chapter 1. In the twenty-first century, however, some aspects have been contested on the premise of economic harms done to landowners. For example, in 2004, 61 percent of voters passed Ballot Measure 37, requiring state and local governments to either waive land use regulations or compensate landowners when a regulation reduces a property's fair market value. Measure 37 was subsequently modified by Measure 49, which reduced the number of properties eligible for Measure 37 claims. Nonetheless, a number of Measure 37 claims have been approved, notably along the I-5 corridor and in central and northeastern Oregon.[13]

Land Use Planning Effectiveness: Positive Impacts and Limitations

Oregon's unique statewide land use planning system, along with innovative land use decision-making at local levels, has resulted in a range of positive impacts that should be celebrated. These are summarized in the following pages, as are some of the limitations of the program. Notably, some of the benefits and challenges seem contradictory, reflecting the underlying tension between the program's twin goals of conservation and development. Here we briefly discuss some of the broad highlights.

Protection of Resource Lands, but No Guarantee of Positive Environmental Benefits

Goals 3 and 4 require jurisdictions in Oregon to identify and protect farms and forestland, including by establishing minimum lot sizes and restricting some development. The American Farmland Trust has consistently rated Oregon's approach as among the most effective in the nation at preserving farmland.[14] As an indicator of efficacy, the number of acres of farm- and forestlands converted per new resident to low-density residential and urban uses in Oregon slowed dramatically after the adoption of county comprehensive plans in 1984.[15] As shown in figure 7.1, from 2005 to 2014, only about 0.2 acres of resource land were converted to residential or urban uses per new resident, compared to over 0.9 acres per new resident from 1974 to 1984.

Meanwhile, the value of farm sales has increased significantly in Oregon since the establishment of the land use planning program. For example, in the Willamette Valley, farm sales increased 2.7-fold, from about $270 million in 1964-82 to about $715 million in 1982-2017 (in constant 2021 dollars).[16] Put differently, in 1982, the total value of farm goods sold was about $1.8 billion, rising to more than $2.5 billion in 2017, or about 40 percent more in inflation-adjusted 2021 dollars. Oregon's remaining farm base has the potential to contribute to food systems resilience and carbon sequestration, among other public benefits.

Oregon's land use planning program has been particularly effective in preserving forests, which are important for habitat, logging, recreation, and landscapes. Nearly 98 percent of the nonfederal land in wild forest use and almost 90 percent of land in mixed forest/agricultural use in 1974 remained in the same use in 2014—much higher than in Washington State.[17] Compared to other western states,

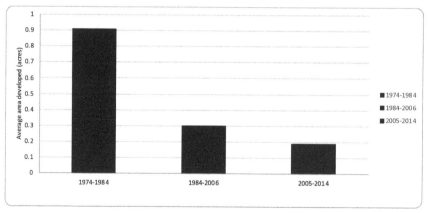

Figure 7.1. Average area (in acres), per new resident of nonfederal land, changing from resource to low-density residential or urban uses in Oregon, 1974-2014. *Source*: Gary J. Lettman, Andrew N. Gray, Dan Hubner, Joel L. Thompson, and John Tokarczyk, "Land Use Change on Non-Federal Land in Oregon and Washington—2018 Update," accessed January 17, 2024, https://www.oregon.gov/odf/board/bofarchives/20180905/BOFSR_20180905_07_01_Land%20Use

Oregon also has a lower percentage of housing in the wildland urban interface; this reduces the risk and impacts of wildland fires.

These successes in terms of farm- and forestland protection are not permanent, however. Between 1989 and 2017, over 50,000 acres and over 17,000 acres of forest and mixed farm- and forestlands were added to urban growth boundaries or rezoned for rural development.[18] American Farmland Trust estimates that between 2001 and 2016, nearly two-thirds of the farmland converted was Oregon's highest quality (most productive, versatile, and resilient).[19] Another significant issue is the increasing fragmentation of working lands and the proliferation of private residences, notably in parts of the Willamette Valley and central and southern Oregon. Patchwork development cuts off producers from leased fields and brings farm equipment into conflict with commuters on roadways, for example, in western Washington and Yamhill Counties. Where houses have proliferated in forestlands, like in Douglas County, wildland firefighters are exposed to more dangerous firefighting situations (electricity, tanks, flammable fluids, toxic smoke from building materials, etc.) as they try to protect the residences.

Another limitation is that simply protecting working lands does not guarantee ecological management or community benefits. Certain industrial approaches to agriculture and forestry have well-documented negative environmental impacts, including stream and groundwater pollution, degraded habitat and biodiversity loss, and soil compaction.[20] For example, in Polk County, Falls City temporarily shut down its water treatment plant because it was clogged with runoff from logging operations. Lost Valley Dairy, in Morrow County, has repeatedly mismanaged manure and wastewater, threatening local water supplies.[21] Additionally, industrial farming and forestry are significant sources of greenhouse gas emissions in Oregon and exacerbate the climate change impacts discussed in chapter 3.[22]

Compact and Mixed-Use Neighborhoods, but Also Sprawling Development Patterns within Urban Growth Boundaries

Oregon's land use planning framework encourages compact and mixed-use development indirectly, by directing jurisdictions to maximize development within their urban growth boundaries. In the state's largest metro region, the UGB has retained its shape over decades, with

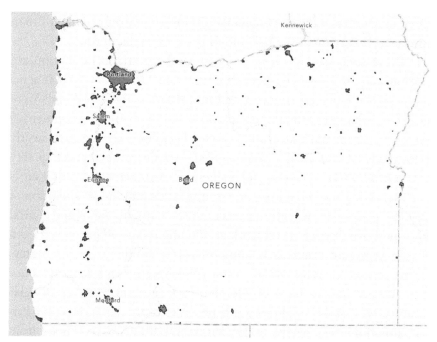

Figure 7.2. Urban growth boundaries (in gray) are a unique feature of land use planning in the state. *Source*: Data Basin, accessed January 17, 2024, https://databasin.org/maps/new/#dataset s=1a6d8ed01a3d44a88b6d2fa4c0b6ff57%20Change%20on%20Non-Federal%20Land%20in%20 Oregon%20and%20Washington%202018%20Update.pdf

only modest expansions to the UGB—a very different scene than in most metropolitan regions across the country. Figure 7.2 shows urban growth boundaries around every major city and metropolitan area in Oregon.

The benefits of compact and mixed-use neighborhoods are well documented. People living in neighborhoods with mixed-use and compact development patterns take fewer car trips and are more likely to walk and use transit, which means less associated air pollution and greenhouse gas emissions. There are social benefits of compact development as well, including lower rates of car crashes, stress, and obesity.[23] Sprawling development, in comparison, is inefficient and compromises water and air quality and ecological functioning. Extensive paved surfaces contribute to the problem of "heat islands," discussed in chapter 3. Sprawl is also linked to physical inactivity, stress, traffic fatalities, poorer health outcomes, increased emergency response times, and longer commute distances and times.

Oregon's older downtowns in medium-sized cities, such as Ashland, Astoria, Baker City, Corvallis, Hillsboro, and La Grande, are exemplars of compact development at a scale appropriate to the size of their region. Meanwhile, many of Oregon's larger cities are planning for compact and connected neighborhoods. For example, Portland's Climate Emergency Workplan, adopted in 2022, calls for complete neighborhoods where residents can walk or bike to access their daily needs.[24]

In suburban Washington County, Orenco Station is an example of transit-oriented greenfield development, where new residential, retail, and office space were constructed within close distance to a light rail station and walking connections were prioritized. Many places in the Portland suburbs have density levels of approximately four thousand people per square mile, twice as land-efficient compared to the nation as a whole.[25] Another sign of increasing infill is the fact that new single-family homes in the Portland metropolitan area today uses about half as much land as one built in 1980, shortening travel distances between homes and other locations.[26]

Oregon also has its share of sprawling development patterns, however, mostly within existing UGBs, though some predate the land use program. A national study of sprawl ranked metropolitan Portland as "mediocre," meaning it had plenty of evidence of sprawling development.[27] Other Oregon counties, especially Columbia, Polk, and Yamhill, also showed high rates of sprawl. A few examples of sprawling development in Oregon include the corridor of strip malls along I-84 running from East Portland out to Troutdale; the I-5 corridor south of Portland down to Wilsonville; gated luxury housing developments and strip retail along Highway 101 on the northern coast; and "loop and lollipop" curvilinear cul-de-sac developments in Douglas County.

It is difficult and cost-ineffective for transit agencies to serve communities with sprawling patterns, despite the need as lower-income households are pushed to such areas owing to rising costs in inner neighborhoods. Across most of Oregon (with the exception of small parts of the Portland metropolitan area and the Willamette Valley), only a small percentage of residents live within five minutes walking of a transit stop.[28]

Infill Development, but Also Under-Utilized Land within Urban Growth Boundaries

Goal 14 requires Oregon's towns and cities to look for capacity within UGBs to accommodate growth via infill development before looking to expand their boundaries. The requirement has had measurable success. Over three-quarters of the net new housing units in the Portland UGB between 2007 and 2016 were from redevelopment and infill, far exceeding previous forecasts.[29] Other cities and towns outside of the Portland region also promote infill. For example, Bend's Comprehensive Plan update in 2016 focused on (in addition to some UGB expansion) denser infill development within the city.[30]

Yet there are large numbers of vacant and underutilized lands within UGBs across the state. Buildable land inventories prepared by municipalities are likely both over- and undercounts of the land available for more intense development, but the statistics from across Oregon remain notable:

- The Dalles: 480 acres/3,689 units of buildable residential land, more than double the 232 acres/1,769 needed units identified in its 2016 analysis.[31]
- Medford: 4,658 acres of total buildable land, more than half of it vacant, in its 2007 analysis.[32]
- Nyssa: at least 165 more buildable acres than needed to accommodate residential land needs in the next twenty years, according to a 2014 analysis.[33]
- Portland: estimated zoned land capacity for over 1.3 million homes within the UGB, and identified buildable land supply for 229,200 to 364,300 additional homes, in a 2018 analysis.[34]

Even though there is a lot of buildable land and the benefits of compact development are well known, much recent development within UGBs has not been done at urban densities. A study of twenty-nine cities and five counties in Oregon found that development at low densities (around 1.5 dwelling units per acre) is occurring within the "urbanizable area" reserved for urban use.[35] This pattern constrains available land supply, causes more frequent future UGB expansions, and leads to non-contiguous, leapfrog development that defeats the intent of Goal 14.

Diverse and Mixed-Income Neighborhoods, but Also Segregated and Inequitable Neighborhoods

Racially diverse and mixed-income neighborhoods are important for a number of reasons, including better chances of upward mobility for children of low-income families.[36] Compared to other regions in the United States, the Portland region has more racially and ethnically mixed neighborhoods.[37] But Oregon also has both racially and economically segregated and inequitable neighborhoods. The causes of this segregation go back decades. The Oregon Health Authority calculated the statewide Black-white segregation index at 63, on a scale where 0 is complete integration and 100 is complete segregation. Counties including Crook, Deschutes, Jackson, Linn, Umatilla, and Yamhill had rates above 66.[38]

In the Portland region, the Regional Equity Atlas (not recently updated) has been an important tool for highlighting enduring inequities in land use–related benefits and burdens. Residents have uneven access to benefits like transit, parks and open space, and are unevenly exposed to burdens like urban heat islands and other climate change risks (the latter is discussed in chapter 3). Looking to 2050, an imperative for land use planning is to improve the built environment where historically marginalized residents live, and accompany those investments by anti-displacement strategies and investments in affordable housing to ensure investments don't lead to eco-gentrification.

Protected Working Lands, but Also Inequitable Economic Benefits

There are major inequities in who benefits from Oregon's protected resource lands. For example, on private forestland, Oregon has implemented lower taxes and weaker environmental protections compared to neighboring states. These policies mainly benefit corporate owners and timber investment management organizations (TIMOs) like Weyerhaeuser, which has doubled the size of its land holdings in western Oregon recently and now owns 1.5 million acres.[39] Yet Oregon has fewer forest sector jobs per acre and collects a smaller tax share of logging profits than Washington or California. Notably, county governments in western Oregon are collecting 85 percent less in tax revenue from private timber companies than they were in the early 1990s, or only around $20 million per year. County and city governments, already struggling with high poverty and unemployment rates, have had to raise taxes on residents and small businesses to sustain their budgets and make devastating decisions like closing libraries or cutting funds to public safety and law enforcement.

As one example in Polk County, more trees are cut today than decades ago, yet timber-related jobs and services and timber tax contributions to the county have dropped. The elimination of the severance tax and lower property taxes for private timber companies have cost the county at least $100 million from 1991 to 2021. The county recently closed its library owing to budget challenges. Meanwhile, Lincoln County used to collect an average of $7.5 million a year in severance taxes but in 2021 collected just under $25,000.

Cost-Effective Development, but also Rising Costs

There is generally a consensus among scholars and analysts that compact patterns of development are more cost-effective relative to sprawl. Compact development is associated with higher tax revenues and reduced local government spending over the long term on a per capita basis.[40] Put another way: less space between buildings means shorter sewer lines, water lines, and roads to build and maintain over time. This is critical especially because governments typically under-plan for long-term maintenance costs.

As an example of the cost-effectiveness, a recent study showed that downtown Eugene, with its compact combination of shops, offices, and apartments, has a much higher per-acre taxable value than other parts of town characterized by single-family residential neighborhoods and big box retail. In addition, downtown's dense development consumes less land, pavement, and water and sewer pipes than other parts of the city.[41] Like Eugene, other Oregon cities and towns benefit economically in the long run from their efforts to sustain and expand compact development. Meanwhile, residents of more compact development often pay less on their transportation costs, leading to their overall reduced combined housing and transportation cost burden relative to residents of more sprawling areas.

That said, long-term cost efficiencies are often not experienced in the here and now by residents who need it most. In fact, housing in close-in, compact, walkable neighborhoods is limited and thus priced at a premium, shutting low-income households out of the benefits of low transportation costs and the lower shared costs of infrastructure maintenance.[42] In many places in Oregon, low-income earners pay more than half of their income on combined housing and transportation costs.[43]

Hazard risks are raising the costs for residents, taxpayers, and government in the short and long term. While less of Oregon's housing is built in the urban wildland interface compared to other western states, the cost of protecting these homes and lives from fires is nonetheless increasing. More than 107,000 homes in Oregon, worth $12.7 billion and representing 8 percent of the state's housing supply, face high or very high risk of wildfire.[44] In 2018, state and federal agencies spent $533 million fighting wildfires in Oregon. Wildfire also leads to increased risk of flooding and landslides, transportation closures, home loss, and other negative impacts. Besides fire hazard, many Oregon communities also are at risk of flooding and other impacts of sea level rise.[45] These issues are discussed more in depth in chapter 3.

Another major challenge is that Oregon's aging infrastructure needs maintenance as well as seismic and climate-related upgrades; this is a costly proposition. In 2019, the American Society of Civil Engineers gave Oregon infrastructure an overall grade of C– and evaluated four categories (out of ten) of infrastructure—dams, energy, levees, and wastewater—as being in poor condition. The estimated cost to repair aging wastewater systems alone is over $5 billion in the next fifteen years. In addition, nearly 20 percent of Oregon bridges risk becoming structurally deficient in the near future. House Bill 2017 improved funding for bridge infrastructure, but maintenance costs are forecasted to keep growing. One study estimates $10 billion needed in infrastructure repairs and replacement in the Portland region alone by 2035.[46]

Regional Land Use Issues
RESERVATION/TRIBAL LAND

Each reservation in Oregon has particular land use planning challenges and priorities. As one example, the Confederated Tribes of the Umatilla Indian Reservation (CTUIR) cannot exercise full land use authority on their reservation because nearly half of land on the reservation is owned by non-Indians. Meanwhile, the *Brendale v. Confederated Yakima Indian Nation* (1989) decision gives jurisdiction over non-Indian fee landowners to nontribal governments.[47] CTUIR has spent much effort subsequently in developing intergovernmental agreements with states and counties to mitigate the problems caused by the *Brendale* precedent. CTUIR is also working to build partnerships with farmers and the irrigation community to protect common interests around water and salmon. They also are shifting their self-advocacy beyond treaty rights protection to land acquisition (particularly of the reservation land owned by non-Indians) and sustainable resource management. They recently purchased 2,400 acres of their historical homeland in western Umatilla County and 8,700 acres in southeastern Washington. Not all Oregon tribes have the resources to engage in land acquisition, however.

CENTRAL OREGON

Central Oregon, notably the area around Bend, Prineville, Redmond, and Sisters, is growing rapidly in population. While growth potentially brings the positives of jobs and taxes, unmanaged growth can have negative impacts on housing costs, traffic, and to the small-town feel and scenic landscapes. There is debate about whether to accommodate growth through urban infill or through growth on the fringe and via large-lot development, the latter of which will be unlikely to address housing cost concerns and will lead to future high maintenance costs. Another controversial issue in the region is leisure development in rural areas, including vacation resorts, luxury "ranchettes," and private hunting grounds. The region is currently home to at least ten large, gated resort developments. Though these projects may generate jobs and taxes, they also disrupt ecosystems and typically serve the needs of wealthy vacationers without addressing local housing and employment needs. Mitigating wildfire risk and damage is also an ongoing priority. The City of Sisters has almost yearly fire-related evacuations, and significant investments were made to Redmond Municipal Airport to expand evacuation capacity.

COLUMBIA RIVER GORGE

The eighty-five-mile-long Columbia Gorge National Scenic Area has permanent protections of its scenic and natural resources, with some areas reserved for economic development and residential accommodations for its 55,000 residents. There are thirteen urban areas in the scenic area; the Oregon side includes Cascade Lakes, Hood River, and Mosier. The Gorge Commission recently updated the Gorge 2020 plan with a new chapter on climate change, expanded buffers around seven rivers, and revisions to planning for natural resources and recreation area. The plan includes an expansion of urban areas by 2 percent, or fifty acres. A hot issue in the region is rising housing and land prices, the latter of which threatens the economic viability of farming into the future. Another issue, especially in Wasco County and farther east, is the competition for land for solar and wind energy development. The Department of Land Conservation and Development recently developed new rules for wind and solar energy siting on agricultural land based on input from energy providers and conservation groups, though concerns remain that corporations and private landowners will be the ones to benefit, not rural communities more broadly.

EASTERN OREGON

Parts of eastern Oregon face economic and population stagnation, though less stark than in other parts of the United States. In some communities, the demographics are changing, with rising proportions of older residents (e.g., Wallowa and Wheeler Counties) and Hispanic/Latino residents (e.g., Malheur County), as discussed in chapter 2. Eastern Oregon communities face unique land use challenges, including revitalizing their historic downtowns after decades of building sprawling development, attracting and retaining residents and businesses, planning appropriately (including for housing) for their changing populations, and addressing anticipated water constraints and other environmental issues. In terms of downtown revitalization, there have been some successes in Baker City, La Grande, Ontario, and Pendleton, which have seen a varying degree of resurgence in both residential and retail use in recent decades. Eastern Oregon leaders have varied views on land use planning. Some argue that restrictive land use planning compounds eastern Oregon's economic growth woes and have sought to limit state land use planning in their area to favor development opportunities for individual landowners, including more rural residential development.[48] But a reduction in state planning mandates is unlikely to mitigate the region's larger challenges and may in fact deepen them.

COAST

The coast of Oregon has unique factors in terms of land use planning, including limited buildable terrain, demand for oceanfront housing, coastal hazards areas (erosion, flood, landslide, tsunami, and sea level rise), and aging or missing infrastructure. More than 80,000 acres of land, a strip a half mile wide on both sides of Highway 101 stretching for 125 miles, is zoned for development because the land was "excepted" from state land use goals intended to protect farm- and forestlands.[49] In past decades, most coastal development has been outside of urban areas. Development, primarily of second homes and expensive vacation properties, has sprawled along the coastline, increasing daily and seasonal traffic along Highway 101 to the extent that Lincoln County has developed traffic congestion safety measures.[50] The land use planning strategies that create efficient mixed-use neighborhoods in urban areas like Portland might unintentionally fuel resort areas and vacation home development on the coast. Going forward, a major challenge will be to reorient development for permanent local residents rather than occasional visitors.

Goal 18's protection of public access to the beach prevents developed lots from using shoreline hardening techniques such as the installation of riprap. The restrictions—intended to avoid the negative environmental impacts of hardening and to ensure public access—put some homes at risk from waves and sea level rise. These sorts of conflicts will only increase alongside climate change.

PORTLAND METROPOLITAN REGION

The Portland metropolitan region, home to more than two million people, is well known for its coordinated regional planning by the multicounty agency known as Metro (discussed briefly in chap. 1). Metro and local jurisdictions have channeled much of the region's recent population and job growth into identified growth centers. While the region has less sprawl than many counterparts, there are ongoing concerns about traffic congestion, vehicle miles traveled, uneven development, and quality of life. Meanwhile, significant stretches of the region, including those near transit and urban centers, remain underdeveloped relative to their zoned capacity and to the ideals of compact, multimodal development. There are political and other challenges to promoting more compact development, including that the region's twenty-four cities and three counties are not always on the same page. Another challenge is that neither Oregon nor Metro has authority or much influence over development patterns across the Columbia River in Clark, Cowlitz, and Skamania Counties in Washington State. These areas continue to grow, mainly in terms of single-family sprawling development patterns, in part owing to residents being drawn by the lower costs of housing relative to the Portland region and by the lack of a state income tax. The future of downtown and parts of inner Portland are in flux, amidst high office and retail vacancies, a lack of pedestrian traffic relative to before the pandemic, an increase in crime, a visible increase in homeless residents, and a drop in development demand. These realities challenge long-held planning assumptions that downtown Portland will be the geographic home to much of the region's new employment and residential development, and raise questions about transit planning (discussed in chap. 8).

SOUTHERN OREGON

Southern Oregon is home to a lot of working lands and to medium-sized towns like Ashland, Grants Pass, and Medford. The region historically had a lot of logging activity, though timber-related employment and revenue have declined in recent decades with increases in industrialization and changes to timber tax policy. The region has also been a hotspot for debates over resource land and rural residential zoning. For example, Douglas County commissioners pursued changing the designation of nearly 35,000 acres (about fifty-five square miles) in farm and forest zones to "non-resource transitional lands," which would have enabled more rural low-density development. They later backed off the effort.[51] Some land use goals for the region looking ahead to 2050 are providing affordable housing and living wage jobs, helping historic downtowns thrive after decades of building competing sprawling development, and addressing increasing wildfires and water scarcity, the latter of which threatens the future of tourism in the region.

WILLAMETTE VALLEY

The Willamette Valley, extending south of the Portland metropolitan region, is the agricultural heartland of Oregon. It some of the best farmland in the country, situated close to major population centers and

I-5. The region used to be dominated by oak woodlands, oak savanna, grassland, riverine, and wetland habitats, but it has been significantly altered by development and farming since the 1850s.[52] One of the main land use planning issues for the region is planning for where and how the growing number of residents will live and get around, while minimizing negative environmental impacts and preserving the base of working lands. Another issue is development pressure on agricultural land from aggregate mining, utility and communication facilities, energy development, and rural residential and industrial development.[53] Yamhill and Marion Counties have seen extensive pressure for solar development. While some of these uses are complementary to ongoing farming, there is an overall threat of a tipping point after which farming is no longer viable. Another major issue looking ahead to 2050 is how to promote resource land use—including farming—that is environmentally responsible and benefits local communities.

Challenges to More Effective Land Use Planning

Compared to the rest of the United States, Oregon has a land use planning system with measurable positive impacts, providing a good foundation for addressing challenges like social justice, climate change, and other hazards. It is predictable and consistent, and while there are critics, many developers and planners find its predictability to be useful. Nevertheless, planning for the future asks us to think big, and to do so, we must confront the real challenges and threats.

One of the overall challenges is that Oregon's planning system is constrained in its influence. It was developed mainly to provide guidance around orderly development, not to fundamentally challenge the dominant patterns of private property ownership and financial "highest and best use" of land. Comprehensive plans and zoning regulations function more as "offers" to developers and landowners, who can choose to either maximize the use of their land under current zoning or wait for development conditions to become more profitable, which entails leaving land in prime locations, such as along transit lines, vacant or underused while awaiting appreciation. The drive for profit also means that in central Oregon, along the coast, and in the Portland region, developers build large luxury houses rather than "missing middle" housing. Another implication is owners of working lands may do short- or long-term environmental harm, such as by stripping the topsoil via mechanized farming, or cutting down trees at a rate faster than regrowth, for short-term returns. Increasingly, Oregon land is owned by investor groups and corporations, not locally based families. For example, at least two-thirds, and possibly up to 90 percent, of western Oregon's private forests are investor owned.[54] Investor-owned companies tend to value short-term profits over long-term sustainable management and community relationships. Farmland is increasingly corporate owned as well. There are similar trends of the financialization of the urban and suburban residential market, as discussed in chapter 6.

A second challenge is that land use planning in Oregon is often practiced in isolation from other related efforts. Despite efforts at regionalism through metropolitan planning organizations (MPOs) like Metro, transportation, land use, and housing are often planned in silos. MPOs distribute transportation funds to local jurisdictions without conditions to meet other planning goals, such as those related to housing. For example, the TriMet transit authority invests in new light rail infrastructure with the hope—but not the mandate—that local jurisdictions will change their land use to be more supportive of transit (e.g., as with the Orange Line, though development patterns near it are slowly changing).

In many ways, Oregon has yet to match its land use policy with relevant cross-sectoral policies. For example, factors beyond land use are important for the ongoing viability of farming and forestry, such as ownership, markets, and profit margins for farmers. When farmers of all scales can make sufficient livelihoods from farming, they are less likely to convert their land to other uses. Yet farmland prices have risen across the state,[55] and many farmers struggle to afford land or secure tenure. Another example comes from property taxes. As chapter 13 discusses, the current tax systems perpetuate inequitable land use patterns. Meanwhile, Oregon's approach is not always backed by supportive federal policy and funding. The federal government's influence in Oregon in past decades has largely been through massive investments in auto-oriented transportation infrastructure and support for suburban styles of development. As of this writing in 2021, President Biden's Build Back Better Plan will direct nearly $2 trillion to roads and bridges, public transit, ports and airports, and water infrastructure.

Preliminary analysis of the bill suggests it will not dramatically alter land use in the way this chapter promotes.

A third shortcoming is that local governments across Oregon are trapped in a cycle of relying on growth for their budgets, an issue not well addressed by the program. To maximize short-term revenue, municipal governments sometimes encourage industrial and office parks, shopping and strip malls, and resort developments—even when it means converting farmland and other valuable resource and habitat land or forgoing a more sensible location. Neighboring jurisdictions may compete for some of the same businesses instead of collaborating to locate those uses to maximize regional benefit. For example, Washington County has some of the best farmland in the state but has rezoned a lot of it for industrial and commercial development—much with sprawling development—in recent decades. Meanwhile, in parts of Oregon where there is not growth, governments face revenue shortages. If there are no other models of funding local budgets, development pressure will continue.

Alongside this reliance on growth for revenue, local jurisdictions do not tend to budget for long-term maintenance costs. Much of Oregon's infrastructure was built using federal funds in the 1960s through 1980s. Since that time, federal funding has declined while infrastructure has aged. Now, local communities are responsible, with some incomplete support from the state, for ongoing operation and maintenance of levees, once built with federal funding. The American Society of Civil Engineers has rated about 30 percent (113 miles) of Oregon levees as "Unacceptable." Local governments recoup some of the initial costs of infrastructure through systems development charges (SDCs). But few, if any, local governments in Oregon charge accurate or sufficient SDCs for the full life cycle of infrastructure, making long-term maintenance a perpetual burden for taxpayers. Local governments are also hesitant to raise SDCs because most jurisdictions badly need more housing supply, and additional costs may reduce developer interest. A larger issue is that since SDC revenue cannot be used to pay the ongoing service costs of infrastructure, cities and counties must find other revenue sources, many of which are limited or diminishing. These include fuel taxes (discussed in chap. 8), property taxes (capped and constrained by several ballot measures, as discussed in chap. 13), voter-approved bonds, ratepayer payments, and even municipal general funds, which also pay for essential services like firefighting. Meanwhile, Oregon does not have sales tax and has lower corporate tax rates than many other states. Climate change is already affecting infrastructure and is expected to accelerate operating and maintenance deficits.

While infill development is often touted as a more cost-effective land use approach than sprawl over time, its upfront development costs are significantly higher. In close-in urban and suburban and high-amenity areas, such as inner Portland and downtown Ashland, Beaverton, Bend, and Hood River, land values tend to be higher and parcel sizes smaller. In addition, development in existing urban areas often requires more tailored architecture and design, compared to "greenfield" development where spec housing, commercial strip malls, and large industrial buildings with parking lots can be built relatively easily. Existing development patterns consisting of busy car-oriented highways and strip retail (such as along parts of Highways 97 in central Oregon, 99 in the Willamette Valley, and 101 on the coast) are difficult to transform to more walkable, mixed-use environments, and are not always attractive to developers. System development charges, while necessary to balance municipal budgets, compound the costs of infill development. On the North Coast, SDCs are typically around $15,000 to $30,000 per connection, a barrier to badly needed housing development.[56] Independent service districts in urban unincorporated communities like Pacific City often manages these SDC charges, which means that SDC discounts or deferrals may not be coordinated with a county housing plan. Altogether, these challenges contribute to underdeveloped land within existing UGBs.

A fourth challenge is that some land use measures have been weakened incrementally over the decades. As one example, the state legislature has recognized that some farm-related and nonfarm uses are appropriate in EFU and mixed farm-forest zones. Today, more than fifty uses other than farm use (up from six in 1963) are allowed in an EFU zone. The expanded list of allowed uses allows farmers more flexibility in earning farm-related income. Not all of the allowed uses are clearly related to farming, however, and they threaten the future of the overall agricultural land base.

At the local level, "ballot box zoning"—which is when local initiatives undo carefully planned procedures, like UGB decisions and land use policies—is a political threat. The North Bethany County Service District for Roads (NBCSDR) was approved in 2011, and thus residents have helped finance the new roads. This is just one case where new development did not pay for itself, and where ballot box voting has undercut the intended thoughtful approach of the land use planning system.[57]

A fifth major challenge is that while the state system provides a framework, small jurisdictions lack the staff and expertise to do land use planning effectively. There is some dedicated state funding to support larger cities in updating comprehensive plans and implementing ordinances, but little is available to counties. Some rural counties and cities lack the funds to pay the prevailing wage for a planner, leaving them unable to recruit and retain staff with deep land use planning experience. Many rural planners shoulder additional responsibilities in their jurisdictions. DLCD regional representatives assist understaffed communities, but that has not been enough to counter a pattern of inconsistent adherence. This is a notable challenge, even as there have been some important positive additions to the land use program in recent years, including the expansion of zoning for missing middle housing and rulemaking for climate-friendly and equitable communities. Many local planers support these changes but are concerned by the additional burdens, which often do not come with additional resources, placed on stretched planning departments.

The lack of resources affects not just planning, but also implementation. Many counties do not have the staff or resources to effectively monitor whether, for example, approved emergency hardship dwellings or farm assistance dwellings are ultimately used for their intended purposes.[58] Notably, almost all land use–related enforcement is driven by complaints. Another example is that county tax assessors don't monitor lands to ensure that people getting tax breaks for farming or forestry are actually doing the activity.

Possible Futures: Illustrative Comparisons

With a million-plus people joining Oregon's population between 2020 and 2050, requiring another 500,000 or so homes, a land use question is: Where should they go? To illustrate some possible approaches, we offer three different land use scenarios statewide: Business as Usual, Sprawl, and Smart Growth. We used the platform Urban Footprint to project the impacts of these different scenarios in the central Oregon, Columbia Gorge, North Coast, and South Coast regions. Because Portland already receives a lot of scholarly and planning attention, Metro has a robust regional land use planning capacity, and because the region is so jurisdictionally complex, it is not included in the analyses.

- Sprawl: This scenario entails a loosening of Oregon land use planning requirements, residential development that is composed of mainly detached single-family residences, and an expansion outward from existing urban growth boundaries along major roads.
- Business as Usual: In this scenario, there is a continuation of recent development patterns, meaning the continued expansion of mainly single-family detached residences, with some infill containing single-family and multifamily residential and mixed-use development.
- Smart Growth: This scenario assumes no expansion of urban growth boundaries and instead consists of densification via infill development, consisting mainly of multifamily development in urban centers and along major transit corridors and roads within urban growth boundaries.

Tables 7.1 and 7.2 show that the Smart Growth scenario had by far the most environmental and social benefits, including reduced vehicle and building emissions and lower fuel and residential water costs per household, as well as a greater percentage of residents living within walking distances to schools. But even the Smart Growth scenario does not achieve huge reductions in number of dwellings in risk zones (many already exist, and some risk zones are expected to expand) and mode share splits. These goals will need to be addressed by other efforts outside of these scenarios, such as building for hazard resilience and enhancing transportation infrastructure for transit, walking and biking, as discussed in chapters 3 and 8.

This analysis is an incomplete model that only considers some data. It misses data on farmland loss or saved and impacts to residential

Table 7.1. Comparison of Different Land Use Scenarios in 2050

	Sprawl Scenario	Business as Usual Scenario	Smart Growth Scenario
Large-lot single-family dwelling units	↑↑	↑	↑
Multifamily dwelling units	↑	↑	↑↑
Vehicle emissions per household and building emissions per household	↑	↔	↓
Fuel and residential water costs per household	↑↑	↑	↓
Number of dwelling units in risk zones	↑↑	↑	↑
Annual vehicle miles traveled per household	↑	↑	↓
Mode share by people taking transit, walking, or biking	↔	↔	↔
Percentage of residents living within walking distance of schools	↓↓	↑	↑

Source: Author analysis using Urban Footprint.

segregation by race or income) and is based on a lot of assumptions that may not remain true. Nevertheless, it provides some guidance that infill development—compared to other approaches—is a more environmentally and socially sound land use strategy to accommodate more than one million new residents.

Big Ideas

Oregon's expected population growth presents an opportunity to revitalize urban neighborhoods and small towns, promote more environmentally sustainable ways of living, develop more fiscally sound infrastructure, and foster social equity—if we employ appropriate land use planning strategies. But without purposeful change, we will end up with more sprawl, segregation, negative environmental impacts, reduced resiliency to climate change, and higher costs. Below we highlight five categories of big ideas to promote better land use, with some specific actions in each one. These big ideas depend upon the basis of the land use planning program, but they also go beyond it.

LAND USE

Table 7.2. Detailed Comparisons of Different Land Use Scenarios in 2050

	Central Oregon				Columbia Gorge			
	Base 2020	Sprawl 2050	Business as Usual 2050	Smart Growth 2050	Base 2020	Sprawl 2050	Business as Usual 2050	Smart Growth 2050
Population	198,092	400,000	400,000	400,000	51,063	65,000	65,000	65,000
Large-lot single-family dwelling units	76,993	163,745	125,496	113,667	18,264	23,986	21,973	18,857
All multifamily dwelling units	15,491	15,671	17,303	33,825	3,982	3,951	4,013	4,839
Annual passenger vehicle emissions per household (metric ton), rounded	23	27	24	20	21	24	22	19
Annual building energy emissions per household, not rounded since differences are minor (<1)	4.66	4.97	4.65	4.34	4.19	4.32	4.25	4.04
Annual fuel costs per household	$8,111	$9,316	$8,336	$7,093	$897	$1,573	$1,418	$803
Annual residential water costs per household	$970	$3,462	$2,026	$755	$7,423	$8,480	$7,796	$6,805
Dwelling units in special flood hazard zones	0	0	0	0	0	0	0	0
Dwelling units in fire hazard severity zones	33,338	120,230	77,545	54,387	8,393	12,992	12,645	9,246
Dwelling units in sea level rise risk areas	0	0	0	0	0	0	0	0
Per household annual vehicle miles traveled	59,779	68,490	61,404	52,425	51,819	59,200	54,592	47,523
Mode share: auto/transit/walk or bike (%)	94/1/5	91/2/7	93/1/6	93/1/6	95/1/4	95/1/4	95/1/4	94/1/5
Percentage of residents within 15 minutes of school access	30	26	33	17	27	21	22	22

	North Coast				Southern Oregon			
	Base 2020	Sprawl 2050	Business as Usual 2050	Smart Growth 2050	Base 2020	Sprawl 2050	Business as Usual 2050	Smart Growth 2050
Population	171,831	206,000	206,000	206,000	453,685	572,000	572,000	572,000
Large-lot single-family dwelling units	77,091	90,583	88,719	79,764	158,312	206,593	188,742	168,979
All multifamily dwelling units	17,933	17,776	17,748	19,444	35,055	34,382	41,194	49,495
Annual passenger vehicle emissions per household (metric tons)	19.39	19.68	18.51	17.52	20.48	19.79	20.21	17.93
Annual building energy emissions per household	4.16	4.26	4.23	4.06	5.73	5.88	5.69	5.47
Annual fuel costs per household	$6,944	$7,049	$6,628	$6,274	$7,488	$7,235	$7,387	$6,554
Annual residential water costs per household	$829	$1,379	$1,077	$772	$174	$700	$261	$204
Dwelling units in special flood hazard zones	6	6	6	6	32,749	53,374	38,925	36,197
Dwelling units in fire hazard severity zones	11,641	13,607	12,818	14,104	9,481	10,450	12,847	14,592
Dwelling units in sea level rise risk areas	13,455	15,865	15,564	15,545	0	0	0	0
Per household annual vehicle miles traveled	49,305	49,941	47,082	44,681	58,087	56,774	57,568	51,758
Mode share: auto/transit/walk or bike (%)	95/1/4	95/1/5	95/1/6	94/1/5	94/1/5	94/1/5	94/1/5	93/1/6
Percentage of residents within 15 minutes of school access	20	18	19	21	41	33	36	40

Note: The 2050 population is estimated; see chapter 2 for more details on projections.

Source: Author analysis using Urban Footprint.

Dramatically Incentivize and Require Infill Development

For Oregon to achieve the smart growth scenario described above, we need to significantly ramp up urban infill and compact development, and curtail most UGB expansion. One strategy is to more effectively use buildable land inventories to spur the redevelopment of undeveloped lands, especially underutilized parking lots and vacant commercial and retail space. Conceptually, nearly all of metropolitan Oregon's demand for new homes and jobs can be accommodated on existing parking lots, at modest heights (i.e., not expensive high-rise towers), along corridors and existing transit lines, while still accommodating current surface parking needs through more efficient parking management and promotion of multimodal transportation. A second strategy is to reimagine rezoning on a bigger scale than HB 2001, to open lower-density neighborhoods to a broader range of multifamily housing options. A third related strategy is to lower the costs of infill development, for example, reducing permitting fees, shortening approval time lines, and loosening requirements (e.g., by having preapproved standard designs for backyard accessory dwelling units and missing middle housing). Perhaps cities could experiment with competitions and marketing of infill projects.

One untapped opportunity is for local government to open some of their publicly owned land to infill development. The City of Portland, for example, owns 40 percent of land as right-of-way. Some wider and less traveled streets—including in a less busy downtown post-pandemic—may be reimagined as land for infill housing development, with *woonerf*-style streets. Portland and other cities can get inspiration from other city's land use strategies, like Barcelona's super blocks, to convert existing parking lots and roadways into much-needed residential development and green spaces. A fourth related strategy is to reduce low-density development within existing UGBs. The Department of Land Conservation and Development should encourage or require cities to update urban growth management areas (UGMAs) with stronger provisions that give cities more oversight over land inside the UGB[59] and consider adopting an administrative rule requirement that cities must review their UGMAs as a component of any UGB amendment. A final big strategy is to coordinate all UGB expansions at the regional rather than local level, so that some cities and towns can allot their growth to neighboring cities willing to allow more infill development. Regions should be restricted from expansions if they have buildable land anywhere within the existing UGBs, instead encouraging such trading allotments.

Promote Coordinated Land Use and Transportation

A second big idea is to promote climate smart planning via coordinated land use and transit planning. Local governments in Oregon have been required to make coordinated land use and transportation plans for decades, though this has not always been operationalized with reducing greenhouse gas emissions at the forefront. DLCD's recently completed rulemaking on climate-friendly and equitable communities encourages such coordinated planning, to a degree. The rules require some communities (of minimum size, among other factors) to adopt regulations allowing walkable mixed-use development along with higher-density development transit corridors and downtowns. The rules reduce or remove costly parking mandates and give communities more options for managing parking. Altogether, the rules seem poised as an important strategy to better coordinate land use and transportation planning, though implementation is dependent on specific city leadership and developer action. A bigger idea would be to go beyond allowing and encouraging, and actually requiring, though that would likely face pushback from local communities, especially if those requirements did not come with resources and implementation support.

Permanently Protect Resource Lands and Require Community-Oriented Stewardship

A third big idea is that high-value resource lands should be permanently protected, recognizing their potential value for carbon sequestration, community food security, and other ecosystem services. One strategy that may be of use is to put easements on two or three sides of UGBs to protect high-value resource and land, and to limit UGB expansion in one direction only (though this would not be needed if UGB expansions were curtailed outright). Another strategy is to expand the number of counties practicing transfer of development rights (TDR), by adopting DLCD's model code for Measure 49 transfer, by making the TDR program attractive to participants, and by coordinating regional or state efforts. Owners of resource lands would ideally transfer their development rights to nearby cities and towns to support infill and increased urban densities. A third strategy is to require alternative siting analysis for high-impact uses as well as cumulative impacts analysis in rural areas/resource lands experiencing high development pressure.[60] At the same time as reducing development, farming landowners should be supported in having sufficient affordable housing options (e.g., by enabling more cluster cottage-style communities on farmland) to enable cooperative farming approaches, though this needs to coupled with maximum house sizes and second-home ownership restrictions to reduce the risk of luxury mansion development for amenity owners (as in British Columbia).

Strategies to permanently protect land should go further, however, to ensure that the use and management of the land promotes environmental and community benefits. For example, Oregon should increase carbon sequestration on farm- and forestland while also benefiting workers and rural communities through strategies like land reform (further discussed below), where private industrial forestland is transferred to locally owned and operated social benefit enterprises.[61] Reduced tax assessments for farming and forestlands could be focused more on farms and forestland that benefit local workers and communities, while amenity owners should pay more.

Assess for Long-Term Costs and Tax for the Desired Land Uses

A big idea to improve land use in Oregon is to fully assess for long-term costs and to tax for the desired land uses. One strategy is full cost accounting on infrastructure and, relatedly, requiring the cumulative assessment of the fiscal impacts of land use decisions. A second strategy is to set impact and development fees on a per acre, gross land, or square-foot basis, rather than a per unit basis to reflect the true infrastructure costs. This would have the impact of lower SDCs for compact development.

Other fiscally related strategies are changes to timberland, property, and other taxes. If Oregon taxed timber owners the same as its neighboring states California and Washington, it would generate tens of millions of dollars more for local governments.[62] It is also time for Oregon to consider a land value tax, long promoted by economists over a tax on development (discussed in chap. 13). A land tax would incentivize the development of underutilized land in areas with high land values, such as inner Portland. A land tax would also blunt the current tax penalties associated with adding density to a single-family lot via an accessory dwelling unit or similar structure. Recent research confirms that land value taxes would lead to more widespread economic equality.[63] A new land value tax structure would require mitigation to prevent negatively affecting groups like low- and fixed-income homeowners who own property in high-value areas.

Another tax idea is regional tax-base sharing, such as that used in the Minneapolis/St. Paul region, a strategy that might be most appropriate in the Portland metropolitan region. Tax-base sharing encourages suburbs and central cities to cooperate—rather than compete—on regional economic development goals and leads to a more equitable distribution of tax burdens and public services.

Another category is taxing undesired land uses, for example, segregation. Oregon could levy an additional property tax on every community that has a housing stock where less than 10 percent of the units are considered affordable. The funds could then be distributed to the towns with the greatest need, which have also already done their part to create affordable housing, they could be used to develop more affordable housing, or they could provide direct subsidy to poor families facing housing insecurity. A related strategy is to tax parking lots to spur their development into housing. In Salem, for example, there is vast land waste dedicated to parking lots for state office buildings and churches alongside a growing housing crisis.

Land Reform

A final big idea is land reform. Oregon is no stranger to land reform, having participated in the redistribution of Native land to corporations and individual white settlers in the nineteenth century. With the rise in the consolidation of ownership of resource land as well as urban land, it is a good time for Oregon to learn from the successes and limitations of historical and contemporary land reform efforts in Ireland, Mexico, and Scotland, among others. One strategy is to promote "Land Back" reparation practices, by transferring ownership and management of historic tribal lands to Oregon tribes and Native communities. Another is to advance community ownership of land, such as via community land trusts. One example of land reform comes from Scotland, which set a target of one million acres of land under community ownership by 2020.

Notes

The authors thank Brian Campbell (American Planning Association, Oregon Chapter), Victor Cesar (Vancouver Housing Authority), Katherine Daniels (previously with Oregon Department of Land Conservation and Development), Taren Evans (Coalition of Communities of Color), Hilary Foote (Department of Land Conservation and Development), Mary Kyle McCurdy (1000 Friends of Oregon), Dave Siegel (American Planning Association Oregon Chapter), and J. D. Tovey (Confederated Tribes of the Umatilla Indian Reservation) for their constructive feedback.

1 Julia Freedgood, Mitch Hunter, Jennifer Dempsey, and Ann Sorensen, *Farms under Threat: The State of the States* (Washington, DC: American Farmland Trust, 2020), https://s30428.pcdn.co/wp-content/uploads/sites/2/2020/05/AFT_FUT_StateoftheStates-1.pdf.
2 Arthur C. Nelson, personal communication, 2022.
3 Oregon Chapter of the American Planning Association, "Tribal Planning (OAPA Webinar)," YouTube video, February 21, 2019, https://www.youtube.com/watch?v=5NlP7ed5zm0.
4 David G. Lewis, "A Short History of Oregon Tribes," *Quartux Journal*, August 9, 2018, https://ndnhistoryresearch.com/2018/08/09/a-short-history-of-oregon-tribes-in-the-contemporary-era/.
5 David G. Lewis, "Did the Grande Ronde Tribes Get Paid for All Their Ceded Lands?," *Quartux Journal*, July 25, 2017, https://ndnhistoryresearch.com/2017/07/25/did-grand-ronde-tribes-get-paid-for-all-their-ceded-lands/.
6 "Our Story," Confederated Tribes of Grande Ronde, accessed December 28, 2023, https://www.grandronde.org/history-culture/history/our-story.
7 "Introduction to Oregon Tribes," Oregon Blue Book, accessed December 28, 2023, https://sos.oregon.gov/blue-book/Pages/national-tribes-intro.aspx.
8 Richard Rothstein, *The Color of Law: A Forgotten History of How Our Government Segregated America* (New York: Liveright, 2017); Keeanga-Yamahtta Taylor, *Race for Profit: How Banks and the Real Estate Industry Undermined Black Homeownership* (Chapel Hill: University of North Carolina Press, 2019).
9 Jena Hughes, *Historical Context of Racist Planning: A History of How Planning Segregated Portland* (Portland, OR: Bureau of Planning and Sustainability, 2019), https://beta.portland.gov/sites/default/files/2019-12/portlandracistplanninghistoryreport.pdf.
10 Jenny H. Liu and Jeff Renfro, *Oregon Property Tax Capitalization: Evidence from Portland* (Portland, OR: Northwest Economic Research Center, 2014), http://media.oregonlive.com/portland_impact/other/locreport.pdf; Elliot Njus, "Tax Breaks for Gentrifiers: How a 1990s Property Tax Revolt Has Skewed the Portland-Area Tax Burden," *The Oregonian*, September 11, 2015, https://www.oregonlive.com/business/2015/09/measure_50_winners_and_losers.html.
11 Nigel Jaquiss, "You Call This a Farm? Urban Farmers and Foresters Are Benefiting from a Gaping Property Tax Loophole," *Willamette Week*, March 20, 2015, https://www.wweek.com/portland/article-24213-you-call-this-a-farm.html.

12. "Oregon Department of Transportation: 2006 Transportation Plan Survey," Oregon Values and Beliefs Center, accessed February 28, 2024, https://oregonvbc.org/study-topic/community-planning/. Note the survey is among the most comprehensive attempts to understand the values of Oregonians, but it has limits. According to the project itself, "the goal is not to offer an ultimate statement of Oregon values but rather a baseline of information from which to draw inferences and a platform for more detail as circumstances permit."
13. "Measure 49 Analyzer," Oregon Explorer, accessed December 28, 2023, tools.oregonexplorer.info/OE_HtmlViewer/Index.html?viewer=m49.
14. Freedgood et al., *Farms under Threat*.
15. Gary Lettman et al., *Forest, Farms and People: Land Use Change on Non-Federal Land in Oregon 1974-2014* (Salem: Oregon Department of Forestry, 2016), https://ir.library.oregonstate.edu/concern/technical_reports/0c483p903.
16. Nelson, personal communication, 2022.
17. Lettman et al., *Forest, Farms and People*.
18. Oregon Land Conservation and Development Commission, *2016–2017 Oregon Farm and Forest Report* (Salem: Oregon Land Conservation and Development Commission, 2019), https://www.oregon.gov/lcd/Commission/Documents/2019-01_Item_12_Farm_Forest_Report.pdf.
19. Freedgood et al., *Farms under Threat*.
20. Tony Schick, Rob Davis, and Lylla Younes, "Big Money Bought Oregon's Forests. Small Timber Communities Are Paying the Price," Oregon Public Broadcasting, June 11, 2020, https://www.opb.org/news/article/oregon-investigation-timber-logging-forests-policy-taxes-spotted-owl/.
21. Tracy Loew, "Oregon Mega-Dairy Lost Valley Farm Fined $187,320 for 224 Environmental Violations," *Statesman Journal*, October 16, 2018, https://www.statesmanjournal.com/story/tech/science/environment/2018/10/16/oregon-megadairy-lost-valley-farm-fined-environmental-violations/1659452002.
22. Samantha Krop, "Oregon Department of Forestry Fails to Step Up to Their Climate Responsibility," Oregon Center for Sustainable Economy, July 1, 2020, https://sustainable-economy.org/oregon-department-of-forestry-fails-to-step-up-to-their-climate-responsibility/.
23. Smart Growth America, *Measuring Sprawl 2014* (Washington, DC: Smart Growth America, 2014), https://smartgrowthamerica.org/wp-content/uploads/2016/08/measuring-sprawl-2014.pdf.
24. City of Bend, *City of Bend Comprehensive Plan* (Bend, OR: City of Bend, 2016), https://www.bendoregon.gov/home/showdocument?id=42053.
25. Hart Schwartz, "Land-Use Zoning and Fuel Consumption: Portland's Urban Growth Boundaries," *The Fuse*, accessed 2018, http://energyfuse.org/land-use-zoning-fuel-consumption-portlands-urban-growth-boundaries/.
26. Metro, *Urban Growth Report: 2018 Growth Management Decision (Discussion Draft)* (Portland, OR: Metro, 2018), https://www.oregonmetro.gov/sites/default/files/2018/07/09/2018_UGR-summary-07092018.pdf.
27. Smart Growth America, *Measuring Sprawl 2014*.
28. The website Urban Footprint provides analysis; see https://urbanfootprint.com/.
29. Metro, *Urban Growth Report*.
30. Tyler Leeds, "Bend to Not Just Grow Out, But Up," *Bend Bulletin*, March 19, 2016, https://www.bendbulletin.com/localstate/bend-to-grow-not-just-out-but-up/article_4d228a93-90d9-5bd2-9d8b-d7a4782586ca.html.

LAND USE 207

31 Steve Harris, "The Dalles: Urban Area and Urban Growth Boundaries" (PowerPoint presentation, September 17, 2018), http://www.gorgecommission. org/images/uploads/meetings/20180917_Steve_Harris_UGB_slides.pdf.
32 City of Medford Planning Department, *Medford Comprehensive Plan: Buildable Land Inventory* (Medford, OR: City of Medford Planning Department, 2008), https://www.medfordoregon.gov/files/assets/public/planning/documents/comp-plan/7_buildable-lands-inventory_2008.pdf.
33 Bill Searles, *Report and Recommendation for City of Nyssa* (Nyssa, OR: Malheur County Planning, 2018), https://www.malheurco.org/wp-content/uploads/Departments/Planning/Documents/2018-08-013.pdf.
34 Metro, *Urban Growth Report*.
35 Rebecca Lewis and Robert Parker, "Exurban Growth inside the Urban Growth Boundary? An Examination of Development in Oregon Cities," *Growth and Change* 52, no. 2 (2021): 885–908.
36 Joe Cortright, "Why Integration Matters," City Observatory, June 14, 2018, https://cityobservatory.org/why_integration_matters/.
37 Joe Cortright, "America's Most Diverse Mixed Income Neighborhoods," City Observatory, June 18, 2018, https://cityobservatory.org/admin/.
38 Oregon Health Authority, *Residential Racial Segregation Index by County, Oregon, 2013–2017* (Salem: Oregon Health Authority, 2019), https://www.oregon.gov/OHA/PH/ABOUT/Documents/indicators/segregation-county.pdf.
39 "Documenting Forest Ownership in Oregon," Coast Range Association, accessed December 28, 2023, https://coastrange.org/challenging-wall-street-forestry/ownership/.
40 Ted Sweeney, *More Extensive Is More Expensive: How Sprawl Infrastructure Bankrupts Oregon Communities, and What We Can Do about It* (Portland: 1000 Friends of Oregon, 2013), https://friends.org/sites/default/files/2019-04/More%20Extensive%20Is%20More%20Expensive%202013.pdf.
41 City of Eugene, *Mapping Value in Eugene, Oregon: A Practical Guide to Understanding Taxes, Land Use, and Quality of Life in a Great City in the Northwest* (Draft) (Eugene, OR: City of Eugene, 2017), https://www.eugene-or.gov/DocumentCenter/View/35447/Mapping-Value-in-Eugene-Booklet-July-2017?bidId=.
42 Charles Marohn, "The Growth Ponzi Scheme," Strong Towns, May 18, 2020, https://www.strongtowns.org/the-growth-ponzi-scheme.
43 "H+T Affordability Index," H+T Index, accessed September 11, 2020, http://htaindex.cnt.org/map/.
44 Ashlee Fox, *A New Vision for Wildfire Planning: A Report on Land Use and Wildfires* (Portland: 1000 Friends of Oregon, 2018), https://friends.org/sites/default/files/2019-04/Apercent20Newpercent20Visionpercent20forpercent20Wildfirepercent20Planningpercent202018.pdf.
45 Analysis completed in Urban Footprint by report authors; see https://urbanfootprint.com/.
46 Sweeney, *More Extensive Is More Expensive*.
47 "Cayuse-Umatilla-Walla Walla," Confederated Tribes of the Umatilla Indian Reservation, accessed February 22, 2024, https://ctuir.org/departments/economic-community-development/land-management/.
48 Carl Abbott, "Land Use Planning," *The Oregon Encyclopedia*, updated June 28, 2022, https://oregonencyclopedia.org/articles/land_use_planning/#.XqdJFmhKg2x.

49. R. Liberty, *The Future of the Oregon Coast: Can It Be Saved from Sprawl?* (Portland: 1000 Friends of Oregon, 1999).
50. Paul Koberstein, "Where'd They Put the Ocean?," *Cascadia Times*, accessed 2018, https://www.times.org/treasures-of-the-oregon-coast/2018/3/13/whered-they-put-the-ocean-sprawl-obstructs-views-pollutes-beaches-and-mars-oregons-scenic-shoreline.
51. "Non-Resource Land," Farm and Forest, Department of Land Conservation and Development, accessed December 28, 2023, https://www.oregon.gov/lcd/FF/Pages/Non-Resource-Land.aspx.
52. "Willamette Valley Farm-Related Issues as Described in the OR Conservation Strategy (2006)," Oregon State University College of Agricultural Sciences, July 27, 2011, https://agsci.oregonstate.edu/oregon-vegetables/willamette-valley-farm-related-issues-described-or-conservation-strategy-2006.
53. Nicholas Chun, "Identifying Clusters of Non-Farm Activity within Exclusive Farm Use Zones in the Northern Willamette Valley" (master's thesis, Portland State University, 2017).
54. Emily Green, "Cut and Run Dry: Do Oregon Tax Laws Favor the Timber Industry?," Street Roots, September 7, 2018, https://news.streetroots.org/2018/09/07/cut-and-run-dry-do-oregon-tax-laws-favor-timber-industry.
55. Megan Horst, "Changes in Farmland Ownership in Oregon, USA," *Land* 8, no. 3 (2019): 39.
56. Tillamook County Housing Commission and FCS Group, *Tillamook County Housing Needs Analysis* (Tillamook County Housing Commission and FCS Group, 2019), https://www.co.tillamook.or.us/gov/ComDev/HousingCommission/Documents/Tillamookpercent20HNApercent20Finalpercent20Reportpercent20v2.pdf.
57. Sweeney, *More Extensive Is More Expensive*.
58. Amber Shackelford, *Death by 1000 Cuts: A 10-Point Plan to Protect Oregon's Farmland* (Portland: 1000 Friends of Oregon, 2020), https://friends.org/sites/default/files/2020-06/Deathpercent20Bypercent201000percent20Cuts_2020.pdf.
59. Lewis and Parker, "Exurban Growth inside the Urban Growth Boundary?"
60. Shackleford, *Death by 1000 Cuts*.
61. "Climate and Oregon's Industrial Forests: A Green New Deal Proposal," Coast Range Association, accessed December 28, 2023, https://coastrange.org/gnd-proposal/.
62. Schick et al., "Big Money Bought Oregon's Forests."
63. Portland State University, "Portland Land Value Tax Would Improve Equity for Homeowners, Incentivize Development," *EurekAlert!*, August 14, 2019, https://www.eurekalert.org/pub_releases/2019-08/psu-plv081419.php; Joshua Vincent, "Non-Glamourous Gains: The Pennsylvania Land Tax Experiment," Strong Towns, March 6, 2019, https://www.strongtowns.org/journal/2019/3/6/non-glamorous-gains-the-pennsylvania-land-tax-experiment.

8
Transportation
JOHN MACARTHUR

This chapter discusses Oregon's transportation system in terms of how it provides Oregonians with access and mobility as well as its environmental, equity, and social impacts. A range of possible futures for Oregon's transportation system in 2050 are discussed along with the barriers facing the state and its residents. Finally, it presents four big ideas to guide us to a more sustainable, resilient, and equitable 2050.

At its ideal, a comprehensive, affordable, and equitable transportation system allows all Oregonians to connect to jobs, schools, family, and friends through the use of personal vehicles, transit, biking, rolling, and walking. The current transportation system is more than a hundred years old and has influenced the way the built environment and our communities have formed. Though the system has served the state well in some ways, it has added to inequities within communities around state, as in the destruction of the Albina Community in north Portland with the construction of Interstate 5 in the 1960s, and it has created negative externalities, such as air pollution and contributing to a decrease in physical activity. Today's transportation sector faces pressing issues, including its contribution of greenhouse gas (GHG) emissions, high-inflation costs of construction, aging and structurally deficient infrastructure, potential seismic and climate change threats, lack of funding, congestion and travel times, safety outcomes, and inequitable distribution of benefits and burdens.

We find ourselves at a critical juncture in transportation decisions and planning. As we look to 2050, some key questions are: How do we transform the current system to be more sustainable, resilient, and equitable to meet the future needs of Oregonians? Do we continue to build capacity in the roadway system to meet the current demand for cars, or do we look at other means to repurpose and transform the infrastructure into a next-generation system? As technology accelerates, how does the state keep pace with investments and demands of new modes, such as autonomous vehicles and connective technologies? Oregon can harness these technologies to purposefully meet societal goals, or we can be driven by these technologies. Do we maintain a status quo of car-centric infrastructure and live with the ramifications? How do we do things differently to meet the challenges of 2050 and beyond, so that the next generations of all Oregonians can thrive and live in an equitable and sustainable way?

Background and Context in Oregon

As discussed in previous chapters, Oregon is one of the more geographically diverse states in the United States, and it is largely rural. The population is concentrated in the Willamette Valley, which stretches from Portland to Eugene. Meanwhile, ten of Oregon's thirty-six counties have six or fewer people per square mile and thus are considered "frontier" counties.[1] Oregon's large land area is connected by 79,266 miles of public roads.[2] The state highway systems consist of around 7,400 miles of roads and an additional 36,800 miles of county and city roads. There are approximately 8,160 state, county, city, and other publicly owned bridges and culverts, of which only 20 percent are rated in good condition.[3] The needs to address these deficiencies are heightened by an awareness of growing impacts of climate change and that Oregon faces a significant chance of a massive 9.0-magnitude earthquake in the Cascadia Subduction Zone (as discussed in chap. 3), which puts older bridges at significant risk.

In 2010, the Oregon Household Activity Survey (OHAS) was conducted to understand the travel behavior characteristics of Oregon residents.[4] Households reported making 9 daily weekday trips on average, spending a combined three hours a day traveling a total of 60 miles across all household members. On a per capita basis, this means each person takes on average 3.7 trips per day, traveling a total of 26 miles. These values are slightly higher than the national averages.[5] For people living in rural Oregon, they take fewer trips (3.5-person trips) but travel farther (44 miles a day). On a typical weekday in 2010, Oregonians made almost 14 million trips, traveling 86 million miles to partake in a variety of activities. Of those trips, 82 percent were by automobile, accounting for 94 percent of miles traveled. Making up the other 6 percent of the miles traveled, 10 percent were walk trips, 3 percent were by bike, and 5 percent were by transit and school bus.[6] In more urban areas, auto trips comprised about 70 percent, and transit and school bus were about 7 percent, whereas in rural areas, people relied almost solely on cars for trips.

Mobility, or the ability to get around, is crucial to the health and well-being of all Oregon residents. For people with disabilities, younger and older adults alike, loss of mobility means loss of independence and the ability to access medical and preventive health care, get a job, engage in physical and social activities, and shop for fresh food. The OHAS data show that older adults and people with disabilities made fewer trips than the average traveler in Oregon, most likely because they lacked adequate transportation options, especially if they were not able to drive themselves. For Oregonians with those limitations (and chap. 2 notes the increasing proportion of older adults by 2050), it is important that the state enhance its transportation system to enable nondriving options like walking, biking, and transit. This will be easier in some areas, and a significant challenge in others.

The connection of land use, economic development, and transportation is important to consider when discussing long-term planning. In Oregon, land use and transportation have been intentionally linked since the early 1970s, when SB 100 was passed to encourage more comprehensive land use planning. SB 100 has nineteen interconnected goals to create an institutional structure for statewide planning. Direction on land use planning is set by the Department of Land Conservation and Development (DLCD), and the Oregon Department of Transportation (ODOT) provides supportive state transportation policy related to land use. In 1991, DLCD and ODOT adopted the Transportation Planning Rule, which created the Transportation and Growth Management Program (TGM) to enable the integration of land use and transportation planning, with the mission to create livable places with diverse transportation choices. TGM recognizes that land use decisions affect transportation options and transportation decisions influence land use patterns. TGM provides direction and support to local agencies for adopting smart growth principles that enable communities to be livable and economically vital, while meeting transportation needs of all residents.

To facilitate the goals of SB 100 and TGM, Goal 12 (Transportation) requires cities, counties, and the state to create a transportation system plan (TSP) to consider and support all relevant modes of transportation (air, water, rail, highway, transit, bicycle, and pedestrian) in providing access to jobs, goods, and services for all residents, while also meeting environmental and social equity goals.[7] Local TSPs highlight and communicate local needs and priorities for state funding. Regional transportation plans (RTPs) developed by metropolitan planning organizations (MPOs) look at the connections between communities, infrastructure, and facilities necessary for the transportation system to function at a regional level.[8] RTPs also identify funding for regional priority projects. The two are required to be consistent with each other and with the Oregon Transportation Plan. In turn, ODOT projects are meant to be developed consistently with both state and local plans, in the hope of meeting both local and regional needs and statewide goals.

Though the state has a comprehensive land use and transportation framework that should provide the means and way to meet statewide goals, especially environmental, we are drastically behind in our goals in reducing GHG emissions and providing equitable, affordable, multimodal options to all Oregonians.

Current Factors Influencing Travel in Oregon

There are challenges and influencing factors that are important to consider in planning for 2050. This section discusses how population trends, the economy, current land use, safety and health impacts, transportation emissions, and climate change are currently shaping Oregon and must be addressed moving toward 2050.

As described in chapter 2, Oregon has been growing in population at 1 percent per year and is expected to reach about 5.4 million by 2050, 1.2 million more than in 2020. This population will not only grow in the Portland metropolitan region, but also throughout the I-5 corridor. We will see communities expand quickly, and city planners will need to keep pace with the accompanying economic growth and subsequent infrastructure and housing needs. This growth will increase demand for transportation.

As highlighted in chapter 2, we will see a changing demographic population and higher growth in urban areas around the state. With around 60 percent of people living in the Willamette Valley and 58 percent of the population in metropolitan areas—Bend, Corvallis, Eugene/Springfield, Medford, Portland, and Salem/Keizer—we expect these areas to continue to densify. Although all parts of the state are expected to grow, by 2030, highly populated counties will have densities ranging from 345 to 1,800 people per square mile, while parts of eastern Oregon will continue to average 1 or 2 people per square mile.

Oregonians are also getting older and more ethnically diverse. In 2020, about 19 percent of the population was 65 years and older, but that percentage is expected to grow to 23 percent by 2050 as the baby boomer generation ages. In some rural counties, more than 20 percent of residents were over age 65 in 2010, and these counties are losing population. In 2020, approximately 25 percent of Oregonians were members of Black, Indigenous, and people of color (BIPOC) communities, of which about 14 percent were Hispanic/Latino. The BIPOC population is expected to continue to grow and make up an even larger percentage by 2050.

As we look to 2050, the changing demographics will certainly create challenges and opportunities for the current transportation system. For example, while many baby boomers and Generation Xers will continue to rely on driving as their primary means to travel as they get older, by 2050, the youngest of the baby boomer generation will be in their mid-80s and possibly unable to drive safely. The loss of that ability can mean isolation and lack of access to essential services and connections to the community. In contrast, the transportation preferences among younger generations are dramatically changing. Younger adults in urban areas are driving less, and many show a clear preference for other options like biking, walking, using transit, and ride-hailing.[9] The millennial generation is the first generation in decades that drives less than their parents, and fewer young people in this cohort are getting driver's licenses. The rise of mobile technologies and the sharing economy have also changed how younger people connect with their peers, how and where they choose to live, where they work, and consequently how they travel. The demographic data underscore that the existing transportation system will not meet the needs of Oregonians in the future.

With the expected growth in population over the next thirty years, Oregon hopes to grow its economic base and opportunities. This growth will put pressures on decision-makers to maintain fast, efficient transportation for people, goods, and services. By 2030, 122 million freight tons will move through the system, mostly by truck, with growing demands on the system and likely more congestion over extended periods of peak-hour traffic.[10]

The efficient movement of goods and services depends on a well-developed and well-maintained transportation infrastructure, especially as the US economy has shifted to just-in-time freight delivery. This shared demand for highway capacity can create extreme congestion and increased cost to both the traveling public and goods. The state faces pressure to address this issue by increasing highway capacity to minimize congestion and improve travel times, but it can cost billions of dollars. Growing evidence shows that increasing highway capacity is a short-term fix because it creates induced demand, perpetuates a cycle of expanding capacity, and promotes car-centric planning and investments.[11] High-cost highway expansion projects do not reduce congestion and emissions.

In 2019, the state's urban area drivers experienced 102 million hours of delay, costing $2.2 billion and causing an excess of 464,000 tons of GHGs.[12] These costs of congestion are the value of extra travel time (or delay) and the extra fuel consumed by vehicles traveling at slower speeds. A person in the Portland region will spend an additional 68 hours annually in their car due to delay, costing them $1,424 in lost time and fuel cost. Accidents, stalled vehicles, weather, work zones, and other incidents cause about 50 percent of travel delay.

Global economic policies and politics, reflected in the world's oil supply and inflation, are being highlighted in the economy after COVID-19 and are creating uncertainties and instability that may cause unpredictable worldwide supply and transportation impacts in the next thirty years. Peak oil and the rising cost of transportation fuels are major concerns. Transportation fuel costs tend to be higher in Oregon because of the region's distance from a limited number of refineries and fuel supplies. In 2022, gas prices reached a ten-year high; Oregon typically ranks in the top-ten most expensive gas prices in the country.[13] The reliability of fossil fuels for transportation significantly affects the

Oregon economy. To maintain competitive (and reasonable) commute times, retain and attract businesses, and support efficient movement of freight, we need to think beyond highway expansion projects to more aggressive and innovative vehicle miles traveled (VMT) reduction strategies and the shift to alternative fuel and fuel-efficient vehicles.

Adding to the problems with relying on fossil fuels for Oregon's transportation needs, funding for transportation is inadequate and uncertain owing to the connection to fuel tax. The motor vehicle fuel tax funds highways, but over the next twenty-five years, inflation will reduce the tax's spending power by 40-50 percent because it is not indexed to inflation. In addition, as vehicles have become more fuel efficient (including electric cars), the amount of funds being raised by fuel tax is quickly diminishing and will continue to do so.

Oregon's current transportation system contributes heavily to climate change and other environmental problems, such as air pollution, noise pollution, water pollution, and habitat loss, and it represents one significant way the state can decarbonize our economy.[14] And the transportation system itself is vulnerable to the impacts of climate change. This section focuses mostly on GHG emissions owing to the climate imperative, but it also discusses the strategies of mitigation to reduce other environmental and health impacts.

Transportation is inextricably linked to the state's goal to reduce GHG emissions to levels that are at least 75 percent below 1990 levels by 2050.[15] Transportation activities are the largest contributor of Oregon's GHG emissions (40 percent in 2017) and make up 32 percent of the energy used in the state.[16] Light-duty vehicles alone constituted 19 percent of energy use. Of the emissions generated, nearly 60 percent are from light-duty vehicles, while about 27 percent are from heavy-duty vehicles.[17] GHG emissions could have increased by 33 percent from 2000 to 2025 without taking any action, mainly because of increased driving and the projected population growth.[18] Passenger vehicle emissions are nearly 20 percent higher than their proportionate share of the 2020 GHG reduction goal, and current transportation trends indicate Oregon will continue to fall short of the state's future GHG goals, despite current statewide efforts.

In 2018, the transportation sector contributed 38 percent of statewide emissions (24 million metric tons of carbon dioxide equivalent, or

$MTCO_2e$).[19] Within the transportation sector, an estimated 54 percent of combustion emissions are generated from passenger vehicles and light-duty trucks, and approximately 30 percent come from heavy-duty vehicles.[20] Statewide passenger vehicles and light-duty trucks are responsible for approximately 17 percent of emissions from all sources. Diesel is the second-largest contributor of emissions, at almost 8 million $MTCO_2e$.

Vehicle emissions are a factor of both the type of fuel consumed and the number of miles driven. Though total VMT increased 13 percent between 2000 and 2018 while the population increased by 23 percent, we have seen a leveling-off of VMT since 2008.[21] Figure 8.1 shows that the average annual VMT per capita in Eugene, Portland, and Salem remained steady since the early 2000s while increasing in the rest of the country. Though this trend shows a slight decline in VMT per capita and the short-lived declines during the COVID-19 pandemic in 2020, the decline is less than is needed to meet statewide goals. Since 1990, emissions in the transportation sector have increased 15 percent along with a 37 percent increase in overall VMT, which highlights the growth of the system and the demand of the population.[22]

The State of Oregon has been working to reduce the production and impacts of greenhouse gas. In 2009, the Oregon Jobs and

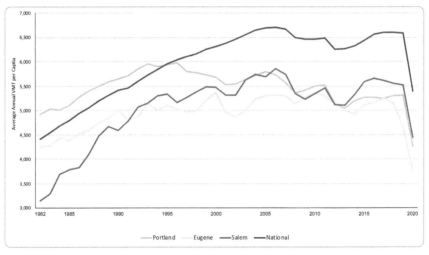

Figure 8.1. Average annual vehicle miles traveled (VMT) per capita in Eugene, Portland, and Salem compared to the national average. Created by the author using data from "Urban Mobility Report," Texas A&M Transportation Institute, accessed January 17, 2024, https://mobility.tamu.edu/umr/

Transportation Act (HB 2001) included several key measures related to transportation GHG mitigation and provided support to conduct metropolitan scenario planning.[23] Also in 2009, House Bill 2186 authorized the Oregon Environmental Quality Commission to adopt a low-carbon fuel standards program for Oregon, particularly addressing medium- and heavy-duty trucks.[24] In 2018, the Oregon Transportation Commission incorporated a GHG emission reduction into the Oregon Transportation Plan. The plan sets out a vision and strategies to reduce GHG emission by 60 percent from 1990 levels. In 2020, Governor Kate Brown elevated the state's GHG reduction responsibilities through an executive order that requires the development of specific guidance, actions, and strategies across state agencies.[25]

To create an integrated statewide effort to reduce GHG emissions from the transportation sector and meet Oregon's GHG reduction goals, the Oregon Sustainable Transportation Initiative (OSTI) was created. The OSTI is a joint effort between ODOT, the DLCD, the Department of Environmental Quality (DEQ), the ODOE, and other stakeholders. Through committees, OSTI works on the development and implementation of the Statewide Transportation Strategy (STS), which is a state-level scenario planning effort that highlights strategies to reduce GHG emissions from the transportation system, such as vehicle and fuel technologies and land use decisions.[26]

Both the Oregon Global Warming Commission and Oregon Transportation Commission highlight the need to encourage the use of hybrid, electric, and other alternative-fuel engines, to increase public transit, and to guide land use and transportation choices. The state is targeting a 15-million-ton reduction in GHGs from transportation by 2050. Half of the reductions will come from the replacement of older vehicles with zero-emission vehicles (ZEVs), such as electric vehicles (EVs) and alternative fuels like biofuels. The other half of the planned reduction will come from changes to transportation planning and the built environment designed to reduce VMT and transportation demand management (TDM), and increase of public transportation and active transportation. Figure 8.2 shows Oregon's past and projected GHG emissions compared to statewide 2050 goals. The transportation sector makes up a significant portion of the GHG emissions. Under current

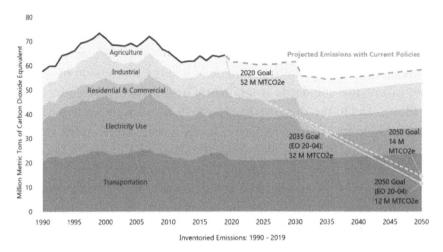

Figure 8.2. Oregon's past and projected greenhouse gas emissions compared to goals. *Source*: "Transportation," Oregon.gov, accessed February 28, 2024, https://www.oregon.gov/energy/energy-oregon/Pages/Transportation.aspx

policies, that will decrease only by a small amount and will not meet the 2050 goal of 14 million MTCO$_2$e.

One of the statewide strategies that needs to be accelerated to meet the state's greenhouse gas reduction targets is significantly higher adoption of EVs across the whole transportation sector. In Oregon, ZEVs are electric vehicles, including electric battery vehicles (BEVs) or plug-in hybrid electric vehicles (PHEVs). Fuel cell electric (hydrogen) vehicles are also a promising technology, but they are not currently easily available in the United States and Oregon. As there are barriers to adoption of ZEVs, such as lack of charging infrastructure and the high purchase cost, the US government has recently committed $5 billion to states and local communities over the next five years to build a convenient, reliable, and affordable EV charging network across the country.[27] Additionally, federal and state incentives help reduce the up-front cost of an EV to be more comparable to a gasoline vehicle. For many EVs, the total cost of ownership is less than an equivalent gasoline vehicle, especially if owners can charge at home.

Meeting the statewide ZEV goals will significantly reduce the state's overall GHG emissions while reducing harmful pollutants, saving consumers money, and producing complementary benefits to the state's rapidly decarbonizing electrical grid. Oregon's ZEV adoption goals are as follows.

- By 2020, at least 50,000 registered motor vehicles will be ZEVs.
- By 2025, at least 250,000 registered motor vehicles will be ZEVs.
- By 2030, at least 25 percent of registered motor vehicles, and at least 50 percent of new motor vehicles sold annually, will be ZEVs.
- By 2035, at least 90 percent of new motor vehicles sold annually will be ZEVs.[28]

In 2021, there were approximately 3.5 million registered vehicles in Oregon using more than 1.5 billion gallons of gasoline annually, with an average fuel efficiency of 23 miles per gallon. As of December 2021, a total of 46,600 electric vehicles were registered in the state, of which 30,200 were BEVs and 16,400 were PHEVs. Adoption rates of ZEVs are much lower than among medium- and heavy-duty vehicles, mostly owing to the availability of models. EVs represent 1.3 percent of vehicles registered in the state and around 2 percent of new vehicle sales. There are approximately 2,100 public chargers in 900 locations throughout the state.[29] While ZEVs are increasingly popular, the state did not achieve its goal of 50,000 registered ZEVs by 2020, and it is not on track to achieve the 2025 or 2030 goals without significant changes in the market or the economy, or without drastic policy measures.

Though EVs are important part of Oregon's strategy to meet 2050 climate goals, we can't solely rely on EV adoption.[30] It will take a mixture of vehicle technology advancements, low-carbon fuels, system improvements, multimodal options, demand management, pricing, and land use decisions. There will be policy and philosophical debates over which of these strategies should be relied more on more, technology improvements or demand management. There is sufficient evidence that a multifaceted approach of complementary strategies is needed to reduce VMT.[31] As Susan Handy, professor in the Department of Environmental Science and Policy at the University of California, Davis, points out, "Make it possible to drive less, help people see how to drive less, help people to want to drive less and stop encouraging people to drive more."[32]

The other side of the climate equation is that much of the state's transportation system is vulnerable to the direct and indirect effects of climate change. As stated in chapter 3, climate change will have profound effects on the state, such as extreme storm events and flooding, rising sea levels and storm surge, coastal erosion and landslides, and higher temperatures and wildfire risks. These impacts could leave some communities isolated and uninhabitable, and rebuilding or maintaining our transportation systems to withstand such impacts will cost billions. To add to the uncertainty, Oregon will at some point experience a 9.0-magnitude earthquake caused by the Cascadia Subduction Zone. This may result in a tsunami of up to 100 feet in height that will devastate the coastal area—destroying communities and damaging roads, bridges, and buildings. Though the state, ODOT, and local jurisdictions are developing strategies and investing in infrastructure to make the transportation system more resilient to these hazards, there is great concern over the cost and resources needed to appropriately respond to the threats.[33] These discussions and decisions are challenging policymakers, planners, engineers, and communities to rethink how we invest with limited resources in the transportation system. In some cases, this might mean abandoning assets or prioritizing specific corridors. If an "ounce of prevention is worth a pound of cure," then we need to look beyond building us out of the problem and instead invest in resilient, multimodal solutions to address climate change at the cause.

Land Use

Oregonians' transportation choices, and therefore VMT, is driven in large part by the land use planning decisions made at local and regional levels. Designing and building communities that allow for and encourage the use of biking, walking, transit, and other low-carbon modes of transportation will decrease emissions, create more livable communities, and encourage more physical activity and potentially more equitable economic benefits. But that is not how a lot of the state has been developed. Local governments sometimes make land use decisions that affect housing development, often locating it far from employment centers and opportunities. These decisions also place major trip destinations—such as grocery stores, schools, colleges, and hospitals—far away from where people live without supporting multimodal access and options, thus creating the need to use cars and adding to higher levels of traffic, congestion, and air pollution. In addition, these land use decisions, along with gentrification, have led to racial and social inequities, as lower-income families are forced into long commutes.

In the next twenty-five years, Oregon faces the challenges of integrating the state and local transportation systems with growing land use needs, a worsening affordable housing crisis, a shortage of urban and suburban industrial land, and uncertain population growth and development patterns. Land use is inextricably linked to the transportation system, but the policies and agencies that oversee the linkage are not always in sync. While land use affects the viable transportation options available to people, ODOT does not have direct authority over land use policies and decisions. As stated above, to encourage a more comprehensive land use planning program, SB 100 Goal 12 (Transportation) requires cities, counties, and the state to create a transportation system plan. The hope is for these plans to support a variety of transportation modes to provide access to jobs, goods, and services for all residents, while also meeting environmental and social equity goals.

One of the barriers to reforming our transportation system is parking.[34] Parking incentivizes more car ownership and driving. Availability of parking allows for the reliance on cars for trips. As a significant part of land use and transportation planning, parking has shaped the design, environment, and economies of our communities. Parking exerts a strong influence on the built environment and is interwoven into zoning and development decisions and government mandates. Many Oregon communities have mandatory parking minimums, which require real estate developers to include a certain number of parking spaces in anything they build, from commercial properties, grocery stores, to churches.

Though cities like Bend, Portland, and Salem are addressing the issue of parking by reducing or eliminating parking minimums and increasing the cost of parking as ways to manage demand, these tend to be for downtown districts or urban cores. Other areas, especially suburban commercial areas, are still building excessive parking. Many parking policy reformers and advocates are proposing policies that discourage excess supply and encourage better use of existing parking supply, including removing off-street parking requirements, imposing impact fees for new parking stalls, restricting new surface lots and impermeable surfaces, and instituting dynamic demand pricing.[35]

As described in chapter 7, if land use planning and the transportation system better support each other, Oregonians could have more options for travel and lower travel times. Businesses could use the most cost-effective transportation option. To manage effective integration of land use and transportation policies, interjurisdictional communication and cooperation are required. The state and local transportation system could function as one system and use technology that operates across jurisdictions and modes of transportation. State agencies must work with local governments and metropolitan planning organizations to develop strategies to promote more sustainable land use planning. For example, pairing land use planning, policies, and incentives with transportation electrification could accelerate adoption to meet the goal of transitioning to a decarbonized system.

Safety and Health

Public health is largely determined by the "social determinants of health," which include the conditions in which people are born, grow up, live, and work in, as well as economic conditions and the built environment in which people live. Transportation provides an important linkage to the physical and social environment and relates to public health in several areas. For example, the availability and circumstances of how people move (walking, biking, public transportation options, and auto use) and what they can access (work, their community, essential and social services) have different impacts on an individuals' level of physical and mental health outcomes.

In 2021, on Oregon's roadways there were over 45,000 motor vehicles related crashes, killing 599 people and injuring 35,945.[36] Pedestrians and bicyclists made up 97 (19.6 percent) of those killed and 1,677 (4 percent) of those injured on roads. These numbers have been consistent for the last decade, even as VMT has slightly declined. The current fatality rate is 1.37 lives lost per 100 million vehicles miles traveled.

In addition to safety-related issues, there are significant transportation-related impacts to health. Lack of physical activity increases the rates of obesity, cardiovascular disease, and diabetes, while exposure to vehicle emissions is linked to higher rates of respiratory disease, cardiovascular disease, adverse pregnancy outcomes, climate change, and environmental hazards (e.g., extreme heat). Air pollution increases the risk of premature death, asthma attacks, cancer, and other adverse health impacts. The most common transportation-related air pollutants are fine particulate matter (PM 2.5), air toxics, and ground-level ozone and smog. Long-term exposure to fine particulate matter has been associated with adverse health outcomes such as reduced lung function and the development of chronic bronchitis, heart disease, and cancer. Short-term impacts, such as asthma, can be caused by elevated ozone concentrations, mostly affecting people with respiratory problems, the elderly, and children. These health outcomes disproportionately affect minority and low-income communities, which are often located near high-traffic corridors, within five hundred feet of highways and interstates.

In 2020, approximately 30 percent of Oregon adults were obese. That proportion has increased since 1990, when 10.7 percent of Oregon adults were obese.[37] Rates of obesity are disproportionately higher in the BIPOC populations where adult African Americans (35.8 percent), American Indian/Alaska Natives (40.6 percent), Hawaiian/Pacific Islanders (45.1 percent), and Hispanics (37.0 percent) are more likely to be obese than whites (28.8 percent) or Asians (9.5 percent). In addition, African Americans are three times as likely and American Indian/Alaska Natives are twice as likely to have diabetes compared to non-Latino whites. Overall, 17.7 percent of Oregon's adults reported that during the past month they had not participated in any physical activity.[38] Also alarming is the increasing rates for childhood and youth obesity, which are currently around 30 percent.[39] The importance of maintaining regular physical activity has measurable health benefits, such as reducing health risks of cardiovascular disease and Type 2 diabetes. Even moderate amounts of active transportation such as walking, biking, and walking to transit stops can result in important health benefits for Oregonians. Awareness of public health and its relationship to active transportation is increasing nationwide and in Oregon. For the past ten years, ODOT and the Oregon Health Authority's Public Health Division have been coordinating efforts in policy, planning, and data-sharing through a bi-agency agreement to identify, develop, and promote connections between public health and transportation.

The Safe Routes to School Program (SRTS) educates and encourages children to safely walk and bike to school. The SRTS program receives $16 million in state highway funding annually.[40] This money goes to communities for infrastructure and non-infrastructure grants, and provides technical assistance to create safe walking and biking routes through investments in crossings, sidewalks, and bike lanes, flashing beacons, and education and outreach to kids and families to ensure awareness and safe use of walking and biking routes.

Looking to the Future

Oregon's transportation system will certainly look different in 2050, and the state can proactively shape its future. Technology aims to improve the way that vehicles and people interact within the transportation system, but uncertainties about the economy, global oil supply, and impacts of climate change will result in unforeseen impacts. As we have seen with the COVID-19 pandemic, unexpected events can have dramatic short-term influence on our lives. They can also cause a useful reevaluation of how we live and work. Do these types of short-term impacts fundamentally change travel patterns and commuting, or will we rebound to pre-pandemic ways? Locally, the potential regional devastation of the Cascadia Subduction Zone earthquake looms large with the public and policymakers. Certainly, the state does not have the financial means to make communities 100 percent earthquake ready. How best should we invest in resiliency with the limited funds we have available? The state's ability to meet these challenges, or at least respond as effectively as possible, depends on the way we work together to change the way we do things, manage the transportation system, better integrate land use, transportation and economic decisions, and fund a sustainable transportation system.

As presented in chapter 7, there are a range of possible future scenarios for Oregon in 2050. We have the benefit of planning now for how we want Oregon to respond to increased population and to promote economic growth while meeting our sustainability and equity goals and minimizing societal and environmental impacts. Because land use and transportation are tied together, this discussion adopts the statewide scenarios presented in chapter 7: Business as Usual, Sprawl, and Smart Growth. These different scenarios were run for four different regions of

Oregon—central Oregon, Columbia Gorge, the North Coast, and the South Coast. The Portland metropolitan region was not included in the scenarios, but we will discuss future projections based on Metro's 2018 Regional Transportation Plan, based on the Climate Smart Communities Scenarios.[41] (The Climate Smart Communities Scenarios Project responds to a state mandate to reduce greenhouse gas emissions from cars and small trucks by 2035.)

All of the scenarios involved a similar projected population increase in each region, based on estimates from the Portland State University Population Research Center. These scenarios and the analysis are intended to be illustrative only, and the specific numbers should not be considered exact projections.

As shown in chapter 7, land use patterns involving sprawl ultimately will lead to worsening social and environmental outcomes, while land use patterns involving more infill ultimately will have the most positive environmental and social benefits. Only in the Smart Growth Scenario do we see declines in vehicle emissions per household and declines in per household annual vehicle miles traveled. Even in this scenario we don't see significant changes in mode share among auto, transit, and bike. This is not totally surprising given the current travel patterns of the region and the low level of transit availability and investment. In the Portland region, Metro has used the Climate Smart Scenario project and the 2018 Regional Transportation Plan as key tools for implementing the 2040 Growth Concept, a long-range strategy for land use and transportation policies, planning, and investments with the intention to reduce the region's carbon footprint.

These scenarios are highly dependent on population and existing land use policies and patterns that will control development in the next thirty years. By focusing on land use development, especially in growing population centers outside of the Portland region, the state can try to minimize VMT through enhanced access in growing urban areas. The struggle for Oregon is how to expand investments in walking, biking, and transit to manage VMT. An example of this approach is in Metro's Climate Smart Strategy, which provides nine place-based strategies that could be implemented across the state by tying investment to incentives and support for policies, programs, and projects that meet this approach.

1. Implement adopted local and regional land use plans.
2. Make transit convenient, frequent, accessible, and affordable.
3. Make biking and walking safe and convenient.
4. Make streets and highways safe, reliable, and connected.
5. Use technology to actively manage the transportation system.
6. Provide information and incentives to expand the use of travel options.
7. Make efficient use of vehicle parking and land dedicated to parking.
8. Support Oregon's transition to cleaner, low-carbon fuels and more fuel-efficient vehicles.
9. Secure adequate funding for transportation investments.[42]

Metro's strategy focuses on making regional connections through an approach of centers and corridors, where local development can support livable communities by investments in walking, biking, and transit. The strategy also supports the movement of people and goods through corridors that connect the region through sustainable mobility.

Mobility, the ability to get around and access essential services, jobs, and opportunities, is crucial to people's needs and to building vibrant communities in Oregon. Mobility provides independence and the capacity to get to and from work or school; shop for fresh food, clothing, and other daily needs; participate in physical and social activities; engage in and contribute to community affairs; and gain access to health and social services. These activities are crucial to the health and well-being of all Oregon residents. Public transportation provides mobility and access for those who, for a variety of reasons, do not or cannot use a private vehicle. In rural areas, however, where population densities are low and places are spread out, public transportation may be limited or even nonexistent. Meeting at least part of this demand through improved transit service could have considerable social, economic, and health benefits—both for the individuals served and for their broader communities.

This type of multimodal approach to the other regional areas in Oregon may help people live healthier lives and save businesses and households money by reducing air pollution, increasing physical activity, and reducing cost of travel with fuel-efficient vehicles. By creating multimodal options, we can reduce delays in transportation and promote the efficient movement of goods.

From an initial glance at the scenarios for both the four regions and Portland Metro, we are not seeing significant reductions in VMT or a mode shift away for car travel. Currently, the 79 percent auto mode split consists of 43 percent drive-alone and 36 percent shared car trips. A focus of the region and other parts of the state should be to shift more of those drive-alone trips to shared car trips. This could include carpooling or shared mobility services, such as ride-hailing or ridesharing services. Ultimately, to reduce VMT in the regional context, public transportation will need to be significantly enhanced to shift people out of cars and into buses and rail. In addition to public transportation investments, pricing and policy levers will need to be put in place to provide needed incentives.

Joe Cortright, in an article on City Observatory, critiqued Metro's current regional strategy as relying too heavily on optimistic assumptions of vehicle fuel economy projections, electrification, vehicle fleet size and composition, and cleaner fossil fuels.[43] Roughly 90 percent of the planned reduction in per capita GHGs are associated with actions over which the region has no control, such as vehicle fuel economy and availability of affordable ZEVs. The regional strategy focuses far less on what local actions and investments the region can do to reduce single occupancy vehicles and VMT, such as public transportation. Basically, even though the region promotes an active transportation-first policy, planning is still in place for a car-centric approach. This can be seen in both the I-5 bridge replacement and the I-84/Rose Quarter Expansion projects, projects that fundamentally improve highway capacity and travel times for cars and trucks.

Of many critiques, Cortright shows that the RTPs over the years consistently predict high levels of transit growth. Figure 8.3 shows the predicted ridership from the last four RTPs and the actual transit ridership. To meet 2040 goals, the region would need to double daily ridership levels. The importance of transit in meeting regional VMT and GHG goals should be a cornerstone of our statewide and regional

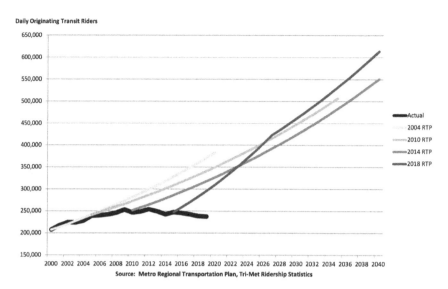

Figure 8.3. Predicted and actual transit ridership in Portland based on regional transportation plans, January 2020 to March 2023. *Source*: Joe Cortright, "Metro's Failing Climate Strategy," City Observatory, December 30, 2021, https://cityobservatory.org/metros-failing-climate-strategy

approach. The findings also demonstrate that more investment, actions, and resources will be needed to ensure the region achieves GHG reduction goals.

What Is Needed as We Move toward 2050

Oregon faces a lot of challenges as it moves toward 2050. A critical element in ensuring that we meet our goals and create vibrant, livable, and sustainable communities is the transportation system. Much of the discussion in this chapter has been driven by our need to reduce the carbon footprint of Oregon's transportation sector. Sometimes this goal can drive discussions, narratives, and decisions without focusing on the broader benefits of enhancing mobility options and accessibility of Oregonians. Because climate change is still extremely politicized in the United States and in Oregon, we need to elevate the benefits of health, accessibility, equity, and economic development. Though many climate-forward policies have co-benefits of health, safety, and equity, some do not. A focus on switching the fleet to 100 percent clean energy does not reduce VMT, improve safety outcomes, or address the need to manage the growing demands on the system.

In addition, those with limited mobility options, older adults, low-income individuals, and those with disabilities will be still struggling to access essential services, jobs, and friends and family.

Oregon should be looking at a broader suite of options and opportunities to meet these goals. Because of the growing urban populations by 2050 and a continuing greater urban and rural divide, it will not be without some unflinching policies that go beyond transportation and into land use, housing, and economic development to meet the state's goals and to overcome the state's challenges moving toward 2050. To accomplish these goals and outcomes, Oregon must reduce VMT, rapidly transform the fleet of cars and trucks to low-carbon fuels, levy fees or taxes for the use of roads, harness the potential of technology to reduce traffic deaths, and increase mobility for all.

One of the most critical steps is to develop a statewide multimodal approach to reduce VMT. As important as the "greening" of the fleet is to meet climate goals, the real need is to double down on VMT reduction. This approach needs to be bold and intentional. VMT reduction policies can take the form of incentives or pricing, regulations, and infrastructure investments that disincentivize the use of single-occupant vehicles and enhance the attractiveness of active transportation. Any of these policies need to have components that directly enhance social equity by increasing mobility, health, and economic well-being in disadvantaged communities by empowering communities to prioritize actions that disincentive single-occupancy vehicle trips.

At the basic level, more funding needs to focus on expanding public transportation services, shared micromobility options such as scooters and e-bikes, and walking and bicycling infrastructure throughout the state. As the population grows over the next thirty years, land use development and transit service need to keep or exceed the pace of people coming into the state and the growth of cities. If they do not, then people will choose to live in lower-density areas, with less access to work opportunities and daily needs, and may feel forced to drive a car. Cities like Bend, Eugene, Medford, and Salem will continue to grow in the next thirty years, from medium-sized to larger cities, hopefully containing growth within urban growth boundaries. The Portland metropolitan region will be challenged to maintain growth within urban areas, as cities like Gresham, Hillsboro, and Wilsonville become larger population centers. These cities will need to work with TriMet and regional partners to improve the efficiency of the existing transportation system to make it more reliable and improve coverage, so people are encouraged and able to use transit, along with walking and biking, to get to work, school, and other locations.

One of the biggest opportunities for the state to truly address VMT reduction and enhanced regional mobility is intercity transit, which has the potential to grow the economy, shrink mobility inequalities, and help to meet statewide carbon goals. Currently, the state is served by intercity bus and passenger rail service that links metropolitan regions, towns, cities, and rural areas throughout the state. Amtrak Cascades passenger rail service provides a critical link between Eugene, Oregon, and Vancouver, British Columbia (fig. 8.4). Intercity Bus includes a mix of public and private providers that fill critical connections, mostly in the Willamette Valley. Both Intercity Bus and Amtrak in Oregon are limited in operations and don't meet

Figure 8.4. Map of the planned Cascadia Rail system, 2050. *Source*: Cascadia Innovation Corridor, Cascadia Vision 2050: How the Cascadia Innovation Corridor Can Serve as a Global Model for Sustainable Growth (Cascadia Innovation Corridor, 2020), https://connectcascadia.com/cascadia-vision-2050-how-the-cascadia-innovation-corridor-can-serve-as-a-global-model-for-sustainable-growth/

the current or future needs of connecting communities in Oregon and the Pacific Northwest region. Based on the Oregon Public Transportation Plan, to meet the unmet transit needs in the state, the current budget of $900 million, which is underfunded by $400 million, would require $2 billion (in 2013 dollars) by 2045.[44]

A critical component to enhance regional connectivity and reduce VMT is the increased frequency, reliability, and connectivity of regional rail. One the most discussed projects is the Cascadia megaregion high-speed rail project, which connects Eugene to Seattle and Vancouver, British Columbia.[45] The governors of Oregon and Washington and the premier of British Columbia have been working under a memorandum of understanding to lay the groundwork for high-speed rail along the I-5 corridor. With recent prospects for federal funding, there is an opportunity to move forward on the planning and building the rail line. With the project costs of $24 to $42 billion in 2017 dollars, the projected annual ridership could range from 1.6 million to 2.5 million by 2035.[46] Not only does a regional rail create the backbone for statewide travel, but it also allows for more local transit connections to be established to provide multimodal regional travel. In addition, a project at this scale can truly create a Cascadia megaregion that can drive economic development for the state.

Another key step is to adopt innovative pricing for road use. One of the most important mechanisms the state and local municipalities have to influence people's travel behavior and significantly reduce VMT is pricing for parking and use of roads. Implementing pricing actions can manage demand and recover the full cost of travel and environmental impacts of roadways. Oregon has been leading nationally on shifting from a state gas tax to a road usage fee through its OReGO pay-by-the-mile program. As drivers transition from gas and diesel to electric vehicles, it will be important to look for an alternative in collecting fees for using the roads, such as a pay-by-the-mile charging system. Road usage charging is advancing quickly around the United States and may be the most impactful transportation innovation since Oregon implemented the nation's first gas tax a century ago. If implemented appropriately, a new funding model and the technology to deploy the program can facilitate a shift away from fossil fuels using a technology-based solution that assesses drivers fairly for their road use. The state will need to quickly move from the pilot phase to fully deploy the system in new vehicle models and to even look at implementing requirements on older models.

Onboard technology for road usage fees is only the first step and looks only at recovering diminished fuel tax funds, which have traditionally been used for road maintenance, preservation, and improvement projects. Once there is technology to track road usage on vehicles, we can move forward with other pricing strategies, such as congestion pricing and highway tolling, and cordon and dynamic parking pricing. Regional modeling shows that by 2027, almost one-third of the region's roads will be congested or severely congested.[47] Tolling has become a topic of much greater interest in the Portland region over the past few years. In 2017, the Oregon State Legislature directed the Oregon Transportation Commission (OTC) to seek federal approval to implement tolling on I-5 and I-205 in the Portland metropolitan area to address congestion through the passage of House Bill 2017 ("Keep Oregon Moving"). ODOT conducted a feasibility analysis between 2017 and 2018 to identify and explore different tolling scenarios on these highways and is currently working on developing the pilots. By implementing congestion pricing strategies, we can charge people for driving or using roadway space and encourage other transportation modes or carpooling. These charges can vary based on different factors, for instance, how congested the roads are, the time of day, or what type of vehicle is using the road. By applying a charge, pricing can help people consider the impact of their travel choices and encourage certain behaviors (like carpooling, traveling at off-peak hours, or using other, nondriving options when possible).

To be more intentional with pricing strategies and to create a more equitable and sustainable transportation system, the City of Portland created the Pricing Options for Equitable Mobility (POEM) project. The city recognized that it needs to develop pricing strategies both for the city and to be used as a framework for regional strategies to meet the challenges of and better manage the roads. The POEM project also used an equitable mobility framework to inform decision-making around pricing strategies that prioritizes extending benefits, reducing disparities, and improving safety for BIPOC communities. One of the key recommendations for the project was that funds generated for any pricing strategy, whether on city or state roads, should be used to advance climate, equity, and mobility outcomes. This means investing in local communities and prioritizing transportation demand management and multimodal options to ensure and enhance these options.

Oregon should also make policies that accelerate the adoption of ZEVs and low-carbon fuels. Zero-emission vehicles are an important strategy for transforming our transportation system, especially for trucking/movement of goods and other transportation not related to individual or household travel behavior. Broader use can be encouraged through increased vehicle sales mandates and targets, along with expansion of electricity and hydrogen fueling infrastructure. Continued focus needs to be on low-income households and underserved communities to ensure they are not the last households to shift from gasoline-powered vehicles. Not only do these households face financial constraints that make purchasing difficult, but often they don't own their homes or have control over installing charging infrastructure. The State of Oregon and urban areas like Portland and Eugene have started focusing on zero-emission vehicles and low-carbon fuel policies, but there needs to be significantly more investment in this area. This effort could be boosted with the Infrastructure Investment and Jobs Act 2021, which will send an additional $1.2 billion to the state in 2022-26, of which $52 million is allocated for the expansion of electricity and hydrogen-fueling infrastructure.

It will take several strategies designed to increase consumer awareness, ensure equity in access to EVs, and continue the build-out of the charging and hydrogen-fueling infrastructure needed to support widespread ZEV adoption. Even with the influx of federal funds for infrastructure investments, Oregon will still need to do more. Oregon's ZEV goals in 2025, 2030, and 2035 require big leaps forward, and the state is not currently on track to meet them—but the opportunities to support EVs are growing. It will take a lot of work for the state and its partners to move quickly toward achieving the 250,000 registered ZEV goal by 2025. By 2050, all new vehicles sold in the state will need to be zero emissions. Oregon should continue to follow and adopt California's rules and standards related to both passenger vehicles and medium- and heavy-duty vehicles. In addition to strengthening sales targets for ZEVs, Oregon can continue a robust ZEV rebate program, especially for low-income households. In 2021, the Oregon Legislature increased the amount of the Oregon DEQ's Charge Ahead ZEV rebate, bringing the total potential amount of rebate dollars available to low-income Oregonians to $7,500. Another lever Oregon should be using is strengthening the low-carbon fuel standard to reduce the average carbon intensity of transportation fuels.

To boost consumer confidence in shifting to EVs, potential regulatory action along with a number of complementary state actions will be essential, including ensuring consumer incentives to bring down the initial purchase price of vehicles, building out a statewide network of charging stations to ensure that EV drivers are able to easily access charging when needed, and accelerating the turnover of fleet vehicles, including in government fleets. It is critical that the transition to ZEVs provide benefits to low- and moderate-income households as well as rural and underserved communities. Geographical areas with greater levels of ZEV adoption have lower levels of local air pollution and vehicle noise.

In these discussions, Oregon planners must also question most of our assumptions about transportation technology. In the past five years, emerging technologies, such as shared mobility and autonomous vehicles (AVs), have disrupted travel behavior and caused transportation planners to question base assumptions on how people will move around in the future. Ride-hailing companies like Uber and Lyft, and micromobility/e-scooter companies like Bird and Lime, came to the market so quickly that it took everyone by surprise, especially regulators, planners, and policymakers. The mobility services, driven by technology companies, focused on market solutions to solve unmet needs particularly in urban areas, not always working with local governments to align with regional goals or practices.

In his book *Three Revolutions*, Daniel Sperling discusses how the three revolutions in transportation—shared mobility, electrification, and AVs—will radically transform how people and goods move around the world.[48] He describes a not-so-distant future where people will no longer own cars. The vehicles that do exist will be fully electrified, have zero tailpipe emissions, and driverless. In a fully automated future, AVs have the potential to eliminate traffic fatalities and injuries while providing greater operational efficiencies, eliminating or minimizing

TRANSPORTATION   235

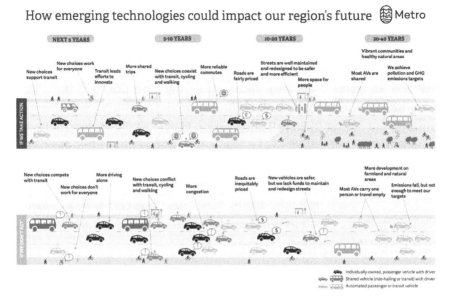

Figure 8.5. Metro's Emerging Technology Strategy. What the region's future could look like if we take action on technology—and if we don't. AV, autonomous vehicle; GHG, greenhouse gas. Metro, Emerging Technology Strategy (Portland, OR: Metro, 2018), https://www.oregonmetro.gov/sites/default/files/2019/01/17/Metro_Emerging_Tech_Strategy_12_2018%20Final.pdf

congestion, increasing convenience and comfort, and enhancing mobility for people who can't drive, especially older adults and people with disabilities. This sounds like a magical future and could eliminate most, if not all, of our transportation issues and concerns. That said, it could also create a future where people feel they can drive farther, causing more sprawl and needs for costly roadway investments. Uncontrolled, we could see a greater divide between the haves and the have-nots, causing even greater equity issues.

As stated above, the evolution to EVs needs to accelerate now, and we need to plan for the current charging needs while also understanding the future charging needs of a 100 percent electric fleet. How many chargers will we need in the state, and will utility companies keep pace with the demand? Of course, the evolution of the technologies is mostly out of the state's control. Advancements in battery and charging technology and vehicles will depend on private and federal investment. But Oregon can encourage smart planning and equitable investment in charging infrastructure and incentivize adoption and proper use. This will include innovative and progressive policies that will allow public utilities and local governments to control strategic investments into publicly available charging. The same goes for AVs and the connected vehicle technology environment. AVs have many applications that are extremely beneficial (such as long-haul trucking routes, automated local delivery, demand response transit, and first- and last-mile connections). Evolution of technology from partial automation (Level 3) to full automation (Level 5) depends heavily on how fast the technology progresses while addressing the policy concerns of liability, licensing, security, and privacy. Figure 8.5 illustrates how the future could look if local communities take action today in embracing emerging technologies, such as connected and autonomous vehicles, as well as what might happen if we don't plan to harness these technologies.

Conclusion

This chapter highlights transportation challenges facing Oregon as we look to a possible 2050 future, and suggests some potential areas of focus for the next three decades. Oregonians are at a critical juncture in transportation decision-making and investments. We can create a more sustainable, equitable, and economically prosperous future, but we will need to make those big choices soon if we hope to meet our 2050 goals. The status quo of a century's worth of car-centric transportation investments and prioritization is not the path forward. Oregonians pride themselves in being trailblazers, independent and innovative. It is time for us to take national leadership in elevating sustainable and equitable modes of transportation, to partner in creating a strong and vital Pacific Northwest economy by investing in regional rail, and to fully decarbonize our transportation system. One of our biggest challenges and opportunities is how we will embrace technology in these efforts. How do we harness these technologies to purposefully meet our goals? We can ride the "Three Revolution" wave, or let it crush us in the surf. For certain, we can't sit idly by with any of these actions. It is time to be bold.

Notes

1. "Guide to 2010 State and Local Census Geography—Oregon," US Census Bureau, last revised October 8, 2021, https://www.census.gov/geographies/reference-files/2010/geo/state-local-geo-guides-2010.html.
2. "Oregon: Transportation by the Numbers," US Department of Transportation Bureau of Transportation Statistics, accessed December 29, 2023, https://www.bts.dot.gov/sites/bts.dot.gov/files/states2020/Oregon.pdf.
3. Oregon Department of Transportation, *Oregon Transportation Plan: Interim Products Informing OPTP Development*, vol. 2 (Salem: Oregon Department of Transportation, 2018), https://www.oregon.gov/odot/Planning/Documents/OPTP_Volume2_Final_Feb19.pdf.
4. Stacy G. Bricka, *Personal Travel in Oregon: A Snapshot of Daily Household Travel Patterns* (Salem: Oregon Department of Transportation, August 2019), https://www.oregon.gov/ODOT/Planning/Documents/OHAS-Daily-Travel-In-Oregon-Report.pdf.
5. N. McGuckin and A. Fucci, *Summary of Travel Trends: 2017 National Household Travel Survey*, FHWA-PL-18-019 (Washington, DC: US Department of Transportation Federal Highway Administration, July 2018), https://www.fhwa.dot.gov/policyinformation/documents/2017_nhts_summary_travel_trends.pdf.
6. Bricka, *Personal Travel in Oregon*.
7. "Goal 12: Transportation," Oregon's Statewide Planning Goals and Guidelines, accessed December 30, 2023, https://www.oregon.gov/lcd/OP/Documents/goal12.pdf.
8. MPOs are federally designated and funded organizations that lead transportation planning activities through collaborative governance to allocate federal and other transportation funding resources. Oregon currently has eight MPOs covering the metropolitan areas of Albany, Bend, Corvallis, Eugene-Springfield, Medford-Ashland, Middle Rogue Valley, Portland, and Salem-Keizer. Two Washington state MPOs cover small areas in Oregon, Kelso, and Walla Walla Valley. Oregon is likely to see more MPOs in the near future as more cities reach a 50,000 population threshold.
9. Camile Squires, "Even as They Age, US Millennials Are Driving Less than Older Generations," Quartz, January 7, 2022, https://qz.com/2109753/us-millennials-drive-less-than-older-generations.
10. Oregon Department of Transportation, *Oregon Freight Plan: An Element of the Oregon Transportation Plan* (Salem: Oregon Department of Transportation, revised 2017), https://digital.osl.state.or.us/islandora/object/osl%3A104977.
11. Susan Handy, "Why Sustainable Transport Cannot Ignore Land Use," in *Handbook of Sustainable Transport*, ed. C. Curtis (Cheltenham, UK: Edward Elgar, 2020), 220–29; idem, "Increasing Highway Capacity Unlikely to Relieve Traffic Congestion" (Davis, CA: National Center for Sustainable Transportation, 2015), https://escholarship.org/uc/item/58x8436d.
12. Texas A&M Transportation Institute, *2021 Urban Mobility Report* (College Station: Texas A&M Transportation Institute, 2021), https://mobility.tamu.edu/umr/.
13. "2022 Gas Price News," AAA Oregon/Idaho, updated December 13, 2022, https://info.oregon.aaa.com/2022-oregon-gas-price-news.
14. Jean-Paul Rodrigue, *The Geography of Transport Systems*, 5th ed. (New York: Routledge, 2020), https://doi.org/10.4324/9780429346323.
15. SB 1059: Greenhouse Gas Emissions Reductions Goals, 2010 Or. Laws 468A.205.

16 Oregon Department of Energy, *2022 Biennial Energy Report* (Salem: Oregon Department of Energy, 2022), https://energyinfo.oregon.gov/ber.
17 Oregon Department of Energy, *Energy by the Numbers* (Salem: Oregon Department of Energy, 2020), https://www.oregon.gov/energy/Data-and-Reports/Documents/2020-BER-Energy-by-the-Numbers.pdf.
18 Oregon Office of Energy, *Energy by the Numbers*.
19 David Allaway, Elizabeth Elbel, and Colin McConnaha, *Oregon's Greenhouse Gas Emissions through 2015: An Assessment of Oregon's Sector-Based and Consumption-Based Greenhouse Gas Emissions* (Portland: Oregon Department of Environmental Quality, 2018), https://www.oregon.gov/deq/FilterDocs/OregonGHGreport.pdf.
20 Oregon Department of Environmental Quality, *Oregon Greenhouse Gas Sector-Based Inventory: 1990 through 2015 with Preliminary 2016 and 2017* (Portland: Oregon Department of Environmental Quality, 2019), https://www.oregon.gov/deq/FilterDocs/ghg-sectordata.xlsx.
21 "Regional Integrated Transportation Information System," Oregon Department of Transportation, accessed December 30, 2023, https://www.oregon.gov/odot/Data/Pages/RITIS.aspx.
22 "Oregon Statewide VMT Data," Oregon Department of Transportation, accessed December 30, 2023, http://www.oregon.gov/ODOT/Data/documents/VMT_Statewide.pdf.
23 Oregon State Legislature, 2009 Regular Session, HB 2001, https://olis.leg.state.or.us/liz/2009R1/Measures/Overview/HB200.
24 Oregon State Legislature, 2009 Regular Session, HB 2186, https://olis.leg.state.or.us/liz/2009R1/Measures/Overview/HB2186.
25 "Executive Order 20-04: Directing State Agencies to Take Actions to Reduce and Regulate Greenhouse Gas Emissions," Office of the Governor, State of Oregon, accessed March 5, 2024, https://www.oregon.gov/gov/eo/eo_20-04.pdf.
26 "Every Mile Counts," Oregon Department of Transportation, accessed December 30, 2023, https://www.oregon.gov/odot/Programs/Pages/Every-Mile-Counts.aspx.
27 "Historic Step: All Fifty States plus D.C. and Puerto Rico Greenlit to Move EV Charging Networks Forward, Covering 75,000 Miles of Highway," US Department of Transportation Federal Highway Administration, September 27, 2022, https://highways.dot.gov/newsroom/historic-step-all-fifty-states-plus-dc-and-puerto-rico-greenlit-move-ev-charging-networks.
28 Oregon Senate Bill 1044 (2019), https://olis.oregonlegislature.gov/liz/2019R1/Measures/Overview/SB1044 and https://olis.oregonlegislature.gov/liz/2019R1/Downloads/MeasureDocument/SB1044/Enrolled
29 Go Electric Oregon website, accessed December 30, 2023, goelectric.oregon.gov.
30 Amy Schlusser and Caroline Cilek, *The Path to 2050: A Policy Pathway for Decarbonizing Oregon's Economy* (Salem, OR: Green Energy Institute, Lewis and Clark Law School, 2022), https://law.lclark.edu/live/files/33826-gei-oregon-decarbonizaton-pathway-analysis-2022.
31 Handy, "Why Sustainable Transport Cannot Ignore Land Use," 220–29.
32 Susan Handy, "California's Quest to Reduce Vehicle Miles Traveled," *TR News* 341 (September–October 2022): 14–16, https://www.trb.org/Publications/Blurbs/182869.aspx.
33 Oregon Department of Transportation Climate Office, Adaptation and Resilience Team, *Climate Adaptation and Resilience Roadmap* (Salem: Oregon Department of Transportation, 2022), www.oregon.gov/odot/climate/Documents/ClimateAdaptation_andResilienceRoadmap.pdf.

34 Todd Litman, *Parking Management: Strategies, Evaluation and Planning* (Victoria, BC: Victoria Transport Policy Institute, 2023), www.vtpi.org/park_man.pdf.
35 Donald Shoup, ed., *Parking and the City New York* (New York: Routledge, 2018), https://www.shoupdogg.com/reforms/; "What Is Parking Reform?," Parking Reform Network, accessed December 30, 2023, https://parkingreform.org/what-is-parking-reform.
36 Oregon Department of Transportation, *2021 Oregon Traffic Crash Summary* (Salem: Transportation Data Section Crash Analysis and Reporting Unit, ODOT, 2023), https://www.oregon.gov/odot/Data/Documents/Crash_Summary_2021.pdf.
37 "Behavioral Risk Factor Surveillance System," Centers for Disease Control and Prevention, accessed December 30, 2023, www.cdc.gov/brfss/.
38 "BRFSS Prevalence and Trends Data," Centers for Disease Control and Prevention, accessed April 14, 2022, https://www.cdc.gov/brfss/brfssprevalence/.
39 "Overweight or Obesity—Youth in Oregon," America's Health Rankings, accessed December 30, 2023, https://www.americashealthrankings.org/explore/health-of-women-and-children/measure/youth_overweight/state/OR.
40 "Safe Routes to Schools Program," Oregon Department of Transportation, accessed December 30, 2023, https://www.oregon.gov/ODOT/Programs/Pages/SRTS.aspx.
41 Metro, *2018 Regional Transportation Plan* (Portland, OR: Metro, 2018), https://www.oregonmetro.gov/regional-transportation-plan.
42 Metro, *Climate Smart Strategy* (Portland, OR: Metro, 2015), https://www.oregonmetro.gov/climate-smart-strategy.
43 Joe Cortright, "Metro's Failing Climate Strategy," City Commentary, December 30, 2021, https://cityobservatory.org/metros-failing-climate-strategy/.
44 "Statewide Policy Plans," Oregon Department of Transportation, accessed December 30, 2023, https://www.oregon.gov/ODOT/Planning/Pages/Plans.aspx.
45 Portland State University, *Ecolopolis 5.0: High Speed Rail in Cascadia* (Portland, OR: Portland State University, 2011), 5; https://pdxscholar.library.pdx.edu/usp_planning/5.
46 Washington State Department of Transportation, *Ultra High-Speed Ground Transportation Study* (Olympia: Washington State Department of Transportation, 2018), https://wsdot.wa.gov/publications/fulltext/LegReports/17-19/UltraHighSpeedGroundTransportation_FINAL.pdf.
47 Metro, *2018 Regional Transportation Plan*.
48 Daniel Sperling, *Three Revolutions: Steering Automated, Shared, and Electric Vehicles to a Better Future* (Washington, DC: Island Press, 2018).

PART III

Social Foundations

Part III covers topics not typically addressed in state planning processes, including in Oregon, where the main focus has been on physical planning issues. But truly comprehensive planning must consider how Oregonians are experiencing our state, and make changes if they are not thriving. Together, the chapters in this section discuss the current reality and foresight for Oregon in 2050 around four salient social issues, with cause for both optimism and concern. One common thread across each of these chapters, and the whole book, is that Oregonians often have different experiences and quality of life depending on demographic categories such as race/ethnicity, income level, and place of residence. Looking to 2050, we suggest that a broader embrace of these and other social aspects of planning will lead to a better Oregon, especially for those who are currently not thriving.

Oregon stands out among states in terms of the economic impacts of arts and culture organizations and in residents' participation in related activities; however, the arts community also faces economic challenges. In chapter 9, Richard A. Clucas offers five tangible recommendations to sustain arts and culture in Oregon, including establishing a centralized state agency, dedicating greater state funding, placing more emphasis on the arts in public schools, and ensuring fair and equitable access to the arts, both in demographic and geographic terms.

The story of employment, wages, and other economic factors is one of different Oregons. In chapter 10, Emma Brophy and Jenny H. Liu describe transitions in Oregon's economy. While Oregon is less unequal than the nation at large in terms of the gap between the highest and lowest wage-earners, the state faces striking and increasing discrepancies. The authors identify a range of possible interventions to address the gaps, including higher minimum wages, universal basic income, negative income tax, access programs, expanded social safety nets, and tax reforms.

In chapter 11, Jacen Green and Marisa A. Zapata discuss the visible and rising number of homeless residents across the state. They argue persuasively that homelessness can be solved, primarily through a housing first approach, accompanied by supportive services. The authors emphasize that without significant interventions in housing and related services, homelessness is likely to worsen.

Moriah McSharry McGrath and Melia Chase note in chapter 12 that Oregon's total jail population has increased 316 percent since 1970, with an accompanying rise in the number of prisons and people employed by the criminal justice system. At the same time, Oregon is poorly situated to meet the mental health needs of residents. The authors reflect on positive state initiatives and offer a set of recommendations to accelerate increased strategies of smart decarceration, criminal justice reinvestment, and behavioral health reinvestment.

9
Arts and Culture
RICHARD A. CLUCAS

The arts and culture scene in Oregon is filled with numerous bright spots but also a troubling underside. Take the arts in particular.

Portland has generated broad national attention in recent years for having a thriving arts community. Among the accolades it has received, the city has been identified as one of the most vibrant arts communities in the country, a leader in having the "ultimate creative economy," and the nation's next "art capital."[1] The arts are also thriving outside the city. Hood River has been ranked fourth in art vibrancy among smaller communities nationwide. Thanks to the Oregon Shakespeare Festival, Ashland has become recognized as one of the premiere incubators of new plays outside of New York City.[2] Bend's annual arts festival, Art in the High Desert, has gained national prominence, ranking among the top ten fine arts shows in the nation for three years in a row prior to the pandemic.[3]

The vibrancy of the state's arts community can be seen in data on economic impact and public engagement in the arts. The US Bureau of Economic Analysis (BEA) reported in 2017 that arts and cultural organizations contributed more than $8 billion to Oregon's economy, along with some 68,000 jobs.[4] The US Bureau of Labor Statistics (BLS) recently ranked Oregon among the top three states in the nation in the concentration of jobs in the arts and among the top four states for concentration of jobs for musicians and singers.[5] As for the public, the National Endowment for the Arts (NEA) has ranked Oregon among the top three states for public engagement in many different art forms, including attending live music performances and art exhibits.[6]

These accolades and statistics tell an important story about Oregon. The state's identity has long been wrapped up with environmental awareness, outdoor recreation, land use planning, and natural resources. It is the state that seized public ownership of coastal beaches, passed the nation's first bottle bill, established the most forward thinking land use rules in the nation, and battled over the spotted owl. While this identity has a powerful heritage, one that continues to resonate in the state, it is only part of the story. Oregon is also defined today by its vibrant arts community.

But the story is not all positive. Oregon's arts community may be visibly thriving, but it has also been teetering on the edge of a steep financial precipice, even before the coronavirus pandemic struck. Moreover, the state has devoted little attention to the arts to ensure it continues to thrive and that the arts are accessible to the public in an equitable way. This is unlike other central aspects of Oregon life in which the state has made a concerted effort to plan for a better future. Senate Bill 100, the foundation of the state's planning program, declared the need for comprehensive plans "to assure the highest possible level of livability in Oregon." But the state planning goals that emerged from this law make no mention of the arts and only passing reference to cultural concerns, while devoting an entire section to recreation.[7]

This chapter examines the position of arts in Oregon today and provides guidance on how to ensure that the arts enjoy a healthy future. It also intends to generate discussion on some of the central concerns surrounding the state's broader cultural policies. It is beyond the scope of this chapter to assess the state's entire cultural life, which includes everything from the humanities to libraries to revitalizing downtown business districts to social identities, different languages, and traditions. Even so, the state policies related to the arts are closely intertwined with the policies governing other aspects of the state's cultural life, especially in the structure of the state's cultural bureaucracy. Thus the chapter's focus on the arts is also designed to help start a conversation on the state's cultural policies generally.

Defining Terms

The first step in understanding how the arts and culture are faring in Oregon today, and in planning for a better future, is to explain the meaning of these terms and how they guide the research and recommendations in this chapter. Historically, when policymakers talked about "the arts," they tended to use a narrow meaning tied to a cultural elitist perspective. The term was used to refer to a few specific art disciplines (literature, visual arts, music, dance, theater, and architecture) and was routinely tied to "high culture." In other words, policymakers viewed the arts as a limited range of specific art forms considered superior for their aesthetic, philosophical, or intellectual value. This conceptualization of the arts had a strong Euro-centric patriarchal focus, treating traditional upper-class European arts as superior to those originating in other cultures or the general public. One of the initial goals of the NEA, for example, was to improve Americans by exposing them to what it considered high-quality art.[8]

In the 1960s, public policy about the arts began to change. One of the changes was a democratization in what policymakers considered the arts. Policymakers began to recognize the value of non-Western, feminist, and more populist art forms, including television and popular music. A second change that occurred in this period was a recognition that art policy was not just about the creation of art by professionals but also included efforts to engage the general public in creative activities.

Today, when policymakers talk about the arts, the term has a more inclusive meaning. It still incorporates the traditional arts, but it also includes crafts, folklore, film, video, graphic design, interior design, computer graphics, and much more. It includes the works produced by nonprofit organizations, for-profit entertainment industries, individual artists, professionals, and amateurs. It recognizes the importance of the arts in terms of producers, distributors, consumers, education, and even individuals who take arts-related classes for personal enrichment or their health. There is also a growing understanding that arts policies need to include bringing creative expression into people's daily activities.[9] This chapter treats the arts from this broad, inclusive perspective. Regarding arts policy and the future of the arts in Oregon, the chapter is concerned with how government's involvement can improve the state of the arts across these broad dimensions, not only in helping artists and art organizations, but also providing a place for the arts for all Oregonians.

The word "culture" also has multiple meanings. In some situations, it is used synonymously with the arts. Many universities, for example, offer courses on "cultural policy," which focus solely on the arts. Similarly, some nations have a ministry of culture that is responsible for promoting the arts.[10] Culture has also been used synonymously with the concept of "high art." In this sense, culture is viewed as the highest-quality art. Underlying this meaning of culture is the idea that some creative works are of higher order than others, and culture reflects the intellectual growth from primitive society into a civilized world.[11] Culture can also have an anthropological meaning, one that is rooted in a holistic perspective on communities. It refers to the beliefs, norms, traditions, religious practices, institutions, and languages associated with a particular group of people or society, which are transmitted from one generation to the next. In this definition, culture includes the arts, but it is much broader, also incorporating the humanities, heritage, and history.

This chapter uses this broader definition when discussing culture, recognizing these multiple dimensions. With this in mind, the chapter follows the perspective laid out by Mark Schuster, a leading cultural policy expert, in defining cultural policy. Schuster defines cultural policy as "all the ways that the state assists, supports, or even hinders the cultural life of its citizens . . . a state's cultural policy can be usefully thought of as the sum of its activities with respect to the arts (including the for-profit cultural industries), the humanities, and the heritage."[12]

While the chapter talks about the arts and culture using these broad definitions, the lack of data in the state, and time constraints on this project, mean that there are limits in what this chapter covers. The chapter focuses specifically on the arts part of culture because of how central the arts have become in the state, and because the arts provide a particularly good vehicle to begin talking about bigger issues in the state's cultural policies. Even though the primary focus is the arts, many of the issues surrounding the arts are so closely tied to broader cultural policies in the state that some of these broader policy concerns are also addressed.

Why Arts, Creativity, and Inclusion Matter

With the COVID-19 pandemic bringing despair across the globe, a severe economic downturn, and some of the worst fires in its history, a concern for arts and culture may seem of little relevance when planning for the future of the state. Yet arts and culture are so important in shaping the character of the state that, like other major economic and social concerns, they deserve attention from state leaders.

The arts are specifically considered to have both instrumental and intrinsic benefits to society.[13] Instrumental benefits refer to the ways in which the arts help society achieve social goals. These benefits include providing jobs, income, and other economic gains along with improving physical and mental health, boosting educational achievement, building communities, strengthening cultural identities, improving the livability of neighborhoods, stimulating political dialogue, and challenging social norms, including racist, sexist, and other forms of exclusion. Intrinsic benefits are the personal benefits derived by the individual from participation in or exposure to the arts, including in giving pleasure, improving the quality of life, encouraging critical thinking, learning from other perspectives, building self-awareness, and providing opportunities for self-expression, creativity, and imagination.

It is beyond the scope of this chapter to explain all the benefits derived from the arts, and culture more broadly, but there are some especially important benefits worth emphasizing.

- *Economic benefits.* The arts provide jobs directly to those who make art (dancers, musicians, actors, visual artists, graphic designers, etc.), support its production (venue workers and owners, supply stores, public relations firms, teachers), or benefit from the expenditures of local arts consumers and cultural tourists (hotels, restaurants, bars, transportation workers, parking garages). The money spent on the arts in creating these jobs has a ripple effect on the economy. As those who directly benefit from art-related jobs and businesses spend money in the community, the money flows into other businesses and creates other types of jobs.
- *Health benefits.* A 2019 comprehensive review by the World Health Organization of more than three thousand studies found that the arts, whether undertaken in daily routines or as part of organized programs, can play a major role in the "prevention of ill health, promotion of health, and management and treatment of illness across the lifespan."[14] The comprehensive review provides a litany of health benefits from participating in or experiencing the arts, including lower risks of cardiovascular disease, cancer, dementia, depression, diabetes, and premature mortality. Different types of arts have been found to improve respiratory conditions,

chronic pain, speech pathologies, behavioral problems, obesity, poor motor skills, and much more.[15] Numerous nonprofit and private organizations across the state recognize the health benefits that the arts provide and offer arts-related programs to help individuals who have disabilities, are in high-risk populations, or just want to maintain or improve their health. These include the Studio at Living Opportunities, a social service organization in Medford that opens artistic doors to adults with intellectual and developmental disabilities; the ArtsCare Program in Corvallis, which brings artists into local hospitals to add the arts into the healing process; and the Council on Aging in Bend, which provides Tai Chi and other movement classes to improve the quality of life for seniors, including helping protect against falls.

- *Educational benefits.* Studies on education have found that the arts improve student success across a variety of dimensions. A recent large-scale randomized study by the Brookings Institution found that arts education has "remarkable impacts on students' academic, social, and emotional outcomes."[16] Among other conclusions, the study found that students who received arts experiences had fewer disciplinary problems, greater interest in school, higher standardized writing scores, more compassion for others, and a better ability to think about things in new ways. One recent review by the Oregon Community Foundation of past research reported that arts education—including in dance, drama, music, and visual art—has been found to produce wide-ranging positive benefits that "stay with students throughout their lives."[17] These benefits include improved social skills; greater academic success; higher math, reading, and verbal scores; increased use of thinking strategies; and improved community engagement. Other studies have found a link to improved cognitive development, heightened imagination and creativity, and better problem-solving skills.[18]
- *Cultural Identities.* The arts also play an important role in affirming cultural identities, which provides important societal and individual benefits. For example, urban planners have become increasingly aware of the importance of emphasizing cultural identity and the arts in community development. By including artists at the center of development planning, creative placemaking provides

a means for which a community's heritage, visions, and values—
its identity—can be strengthened and communicated to others.
Creative placemaking thus provides a vehicle for empowering
segments of society that have been traditionally ignored in urban
development.[19] In turn, creative placemaking that incorporates
cultural identity can help build healthier, more equitable, and more
socially just communities.[20] The Asian Pacific American Network
of Oregon's (APANO) creative placemaking program provides a
good example. The organization has been providing placemaking
grants since 2015 to help build cultural identity and encourage
more socially just development, including providing funds for the
heavily praised Jade District in southeastern Portland.[21] The arts
also play a significant role in building cultural identity affirmation
in the classroom. Introducing students to the traditions, language,
and artistic heritage of their own cultural communities helps to
affirm the cultures of nonwhite students, which in turn helps to
create a better learning environment. Studies have found that
affirming cultural identity in the classroom builds trust, improves
student engagement, and leads to better academic and social outcomes.[22] These studies, as well as those in creative placemaking,
make it clear why inclusive arts policies matter.
- *Intrinsic benefits.* Finally, the arts have intrinsic personal benefits
that should not be dismissed in policy considerations. The arts
can captivate the mind, providing those who experience the arts
with new and different perspectives about the world and their own
lives. They can challenge deep-seated feelings and beliefs. The arts
can bring joy, pleasure, and an appreciation of beauty, but they
can also provide a sense of the profound challenges and dark side
of life. They can help expand feelings of empathy and understanding of others. For those who make art, their work can provide an
intense imaginative experience. The production of art can also give
a sense of accomplishment and a deep sense of satisfaction, while
also helping self-understanding.

Arts and Culture Policy

Many Oregon leaders have long recognized the benefits that arts and
culture provide, and at times the state has taken innovative steps to

help bolster both, but arts and culture have generally been a secondary concern, at best, to state policymakers. The policy steps that have been taken tend to be piecemeal and incomplete, leaving the state without a cohesive plan in helping the arts or the state's cultural life.

The state of Oregon did little to promote the arts until the mid-1960s, when Congress enacted the National Foundation on the Arts and Humanities Act of 1965, creating both the National Endowment for the Arts and National Endowment for the Humanities. Included within the act was an incentive program to encourage states to create their own arts agencies. The act offered $25,000 to help states cover the costs for conducting a study of their cultural needs and establishing an official state arts agency.

In response to this incentive, Oregon governor Mark Hatfield appointed a planning council to survey the state of the arts in Oregon and to prepare a plan for creating a state arts agency. Through these efforts, the Oregon Legislature approved Senate Bill 145 in 1967, creating the Oregon Arts Commission (OAC), the state's official arts agency. The legislature did not bother, however, to allocate any funds for the commission; the *Oregonian* wrote at the time that the arts only "got half a loaf."[23] It was not until 1973 that state money was allocated to the program. In the meantime, the commission relied on private contributions to function, among just a few state arts commissions that went without public funding.[24]

At the time of its creation, the OAC was as an independent state agency. But the commission was reorganized in 1993 and made a part of the Oregon Economic and Community Development Department, which is known today as Business Oregon. At the same time, two staff positions within the commission were eliminated.[25]

While the creation of the OAC was a positive step, the state continued to play only a minor role in supporting the arts. At the end of the twentieth century, state funding for the commission was the fourth lowest of any state arts agency in the nation, with the legislature providing only forty-one cents per capita. The arts were not alone in being underfunded. The state did not provide any money for a statewide humanities council, only one of fourteen states in the nation not to do so.[26]

After a newspaper report came out drawing attention to the state's poor record in supporting the arts, Governor John Kitzhaber called an

Arts and Culture Summit in 1998, which brought together some 350 people to develop a long-range agenda for arts and culture in Oregon. The summit led the governor and legislature to appoint a Joint Interim Task Force to develop a plan for the development of Oregon's culture.

The task force in turn led to the creation of the Oregon Cultural Trust (OCT) in 2001, establishing a central agency to work with cultural organizations across the state, including counties, tribal governments, local arts agencies, and five statewide partners (OAC, Oregon Humanities, Oregon Heritage Commission, Oregon Historical Society, and the State Historic Preservation Office).[27] In addition, the act created a cultural tax credit, a program that allows residents to receive a tax credit for a donation to the OCT when they donate a matching amount to a nonprofit organization. As of 2018, the tax credit was raising between $4 to $5 million per year for the trust, 60 percent of which has then been redirected to cultural nonprofits.[28] Of additional importance, the tax credit offered an incentive to encourage donations to nonprofit organizations.

The OCT was highly praised when it was created as a model for supporting arts and culture at the state level and for providing some stability in cultural funding.[29] Despite this initial praise, many involved in the cultural community do not believe the trust has lived up to what was originally envisioned. One of the biggest challenges confronting the trust has been funding levels that are well below what was originally proposed. When the legislature created OCT, there was an expectation that it would have an endowment of more than $200 million to support the arts, humanities, and cultural heritage. As of 2021, the corpus for the endowment fund was just $29 million.[30]

Another criticism has been of the disjointed structure of the state's cultural bureaucracy. While the trust was created to provide centralized direction, the state's various cultural agencies remain largely independent from each other and buried within other agencies that are unrelated to culture. In 2003, the legislature moved the operations of the OCT in with the OAC, with both housed within Business Oregon. The Trust and the Arts Commission remain separate subagencies, with their own independent governing boards, but they share resources and the same executive director. The joint executive director answers to Business Oregon, which has its own separate board.

The state's other major cultural organizations are independent nonprofit agencies or are housed elsewhere. The Oregon Council for the Humanities (Oregon Humanities), created in 1971, and the Oregon Historical Society, created in 1898, are both nonprofit organizations. The Oregon Heritage Commission and the Historic Preservation Office are based in the Oregon Parks and Recreation Department.

There are a few other public or nonprofit agencies that are involved in the state's cultural life. The Oregon Office of Film and Video is located in the governor's office. The nonprofit Oregon Public Broadcasting has roots dating back to 1923 as a radio station associated with Oregon State University; it separated from the state university system and became a nonprofit in 1981.[31] In 1995, the state created the Oregon Tourism Commission (Travel Oregon), which includes promoting cultural tourism among its duties.

Because of this disjointed structure, the OCT is limited in its ability to guide the cultural agencies with a shared vision or to address major issues that cut across the state's cultural life, including issues surrounding diversity and inclusion. The lack of funding and the poorly designed bureaucratic structures mean that the state's cultural life, including that surrounding the arts, remains underfunded and poorly guided.

Given this history, it would be incorrect to say that state leaders have been entirely inattentive to arts and culture, though these issues have clearly been of a lesser concern. The one governor who stands out for his support for promoting arts and culture is Ted Kulongoski (2003-11), who pushed for stronger state financial investment in culture and the creative economy through a 2007 program titled CHAMP (for Cultural, Heritage, Arts, Movies, Historic Preservation and Public Broadcasting). The program led to almost an $18 million increase in public funding for the arts and to Kulongoski receiving an arts leadership award from Americans for the Arts. In addition, Kulongoski is the only governor to have appointed a policy adviser specifically for arts and culture. [32]

Moreover, state policy has focused primarily on providing financial support for nonprofit arts and culture organizations. Much less legislative attention has been targeted toward helping private arts businesses or addressing the myriad other problems confronting the arts community today, including declining audiences, disappearing rehearsal/studio spaces, inequities in opportunities, and limited access in the schools.

Arts in Oregon

Even if state leaders have not made the arts a priority, the arts have done exceedingly well in Oregon. The importance of the arts can be seen by looking at their impact on the state's economy and in the vast number of Oregonians who engage in them. By looking at this impact, it becomes clear that the arts have become a significant part of the state's economy and a defining character of the state's culture.

Numerous studies have found that the arts strongly benefit Oregon's economy. A 2017 study by the BEA found that a large portion of the economic impact from arts and culture comes from supporting industries, such as publishing and broadcasting, which are involved in the production and distribution of the arts, rather than in its creation.[33] But the "core arts and culture industries," which include architecture, performing arts, writers, and independent artists, also have a significant impact.

Drawing on the BEA's data, the National Assembly of State Arts Agencies (NASAA) ranked arts and culture combined as having the third-greatest impact on the state's economy among comparison groups when looking at employment, compensation, and value added (table 9.1), surpassing some economic sectors that have historically been associated with the state.

Table 9.1. Comparing Arts and Culture to Other Sectors of the Economy, 2017

Sector	Employment	Compensation (in millions)	Value Added (in millions)
Retail	211,871	$7,954	$11,546
Construction	99,567	$6,970	$9,989
Arts and Culture	67,958	$4,370	$8,111
Transportation	58,884	$3,693	$6,551
Agriculture and Forestry	44,805	$1,630	$3,702
Utilities	22,416	$1,108	$3,037
Education Services	4,666	$661	$2,077
Mining	1,830	$138	$281

Source: National Assembly of State Arts Agencies, *State Profiles: Comparing Arts and Culture to Other Sectors of the Economy, 2017* (Washington, DC: National Assembly of State Arts Agencies, 2017).

A study that same year by Americans for the Arts (AFTA) on the nonprofit segment of the arts and culture community in Oregon found that it generated $687 million in total economic activity. This included $364 million spent directly by nonprofit arts and cultural organizations and $323 million in spending by their audiences. The report concluded that the arts and cultural industries supported 22,299 full-time jobs and generated some $53 million in local and state government revenue.[34]

In 2017, the BLS produced a location quotient that identified Oregon as having the fourth-highest relative concentration of artists and related workers jobs in comparison with the rest of the nation.[35] The following year, a BLS report identified Oregon as having the fourth-highest concentration of musicians and singers jobs.[36] Job concentration refers to the relative number of people employed in these occupations in the state compared with the relative number employed in them nationwide.

The Portland metropolitan area is one of the major drivers of these employment figures. The 2017 BLS study identified the region as having the ninth-highest total level of employment in the arts of any metropolitan area in the nation. The 2018 study found Portland had the sixth-highest number of musicians and singers. In general, Portland was only surpassed in these areas by the nation's mega-metropolitan areas, or in the case of music, by Nashville.

But arts employment is important beyond Portland. The 2018 BLS study identified both Albany and Eugene as being among the top four metropolitan areas in the concentration of jobs for musicians and singers. It also identified coastal Oregon as having the second-highest number of jobs in this occupational category for any nonmetropolitan area in the nation. Additionally, a 2017 Bureau of Economic Analysis study found that Hood River (5.3 percent) has by far the largest percentage of arts and culture related employment in the state, surpassing Deschutes (3.2 percent), Multnomah (3.2 percent), and Jackson (3.0 percent).[37] One revealing part of the BEA study is that while it showed that urban counties tend to have more arts and culture workers than rural counties, many rural residents are in arts-related occupations.

Another way to measure the economic impact of arts is to count the number of organizations and business involved in the arts. One challenge, though, is there is no map of all the creative places and industries that exist in Oregon. There are some pieces of data that shed light on the wealth of arts entities in the state, however. A 2017 US Census Bureau report identified more than 41,000 establishments across the state involved in the creation of arts, 13,500 involved in the production and distribution of cultural productions, and another 3,100 involved in support industries.[38] OCT has identified 1,555 cultural nonprofits statewide, including 785 in arts and literature. Art-Collecting.com, a private business targeted to art collectors and enthusiasts, lists 114 art galleries in the state and another 48 sites that are associated with the sharing of arts. The Independent Venue Coalition, an arts lobbying organization, reports that performing arts and music spaces put on more than 13,000 events a year, attract 7 million attendees, provide more than 4,000 jobs, and contribute $384 million to the economy. MusicPortland, another lobbying group, has identified 300 venues in the Portland metropolitan area that regularly host live music, which is more than Austin's tourism bureau identifies in its city.[39]

The arts are also central to the state's tourism industry. From the end of the 2007-9 recession until the coronavirus pandemic, the tourism industry was growing strongly, producing almost $13 billion in direct travel spending in 2019 and providing economy benefits to all thirty-six counties in Oregon.[40] In 2016, Americans for the Arts conducted an audience intercept survey of attendees at different arts and cultural events. More than 68 percent of the visitors to the state said that the primary purpose of their visit was "specifically to attend this arts/cultural event."[41] As the report concluded, arts and culture are an important driver in the state's tourism industry, as they are to the economy generally.

Arts Participation

The relevance of the arts to Oregon can be seen not only in its economic impact, but also in the devotion that Oregonians have toward the arts. The National Endowment for the Arts has conducted seven national surveys on adult engagement in the arts since 1982. In the most recent survey in 2017, the NEA ranked Oregon among the top states in several different categories of arts engagement.[42]

- Attending an art exhibit (top three)
- Attending a live music performance (top three)

- Attending a live arts event in a park or outdoor facility (top two)
- Attending a live performing arts event (top six)
- Reading literature (top three)
- Using electronic media to consume art or arts programming (top two)
- Using electronic media to watch or listen to classical music and opera (top two)
- Creative writing (top two)
- Creating visual art (top two)
- Playing an instrument (top seven)
- Creating or performing art (top seven)

The study also found the state's participation rate in the arts was considerably higher than the national average. Put simply, the data show that Oregonians love the arts.

Yet these numbers barely reveal the extent to which creative activities touch people's everyday lives. The numbers say a bit about the health of arts organizations and individual creativity, but they omit a broad swath of artistic activities, many of which are not always recognized as art. These include such activities as children's chalk drawings and clapping games, adult dance exercise classes, community choirs, knitting, scrapbooking, and model-building. In addition, they exclude the culinary arts, which has also brought Oregon national attention. The arts permeate all parts of Oregon life.

Health of the Arts Community

While the arts are an important part of the state's economy and a defining characteristic of the state's culture, a less positive story emerges in looking at the financial health of arts organizations and the government's support of these organizations.

The US Internal Revenue Service provides public access to the tax returns of nonprofit organizations, providing a means to assess the financial health of Oregon arts organizations. Table 9.2 provides a breakdown of the 2017 tax forms filed for all the nonprofit arts organizations identified by OCT, except for the few that filed either a 990-PF (private foundation) or 990-T (exempt organization business) form. Identified are three types of filings. Nonprofit organizations that have annual gross receipts of less than $50,000 can file a 990-N using the Electronic Filing System (e-Postcard). The 990-N form does not provide any detailed information about the financial status of an organization, except whether it made less than $50,000 in the tax year. Nonprofits can file a 990-EZ if they have gross receipts of less than $200,000 and total assets of less than $500,000 at the end of their tax year. Organizations that have higher gross receipts or greater total assets file a 990 form.

The most striking figure in table 9.2 is the large number of nonprofit organizations that either did not file a tax return in 2017 or filed a 990-N form. Combined, more than 50 percent of the arts organizations fall into those categories. In other words, despite the large number of arts organizations in the state, most are small, with limited resources to create art and pay salaries. In addition, almost 19 percent filed 990-EZ forms, meaning they are not particularly better off.

Table 9.3 gives an analysis of the revenue, profit/loss, and net assets for those organizations that filed either a 990 or 990-EZ form. A majority of the arts organizations made a profit in 2017 and ended the fiscal year in the black, though the profits did not have much cushion. The median profit was just $8,473. While most of the organizations made a profit, 116 arts organizations lost money. In addition, most arts organizations did not end the year with particularly robust reserve assets. Given that median revenue for these groups was $193,108 and that most made little profit in the year, the amount of net assets provides little protection for financial emergencies.

Table 9.2. Types of Returns Filed by Arts Organizations, 2017

Type	Number (Percentage)
None	159 (21.1)
990N	242 (32.2)
990Z	142 (18.9)
990	209 (27.8)
Total	752 (100)

Source: Compiled by author from IRS records.

Table 9.3. Revenue, Profit/Loss, and Net Assets for Arts Organizations Filing 990 or 990-EZ Forms

Description	Value
Number	351
Revenue (median)	$193,108
Profit/loss (median)	$8,473
With operating loss	116 (33%)
Net assets (median)	$169,447

Source: Compiled by the author from IRS 990 and 990-EZ tax forms.

Combined, these tables provide a story about arts organizations in Oregon that is not a bright one. While there are some healthy arts organizations in the state, a large percentage of these nonprofit groups live on the edge, relying on a limited amount of revenue and maintaining backup reserves that provide little protection for their long-term survival. It is especially important to note that these figures are from 2017, when the economy was strong, prior to the upheaval in the arts community caused by the coronavirus pandemic. During the pandemic, almost all arts organizations in the state had to cancel events. The lost revenue devastated many organizations, leading some to the brink of collapse, including the Oregon Shakespeare Festival and Art in the High Desert arts festival. Federal and state funds helped artists and arts organizations survive, but attendance at arts events had still not fully rebounded by the end of 2023, while the spigot of government funds had been turned off. These new threats have compounded the preexisting challenges to arts organizations.[43]

The story about government support is similarly bleak. Oregon provides less direct support than most states in funding the arts. According to NASAA, the state legislature in 2017 appropriated $2.1 million to the OAC, the state agency responsible for channeling public funds to art organizations, artists, and local art agencies.[44] While this may seem sizeable, it represented just $0.51 per capita, placing the state among the bottom third in direct public funding. In comparison, total appropriations by state governments nationwide were $1.05 per capita, more than twice Oregon's support.

In addition to this direct support, arts and cultural nonprofits are considered to benefit from the tax incentive created by the cultural tax credit.[45] But these benefits have been limited. As mentioned above, the tax credit has been raising between $4 to $5 million per year for the trust, 60 percent of which has then been redirected to cultural nonprofits.[46] The tax incentive does not appear to generate additional donations to these organizations above the level of giving found in other states, however. Oregon Community Foundation found that Oregonians donated to nonprofit organizations at a lower rate than Americans overall in 2016 and 2017, and that 6.8 percent of total contributions in 2017 went to the arts.[47] This percent directed to the arts is consistent with giving nationally. For example, GivingUSA found that 6.8 percent of private charitable donations nationwide in 2017 went to arts, culture, and humanities.[48] Combined, these numbers indicate that the credit is not a particularly effective incentive. While it does provide a much-needed stable source of funding for the Oregon Cultural Trust, the donations it produces do not compensate for the state's lower level of direct public support, nor has it helped the trust come close to attaining the $200 million endowment originally envisioned.

Access and Equity

Beyond their economic benefits, the arts play a critical role in bringing people together, creating a sense of cultural identity, building communities, and sharing perspectives on life and social issues. Given the central role that the arts play in cultural identity, it is especially important to consider the question of equity in access to the arts.

The challenge in assessing equity in arts organizations is there are little data available to provide a clear answer. There is no comprehensive database that identifies all arts organizations that provide opportunities and experiences to racial and ethnic minorities, different genders, people with disabilities, and other traditionally underserved communities. Nor is there one that provides information on the demographics of arts leaders, nonprofit organization boards, staff, artists themselves, or to art at home.

The OCT database on nonprofit organizations does not identify what arts organizations serve under-represented communities. Nor is there a list that provides this information for the for-profit arts-related businesses.

Whether or not access to arts organizations is being provided equitably to all, there are many notable nonprofit organizations that serve traditionally underrepresented communities, giving the individuals within these communities an opportunity to come together, have a voice, and either create or experience art. The Milagro Theater rightly bills itself as "the premier Latino arts and culture center of the Pacific Northwest." Since its founding in 1985, the southeast Portland nonprofit has provided a platform for Latino playwrights and performers through its English, Spanish, and bilingual plays. The theater has been praised for uniting the Latino artistic community in Portland, while also helping to teach the community about the diversity of Latino culture.

The theater has an education program that reaches into the schools across the Northwest, offering plays and theater workshops that introduce students to Latino culture and encourage community building. The workshops provide an opportunity for students to explore major social and cultural issues, including ones dealing with inclusion and tolerance.[49]

The Rejoice! Diaspora Dance Theater is a predominantly Black contemporary dance company that provides a creative platform for people of color while using dance as a means for political activism. Created by Oluyinka Akinjiola, a former community organizer, Rejoice! offers performances on themes of social justice using dance forms from Africa, the Black diaspora (such as Afro-Brazilian, Afro-Cuban, and capoeira), and western modern choreographers. One of the company's recent productions (*Phenomenally*) offered a tribute to the poet Maya Angelou, a second (*Been Ready*) offered five personal stories that confront racial and gender bias in society, and a third (*To Protect*) addressed race, police brutality, and hate crimes—a concern at the very heart of American politics today.[50]

Nestled among the rolling foothills of the Blue Mountains on the Confederated Tribes of the Umatilla Indian Reservation, the Crow's Shadow Institute of the Arts has received nationwide recognition for its contributions to developing and promoting Native American artists. The nonprofit organization was founded in 1992 by James Lavadour, one of Oregon's premier visual artists and a member of the Walla Walla Tribe.[51] Crow's Shadow offers a residency program and workshops that are designed to help emerging and established Native American artists in both contemporary and traditional art. The institute also sponsors youth and community programs. Its facilities include a world-class printmaking studio, a computer graphics lab, and a print gallery. But its contribution goes beyond the arts; it provides a valuable support structure for promoting Native American culture, developing economic opportunities for Native Americans, and building cross-cultural understanding.[52]

The PHAME Academy is a nonprofit school for the performing and visual arts in northeast Portland, founded in 1984 to provide performance opportunities in singing, dancing, and acting for adults with intellectual and developmental disabilities. Its programs are designed to empower individuals with disabilities, providing a door to "full, creative lives."[53] But the academy does more than just empower the more than one hundred students enrolled; it also helps build identity and a voice for the disabilities community. When PHAME put on the student-written and -produced rock musical *The Poet's Shadow* in 2019, the show's musical director, Matthew Gailey, talked about the value of the production in helping build self-identity and cultural awareness. Gailey told one reporter that the musical gave a historically ostracized part of the population an opportunity to come together and "form a community and their own culture." By collectively doing art, he said, the project gave "that culture a voice to allow that cultural expression to be seen and heard in our community."[54]

There has been growing recognition of the need for greater equity and inclusiveness in providing public funds to cultural organizations. The extent to which OCT, OAC, and other state agencies are distributing resources in an equitable and inclusive manner is beyond the scope of this report. It is in the mission of many of these groups to help underserved communities, however. OCT, for example, includes the nine federally recognized tribes in Oregon within its cultural coalition, ensuring that tribes receive grant money from the trust. OAC expressly identifies the need for "equity and inclusion in the arts" in its vision statement, while Oregon Humanities include equity, difference, and respect within its core values.

While a full analysis of public funding is beyond this report, OAC's annual funding report to the NEA provides a beginning point of what to examine. The NEA requires these annual reports to identify arts organizations that specifically serve traditionally underserved communities. In total, the commission distributed almost $1.6 million through six of its seven grant programs to arts organizations across the state.[55] Of this, more than 17 percent of the funds were specifically directed to organizations that benefit people of color, individuals with disabilities, or other traditionally underserved communities, such as individuals living below the poverty line and youths at risk. For an organization to be categorized as serving a distinct group such as these, the NEA rules require that the organization's final report to the OAC indicate that more than 25 percent of its beneficiaries is identified in that demographic group. Other organizations arts organizations in the state undoubtedly benefit underserved communities but do not meet the NEA's specific threshold.

The final aspect of equity to consider is the availability of arts-related classes in public schools. Oregon's Department of Education has established arts standards for students from elementary to high school. These standards come within five disciplines (dance, media, music, theater, and visual arts). While the state standards recognize the importance of the arts in education, the questions that need to be considered are whether students have access to arts education, and if so, whether it is being done in an equitable way.

Figure 9.1 shows the percentage of elementary, middle, and high schools that provide classes in those five disciplines, as well as for multidisciplinary courses. The figure indicates that most schools across the state provide some arts education, though it is less common overall at the elementary school level, while high schools provide the most diversity in courses. The discipline most frequently taught is music. In elementary schools, arts education is generally equated with music. Middle and high schools also frequently provide music courses. A majority of high schools also provide courses in media arts, theater, and visual arts. Many middle schools also offer these courses, but to a lesser extent. The traditional art that is offered the least is dance. A serious roadblock in providing more diverse arts education is that the state only provides arts-related elementary education certificates in music and visual arts.

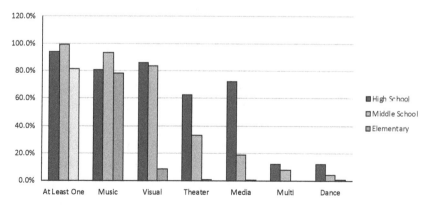

Figure 9.1. Percentage of elementary, middle, and high schools that provide arts education, 2017-18. *Source*: Compiled by the author from Oregon Department of Education arts course datafile.

Figure 9.2A shows the availability of arts education by comparing predominantly white schools (more than 50 percent white) with non-white schools, and figure 9.2B shows non-Title 1 schools with Title 1 schools to determine whether there are disparities in what is offered depending on a school's race and economic levels. To be covered under Title 1, 40 percent of a school's student body must be low income. Overall, these figure do not show a substantial difference among these categories. The biggest disparity is at the elementary school level, where the predominantly white schools have less access to the arts. At the high

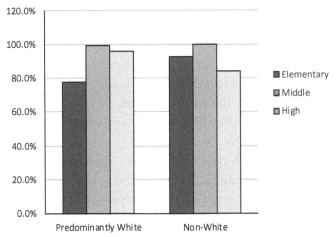

Figure 9.2A. Access to arts education by race by school level, 2017-18.

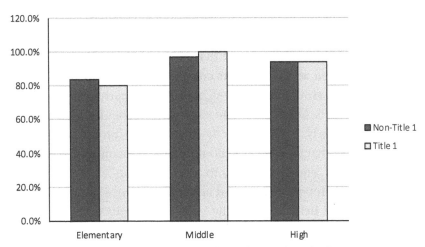

Figure 9.2B. Disparities in course offerings at Title 1 and non-Title 1 schools.

school level, there is a reverse to that, with the predominantly white schools having greater access.

Beyond race and economics, it is important to consider regional disparities in access to arts education. Comparing urban and rural schools, one finds that the availability of arts class is generally comparable at the middle and high school levels, though urban elementary schools tend to offer the arts more than their rural counterparts. These findings suggest that access to arts education is widespread and fairly equitable. But the numbers barely touch the surface in evaluating access to arts education. They only provide a head count as to whether the schools are offering arts-related courses. They do not reveal how many students are accessing these courses. Nor do they say anything about the diversity and number of courses being offered at different schools, and there are differences. For example, the non-Title 1 and the urban schools tend to offer a wider selection of classes than Title 1 and rural schools. The disparity is the most apparent in theater production. Some 71 percent of the urban high schools and 66 percent of the non-Title 1 schools offer theater courses, whereas only 50 percent of the rural and 29 percent of the Title 1 schools do. Similarly, the offering of dance classes is almost nonexistent in rural schools, with only four schools in total offering dance. This is not surprising given that the state does not offer a teaching credential for dance at the elementary or secondary level. Lastly, the figures above reveal nothing about the exposure students receive to non-Euro-centric art forms. Thus they reveal nothing about the inclusiveness of the curriculum.

These conclusions are consistent with past studies. A 2011-12 report conducted by OAC found that 77 percent of all schools across the state provided at least one arts course, though access varied widely by region. More troubling, the OAC found that nearly 65,000 students attending public schools had no access to arts classes by a licensed arts teacher.[56] Similarly, a 2019 study by the Oregon Community Foundation concluded that most K–12 schools offer at least one arts course, but that there is not "equitable access to arts education" across the state.[57] The foundation report also looked at the importance of nonprofit arts organizations in helping to fill the void in arts education. While the contribution of nonprofits is substantial, reaching into every county, these organizations themselves face funding challenges, making it difficult for them to fill the void.

Looking to 2050

This chapter has described the importance of arts in Oregon, the history of arts policy in the state, and the health of the arts community. What are the key takeaways from this information? And what lessons can be drawn from it in planning for Oregon in 2050?

There are five main takeaways:

1. The arts are thriving in Oregon, or at least they were before the coronavirus pandemic. Portland and other communities across the state have been recognized nationwide for the vitality of their arts communities. Employment in the arts is among the highest in the nation, as is the public's engagement. Arts organizations and establishments are flourishing across the state, not just in Portland. Most public school students have some exposure to arts education.
2. The arts, along with other cultural organizations, are a significant contributor to the economy, pumping billions of dollars into the community and creating jobs across the state. The economic benefits are not limited to arts organizations themselves. Businesses that support the arts industry and those that cater to arts consumers also benefit, including in cultural tourism.
3. Arts organizations provide many opportunities for underserved communities to be involved in the arts. Milagro Theatre, Rejoice!, Crow's Shadow, and PHAME are just a few of the distinguished organizations that provide opportunities for different cultural groups, people with disabilities, seniors, at-risk youths, and other traditionally underserved communities to create or engage in the arts.
4. While the state has many arts organizations, most of them have limited revenue and maintain little reserves to protect against crises. The state's cultural tax credit has been praised for helping "to insulate arts and culture funding in Oregon against . . . uncertain future trends," yet art organizations in the state are not well insulated. As for financial support, Oregon provides far less money to the arts than most states, and Oregon residents provide less in

charitable giving than Americans generally. It is important to keep in mind that the financial challenges confronting arts organization shown in this chapter were from 2017, when the economy was strong. With the spread of the coronavirus pandemic and the recession it triggered, the position of art organizations and artists is worse than reported in this study.[58] These organizations and artists received some protection during the heart of the pandemic thanks to the inflow of federal COVID relief funds, but the federal money provided only a stopgap measure to the problem.[59] Financial challenges are undoubtedly the most wicked problem confronting art organizations and artists, but there are others as well, including declining audiences, the disappearance of rehearsal/studio space in urban areas, inequities in opportunities, and a deemphasis in schools and universities.

5. Much is not known about the arts in Oregon, as well as cultural life generally. While the OCT has a listing of cultural organizations across the state, and the US Census Bureau provides some data on cultural establishments, there is no comprehensive inventory of all the arts organizations and businesses in the state, one that considers not only nonprofits but also creative spaces, performing arts venues, galleries, art suppliers, movie theaters, music groups, and others that create art, provide support for artists, or help make art available to the public. Data are also limited on how Oregonians engage in creative activities on a day-to-day basis. As a result, the figures in this study far underestimate the importance of arts and culture to the state. In addition, while many outstanding organizations provide benefits to the underserved communities, the lack of data makes it impossible to assess whether access to these organizations and to public funding is equitable. It may be that more data have been collected and analyzed, but there is certainly no central clearinghouse sharing this information, despite how important arts are within the state.

Given these takeaways, what can be done to build a healthy arts future, one that provides greater protection to artists and art organizations, ensures equitable access to all groups and across the state, and enhances creative opportunities for all Oregonians? Here are five essential steps that should be taken:

1. Make the arts (and culture) a more explicit and meaningful part of the state's planning concerns. The state's planning goals recognize recreation, economic development, public facilities, transportation, and other factors that are critical for reaching SB 100's goal of having "the highest possible level of livability in Oregon." Yet by leaving out the arts in its planning concerns, the state is ignoring a central component of livability.
2. Restructure the state's cultural bureaucracy. Under the current disjointed organization, the cultural bureaucracy lacks the cohesion and resources needed to ensure a healthy arts future. The OCT was created to provide such cohesion, but it cannot do so buried in an agency (Business Oregon) that is not focused on culture while the other segments of the cultural bureaucracy are housed elsewhere. The siloed nature of cultural agencies encourages division, competition, myopia, and unhealthy tension. As a single merged agency, the different cultural agencies would be in a better position to work together, while the OCT could then play the role for which it was created—helping to provide vision and support across the state's cultural life, including to the arts. For this agency to be effective, the agency's director needs to answer directly to the governor so that cultural concerns reach the state's leading policy actors. A centralized agency that answers to the governor would then be in a better position to work cooperatively and effectively with all the groups that are involved in arts (and culture generally), including nonprofit organizations, the private sector, foundations, corporate supporters, local governments, county arts agencies, public schools, and higher education. It would also be in a better position to assess the health of cultural life in Oregon, to address the needs of the public, and to advocate for arts and culture communities.
3. Provide adequate funding for the arts and culture. With many of the state's artists and arts organizations living on the edge, Oregon needs to provide protections to ensure their survival. At minimum, this means that policymakers should take steps to ensure

that the OCT is provided the $200 million endowment that was originally envisioned. Yet the financial support needs to go beyond just helping artists and art organizations. If the state creates an independent cultural agency, it needs to provide the infrastructure to ensure that the agency can survive. This means providing adequate staff support, including in accounting, clerical, information technology, and development. There should also be funds for research. One of the challenges in this chapter was finding data to assess the state of the arts in Oregon. In many areas, data are not available. Moreover, this chapter focused solely on one segment of cultural life—the arts community. If the state is to ensure a healthy future for Oregon's cultural life, similar studies need to be done on other aspects of culture. Research requires financial support. Lastly, many arts organizations and local communities are lacking in facilities to produce and perform their art. Support for capital projects is needed.

4. Emphasize arts in the schools. Countless studies have found a positive relationship between arts education and student success. This recognition has led many policy leaders to call for the arts to be added to curricular requirements. Moreover, K–12 education provides the foundation for later engagement in the arts. Thus arts education is essential to the future health of the arts community. The state needs to include an arts education mandate with resources at the K–12 level, and it needs to expand the types of education certificates available so that dance and theater can become accepted parts of the curriculum.

This greater emphasis on the arts needs to be brought into higher education as well. In many communities across the country, colleges and universities serve as a central hub in bringing the arts together. In Oregon, the arts have suffered in higher education. In the past few years, the state has seen the closing of two colleges that strongly supported the arts, Marylhurst University and Oregon College of Art and Craft. At the same time, the University of Oregon shut down its White Box art gallery, while Lewis and Clark College turned its Hoffman Gallery over entirely to student work.[60] Portland State University has made an attempt to expand its engagement in the arts in recent year by opening the Jordan

Schnitzer Museum of Art in 2019, getting legislative approval in 2021 for a new building that will bring the university's art and design programs together under one roof, and putting forward a bid to build a major performing arts venue to replace Portland's aging Keller Auditorium. Yet the university has in other ways given little attention to the arts. The university's decision to eliminate its dance department in the 1990s still reverberates, setting the dance community back for several years and making many in the local arts community skeptical about the university's commitment to the arts. More recently, Portland State University's Theatre Arts Program was targeted for potential dismantlement as part of the university's Program Review and Reduction Process.[61] For a university with a motto of "Let Knowledge Serve the City," and a metropolitan area in which the creative industries are central to its economy, the university could be doing much more to help build and support the arts community beyond these recent steps. Such support would not only bolster these industries but also help revitalize downtown Portland, while ensuring the continued vitality of the arts in the region.

5. Ensure fair and equitable access to the arts, both in demographic and geographic terms. There are so many different instrumental and intrinsic benefits associated with the arts, it is essential that they are accessible equally to all Oregonians. The best way to ensure that the arts are accessible to all is by following through with the four preceding recommendations. Including the arts in the state's planning efforts will better ensure that the arts are being made accessible in a fair manner. By creating a more organized cultural bureaucracy, it will enable the Oregon Cultural Trust to take a broader view of the cultural landscape and to address major policy concerns, including inequities across the state's cultural life. By providing adequate funding, it will help build an inclusive and healthy future for artists and arts organizations. Moreover, providing adequate funding will enable OCT to conduct more detailed studies on access to arts and culture, which will in turn allow it to identify and address areas in which there is inequity. Finally, by emphasizing education more strongly in the schools, requiring an arts education mandate, and using a curriculum that provides for

cultural identity affirmation, it will lead to a more just education system, one in which students across the state are assured of the benefits that come from arts education.

Combined, these five recommendations will help ensure that Oregon is arts healthy in 2050. As a defining characteristic of the state in recent decades, the arts help to build its reputation nationwide, provide jobs locally, and make the state especially livable. To ensure that the arts retain their importance in 2050, policymakers need to include the arts on the state's policy agenda and treat them in the same positive, visionary way they have long approached other vital aspects of Oregon life. These five recommendations are important steps for doing that.

Notes

1 Zannie Giraud Voss and Glenn Voss, "The Top 40 Most Vibrant Arts Communities in America (2018)," SMU DataArts, July 2, 2018, https://dataarts.smu.edu/artsresearch2014/arts-vibrancy-2018; Richard Florida, "One Reason It's So Hard to Become a 'CreativeSuperstar City,'" Bloomberg CityLab, May 28, 2015, https://www.bloomberg.com/news/articles/2015-05-28/one-reason-it-s-so-hard-to-become-a-creative-superstar-city; Peter Plagens, "Our Next Art Capital: Portland?," *Wall Street Journal*, May 2, 2012; Jessica Dawdy, "The Best US Cities for Music Lovers," Culture Trip, February 9, 2019, https://theculturetrip.com/north-america/usa/articles/the-12-best-us-cities-for-music-lovers.
2 Gordon Cox, "How an Oregon Theater Got the Attention of the Tonys, the Pulitzers and Broadway," *Variety*, June 7, 2017.
3 Kristin Thiel, "Art in the High Desert Returns to Central Oregon this Month," Oregon ArtsWatch, August 10, 2023.
4 National Assembly of State Arts Agencies (NASAA), "Creative Economy State Profiles: State Arts and Cultural Production 2017: Oregon," NASAA Dashboard, accessed December 31, 2023, https://nasaa-arts.org/nasaa_research/creative-economy-state-profiles/.
5 US Bureau of Labor Statistics, *Occupational Employment and Wages: 27-1019 Artists and Related Workers* (Washington, DC: US Bureau of Labor Statistics report, May 2017); US Bureau of Labor Statistics, *Occupational Employment and Wages: 27-2042 Musicians and Singers* (Washington, DC: US Bureau of Labor Statistics report, May 2018).
6 National Endowment for the Arts, *Arts Data Profile: State-Level Estimates of Arts Participation Patterns: 2017-2018. Brief #1: Live Performing Arts Attendance—Top-Ranking States* (Washington, DC: National Endowment for the Arts, December 2019), https://artsgovd8.prod.acquia-sites.com/sites/default/files/ADP23-Brief1Access-3.pdf; National Endowment for the Arts, *Arts Data Profile: State-Level Estimates of Arts Participation Patterns: 2017-2018. Brief #2: Art Exhibit-Going—Top-Ranking States* (Washington, DC: National Endowment for the Arts, December 2019), https://artsgovd8.prod.acquia-sites.com/sites/default/files/ADP23-Brief2Access-2.pdf.

7 Oregon has established nineteen land use goals. Goals 1 and 5 mention, in passing, the need to gather information on cultural places and areas. In one short section, Goal 8 ("Recreational Needs") mentions the need for recreation areas, facilities, and opportunities to provide for "human development and enrichment." It then presents a list of activities that should be provided for, which included archeological resources and cultural events. No other mention of cultural concerns is found anywhere else in these or the other sixteen goals.
8 See Donna M. Binkiewicz, *Federalizing the Muse: United States Arts Policy and the National Endowment for the Arts, 1965-1980* (Chapel Hill: University of North Carolina Press, 2004).
9 Kevin Kirkpatrick, *Creating Connection: Research Findings and Proposed Message Framework to Build Public Will for Arts and Culture* (Minneapolis: Arts Midwest and the Metropolitan Group, April 2015).
10 Kevin V. Mulcahy, "Cultural Policy: Definitions and Theoretical Approaches," *Journal of Arts Management, Law, and Society* 35 (2006): 320.
11 Carole Rosenstein, *Understanding Cultural Policy* (New York: Routledge, 2018), 6-7.
12 J. Mark Schuster, ed., *Mapping State Cultural Policy: The State of Washington* (Chicago: University of Chicago Press, 2003).
13 Kevin F. McCarthy, Elizabeth H. Ondaatje, Laura Zakaras, and Arthur Brooks, *The Gift of the Muse: Reframing the Debate about the Benefits of the Arts* (Santa Monica, CA: RAND Corporation, 2004).
14 Daisy Fancourt and Saoirse Finn, "What Is the Evidence on the Role of the Arts in Improving Health and Well-Being? A Scoping Review," in *Health Evidence Network Synthesis*, Report 67 (Copenhagen: World Health Organization Regional Office for Europe), 2019.
15 Fancourt and Finn, "What Is the Evidence?"; Alexa Sheppard and Mary C. Broughton, "Promoting Wellbeing and Health through Active Participation in Music and Dance: A Systematic Review," *International Journal of Qualitative Studies on Health and Well-Being* 15 (2020): 1-19.
16 Daniel H. Bowen and Brian Kisida, *Investigating Causal Effects of Arts Education Experiences* (Houston: Rice University Kinder Institute for Urban Research, 2019).
17 Sonia Worcel, David Keyes, and Zulema Naegele, *How the Arts Advance Student Learning* (Portland: Oregon Community Foundation, October 2017).
18 Georgina Barton, "Arts Based Education in the Early Years," *International Research in Early Childhood Education* 6 (2015): 62-78; Bowen and Kisida, *Investigating Causal Effects*; Yinmei Wan, Meredith J. Ludwig, and Andrea Boyle, *Review of Evidence: Arts Education Through the Lens of ESSA* (Washington, DC: American Institute of Research, 2018).
19 National Endowment for the Arts, *How to Do Creative Placemaking: An Action-Oriented Guide to Arts in Community Development* (Washington, DC: National Endowment for the Arts, 2016).
20 Maria Rosario Jackson, *Creative Placemaking and Expansion of Opportunity* (Detroit, MI: Kresge Foundation, 2018).
21 "Local Visions Fuel Progress in Portland," The Scenic Route: Getting Started with Creative Placemaking and Transportation, accessed December 31, 2023, https://creativeplacemaking.t4america.org/our-eight-approaches/develop-local-leadership-capacity/local-examples/.
22 Madhu Narayanan, ed., *Affirming Cultural Identity* (Seattle, WA: Building Equitable Learning, n.d.), https://equitablelearning.org/books/n7Bw4Xso/a8pACWSp/CvLvCwDr.

23 "Legislature Takes Major Steps to Improve Crime, Correction Facilities," *Oregonian*, June 15, 1967.
24 Richard Harry Stewart, "An Investigation of the First Five Years (1967-1972) of Federal Funding of Music in Oregon through the Oregon Arts Commission," PhD diss. (School of Music, University of Southern California, February 1977); "Oregon Trails," *Oregonian*, April 15, 1968.
25 "Oregon Arts Commission: A Report on 1992-93," *OAC News* (Winter 1993): 9.
26 NASAA, *Cultural Policy Innovation: Review of the Arts at the State Level* (Philadelphia: Pew Charitable Trusts, June 2001).
27 Oregon Legislative Assembly, Joint Interim Task Force on Cultural Development, *The Culture of Oregon* (Salem: Oregon Legislative Assembly, January 2001), https://www.culturaltrust.org/wp-content/uploads/culture_development_summary.pdf; Gustav Alexander Baum, "Searching for Solutions: A Planning Analysis of the Oregon Cultural Trust and Recommendations for Community Arts Managers with Regard to Public Funding of Culture in Oregon," masters capstone (University of Oregon, March 2003).
28 "Impacts of the Oregon Cultural Trust and the Cultural Tax Credit," ECONorthwest, accessed December 31, 2023, https://olis.oregonlegislature.gov/liz/2019R1/Downloads/CommitteeMeetingDocument/160050.
29 NASAA, *Cultural Policy Innovation*, 2; M. Christine Dwyer and Susan Frankel, *Policy Partners Making the Case for State Investments in Culture* (Philadelphia: Pew Charitable Trusts, 2002).
30 D. K. Row, "Oregon Cultural Trust Looks to the Future as It Announces New Grants," *Oregonian*, July 26, 2010; Connor Reed, "The Oregon Cultural Trust Explores Unprecedented $10 Million Coronavirus Relief Fund for Arts Orgs," *Portland Monthly*, March 27, 2020.
31 Kyle Odegard, "OPB to Leave OSU," *Albany Democrat-Herald*, April 29, 2008.
32 Oregon Arts Commission, "Oregon Governor Ted Kulongoski to Receive Americans for the Arts' Leadership Award," press release, January 20, 2010, https://www.oregonartscommission.org/sites/default/files/news/file/01-20-10_Governor-Kulongoski-to-Receive-AFTA-Award.pdf.
33 NASAA, "Creative Economy State Profiles."
34 Americans for the Arts, *Arts and Economic Prosperity 5: The Economic Impact of Nonprofit Arts and Cultural Organizations and their Audiences in the State of Oregon* (Washington, DC: Americans for the Arts, 2017).
35 US Bureau of Labor Statistics, *Artists and Related Workers*. The report notes that "these estimates are calculated with data collected from employers in all industry sectors, all metropolitan and nonmetropolitan areas, and all states and the District of Columbia."
36 US Bureau of Labor Statistics, *Musicians and Singers*.
37 US Bureau of Economic Analysis, *Employment by Industries, 2017* (Washington, DC: US Bureau of Economic Analysis, 2017).
38 US Census Bureau, *2017 County Business Patterns and 2017 Nonemployer Statistics* (Washington, DC: US Census Bureau, 2017).
39 "Music Venues and Festivals," MusicPortland, accessed December 31, 2023, https://musicportland.org/music-venues-festivals; "Austin Music Venue Guide," Visit Austin, accessed December 31, 2023, https://www.austintexas.org/music-scene/venue-guide/.
40 Dean Runyan Associates, *Oregon Travel Impacts: Statewide Estimates, 1992-2019* (Portland, OR: Dean Runyan Associates, April 2020).
41 Americans for the Arts, *Arts and Economic Prosperity 5*, 10.

42 "The 2017 Survey of Public Participation the Arts," National Endowment for the Arts Office of Research and Analysis, posted September 2018, https://www.arts.gov/impact/research/arts-data-profile-series/adp-18.

43 Thiel, "Art in the High Desert Returns to Central Oregon"; Lizzy Acker, "Oregon Arts Organizations Struggle as Audiences Are Slow to Return and Money Dries Up," *Oregonian*, December 13, 2023; Cultural Advocacy Coalition, *COVID-19 Oregon; Arts and Culture Sector Impacts* (Portland, OR: Cultural Advocacy Coalition, April 2020), https://www.oregonculture.org/wp-content/uploads/2020/05/FINAL_COVID-19-Oregon-Impacts-1.pdf.

44 NASAA, *State Arts Agency Revenue, Fiscal Year 2017* (Washington, DC: February 2017), https://nasaa-arts.org/wp-content/uploads/2017/04/NASAA-FY2017-SAA-Revenues-Report.pdf.

45 Joshua Cummins, Milton Fernandez, Jennie Flinspach, Briana Hobbs, Patricia Lambert, Victoria Lee, Brad McMullen, JK Rogers, Juliet Rutter, and Jes Sokolowski, *The Impact of the Oregon Cultural Trust on the Statewide Cultural Policy Institutional Infrastructure: Research Report 2018, 2017-2018 Master of Arts Management Professional Project* (Eugene: Center for Community Arts and Cultural Policy, University of Oregon, June 2018).

46 "Impacts of the Oregon Cultural Trust."

47 "Giving in Oregon 2019," Oregon Community Foundation, accessed December 31, 2023, https://oregoncf.org/community-impact/research/giving-in-oregon-2019/.

48 "Giving USA 2018: Americans Gave $410.02 Billion to Charity in 2017, Crossing the $400 Billion Mark for the First Time," GivingUSA, June 13, 2018, https://givingusa.org/giving-usa-2018-americans-gave-410-02-billion-to-charity-in-2017-crossing-the-400-billion-mark-for-the-first-time/.

49 Beatriz J. Rizk, "Milagro Teatro in Portland, Oregon: An Interview with Founders and Artistic Director Dañel Malan, José González, and Olga Sánchez," *Latin American Theatre Review* 48, no. 2 (2015): 121.

50 Elizabeth Whelan, "Diversity Dances: Rejoice! Diaspora Dance Theater," *Oregon ArtsWatch*, April 30, 2018; Heather Wisner, "Rejoice! Finds Community in 'A Midsummer Night at the Savoy,'" *Oregon ArtsWatch*, November 2, 2018; Adira Freigeist, "Expressing Adversity Through Dance," *PSU Vanguard*, February 25, 2020.

51 See the Crow's Shadow Institute of the Arts website, https://crowsshadow.org/about-us/history/.

52 Paulette Beete, "Grant Spotlight on Crow's Shadow Institute of the Arts," National Endowment for the Arts, May 30, 2018, https://www.arts.gov/stories/blog/2018/grant-spotlight-crows-shadow-institute-arts.

53 See the PHAME website, accessed December 31, 2023, https://www.phamepdx.org/about-phame.

54 Friderike Heuer, "PHAME and Friends Rock Out," *Oregon ArtsWatch*, August 22, 2019.

55 Small operating support grants do not include federal funds, so they were not included in the report. These grants are meant to ensure arts access across the state, especially in rural areas. Thus a more comprehensive analysis would benefit from their inclusion. See Oregon Arts Commission, "101 Small Arts Organizations Receive Fy2020 Operating Grants," press release, February 7, 2020.

56 Oregon Arts Commission, *Access to the Arts in Oregon Schools III* (West Salem: Oregon Arts Commission, 2013).

57 Kim Leonard, Zoe Flanagan, and Elise Cordle Kennedy, *A Snapshot of K-12 Arts Education in Oregon* (Portland: Oregon Community Foundation, June 2019).
58 "Impacts of the Oregon Cultural Trust"; Matthew Dennis, "CAFÉ 451: Oregon Cultural Trust Survey Reveals Dire Numbers of Community Arts Organizations," *Eugene Register Guard*, June 26, 2020.
59 Jamie Hale, "Oregon Lawmakers Approve $50 Million Lifeline for Struggling Arts and Culture Organizations," *Oregonian*, July 14, 2020; Chris M. Lehman, "Performance Venues, Arts Groups Ask Oregon Lawmakers for More Covid Recovery Funds," OPB, December 11, 2022, https://www.opb.org/article/2022/12/11/oregon-arts-venues-pandemic-struggles-ongoing/.
60 April Baer, "What Happened (and What Didn't) with Portland's Creative Space Plan," OPB, March 10, 2019, https://www.opb.org/artsandlife/article/portland-oregon-real-estate-rent-artists-creative-spaces/.
61 "Phase II Unit Narrative Report Summaries Including Provost Responses," Office of Academic Affairs, Portland State University, accessed December 31, 2023, https://www.pdx.edu/academic-affairs/phase-ii-unit-narrative-report-summaries-including-provost-responses#theater.

10
Economy, Wages, and Other Economic Factors
EMMA BROPHY AND JENNY H. LIU

Oregon has been transitioning in recent decades from a resource-based economy focused on timber, agriculture, and similar industries to one that also encompasses clusters related to advanced manufacturing, technology, apparel, and innovations in clean energy.[1] While these high-growth clusters have buoyed Oregon's economy in comparison to the nation at large, the benefits have not accrued equitably among the state's residents. In Oregon, incomes for the lower income percentiles have grown to a greater extent than the national average, while incomes for the higher percentiles have lagged national levels (probably because the state does not have a strong finance or multinational industry presence).[2] In 2013, the top 1 percent of Americans earned 25.3 times more income than the bottom 1 percent, and in Oregon, that number was 18.5, placing Oregon twenty-ninth out of the fifty states in terms of income inequality.[3] The 2019 American Community Survey (ACS) five-year estimates show similar results, ranking Oregon twentieth in terms of income inequality, as measured by a Gini coefficient equal to 0.4586 compared to the United States overall Gini coefficient of 0.4823 (for reference, a Gini coefficient of 0 indicates perfect income equality, while 1 indicates perfect inequality). Although Oregon may be "less unequal" than the nation at large, there remain striking discrepancies between earnings at lower socioeconomic levels and those at higher levels, and those discrepancies appear to be increasing (if more slowly than in the nation at large). At the same time, the recent COVID-19 pandemic crisis has hit hardest in lower-wage sectors and in lower-paying jobs in higher-wage sectors.[4]

This chapter moves from a broad look at the state economy to a narrower focus on the differing economic realities for disadvantaged groups and considers what potential economic policies and strategies moving toward 2050 might be employed to address existing issues. This chapter's examination of the state's economy is broader than only taking on the state land use planning program perspective, though we give attention to how the program has and can better promote economic development in a changing context.

Background

In 2022, Oregon's GDP (gross domestic product) was approximately $297.31 billion, with a total of 2,658,285 jobs and a per capita personal income of $62,303 (all in 2022 dollars).[5] Oregon's economy ranks in the middle of all the states in terms of its overall output and employment. But it is difficult to discuss Oregon as an economic whole because it consists of many varying economic environments. For the purposes of the present discussion, it is most useful to examine two distinct portions of the state: the major metropolitan areas and the rest of the state. When statewide measures are used, Portland and other metropolitan areas overwhelm the data owing to the concentration of economic activity. For example, when looking at the pattern of job loss and recovery following the Great Recession in the late 2000s, it appears that Oregon led the nation, with losses felt here before they were felt on the national stage, and jobs returned more quickly than elsewhere in the country as well. But the data obscure the impact of the recession on more rural areas, which did not display this resilience—in fact, data from the Bureau of Economic Analysis shows that annual job growth rates over the ten-year period between 2010 and 2020 were negative in seven of Oregon's thirty-six counties and less than 0.4 percent in another seven counties, mostly concentrated in eastern and coastal Oregon, more than a decade after the recession's end.

These types of hidden economic stagnation and inequities are common in a variety of contexts, where data from the dominant group obscure the full picture: rural versus urban, those high school versus college completion, high-wage earners versus low-wage earners, and white people versus people of color are just a few examples of possible areas of divergence. While the differences in employment rates and poverty rates between white non-Hispanic and BIPOC (Black, Indigenous, and people of color) Oregonians have been shrinking in recent years, other inequities continue to persist. Where intersectionality of disadvantaged groups occurs, these differences are often heightened. It is necessary to analyze economic phenomena along as many social and demographic continuums as possible in order to derive a clear picture; this is the fundamental goal of this section.

Oregon's labor force (the number of individuals aged 16 or older who have sought work in the last month) is estimated at 2.2 million as of December 2023, and the labor force participation rate, or what percentage of the population is currently employed or seeking work, is around 61.9 percent.[6] This is slightly lower than the labor force participation rate of the nation at large, which is 62.5 percent, but both the state and the nation remain markedly low in comparison to the high observed prior to the Great Recession.[7] During that time, many individuals not only ceased working, but also ceased looking for work. This lag does not appear to be due to enhanced social programs but perhaps their absence: as the authors of a 2018 letter from the Federal Reserve Bank of Dallas point out, the decline in labor force participation has been occurring for twenty years, in contrast to the world at large.[8] While an aging population is the primary contributor to this decline, the authors highlight several additional factors: increased incarceration, poor health and social services provision (including childcare for working parents), and insufficient active labor market policies are all actionable elements that affect the working-age population.[9]

While Oregon is known for the industry sectors mentioned in the outset of this section—primarily natural resource-based products, technology (particularly what is known as "cutting edge" or high-tech), and advanced manufacturing—these are the sectors that make the state unique and do not reflect the actual number of individuals employed in each sector. As figure 10.1 shows, substantial numbers are employed in retail, leisure and hospitality, educational and health services, and professional and business services.[10] (For comparison, the jobs in the signature sectors described above are predominantly located under natural resources and mining, information, and manufacturing in fig. 10.1.) Many of these jobs are comparatively low paying when considered in comparison to the higher-paying jobs found in, for example,

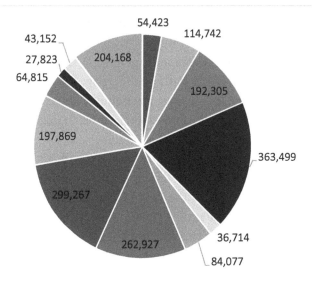

- Natural resources and mining
- Manufacturing
- Information
- Professional and business services
- Leisure and hospitality
- Total federal government
- Total local government
- Construction
- Trade, transportation, and utilities
- Financial activities
- Education and health services
- Other services
- Total state government

Figure 10.1. Oregon nonfarm employment by industry, 2019. *Source*: "Quarterly Census of Employment and Wages (QCEW), Annual 2019," US Bureau of Labor Statistics, accessed January 17, 2024, https://www.bls.gov/cew/

the development of hardware components. Additionally, individuals in these professions are vulnerable to recession, especially under pandemic circumstances, and unemployment claims reflect this fact.

Note that this labor snapshot considers exclusively nonfarm employment (a definition that excludes "proprietors, private household employees, unpaid volunteers, farm employees and the unincorporated self-employed").[11] These types of employment are not included for several reasons: first, agricultural employment is highly seasonal, meaning that many jobs appear and disappear over the course of the year, and the number will vary dramatically depending on when data are collected. Second, many farmworkers are not documented, whether by their employer or as citizens of the United States, additionally rendering data collection difficult. The US Department of Agriculture estimates that 48 percent of all farmworkers do not have a legal authorization to work.[12] Last, while the farm sector appears to be a small portion of overall employment and difficult to estimate accurately, the "farmgate production" and "agriculture support services" industry sectors directly employ more than 90,000 people and are important economic contributors within many rural communities.[13]

Statewide Economic Development Planning

Macroeconomic trends (in 2023, these include inflation, high interest rates, and globalism) and other external factors influence Oregon's economic reality. It is also affected by efforts by the state and by other local and regional actors. One important way the state influences the economic issues discussed in this chapter is through the statewide land use planning program, specifically Goal 9, Economic Development. Goal 9 was officially adopted in 1974 and subsequently modified several times, notably during economic downturns, and thus is mainly focused on generating economic growth.[14] As with most of the other goals, the goal is accompanied by guidelines that are not binding but are rather considered best practices.

Goal 9 remains one of Oregon's most influential economic development efforts, relative to other states. The primacy of the state land use planning and regulation in economic development in Oregon has been contested from the beginning, and it has limits, including its urban orientation and relative lack of relevance to more rural and resource-based communities and those experiencing economic stagnation. Land use lawyer Edward Sullivan and economist Noelwah Netusil discuss some of the interactions of Goal 9 with other goals, like Goal 5 (Natural Resources, Scenic and Historic Areas, and Open Spaces), and they trace the transformation of Goal 9 from a "relatively weak peripheral consideration" to a high-stakes determinant in the land use field.[15]

The purpose of Goal 9 planning is to make sure cities and counties have enough land available to realize economic growth and development opportunities, it and requires them to proactively plan. The Department of Land Conservation and Development (DLCD) website explains:

Under Goal 9, all local governments should have a working inventory of areas suitable for economic growth that can be provided with public services. These inventories primarily focus on planning for major industrial and commercial developments, and having a ready supply of land appropriately zoned and located for those opportunities and local investments. As with all areas of the comprehensive plan, the amount of land planned for economic development should be adequate for a 20-year supply. The economic development plans formed by a city often use one or more market incentives to encourage the type of development a community or county would like to see. These might include tax incentives or disincentives, land use controls, or preferential assessments.

Scholars have observed that there has not been a comprehensive analysis of the efforts to link land use planning and the state's economy. Sullivan and Netusil note that the integration has not been complete, since the Land Conservation and Development Commission (or LCDC, the volunteer advisory commission that, assisted by DLCD, adopts state land use goals and implements rules, ensures local plan compliance with the goals, coordinates state and local planning, and oversees the coastal zone management program) has not engaged robustly with economic policymaking outside of land use. For example, LCDC does not typically collaborate directly with economic development districts (EDDs). Meanwhile, Business Oregon (discussed below) has not gotten greatly involved in land use planning. They also question the effectiveness of Goal 9 efforts, in part owing to the disconnect of Goal 9 requirements—which are locally focused—from the realities of regional economies, the need for resources to implement the plans, and the lack of monitoring, evaluation, and adaptation. The authors additionally note weaknesses in the methodologies prescribed for economic opportunity analyses as part of this goal. A final limit is that the kind of planning described in Goal 9 is not particularly relevant to much of eastern, southern, and coastal Oregon. The type of economic development that would be relevant to these communities is vastly different than what is supported by or prescribed by the kind of planning in Goal 9. Another issue is that these communities have limited planning staff and technical capacities. The state has occasionally offered funding to communities to enable them to do economic planning work, but the funding is limited, inconsistent, and does not address the larger issues.

Additional to Goal 9 efforts, Business Oregon is the state's economic development agency.[16] Its mission is to invest in Oregon businesses, communities, and people to promote a globally competitive, diverse, and inclusive economy. Business Oregon has identified six target industry groups—advanced manufacturing, business services, food and beverage, forestry and wood products, high technology, and outdoor gear and apparel—that provide Oregon with unique opportunities for growth, high-wage jobs, innovation, and statewide prosperity. In 2017, the department published a new strategic plan to guide economic development over the next five years. The plan's five priorities are to innovate Oregon's economy, grow small- and middle-market companies, cultivate rural economic stability, advance economic opportunity for underrepresented people, and ensure an inclusive, transparent, and fiscally healthy agency. Business Oregon administers more than eighty grant, loan, tax incentive, and other programs to further the development of businesses, communities, and economies in Oregon, though demand is typically higher than funding levels. At the local level, a range of EDDs, agencies, and organizations do on-the-ground work. These range from Prosper Portland, the economic and urban development agency for the City of Portland, to the Northeast Oregon Economic Development District, which provides financial, technical, and educational resources for entrepreneurs, nonprofits, and municipalities in Baker, Union, and Wallowa Counties.

Economic Equity in Oregon

Economists typically consider efficiency (related to economic growth and development) and equity as the main criteria to assess the economy, often noting substantial trade-offs between efficiency and equity when unequal weight is placed on achieving economic growth. As such, economic equity describes the differences in employment patterns, wages, and wealth between different demographic groups and geographic areas where state data are available.

Racial Equity in Oregon

Oregon is known as a racially and ethnically homogenous area, but in recent years, it has been changing: between 2013 and 2022, racial diversity increased at a rate greater than that observed in the rest of the nation, and the share of nonwhite residents reached 21.3 percent (13 percentage points below the national average).[17] As is the pattern in much of the country, Oregon's residents of color (with the exception of the Asian population) experience lower wages, higher unemployment rates, lower rates of college education, and typically work lower-paying jobs and industries (sources below).

It is challenging to describe Oregon as an economic whole owing to large disparities in economic characteristics between urban and rural areas. Counties with major metropolitan areas such as Deschutes and Multnomah have gained 17.64 and 6.21 percent in labor force from 2017 to 2022, respectively, while rural counties in eastern Oregon such as Wheeler and Baker have lost 4.05 and 3.41 percent of their labor force, respectively, during the same period.[18] Furthermore, income levels of households across geographic regions follow a similar pattern, with more urban counties such as Washington and Clackamas having $100,121 and $95,740 in median household income (in 2022 dollars), respectively, and rural eastern Oregon counties such as Lake, Harney, and Malheur having a median household income around or just below half of Washington County's level (between $45,462 and $54,663).[19] These statistics reflect the deepening urban-rural economic divide in the state and mean that additional attention must be paid toward bridging this gap for future economic prosperity.

According to the 2022 American Community Survey, labor force participation is higher for most nonwhite residents than for white residents, meaning that the percentage of the population either working or looking for work is higher (table 10.1). Some of this can be attributed to demographic reasons, as older populations gradually leave the labor force (overall labor force participation drops to 55.7 percent in the 60–64 age group, and to 24.1 percent in the 65–74 group), and there is a lower level of racial diversity within this same group. Labor force participation is lowest for American Indians and white alone groups, but American Indians also face the highest unemployment rate (as

ECONOMY, WAGES, AND OTHER ECONOMIC FACTORS 283

Table 10.1. Employment Status by Race and Ethnicity

Group	Total Employment	Labor Force Participation Rate (%)	Unemployment Rate (%)
Population 16+	3,472,552	62.50	5.50
Hispanic/Latino	2,640,429	60.30	5.90
Non-Hispanic white	407,991	78.20	5.10
White	2,794,358	61.00	5.40
Black	62,945	66.60	7.60
American Indian	37,643	61.90	8.30
Asian	158,923	67.10	4.60
Native Hawaiian	13,571	70.40	5.90
Some other race	133,106	72.40	5.70
Two or more races	272,006	68.50	6.50

Source: Created by the authors based on data from "2022 American Community Survey, 5-Year Estimates," Table S2301, US Census Bureau, generated by Emma Brophy, https://data.census.gov/table/ACSST5Y2022.S2301?q=s2301&g=040XX00US41&moe=false

noted previously, low labor force participation typically results in the appearance of lower unemployment rates).

The type of employment varies as well: the second most common industry for nonwhite residents is leisure and hospitality, with an annual median salary of $21,500 between 2018 and 2022, while the second most common for non-Hispanic white residents is retail trade, with an average salary of $31,400. The most common industry for Asian workers in the state is the manufacturing sector.[20] This sector provides one of the highest salaries in the state ($57,800), with overwhelming influence from the semiconductor subsector; other manufacturing subsectors have more middle- to-lower wage jobs. The state median household income (median income being the most common income level, in contrast to average) was $86,780 per year in 2022.[21] Significant wage differences also exist within industrial sectors. For example, the manufacturing sector includes occupations ranging from wood product manufacturing (23,205 employed, or 12.1 percent of the manufacturing sector), with an average annual wage of $64,470, to computer and electronic product manufacturing (41,101 employed, or 21.4 percent of the manufacturing sector), with an average annual wage of $150,406 in 2022.[22] Differential employment by sector is important for another reason: different industries offer varying levels of health (and other) benefits for full- and part-time employees.

Following the Great Recession and pandemic, wage disparity has remained fairly constant (fig. 10.2). This disparity—median household incomes for Black and American Indian households are about $20,000 behind white households and more than $40,000 behind Asian households—is likely due to many factors. One is the differences in job type, which itself is partly related to educational attainment. According to the 2022 ACS, the Asian population has the highest rate of college education, with 54.6 percent holding a bachelor's degree or higher, in comparison to 36.9 percent of whites, 32.5 percent of the Black community, 15.9 percent of Native populations, and 18.9 percent of Hispanic respondents.[23] High school graduate rates vary among racial

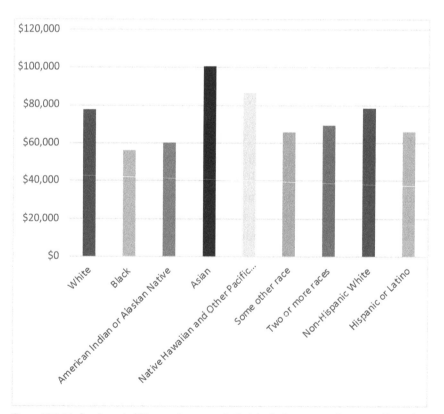

Figure 10.2. Median household income by race and ethnicity in Oregon over January to December 2019. *Source*: Created by the authors based on data from "2019 American Community Survey, 5-Year Estimates," Table S1903, US Census Bureau, retrieved March 1, 2023, https://data.census.gov/cedsci/

groups, but conditional on graduating high school, Oregonians of different races and ethnicities attend college at similar rates. Black and American Indian Oregonians complete college at lower rates, however. Differences in educational attainment do not pertain to the characteristics of groups but instead have wide-ranging causes that include differential treatment of groups within the educational system, access to resources, economic characteristics and stability, and other forms of social prejudice and systemic racism that may affect both enrollment rates and completion rates across groups.

Educational attainment is a strong factor in the determination of wages. In 2019, median earnings for those with a bachelor's degree were nearly double those for individuals who did not graduate high school. Lower rates of high school and college completion appear to be responsible for a lower rate of bachelor's degrees, meaning that interventions geared toward meeting those benchmarks are key.[24]

In addition to wage disparity, wealth disparity (which includes all assets and debts of an individual or household, rather than simply what they are paid in wages) exists between racial demographic groups. In 2022, the Survey of Consumer Finances showed that nationally the median net worth of families differed dramatically by race—close to $285,000 for white non-Hispanic families compared to about $44,900 for Black non-Hispanic families and just under $61,600 for Hispanic families.[25] Differences in wealth arise from complex structural factors such as historically discriminatory housing policies that prevented the accumulation and transfer of generational wealth, as well as lower incomes resulting from discriminatory hiring practices, among many other discrepancies in treatment and access.

A large part of this divergence is likely due to differences in homeownership rates, as homes constitute the largest repository of wealth for most families. A significant gap (more than 10 percent as of 2017) continues to persist in rates between white, non-Hispanic households and minority-led households in the Portland metropolitan area. Homeownership for this group declined steeply during the Great Recession, and while it has since rebounded, it remains lower. This again may be attributed to systemic redlining and other discriminatory practices further described in chapter 6.

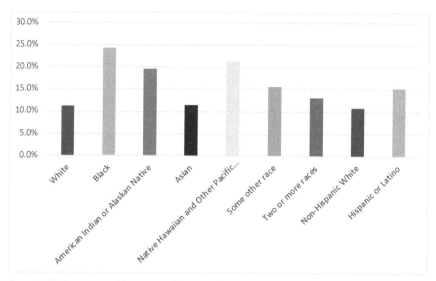

Figure 10.3. Percentage of Oregonians by race and ethnicity living below the poverty line. *Source:* Created by the authors based on data from "2020 American Community Survey, 5-Year Estimates," Table S1701, US Census Bureau, retrieved March 1, 2023, https://data.census.gov/cedsci/

When we move from examining what people have to what they do not have, the picture worsens. The racial poverty gap decreased in Oregon in the early 2020s and is currently the lowest poverty gap in recorded history, which is something to celebrate. But the grim reality is that the gap is still huge. As of 2022, poverty rates in Oregon are much higher for nonwhite residents. As figure 10.3 shows, about one in four of Oregon's Black residents lives below the poverty line (24.3 percent), and the overall share of state residents living in poverty (currently defined as earning less than $14,880 for an individual or $29,950 for a family of four) is at 11.9 percent.[26] This is a stark illustration of the way in which today's economy tends to accrue gains to the higher levels of income, while leaving life unchanged for lower tiers.

Poverty is closely linked with a variety of social and economic problems, as it can both cause and be caused by mental, physical, and social issues. In this way, it is similar to many of the issues of racial equity covered above—it has many systemic causes and is in many ways a "wicked problem." Nonetheless, intervention is possible where the data clearly show differential outcomes, and improved data collection allows policymakers to see where progress is being made.

Oregon displays the same patterns in gender equity as those observed elsewhere in the nation: women face economic disadvantages at home and work, typically earning less and working less than men, even in comparable positions and levels of education. When considering disparities in wages, wealth, and employment, intersectionality is key to analysis, as the compounding impacts of race and gender discrimination are profound. Women of color in particular face unique challenges in comparison to white women. One serious limitation of this discussion is that it considers only binary gender, as we do not yet have data for nonbinary individuals. Future data collection should include nonbinary classification options.

Women in Oregon participate in the labor force at a lower rate than men do—74.3 percent for those between the ages of 20 and 64, compared to 82.1 percent for men in that age range.[27] Women often bear greater childcare responsibilities, which may account for much of this difference (the availability and affordability of childcare is discussed in a later section). Among parents, fathers participate in the labor force much more than mothers, while working-age men without kids and Oregon working-age women without kids have similar labor force participation rates. Women (mothers or not) are also more likely to be employed part time and are more likely to work in lower-paying occupations. When they work in high-paying occupations, they are more likely to earn comparatively lower salaries than their male colleagues, discussed in detail elsewhere.[28]

In Oregon, as in the nation at large, women earn less than men on average. The wage gap rises with both education and income level, meaning that it is least present at jobs that have been considered "low skill." This wage gap is likely due to minimum wage requirements at the lower end of the earning spectrum.[29] Figure 10.4 shows the wage gap at different levels of education. Note that at every instance, women earn less on average than men at a lower level of education; that is, women with a graduate degree earn less than men with a bachelor's degree, women with a bachelor's degree earn less than men with only some college, and so on. On average, women with some college or an associate's degree earn about the same amount as men with less than high school graduate education.

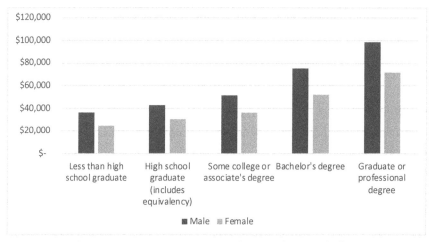

Figure 10.4. Median earnings over January to December 2019 by sex and education in Oregon. *Source*: Created by the authors based on data from "2019 American Community Survey, 5-Year Estimates," Table B20004, US Census Bureau, retrieved March 1, 2023, https://data.census.gov/cedsci/

One often-discussed driver of the gender wage gap is the division of unpaid labor such as housework and care for family members. According to the US Bureau of Labor Statistics' 2022 Time Use Survey, women are more likely to spend time on household upkeep activities on a given day (85.4 percent for women vs. 70.3 percent for men), and they spend more time doing so when they do (2.26 hours for women vs. 1.51 for men). When it comes to childcare, the survey indicates that 26.1 percent of women care for and help household members on any given day (compared to 16.9 percent of men) for an average of 0.64 hours (compared to 0.31 hours for men).[30] For this reason, access to affordable childcare is considered a crucial element in reducing the gender pay gap. A 2015 report from nonprofit organization Child Care Aware of America found that when median income and annual cost of childcare are combined using 2014 data, Oregon ranks second worst in the nation, falling behind only Minnesota.[31] There is also the matter of time off for expectant mothers and parental leave, neither of which are reliably compensated even when available and contribute to lower earnings as well.

In addition to the problem of affordability, the lack of available childcare in proximity to where partners live and work poses another challenge. Even before the COVID-19 pandemic, all Oregon counties were considered "childcare deserts," meaning they lacked adequate childcare capacity for infants and toddlers—measured as regions where there are more than three children for every single childcare space or slot in a program.[32] The lack includes both family childcare homes and centers. And in many counties, parents of preschool-aged children also lack childcare options. From 1999 to early 2020, the number of small family childcare homes saw a big decrease statewide, from about 47,000 slots to about 15,000, while centers and large family childcare homes slots increased by about 26,000. Overall, Oregon (as of early 2020) had 6,000 fewer childcare slots than in 1999, even though the state's population has grown by more than 25 percent during the same period. With some exceptions, the childcare supply in Oregon is scarcer in rural areas than in urban ones. The challenge goes both ways, in that childcare centers and workers struggle to make enough profit, and parents are overstretched in paying for childcare.

Single mothers often feature in discussions of poverty, with good reason. As of 2022 in Oregon, greater than one in five single mothers in Oregon were living below the poverty line (compared to just 4.8 percent of married-couple families).[33] More than one in ten Oregon single moms had an income of less than half of the poverty line, a level termed "deep poverty." Considering the intersection of sex and race, an estimated half of all Black, Latina, and American Indian single mothers were surviving at or below the poverty level.[34]

The reasons why many single mothers find themselves living below the poverty line include the difficulty of running a household on a single income, especially considering that they often face discrimination in the hiring and job markets. The high cost and unreliability of quality childcare pose challenges as well. In 2019, the median household income for single male parents with children under 18 was $66,000 per year, while for single women, it was $42,000.[35]

While inequities related to sexual orientation and gender identity are known to exist, there is a dearth of demographic data collection in this area, so it is difficult to offer much analysis. Recent reports indicate that wage and hiring discrimination may be diminishing for individuals who are lesbian, gay, bisexual, transgender, or queer plus (LGBTQ+) on a national basis, but transgender individuals remain more likely to experience poverty and homelessness. Oregon is routinely considered to be one of the most LGBTQ+-friendly areas in the nation and ranks among the top states in the Human Rights Campaign's 2019 State Equality Index for LGBTQ+ legal protections.[36] Over the past ten years, twenty-seven laws aimed at protecting the rights of the gay and transgender community have been passed, indicating a general atmosphere of support and making Oregon one of the safest places to live with a nontraditional sexual identity.

But legal protection can only tell half of the story—many LGBTQ+ individuals, especially those who are transgender, face substantial challenges based in discrimination. The 2015 US Transgender Survey found that 12 percent of respondents in Oregon were unemployed (three times higher than the state rate at the time), and one in three were living in poverty. One in five reported having lost a job because of their gender expression, and 37 percent reported having been homeless at some point in their lives (12 percent within the last year). While those constitute the explicitly economic survey questions, the survey documents high rates of mistreatment as well, including assault, bullying, and fear of seeking assistance from the police.

The American Community Survey does not collect data on sexual identity or orientation, but it does ask questions about disability, meaning that there are more economic data for this group. The number of individuals with disabilities that respond to the ACS is low (dependent on self-reporting), however, so margins of error are too high in many cases to allow parsing data by disability type, for example. It is also possible that individuals with disabilities do not report them. This section will only cite data that are not rendered meaningless by a large margin of error, and small differences between groups should not necessarily be considered meaningful.

In Oregon in 2022, 14.9 percent of the population identified themselves as living with some form of disability on the American Community Survey, higher than the national prevalence rate of 12.9 percent.[37] Oregonians with disabilities are likely to be older than the general population—while the rate for 18- to 34-year-olds is 9.6 percent and 35- to 64-year-olds is 14.1 percent, it rises to 25.4 percent for those aged 65-74, and 48.7 percent for those over the age of 75. People with disabilities were similarly likely to be male than female (15.0 percent compared to 14.9 percent). Figure 10.5 shows disability rates by race.

ECONOMY, WAGES, AND OTHER ECONOMIC FACTORS   291

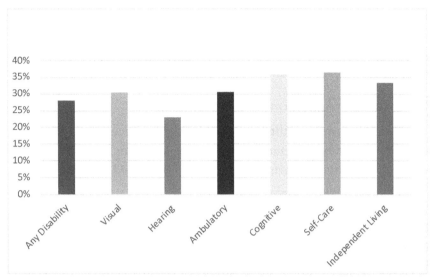

Figure 10.5. Percentage of Oregonians with disabilities by race and ethnicity (all ages). *Source*: Created by the authors based on data from "2019 American Community Survey, 5-Year Estimates," Table S1810, US Census Bureau, retrieved March 1, 2023, https://data.census.gov/cedsci/

Of the 17.2 percent of Oregonians aged 16 and over with disabilities, 27.0 percent were employed. Median earnings were $27,654 per year, $15,000 lower than median earnings for individuals not reporting disabilities.[38] Median household income for households that included working-age adults with disabilities was $62,500, in comparison to $92,800 for families without.[39] The highest median household income was observed for hearing disabilities ($68,800), while the lowest was for "self-care" disabilities, defined as the inability to wash or dress oneself ($48,100). Note that these values are for households that contain individuals with disabilities but are not necessarily headed by them, so this is in many cases a measure of caretaker income. Also note that the age categories are slightly different (18-64 vs. 21-64) depending on the specific data source and variable.

Individuals with disabilities are far more likely to be living in poverty—20.6 percent in 2022, compared to 11.6 percent overall in Oregon.[40] In terms of education, 29.2 percent of individuals with disabilities have attained only a high school diploma or equivalent, in comparison to 20.7 percent of the general population in the same year. The rate of college attendance differs less: 36.6 percent of individuals with disabilities have attended some college, compared with 32.9 percent of those without. The rates diverge most dramatically when it comes to college degrees, with only 21.2 percent having obtained a bachelor's degree or more—less than half of the 39.0 percent of bachelor's degree holders in the state overall.

Oregon's Recent Economic Trends

This section briefly outlines some of Oregon's economic attributes that are not centered around equity issues, including Oregon's general economic climate, relative vulnerability to increased automation, and international trade.

Oregon has been one of the fastest-growing states in the nation in recent years, adding jobs at a rapid clip and experiencing a rise in wages in response to a shifting landscape where the manufacturing sector is moving toward certain components like transportation equipment manufacturing and primary metal manufacturing, and away from paper manufacturing, sawmills, and wood preservation. Additional growth is projected in the leisure and hospitality sector, largely "driven by the recovery from the pandemic," but also within higher-paying sectors

Figure 10.6. Oregon's wage and salary growth in comparison to the United States overall, 2005-20. *Source*: US Bureau of Labor Statistics, "All Employees, Manufacturing (MANEMP)," Federal Reserve Bank of St. Louis, accessed March 14, 2022, https://fred.stlouisfed.org/series/MANEMP; and US Bureau of Labor Statistics, "Manufacturing Sector: Output for All Employed Persons (OUTMS)," Federal Reserve Bank of St. Louis, accessed March 14, 2022, https://fred.stlouisfed.org/series/OUTMS

like private health care and social assistance, trade, transportation, and utilities, and professional and business services.[41] Not only are these jobs growing more rapidly now, but in the current economic landscape, they have a strong potential for growth going forward. It appears that Oregon is becoming increasingly well situated to the current global economic climate.

While Oregon's minimum wage increased from $9.25 per hour statewide in 2016 to $14.20 per hour ($15.45 in Portland Metro or $13.20 in nonurban counties) in 2023 and will be adjusted annually based on inflation, inflation-adjusted average wages, reflecting increases in workers' actual purchasing power, have dropped into negative growth territory for workers in most industries in Oregon as of January 2022 owing to persistent high inflation, with the exception of the leisure and hospitality industry.[42] Since the Great Recession, Oregon's wage and salary growth has outpaced that of the nation as well, although the top line is moving the average much more than groups with lower income and wages (fig. 10.6).

One of the reasons that productivity continues to rise in the modern age while wages do not is that automation has in part divorced human labor from output. Figure 10.7 shows indexed manufacturing

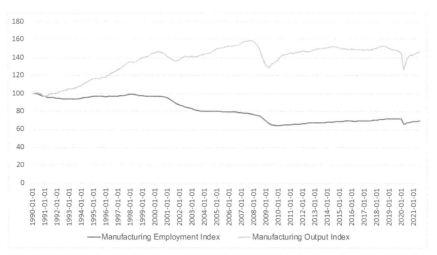

Figure 10.7. National manufacturing employment and output indices, April 1990 to October 2021 (1990 = 100). *Source*: Created by the authors based on data from US Bureau of Economic Analysis, "Total Wages and Salaries, All USA and Oregon-Specific, BLS (BA06RC1A027NBEA)," Federal Reserve Bank of St. Louis, accessed March 14, 2022, https://fred.stlouisfed.org/series/BA06RC1A027NBEA

output versus manufacturing employment. Indices, which normalize values to 100, are used to show how the two measures have diverged over time.

Investments in technology can dramatically increase a firm's profit margin by replacing humans with machines, and while automation can improve life and generate wealth, there is long-standing concern about how the labor market will change as more and more jobs formerly filled by workers are transferred to automated methods. In addition to manufacturing, jobs in food service, truck transportation, administrative capacities, and repair and maintenance occupations are considered by the Brookings Institution to be the most vulnerable to automation.[43] Oregon has a (very) slightly higher proportion of workers than the national average in food service and repair and maintenance, and a 15 percent greater share of workers in manufacturing. These manufacturing jobs are located in the Portland-Vancouver-Hillsboro Metropolitan Statistical Area, where the share of workers in manufacturing is 20 percent greater than the US average.[44] It is vital to ensure that workers displaced by automation are met with adequate resources to prepare them for alternative careers.

International Trade

Like other West Coast states, Oregon engages in more international trade than the national average. Oregon primarily trades with countries on the Pacific Rim, and China and Canada are Oregon's top two trading partners.[45] This means that Oregon is slightly more affected by international trade policy than other states might be, although it is worth noting that the recent trade skirmish with China did not result in any notable deviation from the norm as of 2019.[46] While Oregon's exports as a share of GDP have remained relatively constant at around 8-10 percent since 1997, exports to China have risen from essentially 0 up to 1.7 percent in 2018. In 2019, Oregon exported approximately $7.2 billion to China, ranking third in the nation in terms of absolute export value (behind California and Texas). While US exports to China have been falling in recent years, a trade deal (Phase One) reached in 2020 specified an additional $200 billion in Chinese purchases of American goods above 2017 levels, with $77 billion to be spent in 2020 and $123 billion in 2021. As US exports to China totaled $186 billion in 2017, this would be a significant increase.[47] Oregon can likely expect some increased demand for exports going forward as a result.

Low-wage jobs such as those in retail and hospitality had been hit harder during the COVID-19 pandemic, as many workers in these sectors could not work remotely and public health measures curtailed travel, eating out, and drinking in bars for a considerable period. It was widely reported in April that more than 80 percent of restaurant workers had lost their jobs.[48] As is unfortunately all too typical, in times of economic crisis, those at the lower levels of income experienced the most severe consequences to quality of life. The COVID-19 pandemic crisis hit hardest in lower-wage sectors in Oregon and in lower-wage jobs in higher-wage sectors.[49] Poor Oregonians, already struggling to get by during normal times, are in greater financial duress during economic downturns like the pandemic—an issue for policymakers to prioritize.

Looking forward past the pandemic, we may see some lingering and perhaps permanent impacts on the state and national economy. Some speculate that tourism and large group gatherings (such as concerts, sporting events, and convention center gatherings) will be less prevalent for years to come, though this does not seem to be bearing out wholesale. Meanwhile, it seems likely that online shopping, delivery services, remote work services, and outdoor recreation will continue to experience sustained growth. Meanwhile, in-store shopping, commercial office space, and indoor recreation may continue to be less robust than before the pandemic. In the Portland region specifically, downtown Portland has had a slower economic recovery than comparable cities across the country, with office vacancy rates over 26 percent and lower pedestrian counts than pre-pandemic. At a recent panel discussion about the future of commercial spaces in downtown Portland, panelists did not find it likely that downtown would return to its pre-pandemic numbers, and instead urged local leaders to consider different approaches to economic development, including building more housing.[50]

Additionally, historically high-inflation global supply chain constraints and oil supply issues stemming from Russia's attack on Ukraine, and the resulting significant interest rate hikes by the Federal Reserve to combat inflation, have combined to force Oregon households to spend down their savings. Looking ahead, state economic forecasters predict a mild recession, influenced mainly by ongoing high inflation. The job losses are likely to fall most heavily on the construction, manufacturing, and transportation sectors. They also predict tighter government budgets. Beyond the short term, all of the abovementioned trends, as well as changes that influence housing affordability and net migration, will be consequential to how the state can attract and retain its labor force and businesses.[51]

Big Ideas

Since this book focuses on the state land use planning program, we start this section by calling for an update to Goal 9 to bring it into the twenty-first century. We mainly reiterate the calls made by Sullivan and Netusil, who recommend updating the administrative rules and agency guidelines to better support the transition of the state's economy from primarily a natural resources-based economy to one with ongoing significant natural resource bases and a large portion of economic activity and employment in services and technology. In the densely populated parts of western Oregon, this means planning for economic development elements that address affordable housing and adequate public services and facilities, and including multimodal transportation options to reduce traffic congestion and vehicle miles traveled. These elements are necessary to deal with the economics well as social and political issues faced by the state. As such, improvements to Goal 9 must be influenced by the big ideas and recommendations in other chapters of this book on these topics.

Statewide, economic development planning must also account for risks from climate change, earthquakes, and other hazards discussed in chapter 3. For example, municipalities should be required to locate major employment areas outside of tsunami and flood zones (which are notoriously not accurately mapped by the Federal Emergency Management Agency; see chap. 3), or at least to have plans for resilience against these hazards. Meanwhile, economic development activities must contribute toward the state's goals to reduce greenhouse gas emissions and to position Oregon as a leader in the renewable energy and sustainable economy of the future. This latter part may be especially salient for the eastern part of the state, which faces economic stagnation owing to macroeconomic trends like technological changes (e.g., changes in agriculture and forestry that require fewer workers), globalization, and resource challenges like water scarcity, which will worsen with climate change. In this part of the state, economic development planning should also be better linked with the efforts of Business Oregon and building upon local innovations to adapt their natural resource economies for the current eras.

Another improvement to Goal 9 is to foster consensus-based, regional (rather than municipal) economic development planning. This planning would better match the regional, connected scale at which economies function, rather than treating cities like Portland as separate from others in the region, like Troutdale. Goal 9 could also be better integrated with Goal 1 in that economic opportunities analysis (EOA) processes should be more inclusive and integrating community objectives like social equity, environmental protection, and community resilience. A third improvement is to require a ten-year review period, where planners reflect on whether the assumed growth rate was achieved and make appropriate adaptions. This could be part of a renewed period review program that effectively ended about 2000.[52]

A final area of change to Goal 9 is to broaden the focus from being solely about ensuring a specific quantity of commercial- and industrial-zoned land. Office-based work and retail have changed significantly in past years, including huge shifts to work from home and to online-based retail, and are likely to continue doing so in ways that have big implications for smart land use planning. Goal 9 could do more to encourage mixed-use planning, with better integration of office and commercial space to make "complete communities." Goal 9 could also support both the protection of industrial lands into the future and their evolution into areas that embrace healthy, green, and equitable industrial practices. The City of Portland is already innovating with Clean Industry Hub Planning. The city notes that "concept of a hub is intended to be a space—either physical or virtual—to develop new and cutting-edge technology and clean/closed/circular production practices to benefit Portland industries and possibly other business opportunities."[53] If the hub proves effective, the model could be an inspiration for other municipalities in the state.

Going forward, economic growth and development in Oregon cannot be considered without improvements in economic equity across multiple dimensions. Discrepancies in economic outcomes between demographic groups manifest as wicked problems to solve, as there are many different factors that combine to result in these striking differences. Generally speaking, social justice issues are wicked problems, as they require policy-based solutions that will not work immediately and can be politically contentious. Many of these solutions go beyond the traditional realm of planning to include social and economic policy.

Strategies to address inequality typically focus on crafting broad social policy that provides aid to those at lower socioeconomic levels using income, rather than other identities like race or gender, as the qualifier. The alternative to this approach are strategies that, rather than addressing low income as the qualifier, use the social and demographic traits themselves—for instance, programs that are only available to BIPOC, women, or individuals identifying as LGBTQ+. While the former strategies are often somewhat more politically acceptable, especially to white lawmakers and voters, they often fail to fully address the systemic causes of inequalities and end up disproportionately benefiting white beneficiaries and exacerbating other inequalities along lines of race, ethnicity, and gender. For this reason, programs specifically targeted at identity-based inequities also have their place, as they can be a more explicit effort to address the systemic causes of inequalities (such as poverty) and designed with relevant cultural competency. A challenge is that such programs can face political opposition. For example, a logging company in eastern Oregon and a Mexican business owner in Portland raised lawsuits against a recent program, the Oregon Cares fund, targeted specifically at assisting Black-owned businesses in Oregon during the COVID-19 pandemic.[54]

Below, we summarize some potential approaches to decreasing economic inequality in Oregon. Most of them can be administered on the basis of either economic means or sociodemographic traits. This list is offered as a starting point only. Ideally, attention to economic equity would be combined with efforts to revise Goal 9.

Universal Basic Income

UBI programs provide every citizen with some basic amount of income, with no qualifying level, meaning that everyone receives a payment regardless of income level. The advantage of this approach is that it is simple to implement. The disadvantage is that it is expensive, as it covers everybody and must be of an amount sufficient to reach a reasonable level regardless of who it is administered to. As a result, UBI programs are difficult to implement. In the United States, most basic income projects were short in duration, provided relatively small sums, and were not universal (meaning that the participants needed to qualify for them). The only long-standing program similar to UBI in the United States exists in Alaska, where every resident receives a set identical amount based on its natural resource revenues, although pilot programs in other jurisdictions around the country are currently underway.[55] The fund was established using oil revenues in 1976, and the annual payment amount has varied from $331 to $3,284.

Negative Income Tax

Alternatively, governments can establish a guaranteed minimum level of income and offer rebates to those who fall below that level. The federal and Oregon earned income tax credit (EITC)[56] both operate similarly to a negative income tax (NIT). The advantages of programs like these are that they are effective in reducing regressivity in the tax system and efficiently target low-income households. The disadvantage is that they can be complicated to administer (especially if the eligibility requirements are complex), leaving them vulnerable to error, and that in theory, they can disincentivize individuals from seeking pay increases if doing so would move the worker out of the eligible income tier (although some studies show this effect to be minor or nonexistent). Additionally, programs like the EITC only apply to those who work outside the home and those who file taxes, leaving out the lowest-income households. Similar to UBIs, NITs often encounter a lot of resistance and can be difficult to implement.

Increased Minimum Wage

Increasing the minimum wage affects a relatively small proportion of the population but can result in ripple effects that increase the wages of other low-income earners as well.[57] It is estimated that a higher minimum wage could result in increased wages for up to nearly a third of workers in the United States. The federal minimum wage (currently $7.25 per hour since 2009) has long been recognized as insufficient to meet a reasonable standard of living alone, and raising it would shift the burden of supporting those in poverty from the government to the private sector. The proposed advantages in raising the minimum wage are well known, and include an increased standard of living, improved morale, and potentially increased demand for goods and services. Disadvantages include the possibility of inflation, as companies increase their prices to maintain their profit margins, and the elimination of jobs in order to do the same in response to the increased cost of labor. Additionally, it is possible that it could incentivize companies to rely increasingly on automated processes and technology to reduce the necessary amount of labor. The precise amount of change is unknown and varies substantially across analyses. Recent studies on Seattle's minimum wage increase passed in 2015, which has provided a series of minimum wage hikes, raising it first to $11 an hour and then to $15 an hour over the next four years (with variations depending on the size of the employer and degree of health benefits provided), have provided interesting insights to the real-world dynamics of dramatic wage increase policies. While a 2017 study by researchers from the University of Washington initially found that hours for low-wage employees fell from 6-7 percent (corresponding to a 3 percent increase in wage and resulting in a small net loss of income),[58] a follow-up study in 2018 found that more experienced workers saw their wages increase enough to compensate for reduced hours, while those with less experience came out roughly even.[59] Oregon's minimum wages increased based on inflation starting in 2023 (annual increases are based on any increases to the US city average consumer price index for all urban consumers), and thus the effects will become more evident over time. Although increasing wages addresses part of the problem of achieving a reasonable standard of living, the recommendations provided in chapter 6 to increase housing supply and affordability can function in a complementary manner.

Access Programs

Programs that are designed to subsidize, improve, and provide access to education, health care, job training, childcare, and more are all effective ways to lessen the impact of lower wages on economic outcomes by providing services typically only available to certain income levels to all. Such programs may have a political advantage, as these universal benefits counter arguments that emphasize waste or claim suspicion of recipients to a greater degree than cash payments. For the provision of services like childcare or health care, this works well. When it comes to voucher programs, however, from an economic standpoint, the limitations on use can be a disadvantage: the most economically efficient means of aid can be used in any context—that is, cash—as it avoids any distortion accrued when a particular good that might be less valuable to the recipient is preferred because it is free. Restrictions on how money can be spent may not result in the most efficient use of funds for the individuals using the program. More research is needed into the relative efficiencies of the two program types, especially in the United States, as most research on aid has been performed in developing nations. A recent study from the Democratic Republic of Congo found that recipients of cash payments spent more diversely, while recipients of vouchers were more likely to purchase items that were more durable and could in theory be sold at a point in the future.[60] Direct provision of these services is yet another method to ensure access, but similar to voucher programs or unrestricted aid, the structuring of adequate and sustainable revenue sources (see chap. 13 for a more thorough discussion on government revenue generation) to fund access still presents a challenge. At the time of writing, Multnomah County has started implementing a Preschool for All program that its voters approved in 2020, funded by a "personal income tax of 1.5 percent on taxable income over $125,000 for individuals and $200,000 for joint filers, and an additional 1.5 percent on taxable income over $250,000 for individuals and $400,000 for joint filers" to provide "access to free, high-quality, developmentally appropriate, culturally responsive preschool experiences" for 3- to 4-year old children.[61] This follows a growing number of cities and states that have started to provide universal preschool, and similar efforts are also underway in other Oregon counties and at the state level.

Safety Net Programs

Policies that serve as so-called social safety nets, like food stamps, unemployment insurance, and temporary housing subsidy programs (discussed in chaps. 6 and 11), can reduce inequality by lessening the consequences of a poor economic climate on lower-income households and individuals. These policies are also known as social insurance. The advantages are that they provide support when it is most needed, with disadvantages being that they provide support *only* when it is most needed. They are often insufficient to address systemic inequalities and in the reality of an inequitable labor market and economy that offers few opportunities for people at the bottom of the economic ladder.

Tax Reform

If tax policies are reformed to be more progressive, meaning that higher earners pay a greater proportion of their income than lower earners, then inequality is reduced over time, provided that the policy is effective. See chapter 13 for a deeper look at tax policy in Oregon.

Notes

The authors thank Josh Lehner (Oregon Office of Economic Analysis), Edward Sullivan (land use lawyer), and Noelwah R. Netusil (PhD, professor of economics at Reed College) for providing constructive feedback on drafts.

1. "Oregon's Economy: An Overview," Oregon Employment Department, Workforce and Economic Resource Division, Oregon Blue Book, accessed January 2, 2024, https://sos.oregon.gov/blue-book/Pages/facts/economy-overview.aspx.
2. Josh Lehner, "Oregon's Income Distribution," Oregon Office of Economic Analysis, April 4, 2019, https://oregoneconomicanalysis.com/2019/04/04/oregons-income-distribution.
3. Estelle Sommeiler, Mark Price, and Ellis Wazeter, "Income Inequality in the US by State, Metropolitan Area, and County," Economic Policy Institute, June 16, 2016, https://www.epi.org/publication/income-inequality-in-the-us.
4. Josh Lehner, "Not Fun Friday: Low-Wage Workers and Income Disparities," Oregon Office of Economic Analysis, September 25, 2020, https://oregoneconomicanalysis.com/2020/09/25/not-fun-friday-low-wage-workers-and-income-disparities.
5. "State Annual Summary Statistics: Personal Income, GDP, Consumer Spending, Price Indexes, and Employment," US Bureau of Economic Analysis, accessed February 6, 2024, https://www.bea.gov/itable/regional-gdp-and-personal-income.
6. "Civilian Labor Force in Oregon (ORLF)," Federal Reserve Bank of St. Louis, February 6, 2024, https://fred.stlouisfed.org/series/ORLF.
7. The Great Recession of 2008 was a global slowdown in markets between 2007 and 2009 caused by many factors, one of which was the subprime mortgage crisis in the United States.
8. Alexander W. Richter, Daniel Chapman, and Emil Mihaylov, "Declining US Labor Force Participation Rates Stand Out," *Economic Letter* 13, no. 6 (April 2018): https://www.dallasfed.org/research/~/media/documents/research/eclett/2018/el1806.pdf.
9. Active labor market policies include public job training and creation programs, job search assistance, and other interventions directed at the labor force itself.

10   Government jobs are considered separately from private jobs, as they ebb and flow in response to policy rather than market forces.
11   Maria Hasenstab, "Nonfarm Payrolls: Why Farmers Aren't Included in Jobs Data," Federal Reserve Bank of St. Louis, July 13, 2019, https://www.stlouisfed.org/openvault/2019/july/nonfarm-payrolls-why-farmers-not-included.
12   "Farm Labor: Legal Status and Migration Practices of Hired Crop Farmworkers," US Department of Agriculture, Economic Research Service, April 22, 2020, https://www.ers.usda.gov/topics/farm-economy/farm-labor/#legalstatus.
13   Bruce Sorte, Jeffrey Reimer, and Gordon Jones, *Oregon Agriculture, Food and Fiber: An Economic Analysis* (Corvallis: Oregon State University College of Agricultural Sciences, 2021), https://agsci.oregonstate.edu/sites/agscid7/files/main/about/oragecon_report_2021.pdf.
14   Edward J. Sullivan and Noelwah Netusil, "Oregon's Goal 9: Economic Development and Land Use Planning," *Willamette Law Review* 58, no. 3 (2022): 363-436.
15   Sullivan and Netusil, "Oregon's Goal 9."
16   "Economic Development: Background Brief," Oregon Legislative Policy and Research Office, accessed January 2, 2024, https://www.oregonlegislature.gov/lpro/Publications/Background-Brief-Economic-Development.pdf.
17   Luke Coury, "Race and Ethnic Diversity in Oregon's Workforce," Oregon Employment Department, January 22, 2024, https://www.qualityinfo.org/-/race-and-ethnic-diversity-in-oregon-s-workforce.
18   "2022 American Community Survey, 5-Year Estimates," Table S1701, US Census Bureau, generated by Jenny Liu on February 6, 2024, https://data.census.gov/cedsci/.
19   "2022 American Community Survey, 5-Year Estimates," Table S1903, US Census Bureau, generated by Jenny Liu on February 6, 2024, https://data.census.gov/cedsci/.
20   Coury, "Race and Ethnic Diversity."
21   US Bureau of Labor Statistics, "Real Median Household Income in Oregon," Federal Reserve Bank of St. Louis, accessed February 6, 2024, https://fred.stlouisfed.org/series/MEHOINUSORA672N. As context, the living wage in Multnomah County, Oregon, is calculated by the Massachusetts Institute of Technology's Living Wage Calculator to be at $39,231 before taxes for a single adult living alone, or $69,852 for two adults and one child.
22   "US BLS Quarterly Census of Employment and Wages (QCEW), Oregon Annual 2019," US Bureau of Labor Statistics, generated by Jenny Liu on February 6, 2024, https://data.bls.gov/cew/apps/table_maker/v4/table_maker.htm#type=10&year=2022&qtr=A&own=5&area=41000&supp=0.
23   "2022 American Community Survey, 5-Year Estimates," Table S1501, US Census Bureau, generated by Jenny Liu on February 6, 2024, https://data.census.gov/table/ACSST5Y2022.S1501?q=Educational%20Attainment&g=040XX00US41&moe=false.
24   Josh Lehner, "Economic Disparities, an Ongoing Discussion," Oregon Office of Economic Analysis, June 4, 2020, https://oregoneconomicanalysis.com/2020/06/04/economic-disparities-an-ongoing-discussion.
25   "2022 Survey of Consumer Finances (SCF)," Board of Governors of the Federal Reserve System, accessed February 9, 2024, https://www.federalreserve.gov/econres/scfindex.htm.
26   "2022 American Community Survey, 5-Year Estimates," Table S1701.

27. "2022 American Community Survey, 5-Year Estimates," Table S2301, US Census Bureau, generated by Jenny Liu on February 9, 2024, https://data.census.gov/table/ACSST5Y2022.S2301?q=s2301&g=040XX00US41&tid=ACSST1Y2022.S2301.
28. "Women Still Paid Less Than Men: Oregon's Gender Pay Gap," Oregon Center for Public Policy, April 11, 2016, https://www.ocpp.org/2016/04/11/fs20160411-oregon-gender-pay-gap-women/.
29. Elise Gould, Jessica Schieder, and Kathleen Geier, "What Is the Gender Pay Gap and Is It Real?," Economic Policy Institute, October 20, 2016, https://www.epi.org/publication/what-is-the-gender-pay-gap-and-is-it-real.
30. "American Time Use Survey," Table A-1, US Bureau of Labor Statistics, accessed February 9, 2024, https://www.bls.gov/tus/.
31. Child Care Aware of America, *Parents and the High Cost of Childcare* (Arlington, VA: Child Care Aware of America, 2015), https://www.childcareaware.org/wp-content/uploads/2016/03/Parents-and-the-High-Cost-of-Child-Care-2015-FINAL.pdf.
32. Megan Pratt and Michaella Sektnan, *Oregon's Child Care Deserts 2020: Mapping Supply by Age Group and Percentage of Publicly Funded Slots* (Corvallis: Oregon State University, College of Public Health and Human Service, 2021), https://health.oregonstate.edu/sites/health.oregonstate.edu/files/early-learners/pdf/research/oregons-child-care-deserts-2020.pdf.
33. "2012 American Community Survey, 5-Year Estimates," Table S1703, US Census Bureau, generated by Jenny Liu on February 9, 2024, https://data.census.gov/table/ACSST5Y2022.S1703?q=s1703&g=040XX00US41&moe=false&tid=ACSST5Y2019.S1703 >
34. Audrey Mechling, "A Portrait of Poverty in Oregon," Oregon Center for Public Policy, August 7, 2020, https://www.ocpp.org/2020/08/07/poverty-oregon/.
35. "HINC-04. Presence of Children under 18 Years Old—Households, by Total Money Income, Type of Household, Race and Hispanic Origin of Householder," US Census Bureau, last revised August 9, 2023, https://www.census.gov/data/tables/time-series/demo/income-poverty/cps-hinc/hinc-04.html.
36. Human Rights Campaign, *2019 State Equality Index* (Washington, DC: Human Rights Campaign, 2019), https://hrc-prod-requests.s3-us-west-2.amazonaws.com/resources/2019-SEI-Final-Report.pdf.
37. "2022 American Community Survey, 5-Year Estimates," Table S1810: Disability Characteristics, US Census Bureau, generated by Jenny Liu on February 9, 2024, https://data.census.gov/table/ACSST5Y2022.S1810?q=s1810&g=040XX00US41&moe=false.
38. "2022 American Community Survey, 5-Year Estimates," Table B18140, US Census Bureau, generated by Jenny Liu on February 9, 2024, https://data.census.gov/table/ACSDT5Y2022.B18140?q=disability%20earnings&g=010XX00US_040XX00US41&tid=ACSDT1Y2022.B18140.
39. "Disability Statistics," Cornell University, accessed February 9, 2024, https://disabilitystatistics.org/acs/6.
40. "2022 American Community Survey, 5-Year Estimates," Table S1811: Selected Economic Characteristics for the Civilian Noninstitutionalized Population by Disability Status, US Census Bureau, generated by Jenny Liu on February 9, 2024, https://data.census.gov/table/ACSST5Y2022.S1811?q=disability%20type&g=010XX00US_040XX00US41&moe=false&tid=ACSST1Y2022.S1811.
41. Eric Knoder, "First Quarter 2020: Jobs Increase and Median Wage Rises," Oregon Employment Department, October 8, 2020, https://www.qualityinfo.org/-/first-quarter-2020-jobs-increase-and-median-wage-rises; Felicia Bechtoldt, "Oregon

Jobs Projected to Increase 16 Percent by 2030," Oregon Employment Department, November 22, 2021, https://www.qualityinfo.org/-/oregon-jobs-projected-to-increase-16-by-2030.

42 Dallas Fridley, "Recent Wage Gains Short-Lived as Inflation Reaches 40-Year High," Oregon Employment Department, March 7, 2022, https://www.qualityinfo.org/-/recent-wage-gains-short-lived-as-inflation-reaches-40-year-high.

43 Mark Muro, Robert Maxim, and Jacob Whiton, *Automation and Artificial Intelligence: How Machines Are Affecting People and Places* (Washington, DC: Brookings Institution, 2019), https://www.brookings.edu/research/automation-and-artificial-intelligence-how-machines-affect-people-and-places.

44 "Quarterly Census of Employment and Wages 2022 Annual," Bureau of Labor Statistics, retrieved February 9, 2024, https://data.bls.gov/cew/apps/data_views/data_views.htm#tab=Tables.

45 Josh Lehner, "Oregon's Trade with China (Graph of the Week)," Oregon Office of Economic Analysis, April 11, 2018, https://oregoneconomicanalysis.com/2018/04/11/oregon-trade-with-china-graph-of-the-week/.

46 Josh Lehner, "Oregon's Trade with China (Graph of the Week)," Oregon Office of Economic Analysis, April 5, 2019, https://oregoneconomicanalysis.com/2019/04/05/oregon-exports-strong-dollar-and-trade-tensions.

47 US China Business Council, *2020 State Export Report: Goods and Services Exports by US States to China over the Past Decade* (Washington, DC: US China Business Council, 2020), https://www.uschina.org/sites/default/files/2020_state_export_report_full_report_1.pdf.

48 Jamie Goldberg, "Over 80 Percent of Oregon Restaurant Workers Laid Off or Furloughed Due to Coronavirus Shutdown, Survey Finds," *The Oregonian*, April 22, 2020, https://www.oregonlive.com/coronavirus/2020/04/over-80-percent-of-oregon-restaurant-workers-have-been-laid-off-or-furloughed-due-to-the-coronavirus-shutdown.html.

49 Lehner, "Not Fun Friday."

50 "Downtown Portland as a Commercial Center: A Look Forward," Portland State University, November 15, 2022, https://www.pdx.edu/events/downtown-portland-commercial-center-look-forward.

51 Josh Lehner, "Oregon's Labor Market Is Normalizing," Oregon Office of Economic Analysis, November 30, 2022, https://oregoneconomicanalysis.com/2022/11/30/oregons-labor-market-is-normalizing.

52 Edward J. Sullivan, "The Quiet Revolution Goes West: The Oregon Planning Program 1961-2011," 45 *John Marshall Law Review* 357 (2012).

53 Andrea Durbin, "FY 2021-22 Fall BuMP—Bureau of Planning and Sustainability," September 9, 2021, https://www.portlandoregon.gov/cbo/article/796026.

54 Dirk VanderHart, "New Fund for Black Oregonians Faces Mounting Legal Pressure," Oregon Public Broadcasting, November 25, 2020, https://www.opb.org/article/2020/11/25/oregon-cares-fund-coronavirus-pandemic-black-owned-businesses.

55 "Frequently Asked Questions," Alaska Permanent Fund Corporation, accessed January 2, 2024, https://apfc.org/frequently-asked-questions.

56 The Oregon EITC augments the federal EITC by providing 9 percent of the federal credit as a state tax credit to those who are eligible.

57 Benjamin H. Harris and Melissa S. Kearney, "The 'Ripple Effect' of a Minimum Wage Increase on American Workers," Brookings Institution, January 10, 2014, https://www.brookings.edu/blog/up-front/2014/01/10/the-ripple-effect-of-a-minimum-wage-increase-on-american-workers.

58 Ekaterina Jardim, Mark C. Long, Robert Plotnick, Emma van Inwegen, Jacob Vigdor, and Hilary Wething, *Minimum Wage Increases, Wages, and Low-Wage Employment: Evidence from Seattle*, NBER Working Paper 23532 (Cambridge, MA: National Bureau of Economic Research, 2017), https://www.nber.org/papers/w23532.

59 Ekaterina Jardim, Mark C. Long, Robert Plotnick, Emma van Inwegen, Jacob Vigdor, and Hilary Wething, *Minimum Wage Increases and Individual Employment Trajectories*, NBER Working Paper 25182 (Cambridge, MA: National Bureau of Economic Research, 2018), https://www.nber.org/papers/w25182.

60 Jenny C. Aker, "Comparing Cash and Voucher Transfers in a Humanitarian Context: Evidence from the Democratic Republic of Congo," *World Bank Economic Review* 31, no. 1 (2017): 44–70, https://doi.org/10.1093/wber/lhv055.

61 "Multnomah County Preschool for All Personal Income Tax," Multnomah County, updated February 14, 2023, https://www.multco.us/finance/multnomah-county-preschool-all-personal-income-tax.

11
Homelessness

JACEN GREENE AND MARISA A. ZAPATA

Across the West Coast, people see the visible damage of an ongoing affordable housing crisis in the form of unsheltered homelessness.[1] People living in tents, recreational vehicles, and cars are ever present: under bridges, along freeways, in the woods, and in vacant lots across cities, suburbs, small towns, and rural areas. The crisis is particularly felt in Oregon. Though Oregon's housing costs have been comparably lower to those in Washington and California, over the past decade the state's property values have increased. When access to housing is reduced owing to rent increases, displacement, removal of naturally occurring affordable housing, and more, we see increases in homelessness. Coupled with a rollback of federal investments in affordable housing over the past several decades, accessing and staying in housing becomes harder for people making modest to low wages. In Oregon, the state's prioritization of other issues and structural taxation challenges have resulted in a limited ability, or commitment, to invest in quality housing for people who do not make a living wage.

Compared to other parts of the country, homelessness appears to be a greater problem in Oregon and the rest of the West Coast. This perception reflects the number of people visibly experiencing homelessness while living outside (also called "unsheltered"). In other parts of the country, there have been significant investments in emergency shelter and transitional housing systems, or a relative abundance of "naturally occurring" affordable housing (although such housing may be of a poor quality). Because Oregon developed its homelessness response system at a different time than the East Coast, homelessness service providers have an opportunity to better invest in the solution to homelessness: housing.

The unsheltered population is just a small portion of the people experiencing homelessness. When accounting for people living in shelter and K–12 students and their families living unsafely doubled up, the actual number of people experiencing homelessness climbs into the tens of thousands of people. People of color are most affected, experiencing homelessness disproportionately. Black and Native Hawaiian/Pacific Islander Oregonians are over three times more likely to experience homelessness when compared to white Oregonians, while Native Oregonians experience homelessness at a rate more than double that of white Oregonians.[2]

Homelessness itself is not new to the United States or to Oregon, and its recent increased visibility is only part of what has driven homelessness to the forefront of city politics. Unsheltered people live in spaces where they are trying to survive, well beyond the basic infrastructure that traditionally comes with housing. They are certainly not living in a way imagined by the founders of Oregon's famed state land use system. Without hygiene and waste services, our unhoused community members are forced to manage their own bathroom and trash removal needs however they can. Not surprisingly, people living outside in these circumstances have drawn the attention of their neighbors. Housed Oregonians repeatedly rank homelessness as one of their top concerns in surveys about priority issues. From compassion about unhoused neighbors to not-in-my-backyard leaders to concerns about the impacts of human waste on the environment, the reasons for the rankings vary.

One initial collective outcome of the higher visibility and public concern in the Portland area is that voters recently passed three revenue measures to increase affordable housing and supportive services. The Oregon State Legislature has made unparalleled moves to advance housing supply, rent assistance, access to housing, and supportive services across the state. Localities are experimenting with alternatives to congregate shelter (oriented toward group or community housing needs) in the form of villages with small sleeping pods that include basic infrastructure and sanitation, and using motels left empty during the COVID-19 pandemic as shelter.

Despite these activities in recent years in a place known for its progressiveness, as we finalize this chapter in the winter of 2024, we see the tide shifting in Portland and across the country away from creative solutions. As the housing emergency described in chapter 6 shows no visible signs of resolution, elected officials and community members are calling for camping bans and creating mass camps to which people can be moved. Housing and homelessness advocates are on the cusp of losing their fight to provide the only known solution to homelessness, which is housing.

In this chapter, we provide an introduction to homelessness, including understanding estimates, causes, programmatic and policy solutions, and the futures we foresee based on different values and related policy decisions. We pay particular attention to the impacts of homelessness on people of color. One key argument we make is that homelessness is a solvable issue. We hope the information provided here offers readers a pathway to envision success in the face of a seemingly intractable issue and motivates us all to stem the tide away from temporary shelter and to housing, whether the year is 2024 or 2050.

Origins, Definitions, and Estimates

Homelessness is inextricably linked to the foundation of the United States. As Native American homelessness advocates say, none of them were homeless before 1492. Similarly, 1619 marks the beginning year for Africans and African Americans becoming homeless in the United States. Further entrenching homelessness in the United States, early white, male, affluent colonists brought with them the constructs of private property and ownership. Women were not allowed to own land or structures, while Africans and their descendants were classified as property. People with mental illnesses and substance use disorders were cast aside or locked away. These early forms of homelessness were not viewed as being unhoused. Rather, they were accepted societal positions. The truly homeless were those seen sleeping and living on the street, begging for money, and maybe living with unmet behavioral health needs.

These types of overlooked homelessness from the early years of the nation continue to have repercussions today in the disparities found in homeless populations, how resources are accessed, and by whom. "Homelessness" even has multiple definitions across different federal agencies, which leads to different estimates of the total number of people experiencing homelessness. The US Department of Housing and Urban Development (HUD) defines homelessness as "lacking a fixed, regular, and adequate nighttime residence"[3] and therefore includes only those who are experiencing unsheltered homelessness or who are in emergency shelters and transitional housing. The US Department of Education defines homelessness as youth in grades K–12 who are either homeless under the HUD definition or are living in another person's housing owing to a loss of their home or economic hardship, rather than by choice—a "doubled-up" population.[4] Multnomah County, the City of Portland, and the City of Gresham adopted a definition of homelessness to include people who are doubled up "unsafely," providing resources to those doubled up but not in households with children enrolled in K–12 schools.

These different definitions are not the only important deviation in understanding data sources about homelessness. As a requirement for receiving federal funding to address homelessness, local Continuums of Care (CoCs)—coordinated networks of government agencies and homeless service providers in specific geographies—must conduct a count of homeless individuals at a point in time (PIT) on a single night at least every other year. National PIT counts conducted in 2023 estimated that 653,000 people experienced homelessness across the country.[5] Of these, about 256,600 experienced unsheltered homelessness.[6] Overall homelessness and unsheltered homelessness have risen for the past several years, reaching record highs in 2023.[7] Even within the narrow definition used by HUD, however, PIT counts are believed to understate the true prevalence of homelessness owing to wide variations in methodologies, funding, staffing, training, and motivation between different CoCs.[8] Throughout the year in 2021, nearly 1.21 million people moved through the US shelter system, although this marked a decrease in part because of COVID policies.[9] Black, Indigenous, and people of color (BIPOC) make up a majority of those experiencing homelessness across the country, with Black people alone making up 37 percent despite comprising only 13 percent of the overall US population.[10] The impacts of structural racism on homelessness are discussed in more detail later.

In the 2021–22 school year, roughly 1.2 million enrolled students ages 5 to 18 in the United States were believed to have experienced homelessness.[11] Teachers and staff at local school districts collect and report these numbers by using observed behaviors and characteristics rather than interviews. But parents and adult family members also experiencing homelessness were not included in this estimate and would not have been counted under the HUD definition if they were living doubled up. A count of college and university students experiencing homelessness is not required by the federal government, but a national survey of students at more than 220 two- and four-year institutions found that 17 percent of respondents experienced homelessness in the previous year, according to a definition developed by California State University researchers.[12]

The Homelessness Research and Action Collaborative (HRAC) at Portland State University (PSU) estimated that 20,110 people in Oregon experienced homelessness on a single night in 2023 based on PIT counts.[13] Oregon consistently has one of the highest ratios of unsheltered to sheltered homelessness in the nation,[14] reflecting the fact that Oregon has only about 7,953 year-round emergency shelter and transitional housing beds for people experiencing homelessness.[15] As with national estimates, this reflects a rise in recent years, with PIT counts nearly matching the previous peak reached in the 2008 recession.[16] Many regions across the state switched to more effective counting methodologies during this period, however, so the extent to which this is an actual increase or simply a higher, more accurate accounting regardless of underlying trends is unknown.

Black, Native American, and Hawaiian/Pacific Islander Oregonians all experience homelessness at a rate more than double their proportion of the Oregon population.[17] These disparities are consistent with other areas of inequity, such as income, educational attainment, and the like. Table 11.1 lists racialized rates of homelessness for these and other races.

The data about Latino and Asian community members should be interpreted with caution. First, both Asians and Latinos experience disparities in other areas such as poverty rates, educational attainment, and the like. There are various explanations for why these two communities would appear to have less representation in the homeless population counts. Immigrants are an especially difficult population to count, especially when many people are undocumented and trying

Table 11.1. Racial and Ethnic Disparities in Homelessness in Oregon, 2020 (PIT Count Data)

Ethnicity	Homeless %	Population %
White	81.3%	87%
Black or African American	5.7%	2.20%
Asian	0.80%	4.90%
American Indian or Alaska Native	4.90%	1.80%
Native Hawaiian or other Pacific Islander	1.10%	0.50%
Multiple Races	6.20%	4%
Non-Hispanic/Non-Latino	90.60%	86.60%
Hispanic/Latino	9.40%	13.4%

Source: PIT count data from "HUD 2020 Continuum of Care Homeless Assistance Programs Homeless Populations and Subpopulations, Oregon," US Department of Housing and Urban Development, December 15, 2020, https://files.hudexchange.info/reports/published/CoC_PopSub_State_OR_2020.pdf.

to avoid government attention. Immigrants, especially people who are undocumented, are also ineligible for most federal assistance. While these issues are reasons for undercounting all people of color, they play particularly important roles in undercounting homelessness within the Latino and Asian communities, where there are high numbers of immigrants. Lastly, definitions of homelessness vary culturally, and without better accounting of the doubled-up population, we do not know if Latinos and Asians are simply experiencing another type of homelessness more often. For all of the populations of color, there is also a lack of attention to subpopulations. Data are aggregated, meaning they obscure the differentiated experiences of Asian, Latino, Black, and Native American subpopulations.

While data are missing to illustrate the full extent of homelessness among BIPOC communities, in other areas the data help to illuminate that rates of homelessness are lower among some groups than commonly believed. Contrary to public perception, most people experiencing homelessness, even within the more restrictive HUD definition, do not report living with a serious mental illness or substance use disorder (see table 11.2).

Using the US Department of Education definition shows a dramatically higher rate of homelessness than the HUD definition and PIT counts. Per the mandated schools count, roughly 22,900 public school students and young children in Oregon were believed to have experienced homelessness in the 2022–23 school year,[18] or slightly less than 4 percent of the total student population. In a 2019 survey at fourteen of Oregon's seventeen community colleges, 20 percent of students were found to have experienced homelessness in the previous year.[19] Assuming this proportion holds true at the remaining three community colleges in the state, this would represent more than 52,000 community college students experiencing homelessness in Oregon, not including private and public university students.[20] At Portland State University in 2019, roughly 16 percent of students reported experiencing homelessness in the previous year,[21] an estimated 4,000 students.[22] BIPOC students experienced disproportionately higher rates of homelessness than their white peers, mirroring regional and national trends, with Native American students in particular almost twice as likely as white students to experience homelessness.

PSU's HRAC and Northwest Economic Research Center (NERC) used estimates based on the more expansive and accurate Department of Education definition along with PIT counts and annual service numbers to estimate that roughly 38,000 people experienced some form of homelessness in the Portland metropolitan region in 2017.[23] HRAC and NERC extrapolated the formula used to estimate the total number of people experiencing some form of homelessness in the Portland region across the rest of the state, and the result was a much higher total than other estimates. This formula includes family members of students experiencing doubled-up homelessness (using the most recent average

Table 11.2. Selected Demographics of People Experiencing Homelessness in Oregon, 2020

Demographic	Percentage of Total Homeless Population
Severely mentally ill	17.22
Chronic substance abuse	15.50
Survivors of domestic violence	10.15

Source: PIT count data from "HUD 2020 Continuum of Care Homeless Assistance Programs Homeless Populations and Subpopulations, Oregon," US Department of Housing and Urban Development, December 15, 2020, https://files.hudexchange.info/reports/published/CoC_PopSub_State_OR_2020.pdf.

family size estimates available from American Community Survey data) and multiplies unsheltered PIT counts by a factor of 1.9 (based on other studies looking at the rates at which PIT counts underestimate actual unsheltered homelessness). Using this calculation, an estimated 68,000 people experienced homelessness across Oregon in 2019, with just over 19,000 of them experiencing unsheltered homelessness.[24] Homelessness is widespread across Oregon, with high rates in both urban and rural areas, but an exact comparison is challenging owing to limited data availability in some regions.

These numbers, however shocking they may be, diminish the complex and traumatic individual experiences of the causal factors that lead to homelessness and the experience of homelessness itself. What homelessness is like differs based on the factors which led to it, the individual reality of it, and a person's identity and life experiences. In the next section we discuss the factors that lead to homelessness.

Drivers, Factors, and Connections

Regardless of the definition or the data source, research consistently demonstrates that the main driver of homelessness is a lack of access to stable and safe housing. Multiple studies have demonstrated the connection between the availability and affordability of housing with homelessness, as higher median rent or home prices, lower vacancy rates, and lack of affordable housing are correlated with higher rates of homelessness.[25] The relationship between housing and income is reflected in rates of "cost-burdened" households, which pay more than 30 percent of their income on housing, or "severely cost-burdened" households, which pay more than 50 percent of their income on housing.[26] As mentioned in chapter 6, 22 percent of households in Oregon were severely cost burdened in 2021, with higher rates among Black and Native American households, older adults, and people with a disability.[27] BIPOC households face extensive historical and current discrimination in rental applications in Oregon that affects their ability to access housing.[28]

The primary driver of homeless in housing affordability is obvious. But previous efforts to address homelessness focused instead on making people "housing ready." This orientation resulted in a focus on preparing people experiencing homelessness to take on the perceived responsibility of housing or rewarding people for managing their health or finances well. The idea of housing being something that could only be earned came from the belief that homelessness was the result of irresponsibility or an inability to care for oneself, particularly for people with serious mental illnesses or substance use disorders. In the 1990s, practitioners, advocates, and people experiencing homelessness examined new models to address homelessness. Studies of the "housing first" model, discussed later in more detail, proved that housing was the best way to resolve homelessness. In housing first, housing is provided with no requirements of sobriety or program participation, and services are optional, not required.

This finding solidified the understanding that housing served to both prevent and end homelessness. Yet methods to provide housing to everyone are significantly underfunded. Housing vouchers are provided by the federal government to assist with affordability, but a lack of funding means they are only distributed to roughly 25 percent of eligible households, and a dramatic shortage of affordable units worsens the issue.[29] According to Oregon's new Housing Needs Assessment framework (see below for additional detail), an estimated 139,000 additional units of housing are needed to address current housing shortages across Oregon, with 29,000 of those units dedicated to people experiencing homelessness.[30] Of those units dedicated to addressing homelessness, 89 percent would need to be affordable for households making less than 30 percent of area median family income.[31] An estimate by HRAC and NERC found a much higher level of need, with slightly more than 42,000 units of housing needed for everyone experiencing homelessness in Oregon, of which about 10,500 should be associated with supportive services.

While homelessness is understood as caused by the lack of access to, or ability to afford, housing, other systemic failures amplify the risk for someone to become homeless, including low incomes, disabilities, and more. The intersection of these issues results in a complicated set of related factors, all of which are either caused or worsened by racism and other types of bias. Figure 11.1 shows the common societal infrastructure or systems, which are often referenced in relation to homelessness as pipes. Even in the ideal situation, when the pipes are flowing, discrimination hampers individual and community well-being. Right now, the pipes are broken and leaking into a bucket. Regarding homelessness, the greatest leaks come from the economy and housing systems. Combined with the other leaks, the endless dripping from the pipes have now overwhelmed the bucket and have produced homelessness. Figure 11.1 also highlights ways to think about ending homelessness through creative ways of rethinking the traditional systems.

The intersection of racism and homelessness is a significant systemic issue that causes homelessness in Oregon. The legacy of colonialism and racism gave rise to the fact that "indigenous people of Oregon experience some of the worst outcomes and greatest disparities of any group across all outcomes, including housing."[32] Historically, Oregon took aggressive and damaging steps in its treatment, and exclusion,

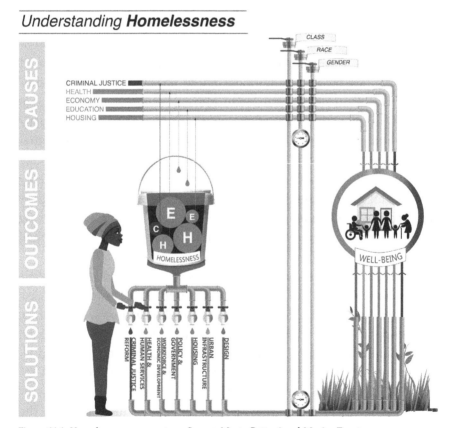

Figure 11.1. Homelessness as a system. *Source*: Marta Petteni and Marisa Zapata

of African Americans, often under the guise of progressive steps to end slavery. For example, in 1845 it was made illegal for Black people to reside in Oregon. Chapter 10 provides more information on these activities and more contemporary, racially motivated housing practices such as redlining, home ownership, tenant protections, and gentrification and displacement. The result of this racialized housing history is a direct line between early racialized actions and the disproportionate rates of homelessness for people of color. Racial discrimination also affects employment and income opportunities; arrest, conviction, and incarceration rates; health and behavioral health treatment; educational attainment; and many other factors.[33]

The criminal justice system also plays a role in creating and perpetuating homelessness. Those affected by the justice system are less likely to obtain employment, secure housing, or receive some services owing to discrimination and policy barriers, increasing their odds of experiencing future homelessness. Nationwide, formerly incarcerated people experience homelessness at a rate almost seven times higher than the general public, increasing to thirteen times higher after multiple incarcerations.[34] People currently experiencing homelessness are disproportionately targeted for policing, especially BIPOC, people with a severe mental illness, and people who have a substance use disorder.[35] Simply experiencing unsheltered homelessness in public has been widely criminalized across the United States and in Oregon.[36] In Portland alone in 2017, people experiencing homelessness represented just over half of all arrests despite comprising less than 3 percent of the population.[37] These arrests were overwhelmingly for nonviolent crimes, and many were for merely procedural offenses.[38]

Addressing at least one area of frequent citation and arrest, the Ninth Circuit Court of Appeals ruled in *Martin v. Boise* that "as long as there is no option of sleeping indoors, the government cannot criminalize indigent, homeless people for sleeping outdoors, on public property, on the false premise they had a choice in the matter."[39] In 2021, the Oregon Legislature passed House Bill 3115 to bring cities into compliance with the Ninth Circuit ruling and ensure that if *Martin v. Boise* was overturned, Oregon would still make progress in protecting people experiencing homelessness.[40]

While only a small minority of those experiencing homelessness are living with severe mental illness or substance use disorders, these health challenges can dramatically worsen economic inequality and criminal justice system interactions that contribute to homelessness. Among individuals experiencing literal homelessness across the United States, about 26 percent are estimated to have a severe mental illness, and 35 percent have a substance use disorder. These rates are lower among those experiencing short-term homelessness and higher among those experiencing long-term or frequent ("chronic") homelessness.[41] About 23 percent of people experiencing homelessness in the Portland metropolitan region in 2023 reported a mental illness, and about 26 percent reported substance abuse.[42] Mental illness and substance abuse frequently co-occur, are often worsened by the traumatic experience of homelessness, and may also occur alongside other disabling conditions such as a physical or developmental disability. It is hard to disentangle the cause and effect of these conditions. In the Portland area, 62 percent of those experiencing homelessness report three or more disabilities.[43] As mentioned above, individuals with a mental illness or substance use disorder are disproportionately targeted by policing, contributing to the fact that roughly half of the adults taken into custody by the Oregon Department of Corrections in 2020 were classified as having a substance "dependence/addiction," while approximately 60 percent either needed or would benefit from mental health treatment.[44] The intersections of mental illness, substance use, systemic and institutional racism, and incarceration dramatically increase the odds of future homelessness, especially for BIPOC community members, who are even more likely to be targeted by police and less likely to have access to effective behavioral health care. The intersection of race, mental health, and policing is explored in more detail in chapter 12.

Among children (up to age 18) and youth (ages 18-25), homelessness is driven by all of the issues listed above, although particular life experiences and identities stand out. More than 80 percent of women experiencing homelessness with their children have previously been affected by domestic violence.[45] Among youth, those without a high school diploma or GED, who have previous involvement in the foster care system, are currently parenting children of their own, or who identify as lesbian, gay, bisexual, transgender, or queer plus (LGBTQ+) are much more likely to experience homelessness.[46] As with all other categories of people experiencing homelessness, children and youth of color are overrepresented, with Black LGBTQ+ youth the most likely among all youth subgroups to report experiencing homelessness.[47]

Climate change is expected to increase the number of people experiencing homelessness and worsen the experiences of people experiencing unsheltered homelessness. In Oregon, more frequent and severe weather events such as floods and fires are displacing increasing numbers of both housed and unhoused people, often destroying housing and shelter in the process. The 2020 Oregon wildfires destroyed four thousand homes, mostly mobile homes, and forced more than two thousand people into emergency shelter.[48] The lost housing was a significant amount of the affordable housing in the area. Housed Oregonians have far better access to disaster relief services than those who are unhoused, with wildfire survivors who were previously experiencing homelessness turned away from shelters that served only previously housed survivors.[49] Hotter temperatures and worsening air quality from smoke, dust, and other particulates are inescapable for those living without shelter. Communities of color, which have been redlined into flood zones, forced through economic necessity to live in less resilient housing, or may lack documentation necessary to secure federal disaster relief, are expected to face greater housing insecurity from climate change. Chapter 3 explores the connection between natural disasters and groups more at risk due to poverty.

Housing insecurity and homelessness are deeply linked to issues of economic inequality; climate change vulnerability; medical and behavioral health accessibility, affordability, and effectiveness; housing affordability and availability; criminal justice; and above all, racism and discrimination. Any attempt to improve and expand race-centered and equity-focused services and supports in the areas listed above could be expected to reduce the number of people experiencing homelessness. Funding and direction for these programs are often the responsibility of government agencies at the federal, state, and local level.

Program and Policy Approaches

Deeply rooted economic inequality, worsened by racism and discrimination and coupled with dramatic shortages of affordable housing, continues to drive increasing homelessness in both the short term and the long term. The good news is that homelessness is solvable for most people, and preventable for almost all. In this section we discuss policy and programmatic approaches that advance the solution to homelessness—housing—which is continually proven by the research. For some people, additional services might be needed beyond the more conventional services we normally provide for housed people (e.g., electricity, roads, sewer). Those additional services might include policy changes or programs for people who have been convicted of felonies or live with severe mental illness, for example.

Because people are currently experiencing homelessness, and housing and services take time to become available even once they are funded, we also include some policy and programmatic approaches that would result in better treatment and support of people experiencing homelessness, mitigating some of its traumatizing and other negative effects of being homeless. Some of the policies and programs could also help prevent and resolve homelessness, and we discuss them as a spectrum of activities. Housing and services should be delivered with an explicit racial equity lens that centers the needs and experiences of BIPOC communities experiencing the greatest disparities in homelessness and housing insecurity, in a way that prioritizes their input and leadership.

Because of the scale of the homelessness crisis, all levels and branches of government have a role to play in enacting public policy to enable these approaches and in providing sufficient funding for successful implementation, either directly through public agencies or indirectly through nonprofits. But current government systems and structures, especially at the local level, may be inadequate for successful coordination and funding at the necessary scale; a reality that should be carefully considered when planning future approaches.

The responsibility of addressing homelessness in Oregon is distributed across a range of state and local jurisdictions. Oregon has eight CoCs, with one for each metropolitan area and one for the balance of the state, comprising a set of government agencies and nonprofits that provide housing, emergency shelter, and services to people at risk of or experiencing homelessness. Each school district in the state has at least one liaison responsible for assisting students and their family members experiencing homelessness, and the Oregon Department of Human Services has a runaway and homeless youth program. Oregon Housing and Community Services manages PIT and Homelessness Management Information System (HMIS) data submission to the federal government and works to address housing insecurity through policy, regulation, and distribution of federal funding via community action agencies located around the state.

The McKinney-Vento Homeless Assistance Act of 1987, which has been repeatedly reauthorized, provides federal funding to address homelessness through regional CoCs. As a requirement of federal funding, school districts and CoCs must conduct periodic counts of the number of people experiencing homelessness. As described above, however, conflicting definitions of "homelessness" complicate these totals. Records of people receiving services are kept using HMIS, a set of data collection and reporting requirements for CoCs and funding subrecipients. Each year, the federal government spends roughly $6.5 billion on homelessness services and a further $59 billion in tax credits and grants on low-income housing and housing assistance programs.[50] But overall federal housing assistance shrunk from 9 percent of nondefense discretionary spending in 2000 to 7.1 percent in 2019, corresponding with an increase of 6 million cost-burdened households.[51]

Housing First and Permanent Supportive Housing

Shelters, either traditional congregate shelters or emerging alternative shelters such as tent encampments or collections of tiny dwellings, are by definition not a solution to homelessness. Even under the narrowest federal definition, someone living in a shelter is still experiencing homelessness. Such approaches can be a useful interim measure if delivered without barriers rather than as a substitute for permanent housing. Truly addressing homelessness requires building enough housing for all those experiencing homelessness, of a form appropriate to their household size and needs, in a location where they can easily access essential services and engage with the broader community, and with associated supportive services as needed. Extensive research has shown that housing should be made immediately available to those experiencing homelessness without preconditions or requirements such as sobriety or involvement in services.[52] One study in Washington, DC, found that people who were severely disabled, alcohol dependent, and previously experiencing homelessness made significant mental and behavioral health improvements within a single year after receiving barrier-free housing linked to voluntary services.[53] Additional supportive or wraparound services are needed on a permanent basis for some people experiencing homelessness who also have a disabling condition. This approach, called "permanent supportive housing," has been widely demonstrated to be highly effective in addressing homelessness. Once someone is stably housed and connected to the wider community, they are more able to engage in services and treatment, more successful in those programs, experience fewer interactions with the criminal justice system, and have better health outcomes, all with an approach that is typically cost-neutral or saves money for society as a whole owing to avoided incarceration, emergency shelter, and medical costs.[54]

But cost savings from permanent supportive housing may not flow back to the organizations that incur the costs to launch and manage such programs, creating a "wrong pocket" program. For example, local health care systems may recognize cost savings from reduced utilization, while local government or nonprofits incur the cost of new programs. One emerging model to address misaligned cost incentives is to have health systems invest in supportive housing, for example, through the Regional Supportive Housing Impact Fund (RSHIF). Health Share of Oregon, the coordinated care organization that manages Medicaid resources in the Portland metropolitan region, administered philanthropic and health system funding for RSHIF to provide housing and services to people at high risk of or experiencing homelessness along with complex medical needs.[55] Such approaches offer promise if they can be scaled up to reach more individuals and extended beyond pilot projects to ensure that they are truly permanent, such as through Medicaid waivers that can provide funding for housing. In late 2023, Oregon received a waiver from the federal government for such a Medicaid program to provide rent assistance to people at risk of or experiencing homelessness.[56]

Given the extensive links between racism, discrimination, and homelessness, any permanent supportive housing program would need to have an approach grounded in racial equity, culturally specific services, and trauma-informed care. A survey conducted by HRAC and local nonprofit advocacy newspaper *Street Roots* that was focused on BIPOC community members experiencing unsheltered homelessness illustrates this need. The top concerns of Black respondents in maintaining housing were living in mixed-race housing or experiencing racism from property managers.[57] For Latino respondents, having someone speak like them when receiving services was critical.[58] And in terms of feeling supported in community, Native Americans listed "fewer experiences of racial discrimination" nearly as often as "food."[59] The ability to successfully access and continue in housing and service programs was linked to being able to do so free of racism and discrimination.

Portland Metro passed a supportive housing services bond in early 2020 to generate tax revenue for programs that help people experiencing or at high risk of homelessness access and remain in housing. Three-quarters of the funding was reserved to support people experiencing chronic homelessness.[60] Multnomah, Washington, and Clackamas Counties developed local implementation plans in early 2021 for their share of the revenue, with overall coordination and oversight provided by the Metro authority.[61] Revenue collection for the measure began in April 2021 with program implementation starting that summer.[62] Although the funding was expected to greatly expand wraparound services for permanent supportive housing, at the time the measure passed, there were not enough designated housing units for the high numbers of people experiencing homelessness in the region. Two recently passed housing regional housing bonds and a new statewide approach for determining housing production needs were designed in part to remedy this gap in affordable and supportive housing.

Affordable and Public Housing

Oregon faces a critical shortage of affordable housing that significantly contributes to homelessness. At least 140,000 new housing units are needed across Oregon (see chap. 6 for additional detail), with 42,000 of those just for people experiencing homelessness. In 2016, Portland voters approved an affordable housing bond that would raise $258 million and leverage additional funding to build 1,300 affordable housing units.[63] By 2020, nearly 1,500 units were either built or in development, exceeding the original goal.[64] A similar bond measure for the entire metropolitan region passed in 2018 and was expected to raise $643 million to construct 3,900 new housing units for 12,000 people, with 1,600 units reserved for extremely low-income households.[65] While these are important steps, a much larger effort to construct new, highly affordable housing would be needed to support everyone in the region at risk of or experiencing homelessness. In 2022, the City of Portland estimated that 20,000 additional units of affordable housing were needed for cost-burdened households at risk of homelessness, with a construction cost of $490,000 per new unit, or $9.8 billion in total.[66] In 2019, the Oregon Legislature passed HB 2003, which requires cities with a population of more than 10,000 to conduct periodic reviews of housing capacity and need, and to develop housing production strategies designed to fill unmet need (also discussed in chap. 6). For perhaps the first time in the nation for any such strategy, cities are required to take into account the number of people experiencing housing insecurity and homelessness as part of their housing need estimates and production strategies.[67] The housing production strategies must also address housing access, affordability, location, and choice for communities of color,[68] addressing elements of systemic racism that directly affect housing insecurity and homelessness. Cities across Oregon are currently working to produce new housing needs analyses, due every six years for large cities and every eight years for smaller cities, along with the associated housing production strategies.[69]

While cities and counties can influence the production, type, and placement of housing, they are ultimately not responsible for the production itself, and these strategies are not guaranteed to result in the creation of needed housing absent other approaches. Multnomah County experimented with a model to build accessory dwelling units (ADUs) in the yards of Portlander homeowners that would house families experiencing homelessness, with the homeowner having an option to purchase the ADU (and possibly evict) the houseless family after five years. The pilot cost more than $550,000 and housed four families.[70] During the COVID-19 pandemic, Oregon was one of many states to launch a project to purchase and utilize motels as temporary shelters, with some being renovated to provide housing. While often pitted against the perceived speed and low cost of shelters, converting motels or purchasing existing housing can often be done much faster at a similar cost. For example, Oregon made 865 new housing units available from converted motels in seven months for less than $75 million,[71] when Portland's "safe rest village" shelters (comprising thirty units of personal occupancy dwellings without individual bathrooms or kitchens) took more than a year to open, at roughly the same ongoing cost per unit.[72] But purchasing or converting existing structures can only go so far—extensive production of publicly subsidized or publicly owned housing will likely still be required to meet existing and projected need.

Rent Assistance

Long-term rent assistance is the provision of indefinite housing subsidies to households that are unable to afford rent or a mortgage. This type of assistance has been shown to be highly effective in addressing homelessness and creating positive outcomes in health, earnings, and reduced incarceration for participants.[73] Limited funding is available, however, even for eligible households through federal rental assistance such as the Housing Choice Voucher Program. State and regional approaches can help fill this gap and address eligibility limitations, if sufficient numbers of vacant housing units are available, but the scale of funding needed may only be available through federal sources.

A major component of the Metro Supportive Housing Services measure was designed to provide long-term rent assistance to households at high risk of homelessness. The funding is allocated to both tenant-based assistance, enabling recipients to choose where they live, and project-based assistance, used to support tenants at specific housing developments. It also aims to create coordinated, simplified screening criteria for eligible tenants across the Portland metropolitan region, and to reduce other barriers for enrollment.[74] In the first year of the program, more than 650 households were placed in permanent supportive housing utilizing long-term rent assistance.[75] One program funded by the measure, Move-In Multnomah, was able to place people experiencing homelessness into 214 private market rentals in only four months.[76] At a yearly cost of $16,636 for each household placed, it would take an estimated $105 million per year to house everyone listed as experiencing homelessness in the 2023 PIT count for Portland and Multnomah County.[77]

Cash Transfers and Basic Income

Rather than providing a rent subsidy, some programs simply deliver direct cash transfers (akin to universal basic income, also discussed in chap. 11) to households in need to spend in whatever areas they deem most important. Such programs provide more agency to households and allow them to prioritize needs based on individual and family circumstances.

While broadly accepted as an effective tool for addressing extreme poverty in developing nations,[78] cash transfers have not been as fully studied in developed nations. The New Leaf Project in Vancouver, Canada, recently tested the concept by awarding $7,500 each to fifty randomly selected individuals experiencing homelessness. This amount was accompanied by a workshop on self-affirmation and personal development. Participant outcomes were tracked for a year and compared to a similar group that did not receive cash aid, but with some members who participated in a similar workshop. Cash recipients spent less time in homelessness, experienced less food insecurity, and retained an average of $1,000 in savings throughout the year despite the high cost of living in Vancouver.[79] In 2023, Oregon launched a direct cash transfer pilot for young people who have experienced homelessness, providing more than a hundred participants with $1,000 in unrestricted income each month.[80] The results will be evaluated by the national organization Point Source Youth, which also helps run the program.[81]

More ambitious proposals would provide ongoing, guaranteed UBI payments either to households in severe need or all households in a region. Studies on UBI and related programs in Canada, Europe, and the United States have shown a negligible impact on overall employment and positive impacts on education, health, and behavioral health, especially among highly disadvantaged groups.[82]

Evictions Prevention

A study in Seattle revealed that approximately 62 percent of tenants who had been evicted ended up experiencing homelessness, with almost 38 percent in unsheltered homelessness.[83] Numerous other studies have demonstrated that evictions are a major driver of homelessness.[84] Evictions disproportionately target Black and Latino renters, especially women,[85] reflecting racial disparities in housing insecurity that are evident in Oregon as well.[86] At the height of the COVID-19 pandemic in February 2021, an estimated 89,000 Oregon households owed back rent, and 200,000 households had little or no confidence in their ability to pay next month's rent.[87] When the eviction moratorium expired in Oregon, a significant number of those households were expected to be at risk of eviction, although numbers were not available in the few months between the end of the moratorium and the writing of this chapter. Assuming that only the 89,000 households who were already behind on rent were evicted, and not the other households that had little confidence in their future ability to pay, up to 55,000 households could end up experiencing homelessness based on rates from the study in Seattle. Using a calculator developed by the University of Arizona, the resulting costs to health, shelter, foster care, and juvenile justice systems was estimated to be $3.3 billion.[88] At that time, the total amount of outstanding back rent owed by Oregon households was $378 million, making it dramatically cheaper for the state to simply provide rent support.[89]

Policies to reduce the rate of evictions—such as laws guaranteeing tenants a right to counsel in eviction proceedings or establishing just-cause requirements for evictions—would be expected to directly reduce the number of people entering homelessness. Programs that provide rental assistance to address housing affordability and reduce eviction for nonpayment, such as the Metro Supportive Housing Services measure discussed above or emergency rental assistance delivered at the state level during the COVID-19 pandemic, are also expected to reduce homelessness.

Decriminalization

Oregon lacks not only enough affordable and supportive housing to effectively address homelessness, but also enough shelter beds to provide even temporary, emergency shelter to everyone experiencing homelessness. Although there is nowhere to go for most people experiencing homelessness, forcing them to sleep, eat, use the bathroom, and carry out other basic functions of life outdoors and in public spaces, those activities are still widely criminalized across the state.[90] Interactions with the criminal justice system increase the odds that people will continue to experience homelessness or return to homelessness after incarceration. Decriminalizing basic human activities for people experiencing homelessness in Oregon would not only help the state abide by the recent Ninth Circuit Court of Appeals decision, but it would also be expected to reduce traumatic police interactions and future homelessness. The passage of House Bill 3115 by the Oregon State Legislature is a first step in that direction. Nonpolice responses to homelessness, described below, offer a related approach.

Given the dramatic increase in the likelihood of experiencing homelessness after incarceration, programs designed to provide housing for individuals returning to society are important to reduce homelessness. In Portland, the Portland Police Bureau and nonprofit homeless service provider Central City Concern partner to provide transitional, supportive housing to individuals reentering society following incarceration. Such programs offer promise if scaled to reach need, are delivered using evidence-based best practices, and incorporate a strong racial equity lens.

Nonpolice First Response Programs

In Portland between 2013 and 2018, "unwanted person" calls regarding people experiencing homelessness, a mental health crisis, or both rose 64 percent to more than 29,000 calls per year and usually resulted in police being dispatched.[91] These calls can easily escalate into violence by police responders, especially against BIPOC community members. The City of Portland agreed to a use of force settlement agreement with the US Department of Justice in 2014 based in part on police violence against people with a mental illness.[92] The city's repeated noncompliance with the agreement[93] demonstrates the ongoing need for alternative approaches in concert with attempts at police reform and accountability.

In response to issues like this, a number of cities across the United States have launched nonpolice first response programs to address behavioral health crises. One of the longest-running programs, Crisis Assistance Helping Out On The Streets (CAHOOTS), has been managed for more than thirty years by White Bird Clinic in the cities of Eugene and Springfield in partnership with local police departments. Under the CAHOOTS model, an unarmed medic and mental health worker are dispatched in response to nonviolent 911, police, or welfare check calls involving a behavioral health component.[94] In 2017, CAHOOTS responded to 17 percent of the City of Eugene's police calls with a budget of $2.1 million and saved the city an estimated $12 million in policing costs.[95] More importantly, programs like this offer the potential to save the lives of community members in situations that might otherwise escalate with a police response.

In early 2021, Portland launched a pilot of the Portland Street Response Program, modeled in part on CAHOOTS and designed in close collaboration with advocates and people experiencing homelessness. In 2022, following an evaluation by HRAC, the program was expanded citywide. Although many other cities in Oregon and across the nation may lack the same level of government scrutiny as Portland under its settlement agreement, the issue is clearly not isolated, and Oregon politicians are leading an effort to expand such programs nationwide. The 2021 American Rescue Plan passed by the US Congress included roughly $1 billion structured as an 85 percent match from Medicaid funding for cities seeking to launch programs based on CAHOOTS, and additional funding has been included in other proposed federal legislation.[96]

In addition to developing new first response programs, reducing the criminalization of unavoidable activities linked to homelessness and reducing the number of people released from incarceration directly into homelessness can lessen the impacts of the criminal justice system in driving homelessness.

Any single policy or programmatic approach listed above is unlikely to be successful alone, even if scaled up to reach all those who need it, without also being linked to a set of other policies designed to address multiple contributing factors of homelessness. Absent these approaches, especially widespread provision of deeply affordable housing and supportive services through a racial equity lens, homelessness in Oregon can be expected to increase even without periodic shocks from natural disasters and economic downturns.

Futures

As planners and communities work to envision Oregon in 2050, we face choices about how to frame that conversation. One current approach to envisioning futures asks us to identify what is unknown and how we might respond. In the case of homelessness, we know what the future will look like. Looking over the history of the United States, we can see consistent policies and decisions that have excluded people from housing. We have made advances in undoing those early decisions, but then, as the funding rollback in public housing in the mid- to late twentieth century demonstrates, we stepped backward. The country offers no right to housing, and recent federal attempts to even moderately reinvest in public housing have met dead ends. Meanwhile, the gap between the wealthy and the poor continues to grow.

What does this mean for the future? There aren't multiple plausible futures for people without means. There is just one, and that one will include people experiencing housing insecurity or homelessness. Will there be more or fewer people experiencing homelessness? That type of planning question presumes that we accept a given number of people living in this circumstance. How much is too many? Does it really matter if it's plus or minus a hundred, a thousand, or ten thousand people in a region experiencing homelessness at the same time? Perhaps instead we should focus on solutions designed to end homelessness, rather than trying to settle on how many people it's acceptable to leave without housing.

When we think about the big ideas for the future that would make a measurable difference in reducing people experiencing homelessness, there are simple yet still controversial policies and programs that need to be scaled up and better implemented. As discussed, this includes tenant protections to prevent homelessness, massive increase in affordable and accessible housing, and implementation of housing first models. To make real strides in preventing and resolving homelessness, all this work must start with building activities for and meeting the needs of people of color.

For us, the big questions for the next thirty years are less about planning, policy, and program implementation than they are about values and commitments. We know how to solve homelessness, and Oregon is currently implementing those solutions at a small scale. The existence of homelessness is a choice for communities to make, and at the moment we have chosen to accept it.

Consider this: using the HUD definition of homelessness, just 0.17 percent of the US population experienced homelessness in 2021. Even looking at what HUD describes as renter households with the worst-case needs, the total percent is 6.26 percent of all US households. In 2021 in Oregon, a $1.9 billion tax surplus was returned to residents.[97] The mortgage interest tax deduction, the largest housing subsidy in the country, largely benefits the wealthiest Americans while costing the federal government $25 billion each year,[98] yet the 2023 proposed federal budget included only $8.7 billion to address homelessness.[99] In Oregon, the state mortgage interest deduction predominately benefits wealthy, white households at a cost of $1.1 billion every biennium,[100] while Oregon Housing and Community Services budgeted $97 million for homelessness services in the 2021-23 biennium.[101] Meanwhile, placing someone experiencing homelessness into a private market housing unit in the Portland region costs less than $17,000 a year,[102] while putting them into a congregate shelter costs $20,000 to $25,000 without even moving them out of homelessness.[103] Saying that we can't resolve homelessness or arguing that the solutions are too expensive reveals a lack of commitment, not the means, to do so.

The big challenge for the next few decades is to ask: Do we want to redistribute resources to people with fewer resources? Do we want to guarantee a right to housing, no matter the cost? Do we want to invest in health care for all, including exceptional care for people with serious mental illness and substance use disorders? Can we reframe our public funding and discussion away from how little should we spend on people in need to how much it will take to help everyone in our communities live affirming lives and to thrive? Our choices for just futures depend entirely on our decisions today about how we want to live in community with one another.

Conclusion

Considering just a few of the data points presented above reminds us of what is at a stake when we allow homelessness to continue. Homelessness increased by as much as 69 percent in Oregon between 2017 and 2023,[104] and as with other elements of homelessness, these impacts fell disproportionately on BIPOC community members. Student homelessness has held roughly steady over that period.[105]

Homelessness is not an intractable problem. Rather, there is a clear and demonstrated solution: housing. The Oregon 2050 project has the opportunity to look at what it would mean to provide safe, stable, accessible, and affordable housing to tens of thousands of Oregonians living with rent burdens and those living without housing. This housing should come with a guarantee of permanence and needed social services. We see the greatest challenge of this work in identifying just how much people care right now about ending these circumstances for Oregonians in need. There may be fewer policies to compare or scenarios to run versus communication messages to develop and community organizing and advocacy to support these efforts.

Oregon can solve and prevent most homelessness. We can end housing insecurity. Why not use 2050 as the goal to do so?

Notes

1. We the authors use the term "homeless" instead of "houseless" and "unhoused," which are more specific in the problem they identify. We use it because that is the term used by federal definitions which drive data collection, funding, and policy. Most importantly, we emphasize that the state of homelessness is an adjective, a symptom of societal problems, and solvable, and not a description of people.
2. "HUD 2020 Continuum of Care Homeless Assistance Programs Homeless Populations and Subpopulations, Oregon," US Department of Housing and Urban Development, December 15, 2020, https://files.hudexchange.info/reports/published/CoC_PopSub_State_OR_2020.pdf.
3. de Sousa et al., *The 2023 Annual Homeless Assessment Report (AHAR) to Congress, Part 1: Point-In-Time Estimates of Homelessness* (Washington, DC: US Department of Housing and Urban Development, 2023), https://www.huduser.gov/portal/sites/default/files/pdf/2023-AHAR-Part-1.pdf.
4. McKinney-Vento Homeless Assistance Act, 42 U.S.C. § 11434a (2017), https://uscode.house.gov/view.xhtml?path=/prelim@title42/chapter119/subchapter6/partB&edition=prelim.
5. de Sousa et al., *Annual Homeless Assessment Report Part 1*.
6. de Sousa et al., *Annual Homeless Assessment Report Part 1*.
7. de Sousa et al., *Annual Homeless Assessment Report Part 1*.
8. Monika Schneider, Daniel Brisson, and Donald Burnes, "Do We Really Know How Many Are Homeless? An Analysis of the Point-in-Time Homelessness Count," *Families in Society* 97, no. 4 (2016): 321–29.
9. Meghan Henry et al., *2021 Annual Homeless Assessment Report (AHAR) to Congress, Part 2: Estimates of Homelessness in the United States* (Washington, DC: US Department of Housing and Urban Development, July 2023), https://www.huduser.gov/portal/sites/default/files/pdf/2021-AHAR-Part-2.pdf.

10 Henry et al., *Annual Homeless Assessment Report Part 2*.
11 "Homeless Enrolled Students by State," ED Data Express, accessed January 3, 2024, https://eddataexpress.ed.gov/dashboard/homeless.
12 Christine Baker-Smith et al., "#RealCollege 2020: Five Years of Evidence on Campus Basic Needs Insecurity" (The Hope Center at Temple University, 2020),
13 14. Greene et al., *2023 Oregon Statewide Homelessness Estimates*.
14 Greene et al., *2023 Oregon Statewide Homelessness Estimates*.
15 "HUD 2020 Continuum of Care Homeless Assistance."
16 "Oregon Homelessness Statistics" (US Interagency Council on Homelessness, 2019).
17 "Homelessness in Oregon: A Review of Trends, Causes, and Policy Options," ECONorthwest for Oregon Community Foundation, accessed January 3, 2024, https://econw.com/project/homelessness-in-oregon-a-review-of-trends-causes-and-policy-options/.
18 Greene et al., *2023 Oregon Statewide Homelessness Estimates*.
19 Hope Center, *Oregon Community Colleges #RealCollege Survey* (Philadelphia: Hope Center, Temple University, 2020).
20 Authors' calculation based on data from "Community College Student Data," Oregon Higher Education Coordinating Commission, accessed February 23, 2024, https://www.oregon.gov/highered/research/pages/student-data-cc.aspx.
21 Greg Townley et al., *Housing and Food Insecurity at Portland State* (Portland, OR: Portland State University, 2020), https://digital.osl.state.or.us/islandora/object/osl:953856.
22 Authors' calculation based on data from "Facts: PSU by the Numbers," Portland State University, accessed February 23, 2024, https://www.pdx.edu/portland-state-university-facts.
23 Marisa Zapata et al., *Governance, Costs, and Revenue Raising to Address and Prevent Homelessness in the Portland Tri-County Region* (Portland, OR: Portland State University, 2019), https://www.pdx.edu/homelessness/sites/g/files/znldhr1791/files/2020-05/RegionalHomelessnessReport.pdf.
24 Estimate created for this chapter and for reflection purposes only. The extrapolation factor for unsheltered homelessness is driven by work in urban regions, and the options for multipliers vary widely.
25 Chris Glynn and Emily B. Fox, "Dynamics of Homelessness in Urban America," *Annals of Applied Statistics* 13, no. 1 (2017): 573–605; William Yu, "Homelessness in the US, California and Los Angeles," in Jerry Nickelsburg, *The UCLA Anderson Forecast for the Nation and California* (Los Angeles: Anderson School of Management, University of California, Los Angeles, 2018); John M. Quigley and Steven Raphael, "The Economics of Homelessness: The Evidence from North America," *European Journal of Housing Policy* 1, no. 3 (2001): 23–336.
26 "Glossary for CPD Maps," US Department of Housing and Urban Development, accessed January 3, 2024, https://files.hudexchange.info/resources/documents/CPD-Maps-Glossary.pdf.
27 "2021 Oregon Housing Profile," National Low Income Housing Coalition, accessed January 3, 2024, nlihc.org/sites/default/files/SHP_OR.pdf.
28 Nikole Hannah-Jones, "Portland Housing Audit Finds Discrimination in 64 Percent of Tests; City Has Yet to Act against Landlords," *The Oregonian*, May 10, 2011, https://www.oregonlive.com/portland/2011/05/a_portland_housing_audit_finds.html.
29 "Homelessness in Oregon."

30 "Homelessness in Oregon."
31 "Homelessness in Oregon."
32 Ann Curry-Stevens, Amanda Cross-Hemmer, and Coalition of Communities of Color, *The Native American Community in Multnomah County: An Unsettling Profile* (Portland, OR: Portland State University, 2011).
33 National Law Center on Homelessness and Poverty, *Housing Not Handcuffs 2019: Ending the Criminalization of Homelessness in US Cities* (Washington, DC: National Law Center on Homelessness and Poverty, 2019), http://nlchp.org/wp-content/uploads/2019/12/HOUSING-NOT-HANDCUFFS-2019-FINAL.pdf; Dereck W. Paul Jr. et al., "Racial Discrimination in the Life Course of Older Adults Experiencing Homelessness: Results from the HOPE HOME Study," *Journal of Social Distress and the Homeless* 29, no. 2 (2020): 184-93; Jeffrey Olivet et al., "Racial Inequity and Homelessness: Findings from the SPARC Study," *Annals of the American Academy of Political and Social Science* 693 (2021): 82-100.
34 Lucius Couloute, *Nowhere to Go: Homelessness among Formerly Incarcerated People* (Northampton, MA: Prison Policy Initiative, 2018), https://www.prisonpolicy.org/reports/housing.html.
35 US Interagency Council on Homelessness, *Homelessness in America: Focus on Individual Adults* (Washington, DC: US Interagency Council on Homelessness, 2018), https://www.usich.gov/resources/uploads/asset_library/HIA_Individual_Adults.pdf.
36 National Law Center on Homelessness and Poverty, *Housing Not Handcuffs*.
37 Rebecca Woolington and Melissa Lewis, "Portland Homeless Accounted for Majority of Police Arrests in 2017, Analysis Finds," *The Oregonian*, June 27, 2018, https://www.oregonlive.com/portland/2018/06/portland_homeless_accounted_fo.html.
38 Woolington and Lewis, "Portland Homeless Accounted for Majority of Police Arrests."
39 Martin v. City of Boise, 920 F.3rd 584 (9th Cir. 2019), https://cdn.ca9.uscourts.gov/datastore/opinions/2019/04/01/15-35845.pdf.
40 Dirk VanderHart, "Two Bills Curbing Camping Regulation Clear Oregon Legislature," Oregon Public Broadcasting, June 9, 2021, https://www.opb.org/article/2021/06/09/oregon-legislature-bills-camping-regulations-encampment-policies/.
41 "Current Statistics on the Prevalence and Characteristics of People Experiencing Homelessness in the United States," US Department of Health, Human Services Substance Abuse and Mental Health Services Administration, last updated December 5, 2023, https://www.samhsa.gov/sites/default/files/programs_campaigns/homelessness_programs_resources/hrc-factsheet-current-statistics-prevalence-characteristics-homelessness.pdf.
42 "2019 Point-in-Time Count of Homelessness."
43 "2019 Point-in-Time Count of Homelessness."
44 "Quick Facts Issue Brief," Oregon Department of Corrections, accessed January 3, 2024, https://www.oregon.gov/doc/Documents/agency-quick-facts.pdf.
45 Yumiko Aratani, *Homeless Children and Youth: Causes and Consequences* (New York: National Center for Children in Poverty, 2009), https://www.nccp.org/wp-content/uploads/2020/05/text_888.pdf.
46 Matthew Morton, Amy Dworsky, and Gina Samuels, "Missed Opportunities: Youth Homelessness in America: National Estimates," Chapin Hall at the University of Chicago, accessed January 3, 2024, https://voicesofyouthcount.org/

wp-content/uploads/2017/11/VoYC-National-Estimates-Brief-Chapin-Hall-2017.pdf.
47 Morton et al., "Missed Opportunities."
48 Matthew Garrett and Ariane Le Chevallier, "Recovering and Rebuilding from Oregon's 2020 Wildfires," Governor's Wildfire Economic Recovery Council, January 4, 2021, https://digital.osl.state.or.us/islandora/object/osl:987568.
49 Maude Hines and Marta Petteni, *Stories from the Outside: Oregon Wildfires 2020* (Portland, OR: Portland State University, 2021), https://www.pdx.edu/homelessness/stories-outside-oregon-wildfires-2020.
50 Gregg Colburn and Clayton Page Aldern, *Homelessness Is a Housing Problem: How Structural Factors Explain US Patterns* (Oakland: University of California Press, 2022): 181-82.
51 Colburn and Aldern, *Homelessness Is a Housing Problem*.
52 Paula Goering et al., *National at Home/Chez Soi Final Report* (Ottawa: Mental Health Commission of Canada, 2014), https://www.homelesshub.ca/sites/default/files/attachments/mhcc_at_home_report_national_cross-site_eng_2.pdf.
53 Sam Tsemberis, Douglas Kent, and Christy Respress, "Housing Stability and Recovery among Chronically Homeless Persons with Co-Occurring Disorders in Washington, DC," *American Journal of Public Health* 102, no.1 (2012): 13–16.
54 Lavena Staten and Sara Ranking, "Penny Wise but Pound Foolish: How Permanent Supportive Housing Can Prevent a World of Hurt," Homeless Rights Advocacy Project, Seattle University, July 12, 2019, https://papers.ssrn.com/sol3/papers.cfm?abstract_id=3419187.
55 "Housing 300 Portland Metro Area Seniors in 2020," Kaiser Permanente, January 20, 2020, https://about.kaiserpermanente.org/community-health/news/housing-300-portland-metro-area-seniors-in-2020.
56 Katia Riddle, "Can States Ease Homelessness by Tapping Medicaid Funding? Oregon Is Betting on It," National Public Radio, October 15, 2023, https://www.opb.org/article/2023/10/15/homelessness-medicaid-funding-oregon/.
57 Marisa Zapata and Shannon Singleton, *Local Implementation Plan Unsheltered Survey Results* (Portland, OR: Portland State University, 2019), https://www.pdx.edu/homelessness/survey-needs-people-living-unsheltered.
58 Zapata and Singleton, *Local Implementation Plan Unsheltered Survey Results*.
59 Zapata and Singleton, *Local Implementation Plan Unsheltered Survey Results*.
60 "Supportive Housing Services: Addressing Homelessness in Greater Portland," Metro, accessed January 3, 2024, https://www.oregonmetro.gov/public-projects/supportive-housing-services/progress.
61 "Supportive Housing Services."
62 "Supportive Housing Services."
63 Portland Housing Bureau, *2020 Progress Report: Portland Affordable Housing Bond* (Portland, OR: Portland Housing Bureau, 2021), https://www.portland.gov/sites/default/files/2021/bondannualreport2021_web.pdf.
64 Portland Housing Bureau, *2020 Progress Report*.
65 "Affordable Homes for Greater Portland," Metro, updated January 2024, https://www.oregonmetro.gov/public-projects/affordable-homes-greater-portland/progress.
66 Establish Key Actions to Increase Affordable Housing Construction, Resolution 37593, City of Portland City Council (October 2022), https://www.portland.gov/council/documents/resolution/key-actions-increase-affordable-housing-construction.

67. "660-008-0050 Housing Production Strategy Report Structure," Oregon Administrative Rules Database, accessed January 3, 2024, https://secure.sos.state.or.us/oard/viewSingleRule.action?ruleVrsnRsn=274770.
68. "660-008-0050 Housing Production Strategy Report Structure."
69. "Housing Needs and Production" (Oregon Department of Land Conservation and Development, 2022).
70. Multnomah County, *A Place for You* (Portland, OR: Multnomah County, 2018), https://multco-web7-psh-files-usw2.s3-us-west-2.amazonaws.com/s3fs-public/A%20Place%20for%20You%20One%20Pager_Aug2018.pdf.
71. Oregon Community Foundation, *Oregon's Project Turnkey Report to the Oregon State Legislature* (Portland: Oregon Community Foundation, August 2021), https://oregoncf.org/community-impact/research/oregons-project-turnkey-report-to-the-oregon-state-legislature/.
72. "Funding for Safe Rest Villages," City of Portland, Office of Commissioner Dan Ryan, last updated May 26, 2023, https://www.portland.gov/ryan/funding-safe-rest-villages.
73. Meena Bavan and David Hardiman, "Findings from PD&R's Multi-Disciplinary Research Team," *Cityscape* 20, no. 1 (2018).
74. "Regional Long Term Rent Assistance Program (Draft 1.18.21)," Metro, January 18, 2021), https://www.oregonmetro.gov/sites/default/files/2021/01/20/Supportive-housing-services-draft-policy-overview-20210118.pdf.
75. "Latest Reports for Metro's Supportive Housing Services Fund Show Counties on Track to Exceed Most of Their Goals" Metro, June 28, 2022, https://www.oregonmetro.gov/news/latest-reports-metro-s-supportive-housing-services-fund-show-counties-track-exceed-most-their.
76. Nicole Hayden, "Multnomah County Experiment That Asked Landlords to Rent to Homeless Individuals Succeeded—But Quickly Ran Out of Money," *The Oregonian*, October 30, 2022, https://www.oregonlive.com/portland/2022/10/multnomah-county-experiment-that-asked-landlords-to-rent-to-homeless-individuals-succeeded-but-quickly-ran-out-of-money.html.
77. Hayden, "Multnomah County Experiment."
78. Francesca Bastagli et al., *Cash Transfers: What Does the Evidence Say?* (London: Overseas Development Institute, July 2016), https://cdn.odi.org/media/documents/11316.pdf.
79. Foundations for Social Change, *Taking Bold Action on Homelessness* (Vancouver, BC: Foundations for Social Change, 2020), https://static1.squarespace.com/static/5f07a92f21d34b403c788e05/t/5f751297fcfe7968a6a957a8/1601507995038/2020_09_30_FSC_Statement_of_Impact_w_Expansion.pdf.
80. Tiffany Camhi, "Homeless Youth in Oregon Rebuild Their Lives with $1,000 a Month Support," Oregon Public Broadcasting, January 26, 2024, https://www.opb.org/article/2024/01/26/homeless-youth-oregon-1000-dollars-a-month-support/.
81. Camhi, "Homeless Youth in Oregon Rebuild Their Lives."
82. Ioana Marinescu, "Summary: Universal Basic Income," University of Pennsylvania, September 25, 2019, https://repository.upenn.edu/cgi/viewcontent.cgi?article=1010&context=pennwhartonppi_bschool.
83. Tara Cookson et al., *Losing Home: The Human Cost of Eviction in Seattle* (Seattle: Seattle Women's Commission and King County Bar Association, September 2018), https://www.seattle.gov/Documents/Departments/SeattleWomensCommission/LosingHome_9-18-18.pdf.

84 Tristia Bauman et al., *Protect Tenants, Prevent Homelessness* (Washington, DC: National Law Center on Homelessness and Poverty, 2018), https://nlchp.org/wp-content/uploads/2018/10/ProtectTenants2018.pdf.
85 Peter Hepburn, Renee Louis, and Matthew Desmond, "Racial and Gender Disparities among Evicted Americans," *Sociological Science* 7 (December 2020): 649-62.
86 Lisa Bates, *Stability, Equity, and Dignity: Reporting and Reflecting on Oregon Tenant Experiences during the Covid-19 Pandemic* (Portland, OR: Community Alliance of Tenants and Portland State University, 2020), https://pdxscholar.library.pdx.edu/cgi/viewcontent.cgi?article=1019&context=hrac_pub.
87 "Household Pulse Survey: Measuring Emergent Social and Economic Matters Facing U.S. Households," US Census Bureau, January 9, 2024, https://www.census.gov/data/experimental-data-products/household-pulse-survey.html.
88 Lisa Bates et al., "Cost of Oregon Evictions Report," Portland State University, February 9, 2021, https://www.pdx.edu/homelessness/sites/g/files/znldhr1791/files/2021-02/Cost%20of%20Oregon%20Evictions%20Report%20%283%29.pdf.
89 Bates et al., "Cost of Oregon Evictions Report."
90 National Law Center on Homelessness and Poverty, *Housing Not Handcuffs 2019*.
91 Katie Shepard, "Portlanders Call 911 to Report 'Unwanted' People More Than Any Other Reason. We Listened In," *Willamette Week*, February 6, 2019, https://www.wweek.com/news/2019/02/06/portlanders-call-911-to-report-unwanted-people-more-than-any-other-reason-we-listened-in/.
92 Maxine Bernstein, "Feds Put City of Portland on Formal Notice of Non-Compliance with Police Use-of-Force Agreement," *The Oregonian*, updated April 6, 2021, https://www.oregonlive.com/crime/2021/04/feds-put-city-of-portland-on-formal-notice-of-non-compliance-with-justice-dept-settlement-agreement.html.
93 Bernstein, "Feds Put City of Portland on Formal Notice."
94 Ben Adam Climer and Brenton Gicker, "CAHOOTS: A Model for Prehospital Mental Health Crisis Intervention," *Psychiatric Times* 38, no. 1 (2021).
95 "What Is CAHOOTS?," White Bird Clinic, October 29, 2020, https://whitebirdclinic.org/what-is-cahoots/.
96 Olivia Young, "$1 Billion for CAHOOTS Act Included in American Rescue Plan," KMTR, March 17, 2021, https://nbc16.com/news/local/1-billion-for-cahoots-act-included-in-american-rescue-plan-03-18-2021.
97 "Kicker Details Confirmed," State of Oregon Newsroom, October 12, 2021, https://www.oregon.gov/newsroom/pages/newsdetail.aspx?newsid=64457.
98 Patrick Condon, *Sick City: Disease, Race, Inequality, and Urban Land* (Amherst, MA: Off the Common Books, 2021).
99 "FY 2023 Proposed Federal Budget for Homelessness," US Interagency Council on Homelessness, March 31, 2022, https://www.usich.gov/tools-for-action/fy-2023-proposed-federal-budget-for-homelessness/.
100 Jayati Ramakrishnan, "Audit of Oregon's Mortgage Interest Deduction Chastises Tax Policy as 'Inequitable and Regressive,' Benefitting Wealthy Homeowners," *The Oregonian*, March 16, 2022.
101 Margaret Salazar an
d Caleb Yant, "Oregon Housing and Community Services Agency Budget Presentation," presentation to the Oregon State Legislature, Joint Ways and Means Subcommittee on Transportation and Economic Development, March 2021.

102 Hayden, "Multnomah County Experiment."
103 "Funding for Safe Rest Villages."
104 Megan Bolton, *2017 Point-in-Time Estimates of Homelessness in Oregon* (Salem: Oregon Housing and Community Services, 2017); Green et al., *Oregon Statewide Homelessness Estimates 2021*.
105 "Unduplicated State Totals (2018-2023)," Oregon Department of Education, accessed February 1, 2024, https://www.oregon.gov/ode/schools-and-districts/grants/ESEA/McKinney-Vento/Documents/Unduplicated%20State%20Totals%2018-23.xlsx.

12
Reinvesting in Rehabilitation
Sites of Incarceration, Mental Health Care, and Substance Use Disorder Treatment

MORIAH MCSHARRY MCGRATH AND MELIA CHASE

This chapter looks at incarceration and how it relates to the availability of facilities for mental health care and substance use disorder treatment—loosely grouping them together under the concept of sites of rehabilitation. While these services are not typically viewed as core land use topics, they have spatial and regional components. Additionally, they are connected to a wide variety of land use and economic development issues, such as housing and jobs.

Like the nation overall, Oregon's prisons and jails burgeoned in the twentieth century, in terms of both number and cost. This growth has been driven by social policy rather than increases in crime, including the shrinkage and fragmentation of the mental health care system that has funneled people into Oregon's prisons. Nationwide, approximately 14 percent of incarcerated people have serious mental illness, and two-thirds are in need of substance abuse treatment.[1] Oregon has been lauded for some efforts to reduce the toll of incarceration and for its notable history of health care innovation. But massive unmet needs for mental illness and substance use disorder services continue to drive the enormous social and fiscal costs of incarceration.

Addressing these dysfunctions is an urgent human rights concern, given the extreme burden of incarceration on people with mental illness and African American and Native American communities. When it comes to people with disabilities, we do not have state-specific data, but Oregon likely reflects patterns of the larger United States, with people with disabilities imprisoned at a rate four times higher than people without disabilities.[2] Similarly, lesbian, gay, bisexual, transgender, and queer (LGBTQ+) people are incarcerated at three times the rate of the population overall. The "poverty to prison" pipeline is also well documented: people with lower educational attainment are at higher risk of incarceration.[3]

As we look to 2050, Oregon can strive for a better balance that enables rehabilitation of people with health problems and for people who have been convicted of crimes. We start by discussing the roots of mass incarceration in Oregon, and then link this to the need for and geography of mental health (MH) and substance use disorder (SUD) treatment. For the sake of brevity, this chapter focuses on adults (age 18+), though youth certainly have critical needs in these areas. Our analysis considers service delivery as well as workforce and economic development aspects of these sectors. From there, we identify pathways for policy innovation, focused on restoring well-being for the Oregonians at greatest risk today: communities of color (particularly Black/African American Oregonians), people with mental illness, LGBTQ+ people, and people with a history of living in poverty.

Oregon's Correctional Landscape

The cost of corrections has risen rapidly, taking money away from spending on schools and other public goods.[4] Incarceration in the United States is a highly racialized phenomenon whose burdens are disproportionately borne by communities of color, in particular Black and African American communities.[5] Incarceration is driven by macroeconomic conditions. For example, a recent study links declining household incomes with both opioid-related deaths and incarceration.[6] Shrinking economies also encourage local governments to use jails as a source of income, renting out beds to other jurisdictions and authorities.[7]

Presently, 85,000 Oregonians are under correctional supervision, with 36,000 of these in a "community-based" program such as parole (conditionally released from prison) or probation (needing to follow a series of restrictions to prevent being jailed).[8] While Oregon is average among US states in terms of the proportion of residents in prison and relatively low in terms of felon disenfranchisement, it ranks a shocking third in terms of proportion of youths in custody,[9] which bears further discussion beyond this project.

Reflecting national patterns, Oregon's incarceration rates vary enormously by race, as illustrated in in figure 12.1: in 2018, Black Oregonians were imprisoned at a rate of 2,061 prisoners per 100,000 people, versus 395 for Hispanic Oregonians and 366 for white Oregonians.[10] Oregon data for Hispanic, Native American, and Asian people are less reliable owing variability/error in the statistics that results from systematic undercounting of people of color;[11] however, Native American rates seem be consistently elevated and Asian/Pacific Islander rates seem be consistently lower than the rate for the white population.

Prisons are big business. A wide variety of vendors sell services to the Department of Corrections and its prisoners as well as purchase of the products of prison labor, such as "made in the USA" apparel. In 1994, Measure 17 amended the Oregon Constitution to require that inmates work forty hours per week; the benefits to prisoners are minimal because these are menial jobs that provide no training for work prisoners might do after their release. Wages are low (generally sixty-one cents an hour) and paid in commissary credits.

Incarceration is expensive for the state. A national report[12] found that Oregon was dedicating four times the funding to corrections than it was on higher education. For the most recent two-year budget, this was approximately $2 billion, or 8 percent of the budget, to

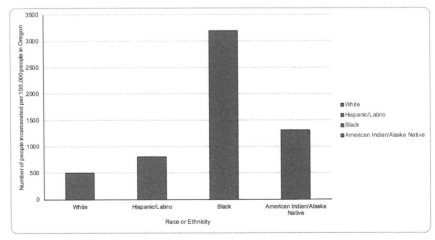

Figure 12.1. Oregon incarceration rates by race. Note that this data set treats Hispanic as a race rather than an ethnicity. *Source*: "Crime and Incineration Dashboard," Oregon Criminal Justice Commission, accessed *February* 28, 2024, https://public.tableau.com/app/profile/cjcdashboards/viz/CrimeIncarcerationDashboardHome/CIHome

corrections.[13] The state projects the population of prisoners will fall sharply from earlier projections owing the impact of House Bills 3194 and 3078, however.

Incarceration has many social costs as well. During incarceration, people are at increased risk of contracting infectious diseases, and the prison population has elevated rates of mental illness, substance misuse, mental illness, disability, and early death compared to the population at large. Formerly incarcerated people encounter many difficulties with "reentry" to the community after their release, including barriers to housing and employment, exclusion from public facilities, and rescinded eligibility for government funding such as student loans. Imprisonment also has neighborhood-level effects, since formerly incarcerated people disproportionately come from and return to communities that have lower levels of health and economic supports.[14] One study found that people in neighborhoods with high incarceration rates had an increased likelihood of mental health problems, even if they had never been imprisoned.[15] Chapter 10 provides additional context about the relationships among race, overpolicing, and housing.

As is common throughout the United States, Oregon's prisons are located in more rural areas. Support for building prisons is generally high among rural residents, but while prisons do seem to have some benefit in terms of slowing the departure of young residents to larger communities/economies, prison labor can undercut local wages.[16] As illustrated in table 12.1, the construction of new facilities accelerated after 1980 owing to mandatory sentencing minimums created by the passage of Measure 11 in 1994. Legislators, elected officials, and the Department of Corrections have discussed building new prisons in Junction City and White City, but neither project has moved forward. Instead, prison closures are becoming more common.

In 2012, the Oregon State Penitentiary-Minimum, built on the state penitentiary grounds in 1964 as Oregon Women's Correctional Center, was shuttered for budgetary reasons.[17] In 2021, Mill Creek Correctional Facility in Salem (Marion County, 308 beds) and Shutter Creek in North Bend (Coos County, 332 beds) closed. Warner Creek Correctional Facility in Lakeview (Lake County, 492 beds) is on the chopping block as well, but many in rural Coos and Lake Counties see economic benefits to keeping the prisons open.[18]

Table 12.1. Oregon's Prisons

Facility	Location	Year Opened	Security Level	Capacity
Oregon State Penitentiary	Salem, Marion County	1866	maximum	2,447
South Fork Forest Camp	Board of Forestry Land, Tillamook County	1951	minimum	202
Oregon State Correctional Facility	Salem, Marion County	1955	medium	895
Santiam Correctional Facility	Salem, Marion County	1977	minimum	440
Eastern Oregon Correctional Facility	Pendleton, Umatilla County	1985	medium	1,646
Powder River Correctional Facility	Baker City, Baker County	1989	minimum	286
Columbia River Correctional Facility	Portland, Multnomah County	1990	minimum	549
Snake River Correctional Facility	Ontario, Malheur County	1991	medium	3,005
Two Rivers Correctional Facility	Umatilla, Umatilla County	2000	medium	1,809
Coffee Creek Correctional Facility	Wilsonville, Clackamas County	2002	all levels (women)	1,702
Warner Creek Correctional Facility	Lakeview, Lake County	2005	minimum	406
Deer Ridge Correctional Facility	Madras, Jefferson County	2007	minimum	1,867

Note: Shaded counties are those deemed "rural" for the purposed of eligibility for funding from the Federal Office of Rural Health Policy. Source: Data from Oregon Department of Corrections.

While the Oregon Department of Corrections runs prisons, county governments run jails, which initially "book" arrested people and hold prisoners for shorter sentences and for less serious crimes. Since 1970, Oregon's total jail population has increased 316 percent to approximately 10,000; the number of women booked increased seventeen-fold. Of people in jail in 2015, 63 percent were pretrial detainees who had been accused of a crime but had yet to go before a judge.[19]

The less populous counties of Wasco, Hood River, Sherman, and Gilliam created a regional authority called NORCOR (Northern Oregon Corrections) that runs a shared facility in the Dalles. Until

2020 NORCOR, generated revenue for these local governments by housing migrants detained by US Immigration and Customs Enforcement (ICE) on a fee-for-service basis. Previously, Columbia, Jackson, Josephine, Klamath, and Umatilla Counties had similar contracts with

Table 12.2. Oregon Top Ten Counties for Jail and Prison Admissions

	JAIL ADMISSIONS, 2015		
County	Number per 100,000 Residents	County	Total
Jefferson	19,997	Multnomah	34,776
Malheur	17,493	Washington	17,173
Coos	13,881	Clackamas	16,138
Lincoln	11,348	Lane	14,756
Grant	11,285	Marion	11,941
Wheeler	11,172	Jackson	11,482
Douglas	10,672	Douglas	6,883
Hood River	10,429	Deschutes	6,779
Clatsop	10,418	Coos	5,226
Wasco	10,354	Yamhill	4,276
	PRISON ADMISSIONS, 2014		
County	Number per 100,000 Residents	County	Total
Marion	333	Multnomah	901
Klamath	322	Marion	693
Jefferson	316	Lane	528
Clatsop	299	Washington	507
Linn	293	Clackamas	364
Lincoln	279	Linn	221
Josephine	274	Deschutes	218
Wasco	252	Jackson	200
Coos	229	Josephine	136
Lane	220	Klamath	134

Note: Shaded counties are those deemed "rural" for the purposed of eligibility for funding from the Federal Office of Rural Health Policy. Source: Adapted from Christian Henrichson et al., "Incarceration Trends in Oregon," in State Incarceration Trends (New York: Vera Institute of Justice, 2019).

ICE. Records show that the revenue from ICE was critical for keeping the Josephine County jail budget balanced.[20]

Multnomah County maintains the largest number of jail beds—1,200—with other urban counties following close behind, with 572 in Washington County and 465 in Clackamas.[21] Looking at the numbers on a per capita tells a different story, however (see table 12.2). Like most of the nation, Oregon's rural areas have high rates of incarceration—with jail admissions in particular skyrocketing. Between 2000 and 2015, the use of pretrial detention has increased by 23 percent in rural areas, while the rate has stayed the same or decreased (by 37 percent in Multnomah County) in the rest of the state.[22] While Marion County, where the capitol and two state prisons are located, has the highest rate of prison admissions, the other top counties are also rural.

The rural prison economy has been driven by economic incentives from the federal government for jail construction as well as violent crimes fueled by rural opiate dependency and joblessness.[23] Substance use and mental health problems both cause people to commit crimes and lead to rural incarceration because the lack of local treatment services means that rural residents who would be referred to treatment if they lived in an urban area end up in their local jail instead.[24]

Oregon's Mental Health Services

In addition to the policy issues mentioned above, incarceration rates are closely tied to the availability of mental health (MH) services. Though there is much to be said about less severe—but also disabling—MH issues like anxiety, which are increasing in prevalence, our focus here is on more severe mental illness[25] and the physical facilities for providing care. The highly visible presence of mentally disturbed people living in the streets has given many Oregonians great concern about this care system.

Oregon ranks fiftieth out of fifty-one US states and territories because of its high prevalence of mental health problems and poor access to care; Oregon's overall rankings have dropped since 2011. Oregon has the second-highest prevalence of adults with any mental illness: 23.6 percent of the population, or 757,000 people.[26] In 2019, about 20 percent of this population received services from Oregon's public mental health programs.[27] As of 2013, an additional 60,000 people—or roughly 8 percent of the population in need—received other addiction services, care in jail or prison, private-pay MH care, or Veterans Affairs (VA) care.[28]

Oregon is also forty-first for access to care, plummeting from the twenty-first position in 2011. Oregon does fare better on uninsurance rates: "only" 8.3 percent of adults with severe mental illness (83,000) lack health insurance, putting Oregon in twenty-fourth place. (This compares to 6.1 percent of Oregon's total population that lacked health insurance in 2021.)[29] But having insurance does not guarantee that a person can access care, since there may be barriers in availability, geography, and language/cultural appropriateness.

There is a powerful interplay among mental health, race, and overpolicing. As mentioned above, many of the high-profile officer-involved killings in Portland and Multnomah County throughout the 2000s and 2010s were of people of color experiencing mental health crises.[30] This makes the lack of access to MH care in Oregon even more concerning. Chapter 10 discusses in detail the relationship between mental health challenges and housing instability.

For clients who do receive care, there is a severe shortage of clinicians of color and culturally competent clinicians. While rates of anxiety and depression have increased among Black and Latino Oregonians, only one-fifth of Oregon mental health professionals are people of color, and only 1 percent are Black.[31] This is in the context of an "immense" provider shortage nationwide that will lead to long waits for care and provider burnout.[32]

One bright spot in the rankings is that Oregon rises to the number two position for MH care provider availability, with one provider for every 210 residents.[33] Additionally, Oregon's policies are viewed more positively than its care record by the national MH community, receiving the grade of B on the Treatment Advocacy Center's scorecard.

The roots of the MH care crisis lie in deinstitutionalization, the mass closure of psychiatric hospitals without other appropriate assistance to people with mental health challenges. The number of Americans in psychiatric hospitals dropped precipitously in the second half of the twentieth century owing to availability of new treatments (specifically, antipsychotic drugs), changing increasing social tolerance of disability, and the push for community-based care. Table 12.3 shows today's continuum of MH care; prior to deinstitutionalization, care was primarily residential, and many people were warehoused rather than receiving any meaningful treatment.

As "one of the largest social experiments in American history,"[34] deinstitutionalization led to a 92 percent reduction in the proportion of people living in public psychiatric hospitals between 1955 and 1994. By 2016, there were 37,679 beds in state hospitals, just 3.5 percent of the historical peak of 558,922 beds in 1955.[35] This loss of beds is an ongoing process, not a one-time event: for example, the number of psychiatric beds available in the United States declined 14 percent in the five-year span from 2005 to 2010.[36] In many instances, people who would have lived in psychiatric hospitals in earlier years today end up in prisons—a painful irony given the fact that the psychiatric reform movement aimed to move mentally ill people out of institutions for more humane care.

As a result, prisons have been deemed "the new asylums." As the number of both public and private psychiatric beds has declined in Oregon, civil commitment[37] has grown less common, and the state hospital only has room to house "forensic patients" who have been accused of a crime. The result is "an inevitable pathway to the nation's jails and the prisons" for people with unmanaged mental illness.[38]

In this context, police have become the de facto first responders to people in mental health crisis. Law enforcement officers often arrest people without charges or jail mentally ill people "for their own safety." Thrust into the role of frontline mental health providers, police are ill equipped to meet the community's needs. Nationally, people with untreated mental illness are sixteen times more likely to be killed in an encounter with law enforcement.[39] Since 2012, the largest police agency in the Oregon—Portland Police Bureau—has been under federal

Table 12.3. Number of State and County Mental Health Care Beds in Oregon

Year	Total
1955	558,239
1976	222,202
1980	156,713
2005	52,539

supervision related to police use of excessive force against people with mental illness. Perhaps contrary to expectation, nationwide trends show that these encounters are most prevalent in small and midsized cities rather than large urban areas.[40]

The goals of the community mental health movement that spawned deinstitutionalization were never realized. Under President Ronald Reagan and the era of "New Federalism," federal programming was ended, and funds were distributed to the states in block grants to spend on all manner of public services. A fragmented care system developed after federal decisions such as the "Institutions for Mental Disease (IMD) exclusion" that disallows Medicaid payment for inpatient services delivered anywhere that has more than sixteen psychiatric treatment slots.[41] This has made it financially unsustainable to run a psychiatric hospital.

Psychiatric facilities can have a huge impact on the surrounding community. For example, when Dammasch State Hospital opened in 1958 to relieve crowding at the State Hospital in Salem, it transformed the economy of rural Wilsonville.[42] After peaking at a population census of six hundred in 1990, Dammasch closed in 1995, having earned a reputation for terrible conditions. The land was redeveloped into the Villebois neighborhood, and the state diverted some of the proceeds from the sale to fund five group homes for people with mental illness.

Facility closures can leave big holes in rural areas. For example, the closure of the Blue Mountain facility (former Oregon State Hospital branch) in Pendleton left local legislators scrambling to propose new uses for the facility that would keep nurses and other skilled staffers employed in the area. In 2016, Oregon had 653 public psychiatric beds at the OSH, which has struggled for decades to provide appropriate care. Major lawsuits in the early 2000s found the state responsible for failing its obligations to:

- house mentally ill people awaiting trial (people are sent to jails instead of health care facilities),
- provide community MH services, and
- provide adequate staffing and treatment, uphold privacy standards, and protect patients from harm at the state hospital.

Despite the allocation of funding by the legislature, problems continued, and the Justice Department ultimately intervened. Worker shortages at the OSH have been so severe that the National Guard has been sent to staff the wards on multiple instances. Over the objections of mental health advocates—who preferred investments in community-based services as was done in Wilsonville—a new campus of the Oregon State Hospital opened in Junction City, fifty miles from Salem, in 2015.[43]

Oregon's private hospitals, both for-profit and nonprofit, provide approximately 220 more inpatient hospital beds, and there were 882 twenty-four-hour residential care beds in 2016.[44] In Portland, multiple health care systems collaborated to open the Unity Behavioral Health Center in 2017 to provide psychiatric emergency services, but this facility has struggled because there are few inpatient beds to which they can transfer patients. After Unity's severe budget challenges were exacerbated by the COVID-19 pandemic,[45] the participating hospital systems (the state's three largest) sued the Oregon Health Authority in 2022 for the shortage of public psychiatric beds, claiming that it forces these private hospitals to house patients in need of long-term care that they do not provide.[46]

After years of debate, in late 2021, the Oregon Health Authority approved a private psychiatric hospital with sixty beds in Wilsonville. Despite their preference for community-based programs (as opposed to inpatient), OHA finally approved the proposal as a way of dealing with the crisis of "boarding" in emergency rooms, where people in need of inpatient care wait indefinitely because no beds are available in other facilities. One study found that 2.1 percent of all emergency room visits in Oregon were boarding psychiatric patients.[47] The state set a quota that 45 percent of the Wilsonville beds be reserved for people referred to the facility by the courts (through civil commitment, protective custody, or a diversion program) to help meet the needs of strained public care systems.[48] Advocates for the facility viewed it as an opportunity for local economic development, citing the company's success with the Cedar Mills Hospital in Beaverton, which relies on patients with "private-pay" insurance.[49] But the parent company, Universal Health Services, withdrew their application with the claim that the state's conditions were financially "untenable."[50]

Beyond inpatient care, mental health services in Oregon are a patchwork of services that makes it difficult to access care. Services were decentralized in 1972, and while local governments initially ran mental health programs that were funded with state money, sixteen counties now contract out this responsibility, increasing the fragmentation of care.[51]

The contracts generally go to nonprofit organizations, which often struggle to stay afloat; this instability puts patients' continuity of care at risk. The largest community-based provider in Oregon has been Cascadia Health (formerly Cascadia Behavioral Health), which is based in Portland but previously served five counties. After a financial crisis in 2008, Cascadia survived only with the support of the Multnomah County government. Today, most of Cascadia's funding comes from the Oregon Health Authority in the form of Medicaid payments. As of this writing, Cascadia has a multimillion-dollar deficit and has requested "bailout" funds costs related to the COVID-19 pandemic and unanticipated loss of state funding.[52] Nationwide, the low reimbursement rates for care (the amount that insurance companies pay providers for services) create a vicious cycle of low employee salaries that cause burnout and high turnover, compromising the quality of care.

Eligible Native Americans can access the Tribal Health System, which operates independently from local mental health authorities. This includes the Northwest Portland Area Indian Health Board and the new Great Circle Recovery Opioid Treatment Program in Eugene, run by the Confederated Tribes of Grand Ronde.

Oregon's aging population, as discussed in chapter 2, also affects the need profile for the state. The Oregon Older Adult Behavioral Health Initiative found that the major barriers to care for older adults: affordable housing, restrictive eligibility criteria, the lack of services in long-term care facilities, the fragmentation of different care types ("silos"), and distance to services. They also singled out eastern Oregon as the region with the most concerning shortage of behavioral health practitioners.

Accessing MH care may be especially difficult in rural areas, where staffing shortages are severe; the result is that many people in need of SUD treatment or MH care end up in emergency rooms at a far greater rate than occurs in urban areas.[53] Table 12.4 maps the geographic distribution of crisis facilities by county, showing the limited services available in rural areas, where the stigma against seeking treatment for mental health issues may also be stronger.[54]

Table 12.4. Mental Health Services Cluster in Urban Areas

Service Area	Number of Mental Health Providers per 1,000 Residents	Service Area	Number of Mental Health Providers per 1,000 Residents
Florence	56	La Grande	0.899
Southwest Portland	5.94	Coos Bay	0.87
Eugene/University	5.01	Mill City/Gates	0.85
Northeast Portland	3.21	Nehalem	0.85
Southeast Portland	2.42	Tillamook	0.83
Newport	2.27	Eugene South	0.81
Portland North Hillsboro/Forest Grove	2.1	Ontario	0.79
		Albany	0.79
Northwest Portland	2.1	Heppner	0.78
Ashland	1.99	Grants Pass	0.78
Salem South	1.86	Burns	0.77
Bend	1.77	Klamath Falls	0.73
Corvallis/Philomath	1.68	Wallowa/Enterprise	0.73
Oregon City	1.67	Arlington	0.72
Lake Oswego	1.49	Portland East	0.72
Hood River	1.33	Boardman	0.7
Medford	1.29	Gold Beach	0.69
Roseburg	1.29	Junction City	0.69
Oregon	1.25	McMinnville	0.69
Beaverton	1.19	Seaside	0.68
Warm Springs	1.17	Gresham	0.66
Astoria	1.12	Redmond	0.65
Milwaukie	1.09	Coquille/Myrtle	0.63
Tigard	1.09	Myrtle Creek	0.63
Pendleton	1.04	Winston	0.62
Newberg	1.04	Madras	0.61
The Dalles	1	Phoenix/Talent	0.58
Lincoln City	0.97	Oakridge	0.56
Sisters	0.97	Brookings	0.55
Reedsport	0.96	Salem North	0.54
Baker City	0.94		

Service Area	Number of Mental Health Providers per 1,000 Residents
McKenzie/Blue	0.52
Siletz	0.48
Cottage Grove	0.47
River	0.46
Springfield	0.46
Port Orford	0.45
Silverton/Mt. Angle	0.43
Veneta	0.42
Cave Junction	0.42
Chiloquin	0.41
Eugene West	0.37
Lakeview	0.37
Hermiston	0.37
Point	0.36
Shady Cove	0.35
Canby	0.35
Woodburn	0.35
Maupin	0.34
Bandon	0.33
Dalla	0.32
St. Helens	0.31
Jordan Valley	0.3
Lebanon	0.3
Sandy	0.28
Applegate/Williams	0.27
Union/Willamine	0.25
Eagle Point	0.24
Glide	0.21
Estacada	0.2
Drain/Yoncalla	0.15
Lowell/Dexter	0.15
Harrisburg	0.15
La Pine	0.13
Sweet Home	0.11

Service Area	Number of Mental Health Providers per 1,000 Residents
Halfway	0.11
North Lake	0.1
Canyonville	0.09
Prineville	0.07
John Day	0.07
Stayton	0.07
Milton-Freewater	0.06
Cloverdale	0.05
Molalla	0.05
Sutherlin	0.04
East Klamath	0
Cascade Locks	0
Glendale	0
Swisshome/Triangle Lake	0
Yachats	0
Powers	0
Merrill	0
Waldport	0
Rogue River	0
Toledo	0
Blodgett-Eddyville	0
Elgin	0
Monroe	0
Irrigon	0
Alsea	0
Condon	0
Moro/Grass Valley	0
Vale	0
Vernonia	0
Scio	0
Wemme	0
Fossil	0
Nyssa	0
Brownsville	0

Source: Oregon Office of Rural Health.

Substance Use Disorder Treatment

Connected to mental health needs is treatment for SUDs,[55] which may be a one-time or recurring need for a patient. Oregon has the fourth-highest adult prevalence of SUDs among US states: 9.8 percent, or 313,000 people[56] and the third-highest unmet need for SUD treatment.[57] Experts attribute the high rates of substance use and misuse to Oregon's underinvestment in prevention services and the lack of integration between MH and SUD treatment.[58] Oregon's housing crisis, discussed in other chapters of this book, plays a role as well. Chapter 10 in particular provides a thoughtful analysis of cycles among substance use, mental health, and housing instability—including the role of trauma and stress stemming from displacement, racism, violence, and poverty.

While substance use by people living on the street is visible to the public, much of substance use happens behind closed doors, and SUD affects all socioeconomic classes. Oregon is thirteenth among US states in the rate of residents receiving SUD treatment: 1,106 stays per 100,000 residents, compared to a national rate of 1,064. The most common treatments in Oregon are for alcohol (52 percent), followed by opiates (24 percent) and stimulants (e.g., methamphetamine) (18 percent).[59] The rate of substance use is even higher. In 2017, Oregon had the highest rates of marijuana use and pain reliever misuse; the second-highest rate of methamphetamine use; and fourth-highest rates of cocaine use, alcohol use disorders, and SUDs.

Access to SUD services is racialized both at the individual level (i.e., a person's access to care) and the community level. Nationwide, counties with a higher percentage of Black residents and Hispanic residents are less likely to have any outpatient SUD facility that accepts Medicaid.[60] Black and Latino people are also less likely than whites to complete the full term of their SUD treatment program, mainly because of housing and employment instability.[61] A 2013 study found that Oregon had one of the biggest Black/white treatment completion gaps among US states. Conversely, this same study found that Latino people completed at a rate slightly higher than whites; structural, not cultural, factors affect these outcomes.[62]

For Indigenous people, the disease transmission, neglect, and militarization of colonization has fomented distrust in accessing services.[63]

Not only has alcohol been a "colonial weapon," but also reservations and so-called Indian boarding schools are carceral spaces,[64] historically using confinement and dispossession in the name of "rehabilitation." Nationally, SUD treatment programs are less effective for Native American people than whites.[65] Seven Oregon tribes operate SUD outpatient programs, and the Native American Rehabilitation Association of the Northwest (NARA) is part of the Urban Indian Health Care Program.

The vast majority of these people who would benefit from SUD treatment also do not seek help. For this reason, experts advise that population-based interventions are a better investment of public dollars than simply opening more slots for inpatient SUD treatment. Population-based interventions reduce substance use through changing social and environmental conditions, such as laws that make it more difficult to obtain alcohol or systematic screening for SUD in medical practices.

The costs of SUD treatment have been increasing, from $134 to $213 for each Medicaid member between 2010 and 2017.[66] One coordinated care organization that studied its claims data found that one major cost of treating opiate use disorders was transportation to and from patients' opiate treatment programs.[67] Many people receiving medication-assisted treatment (MAT) are required to travel every day to the treatment facility to take their medication, such as methadone, under supervision instead of being able to fill a prescription to take home.

Oregon counties vary widely in the rate of inpatient SUD treatment. For example, Hood River County has the lowest rate of alcohol treatment, at 333 people per 100,000 residents, while the statistic for Wheeler County is 941. Only 69 people per 100,000 get opioid treatment in Benton County, compared to 479 in Multnomah County. Multnomah County also has the highest rates of cannabis and stimulant treatment, with Hood River County having the lowest. The number of inpatient treatment slots available ranges from 11 in Clackamas County (one bed per 137,516 residents) to 463 in Multnomah County (one per 1,744 residents). While the absolute number of beds in rural counties was low, many of them have more favorable ratios than urban counties.

There are huge disparities in access to "gold standard" MAT, which uses prescriptions such as methadone or buprenorphine. Multnomah County has the highest number of prescribers of buprenorphine, with 159, or roughly one for every 5,000 residents. Several coastal counties—Clatsop, Columbia, Coos, and Lincoln—have high rates of opiate-related deaths and few available services, similar to Linn and Malheur Counties. Several counties lack any buprenorphine prescribers or opioid treatment programs, such as Tillamook County, which had the highest opioid death rate in the state at 13.42 people per 100,000 residents from 2012 to 2016. For comparison, the rate in Multnomah County was 10.29.[68]

Crosscutting Challenges

The services discussed in this chapter represent a complex patchwork of federal, state, tribal, and local jurisdictions—not to mention community-based organizations and for-profit corporations. Aligning services among all these entities is complex. Oregon policymakers have a philosophical commitment to community-based services, to reduce costs and improve quality of care in areas ranging from disability services, elder care, MAT for SUD, and beyond. But the existing facilities for incarceration, MH, and SUD treatment struggle to deliver these types of services. Although many people have both substance abuse and mental health problems, these conditions are managed separately within the state government, and the SUD treatment sector is highly fragmented.

As a result, people with unmet care needs become "repeat clients" in jails and prisons. One analysis found that these individuals accounted for 9 percent of all people booked into county jails and 29 percent of all booking events (jails and prisons) in Oregon.[69] They were 6.5 times more likely to have a SUD diagnosis and 1.5 times more likely to have been to the emergency department than other Oregon adults enrolled in the Oregon Health Plan, and 29 percent of them had mental health diagnoses. Despite their frequent incarceration, only 2 percent of these people were booked on felony-level offenses against other people. Meeting the SUD and mental health needs of these frequent flyers would alleviate a huge burden on the incarceration system.

Rehabilitation facilities also present the potential for economic development, particularly in rural areas, yet the promise is largely unfulfilled. Corrections jobs have major occupational health risks and offer few career development pathways.[70] Such jobs may seem appealing for Oregonians, however, as they pay relatively high wages and don't require a college degree. The statistics are especially striking for eastern

Oregon, where poverty is high and economic opportunities limited; the median correctional officer wage exceeds $70,000 a year.[71]

There is a nationwide shortage of qualified MH and SUD treatment staff. In particular, there is high turnover and a shortage of practitioners from minoritized racial/ethnic groups.[72] One effort to address these histories is Oregon Administrative Rule 309-019-0175, which set standards for culturally specific providers of SUD treatment and spurred increases in culturally specific SUD treatment providers around the state.

People working at SUD treatment facilities report low wages overall and unmet training needs in critical areas such as MAT. There is a shortage of health care, particularly psychiatric care, few workers in rural areas, and high turnover in paraprofessional jobs owing to poor working conditions and low wages. The costly and time-consuming preparation required for licensure creates huge barriers to people entering the professions. As a result, the workforce is dominated by white, upper-middle-class people and accordingly does not reflect the cultural backgrounds of all Oregon patients. This compromises people's ability to get culturally appropriate care, a problem that grows larger as Oregon's population gets more culturally diverse.

Innovation and Opportunity

Oregon has often taken a different approach from other states, making it an innovator or outlier. In this section, we discuss notable features of Oregon's policy landscape and pathways to more just futures for 2050. Taken together, these strategies aim to decrease the negative impacts of incarceration and stem the "upstream" factors that drive people with SUD and MH issues into prisons.

An overarching goal is reducing the number of people imprisoned. Addressing youth incarceration and the racial inequities in incarceration of youth now is essential for having productive communities in the future. Taking on the broken community-based mental health system could reweave the safety net to help people function at their maximum capacity in their communities and reduce the suffering and violence that is visible on Oregon's streets today. Meeting people's basic needs could reduce homelessness and the resulting exacerbations of mental health and substance use problems. Restorative justice[73] practices could heal harms done without curtailing offenders' life chances through incarceration. Accessible SUD treatment could support all of these goals.

The four major themes in this section are: decarceration, improving service delivery, workforce development, and reducing drug-related harm. Finally, we conclude by discussing how urban planners can contribute to this innovation in their role as stewards of the land use system.

In recent history, Oregonians passed some aggressive "tough-on-crime" policies, but the pendulum is now swinging toward "decarceration," a historical process of changed narratives on the incarcerated and incarceration, innovation across all sectors of the criminal justice system, transdisciplinary policy and practice innovations, and evidence-based strategies.[74] In 1994, the "One Strike, You're Out" Measure 11 set rigid sentencing guidelines. But by 2018, Oregon Senate Bill 1008 on Youth Justice Reform created several mechanisms to reduce the impacts of Measure 11 on minors under 18 years old. Oregon has taken several steps to increase the accountability of the public corrections system, such as ending bail bonds in 1978, not using private prisons, and barring the practice of exporting prisoners to other states in 2001. More recently, the Justice Reinvestment Initiative, created in 2013 by House Bill 3194, has sought to lower correctional spending and reduce the social harms done by incarceration. HB 3194 is expected to save $527 million by 2023.

While laws and policies that have created mass incarceration have often been justified for the purpose of protecting vulnerable members of society from crime, these same policies create more risk for these populations (e.g., Indigenous or transgender women), who are ultimately put at more risk of violence by the policy. Thus putting communities who have been overpoliced and overincarcerated at the head of the decision-making table is a critical next step. As one example, the Oregon Criminal Justice Commission creates important statewide policy; its members are highly regarded correctional employees, lawyers, and elected officials, but most appear to be white, cisgender, and upper middle class. This commission's expertise is incomplete without people who have experienced incarceration and stronger input from Black and Indigenous communities.

Several programs are currently underway to reduce unnecessary detention, which is an urgent need going forward. As discussed in chapter 10, novel collaborations between law enforcement departments and social service providers have nonpolice responses (e.g., Eugene's Crisis Assistance Helping Out On The Streets, or CAHOOTS, and Portland Street Response) to public disturbances caused by people in distress. These programs deescalate disturbances with less likelihood of violence, arrest, or eventual incarceration for people whose disruptive behavior is caused by mental illness or intoxication.

Specialty courts and diversion programs are another important part of Oregon's story. These programs allow people who have been arrested to avoid jail time if they complete a treatment program. The second drug court in the United States started in Multnomah County in 1991, and now many counties across the state have similar programs. Clackamas County started a mental health court in 2003, and programming has since expanded to thirteen other counties. Likewise, the Family Sentencing Alternative Pilot Program (FSAPP), which was created in 2015 by House Bill 3503, established a diversion program for parents convicted of nonviolent crimes to have intensive community-based correctional supervision instead of going to prison. Specialty courts should continue to expand as a way to support family stability and treat people for mental health and SUD problems instead of sending them to jail.[75]

Cash bail, where people pay money to be released from jail until their trial takes place, should end. Oregon's state constitution allows judges to order pretrial detention when there is "danger of physical injury or sexual victimization" if the person is released, but judges tend to use high bail instead, meaning that wealth rather than public safety determines which arrested people are freed. Since wealth is distributed based on race and disability, ending cash bail practice makes Oregon a safer and more equitable state.

Smoothing reentry for people reentering the community after incarceration is an important part of shifting away from a carceral society, where a history of incarceration permanently derails someone's life chances, disrupting their community in the process. In 2015, Oregon implemented a "ban the box" law to prevent employment discrimination against people with criminal records. Oregon is one of twenty states where the requirement includes private as well as government employers.

Oregon also has a history of innovation in service delivery to improve access to healthcare. Since 1975, Oregon has required all insurers to provide mental health coverage, and from 2005, substance abuse treatment coverage was also required. Novel health care delivery systems have increased access to health insurance and integrated MH/SUD services. These systems include the Oregon Health Plan (started in 1994) and its prioritization of preventive care, Medicaid expansion, a lottery for access to care, and Coordinated Care Organizations. More recently, a "Section 1115 waiver" of the IMD provision has enabled the use of Medicaid moneys to pay for SUD treatment in larger psychiatric facilities[76] as well as housing and employment support for participants.

The Behavioral Health Justice Reinvestment Initiative is identifying leverage points where investments in behavioral health would reduce use of criminal justice and health care services. For example, $500 million of general fund and pandemic-related stimulus funds were allocated in 2021 for MH services, housing for people with MH/SUD treatment needs, mobile crisis intervention teams, and peer respite centers for people in behavioral health crisis.[77] This kind of spending, particularly inpatient care, can substantially reduce the number of incarcerated people.[78] The Oregon Health Authority, Department of Corrections, the Oregon Youth Authority, and Criminal Justice Commission have undertaken efforts to streamline MH and SUD care, which should continue.

Prioritizing culturally responsive care for the groups most harmed by historical racism and exclusion is an important strategy for addressing the inequities discussed in this chapter. This work is coming after decades of advocacy by communities of color demanding that the public health system meet their needs.[79] Groups such as Safer Space for Black Lives Matter (BLM) are training clinicians from all backgrounds to be more effective at addressing racism and intergenerational trauma in their practices. To address the workforce issues discussed above, a "pipeline" must be built to bring underrepresented groups such as people who are Black, Indigenous, and people of color (BIPOC), LGBTQ+, disabled, and/or have experiences of incarceration, poverty, or immigration. This might include stronger connections to faith leaders and traditional healers commonly used by many BIPOC Oregonians[80] who are not recognized by the government as part of the formal care systems. The Coalition of Communities of Color has released a series of recommendations[81] to address a wide variety of issues, including data systems and training for nonclinical staff. A critical component of their analysis is that well-being should be considered as a collective experience instead of organizing the entire service system around a Western conception focused on individual treatment for medical disorders.

Oregonians also need to be able to access services during incarceration and other times of vulnerability, and the state has made some headway on this is issue. Measure 57 passed in 2008, requiring the Department of Corrections to provide appropriate treatment services to drug-addicted people who are medium or high risk of reoffending. Red Lodge Transition Services provides culturally specific reentry programming for people from Indigenous backgrounds, and there are also examples of culturally specific programs being provided inside Oregon prisons, such as for Indigenous and Asian incarcerated men. Additionally, Oregonians need care provided in tandem with supportive housing. The Bybee Lakes Hope Center is one model of converting a former jail (Wapato) to a transitional housing environment that provides inpatient care and "one-stop shopping" where people can access counseling, SUD treatment, health care, housing, food support, and more without stigma or the difficulty of pursuing these services through individual bureaucracies.

There are also two major strategies for expanding care opportunities using existing technologies: telemedicine and MAT SUD. The sudden shift to telehealth during the COVID-19 pandemic showed that MH and SUD services can be provided remotely. Telehealth should remain as an important care resource for people who live far from care, have physical mobility challenges, lack transportation options, and/or cannot access culturally relevant care that may not be available in their immediate community. (But remote areas will need broadband infrastructure to use these services.) MAT should be widely available: caps should be lifted on the number of prescribers allowed, and patients should be able to take their medications at home.

Workforce Development

As prisons close and better investments are made in the community MH and SUD treatment system, Oregonians also need new and better career opportunities. For example, scheduled prison closures will eliminate 237 jobs in Coos, Lake, and Marion Counties by 2022.[82] Perhaps these facilities can be converted for community purposes, but regardless of what happens to the buildings, area residents need pathways to human service careers and other jobs, including the remote work that will likely become more common over time.

In our imagined future, Oregon has reinvested in its public education system, including higher education. Every county would have some kind of access to community college coursework, and Oregonians would be able to get credentialed for the wide variety of jobs in the behavioral health sector. Because these jobs vary widely in term of years of training required, creating career ladders is an important component of this training system. In 2019, the Northeast Oregon Area Health Education Center launched the Healthy Oregon Workforce Training Opportunity Program to build the Psychiatric Mental Health Nurse Practitioner workforce. In 2021, HB 2949 created two incentive programs to grow the state's behavioral health workforce, and HB 2086 directed the Oregon Health Authority to establish peer- and community-driven programs that provide culturally responsive behavioral health services.

Recruiting behavioral health professionals from populations that have deep legacies of intergenerational trauma can help heal from the harms of racial terror in the United States and address underrepresentation in the workforce; this is especially important for the Black and Indigenous communities. Furthermore, recruitment must start early: becoming a psychiatrist takes seven to eight years of training *after* the baccalaureate, so students should learn about this career option in high school science classes and have the opportunity for career exploration programs.

The fragmented nature of the MH and SUD system could become a strength if these training programs could take place onsite at the agencies that attempt to serve every corner of Oregon. An additional promising practice already underway is the Mental Health and Addiction Certification Board of Oregon's slate of trainings for unlicensed workers in these industries. This program offers just one example of what a node in long-imagined community care system could look like. In line with the recommendations of mental health advocates, we imagine treatment on demand in smaller community-based settings instead of large psychiatric facilities.

Reducing Drug-Related Harm

Oregon has been a trailblazer in reducing drug-related harm. In 1989, Portland's Outside In started one of the first syringe services program ("needle exchange") in the United States, and service models have evolved to include mobile services and a network of rural harm reduction services. Some programs already underway reduce opiate-related disability and death in rural areas: the federally funded Medication Assisted Treatment-Prescription Drug and Opioid Addiction Project aims to increase the number of physicians prescribing MAT, while the Targeted Response to the Opioid Crisis Program enhances peer support services, focusing on reentry, rural/frontier areas, and Native American communities. Eastern Oregon Opioid Solutions is an innovative trauma-informed program connected to Oregon Center on Behavioral Health and Justice Integration. Oregon's Project ECHO has built systems for telemedicine to improve access to all manner of specialty services in rural Oregon.

In 2020, State Ballot Measure 110 made Oregon the first US state to decriminalize possession of drugs, following what is known as the Portugal Model. The racial and ethnic impact statement prepared prior to the vote suggested that the measure would reduce racial disparities in drug arrest by 95 percent. While possession of drugs for personal use carried no criminal penalties starting in February 2021, it took until August 2022 to create the Behavioral Health Resource Network (BHRN) treatment system, which is funded by cannabis tax revenues and savings from not incarcerating people.

BHRNs are partnerships among public and/or private organizations receiving funding from the Oregon Health Authority that are charged with providing services that are trauma informed, harm reduction focused, culturally specific, and linguistically responsive. Oregon's nine tribal governments are entitled to create BHRNs or use a different service configuration. Services are to be individualized and free of charge and give clients choices about their treatment plan. The goals for the BHRNs are laudable and, if achieved, will be transformative in the pursuit of health justice in Oregon—particularly for their efforts to design out the racialized harms created by earlier approaches to substance use. Implementation and administration remain challenging and uncertain, however.[83] For example, one innovative feature of the program is the use of peer mentors, but their effectiveness is limited when there are limited programs where they can send programs,[84] owing the loss of facilities described above.

Planning for Rehabilitation

These complex, entrenched issues beg the question of how the land use system can play a role in creating a more just future. What is the role for planners, the stewards of the land use system, in shaping Oregon's landscape of rehabilitation facilities?

Historically, planners have been attuned to community opposition new human services facilities, such as the rehabilitation sites discussed in this chapter as well as homeless shelters, schools, hospitals, and group homes for disabled people. This includes NIMBY (not-in-my-backyard) activism as well as more structural processes, such as exclusionary zoning practices that designate suburban land for single-unit housing only. Some older literature[85] focuses on community opposition as a venue for political participation, suggesting that planners can educate opponents by "humanizing" stigmatized population groups or creating "fair share" ordinances that ensure these undesirable facilities are distributed among neighborhoods. They also raise the issue that gentrification can displace human service facilities, which is a huge concern given the issues discussed in chapter 6. Both of these issues could be addressed at the state level by incorporating standards for distribution of facilities as well as programs that support facilities to stay in place or be replaced one-for-one as market pressures threaten their existence. Additionally, the development and preservation of housing discussed in chapters 6 and 12 are essential to reduce the severity of MH and SUD problems and prevent incarceration.

But we can also reconceptualize the role of the land use system to incorporate a more holistic vision of health and well-being, where all processes of criminalization and stigmatization are reduced. The land use system should focus on all residents of the land, allowing the planning process to further expand its focus beyond the demands of landowners. This allows thinking not just about sites to deliver services, but also how to enable all people to feel safe in their communities. For example, Garcia-Hallett et al.[86] identify strategies for planners to interrupt processes that stoke racial inequity: build coalition and community engagement programs that improve police understanding of community issues; protect communities that are criminalized, particularly Latino immigrant groups who fear immigration enforcement; and create equitable processes for enforcing fair housing laws and housing code.

The land use system also needs tools for "daylighting" the racialized impacts of public decisions and the private actions they facilitate. This includes assessing the racial equity impacts of policy decisions as well as doing critical self-reflection about whether demographic analyses and evaluations could unintentionally lead to targeting immigrant enclaves or other vulnerable communities. Likewise, if future corrections facilities become necessary in the future, investments should be carefully vetted to ensure that facilities will be economically beneficial to their host communities.[87]

The planning profession emerged from the social need to address urban inequality, so the land use system of the future should strengthen our capacity to pursue a just future. While planners have historically ignored the existence of formerly incarcerated people, creating a robust reentry ecosystem should be an important part of our mandate for as long as Oregon continues to incarcerate people.[88] Designating physical space for "institutional" rehabilitation facilities is one clear land use function, but planners also have the capacity to normalize and advocate for social services and housing programs. Whether it's called smart decarceration, criminal justice reinvestment, behavioral health reinvestment, or something else, Oregon is pursing initiatives to reduce problems that have profound social and economic costs. Just as the land use system has historically protected the distinctive features of Oregon's physical landscape, we have the capacity to use it as a tool to pursue human well-being as well.

Notes

The authors thank technical advisors Anita Randolph (Oregon Health and Science University/Don't Shoot Portland) and Ken Sanchagrin (Oregon Criminal Justice Commission), as well as Mark Leymon, Nadejda Razi-Robertson, and Katie Wuschke for their input and guidance.

1 Matthew W. Epperson and Carrie Pettus-Davis, "Smart Decarceration: Guiding Concepts for an Era of Criminal Justice Transformation," in *Smart Decarceration: Achieving Criminal Justice Transformation in the 21st Century*, ed. Matthew W. Epperson and Carrie Pettus-Davis (Oxford: Oxford University Press, 2017), 3–28.

2   Julia Acker et al., *Mass Incarceration Threatens Health Equity in America* (Princeton, NJ: Robert Wood Johnson Foundation, 2019), https://www.rwjf.org/en/library/research/2019/01/mass-incarceration-threatens-health-equity-in-america.html.

3   Deborah Johnson, *Connections among Poverty, Incarceration, and Inequality: Policy Brief, Fast Focus Research* (Madison, WI: Institute for Research on Poverty, 2020), https://www.irp.wisc.edu/resource/connections-among-poverty-incarceration-and-inequality/.

4   Christian Henrichson, Joshua Rinaldi, and Ruth Delaney, *The Price of Jails: Measuring the Taxpayer Cost of Local Incarceration* (New York: Vera Institute of Justice, 2015).

5   Michelle Alexander, *The New Jim Crow: Mass Incarceration in the Age of Colorblindness* (New York: New Press, 2020).

6   Elias Nosrati et al., "Economic Decline, Incarceration, and Mortality from Drug Use Disorders in the USA between 1983 and 2014: An Observational Analysis," *Lancet Public Health* 4, no. 7 (July 1, 2019): e326–33, doi:10.1016/S2468-2667(19)30104-5.

7   Carolina S. Sarmiento, "From Jails to Sanctuary Planning: Spatial Justice in Santa Ana, California," *Journal of Planning Education and Research* 40, no. 2 (2020): 196–209, doi:10.1177/0739456x19893743.

8   Ken Sanchagrin, executive director of Oregon Criminal Justice Commission, personal communication, December 7, 2020 .

9   The Sentencing Project, "Detailed State Data," Criminal Justice Facts, 2020, https://www.sentencingproject.org/the-facts/#detail.

10 The Sentencing Project, "Detailed State Data"; The Sentencing Project, "State Rankings," Criminal Justice Facts, 2020, https://www.sentencingproject.org/the-facts/#rankings.

11 Oregon Criminal Justice Commission, *Probabilistic Race Correction for Hispanics* (Salem: State of Oregon, 2018), https://www.oregon.gov/cjc/CJCpercent20Documentpercent20Library/RaceCorrectionTechDocFinal-8-6-18.pdf.

12 American Academy of Arts and Sciences, *Public Research Universities: Changes in State Funding* (Cambridge, MA: American Academy of Arts and Sciences, 2015), https://www.amacad.org/publication/public-research-universities-changes-state-funding/section/1.

13 Hillary Borrud and Noelle Crombie, "Prisons and Preschool: Oregon Governor to Outline Budget Priorities," *Oregonian*, November 28, 2020, https://www.oregonlive.com/politics/2020/11/where-should-oregon-commit-taxpayer-money-pressure-for-both-prisons-and-preschools-as-governor-forges-her-spending-blueprint.html.

14 Juliana van Olphen et al., "Community Reentry: Perceptions of People with Substance Use Problems Returning Home from New York City Jails," *Journal of Urban Health* 83, no. 3 (May 2006): 372–81, doi:10.1007/s11524-006-9047-4.

15 Mark L. Hatzenbuehler et al., "The Collateral Damage of Mass Incarceration: Risk of Psychiatric Morbidity among Nonincarcerated Residents of High-Incarceration Neighborhoods," *American Journal of Public Health* 105, no. 1 (January 2015): 138–43, doi:10.2105/AJPH.2014.302184.

16 Susan E. Blankenship and Ernest J. Yanarella, "Prison Recruitment as a Policy Tool of Local Economic Development: A Critical Evaluation," *Contemporary Justice Review* 7, no. 2 (June 1, 2004): 183–98, doi:10.1080/1028258042000221184.

17 "Budget Crisis Closes Oregon Prison for First Time in 159 Years," *Prison Legal News*, January 30, 2012.
18 Borrud and Crombie, "Prisons and Preschool."
19 Christian Henrichson et al., "Incarceration Trends in Oregon," in *State Incarceration Trends* (New York: Vera Institute of Justice, 2019).
20 "ICE Pays to Use 2 Oregon Jails Despite Sanctuary State Law," Oregon Public Broadcasting, October 26, 2017, https://www.opb.org/news/article/ice-jail-oregon-norcor-josephine-contract-sanctuary-state/.
21 Statistics on the number of jail beds were provided by Ken Sanchagrin at the Oregon Criminal Justice Commission.
22 Henrichson et al., "Incarceration Trends in Oregon."
23 Debby Warren, "Geography of Incarceration Shifts from Urban to Rural," *Non Profit News*, January 21, 2020, https://nonprofitquarterly.org/geography-of-incarceration-shifts-from-urban-to-rural/.
24 Warren, "Geography of Incarceration Shifts."
25 The National Institutes of Health defines "any mental illness" as having a mental, behavioral, or emotional disorder with any level of impairment, whereas "serious mental illness" is the label for people who have one of these disorders and serious functional impairment as a result.
26 Maddy Reinert, Theresa Nguyen, and Danielle Fritze, *State of Mental Health in America 2020* (Arlington, VA: Mental Health America, 2019).
27 "2019 Uniform Reporting System (URS) Table for Oregon," Substance Abuse and Mental Health Services Administration, May 22, 2020, https://www.samhsa.gov/data/report/2019-uniform-reporting-system-urs-table-oregon.
28 "The History of Mental Illness in the State of Oregon," Mental Health Association of Portland, September 20, 2013, https://www.mentalhealthportland.org/about-2/oregons-mental-health-history/.
29 "Health Insurance Coverage of the Total Population," Kaiser Family Foundation, October 28, 2022, https://www.kff.org/other/state-indicator/total-population/.
30 "History of Mental Illness."
31 Donald Orr and Samantha Matsumoto, "Black Oregonians Struggle to Find Mental Health Care amid Increasing Need," Oregon Public Broadcasting, November 4, 2020, https://www.opb.org/article/2020/11/04/black-oregonians-struggle-to-find-mental-health-care-amid-increasing-need/.
32 Reinert et al., *State of Mental Health in America 2020*.
33 Psychiatrists, psychologists, licensed clinical social workers, counselors, marriage and family therapists, and advanced practice nurses specializing in mental health care.
34 WGBH Educational Foundation, "Deinstitutionalization: A Psychiatric 'Titanic,'" *Frontline*, May 10, 2005, https://www.pbs.org/wgbh/pages/frontline/shows/asylums/special/excerpt.html.
35 Doris A. Fuller et al., *Going, Going, Gone: Trends and Consequences of Eliminating State Psychiatric Beds, 2016* (Arlington, VA: Treatment Advocacy Center, 2016).
36 Samantha Raphelson, "How the Loss of US Psychiatric Hospitals Led to a Mental Health Crisis," National Public Radio, November 30, 2017, https://www.npr.org/2017/11/30/567477160/how-the-loss-of-u-s-psychiatric-hospitals-led-to-a-mental-health-crisis.
37 When a court mandates that a person get psychiatric treatment because they are a threat to themselves or others.

38 Joseph D. Bloom, "Civil Commitment Is Disappearing in Oregon," *Journal of the American Academy of Psychiatry and the Law* 34, no. 4 (2006): 534–37.
39 Doris A. Fuller et al., *Overlooked in the Undercounted: The Role of Mental Illness in Fatal Law Enforcement Encounters* (Arlington, VA: Treatment Advocacy Center, 2015), TACReports.org/overlooked-undercounted.
40 Kimberly Kindy et al., "Fatal Police Shootings of Mentally Ill People Are 39 Percent More Likely to Take Place in Small and Midsized Areas," *Washington Post*, October 17, 2020, https://www.washingtonpost.com/national/police-mentally-ill-deaths/2020/10/17/8dd5bcf6-0245-11eb-b7ed-141dd88560ea_story.html.
41 Harold Pollack, "What Happened to US Mental Health Care after Deinstitutionalization?," *Washington Post*, June 12, 2013, https://www.washingtonpost.com/news/wonk/wp/2013/06/12/what-happened-to-u-s-mental-health-care-after-deinstitutionalization/.
42 Josh Kulla, "Former State Hospital Still Shaping Wilsonville," *Wilsonville Spokesman*, October 9, 2013, https://pamplinmedia.com/wsp/196971-51136-former-state-hospital-still-shaping-wilsonville.
43 Christopher David Gray, "Junction City Fills Critical Role over Objections of Chief Advocates," Lund Report, April 13, 2016, https://www.thelundreport.org/content/junction-city-fills-critical-role-over-objections-chief-advocates.
44 "2020 National Mental Health Services Survey (N-MHSS) State Profiles," Substance Abuse and Mental Health Services Administration, accessed January 4, 2024, https://www.samhsa.gov/data/sites/default/files/quick_statistics/state_profiles/NMHSS-US20.pdf.
45 Elizabeth Hayes, "For Unity Center for Behavioral Health, Much Has Changed and Much Remains the Same in the Covid Era," *Portland Business Journal*, August 18, 2020, https://www.bizjournals.com/portland/news/2020/08/18/unity-center-post-financial-crisis.html.
46 Jayati Ramakrishnan, "Hospitals Sue Oregon Health Authority over Failure to Provide Mental Health Facilities for Patients," *Oregonian*, September 28, 2022, https://www.oregonlive.com/health/2022/09/hospitals-sue-oregon-health-authority-over-failure-to-provide-mental-health-facilities-for-patients.html.
47 Jangho Yoon et al., *Emergency Department Boarding of Psychiatric Patients in Oregon* (Portland: Oregon Health Authority, 2016).
48 Nigel Jaquiss, "State Grants Approval for New, Long-Planned Psychiatric Hospital, with Significant Conditions," *Willamette Week*, October 17, 2021, https://www.wweek.com/news/2021/10/17/state-grants-approval-for-new-long-planned-psychiatric-hospital-with-significant-conditions/.
49 Christian Wihtol, "Politicians, Health Care Groups Support Psychiatric Hospital in Wilsonville," Lund Report, April 16, 2020, https://www.thelundreport.org/content/politicians-health-care-groups-support-psychiatric-hospital-wilsonville.
50 Jeff Manning, "Company Abandons Plan for Wilsonville Psychiatric Hospital," *Oregonian*, February 22, 2022, https://www.oregonlive.com/business/2022/02/company-abandons-plan-for-wilsonville-psychiatric-hospital.html.
51 John Fitzgerald and Michael Schmidt, *Analysis of Oregon's Publicly Funded Substance Abuse Treatment System: Report and Findings for Senate Bill 1041* (Salem: Oregon Criminal Justice Commission, September 2019).
52 Nigel Jaquiss, "The State's Largest Provider of Community Mental Health and Addiction Treatment Services Seeks a Bailout," *Willamette Week*, February 3, 2021, https://www.wweek.com/news/2021/02/03/

the-states-largest-provider-of-community-mental-health-and-addiction-treatment-services-seeks-a-bailout/.

53   Shawnda Schroeder and Mandi Leigh-Peterson, *Rural and Urban Utilization of the Emergency Department for Mental Health and Substance Abuse*, Rural Health Reform Policy Policy Brief (Grand Forks, ND: Center for Rural Health, 2017), https://ruralhealth.und.edu/projects/health-reform-policy-research-center/publications.

54   "Rural Oregon Facing Mental Health Issues Alone," *Wallowa County Chieftain*, June 10, 2014, https://www.wallowa.com/opinion/chieftain-rural-oregon-facing-mental-health-issues-alone.

55   SUD is defined as pattern of substance use leading to clinically significant impairment or distress.

56   Reinert et al., *State of Mental Health in America 2020*.

57   Fitzgerald and Schmidt, *Analysis of Oregon's Publicly Funded Substance Abuse Treatment System*.

58   Sophia Prince, "Oregon Had Second-Highest Addiction Rates in the Nation in 2020," Oregon Public Broadcasting/Jefferson Public Radio, accessed February 3, 2022, https://www.opb.org/article/2022/02/03/oregon-had-second-highest-addiction-rates-in-the-nation-in-2020/.

59   Kathryn R. Fingar et al., "Geographic Variation in Substance-Related Inpatient Stays across States and Counties in the United States, 2013–2015," in *Geographic Variation in Substance-Related Inpatient Stays across States and Counties in the United States, 2013–2015*, Healthcare Cost and Utilization Project (HCUP) Statistical Briefs 245 (Rockville, MD: Agency for Healthcare Research and Quality, 2018), http://www.ncbi.nlm.nih.gov/books/NBK537456/.

60   Janet R. Cummings et al., "Race/Ethnicity and Geographic Access to Medicaid Substance Use Disorder Treatment Facilities in the United States," *JAMA Psychiatry* 71, no. 2 (February 2014): 190–96, doi:10.1001/jamapsychiatry.2013.3575.

61   Brendan Saloner and Benjamin Lê Cook, "Blacks and Hispanics Are Less Likely Than Whites to Complete Addiction Treatment, Largely Due to Socioeconomic Factors," *Health Affairs* 32, no. 1 (January 1, 2013): 135–45, doi:10.1377/hlthaff.2011.0983.

62   Stephan Arndt, Laura Acion, and Kristin White, "How the States Stack Up: Disparities in Substance Abuse Outpatient Treatment Completion Rates for Minorities," *Drug and Alcohol Dependence* 132, no. 3 (October 1, 2013): 547–54, doi:10.1016/j.drugalcdep.2013.03.015.

63   David G. Lewis, "A Historical Perspective on Pandemic," Underscore, July 13, 2020, https://www.underscore.news/reporting/historical-perspective-pandemic.

64   James Kilgore, "Mass Incarceration since 1492: Native American Encounters with Criminal Injustice," Truthout, February 6, 2016, https://truthout.org/articles/mass-incarceration-since-1492-native-american-encounters-with-criminal-injustice/.

65   Saloner and Cook, "Blacks and Hispanics Are Less Likely than Whites to Complete Addiction Treatment."

66   Fitzgerald and Schmidt, *Analysis of Oregon's Publicly Funded Substance Abuse Treatment System*.

67   Fitzgerald and Schmidt, *Analysis of Oregon's Publicly Funded Substance Abuse Treatment System*.

68 Oregon Health Authority, *Report on Existing Barriers to Effective Treatment for and Recovery from Substance Use Disorders, Including Addictions to Opioids and Opiates* (Salem: State of Oregon, September 26, 2018), https://dfr.oregon.gov/business/reg/reports-data/Documents/legislature/2018-hb4143-dfr-legislation-reports.pdf.
69 Fitzgerald and Schmidt, *Analysis of Oregon's Publicly Funded Substance Abuse Treatment System*.
70 Blankenship and Yanarella, "Prison Recruitment as a Policy Tool."
71 Bureau of Labor Statistics, "Occupation: Correctional Officers and Jailers (SOC Code 333012)—May 2020," Occupational Employment and Wage Statistics, accessed February 23, 2024, https://www.bls.gov/oes/2020/may/oes_4100008.htm#33-0000.
72 Cummings et al., "Race/Ethnicity and Geographic Access."
73 See "Retributive vs. Restorative Justice," Conflict Solutions Center, accessed January 23, 2022, http://www.cscsb.org/restorative_justice/retribution_vs_restoration.html for discussion of this approach.
74 Epperson and Pettus-Davis, "Smart Decarceration."
75 See Nicholas Freudenberg and Daliah Heller, "A Review of Opportunities to Improve the Health of People Involved in the Criminal Justice System in the United States," *Annual Review of Public Health* 37 (2016): 313–33, doi:10.1146/annurev-publhealth-032315-021420 for discussion.
76 "Substance Use Disorder 1115 Demonstration Waiver," Oregon Health Authority, accessed December 31, 2022, https://www.oregon.gov/oha/HSD/Medicaid-Policy/Pages/SUD-Waiver.aspx.
77 Peter Wong, "Oregon Funds 'Historic' $500M for Mental Health Services," *Portland Tribune*, October 13, 2021, https://pamplinmedia.com/pt/9-news/524885-418324-oregon-funds-historic-500m-for-mental-health-services.
78 Jangho Yoon and Jeff Luck, "Intersystem Return on Investment in Public Mental Health: Positive Externality of Public Mental Health Expenditure for the Jail System in the US," *Social Science and Medicine* 170 (December 1, 2016): 133–42, doi:10.1016/j.socscimed.2016.10.015.
79 Research Justice Institute, *Investing in Culturally and Linguistically Responsive Behavioral Health Care in Oregon* (Portland, OR: Coalition of Communities of Color, 2021).
80 Research Justice Institute, *Investing in Culturally and Linguistically Responsive Behavioral Health Care*.
81 Research Justice Institute, *Investing in Culturally and Linguistically Responsive Behavioral Health Care*.
82 Mill Creek in Marion County closed in June 2021, resulting in the loss of fifty-two jobs. The closure of Shutter Creek in Coos County in January 2022 resulted in the loss of a hundred jobs. Lauren Dake, "Gov. Kate Brown Moves to Close 3 Oregon Prisons," Oregon Public Broadcasting, January 15, 2021, https://www.opb.org/article/2021/01/15/oregon-kate-brown-prison-closures/.
83 Oregon Health Authority, *Too Early to Tell: The Challenging Implementation of Measure 110 Has Increased Risks, but the Effectiveness of the Program Has Yet to Be Determined* (Salem: Oregon Health Authority, 2023).
84 "Peer Mentors Are Key to Oregon's Measure 110 Success, but They Are Working in a Broken System," Oregon Public Broadcasting, January 9, 2023, https://www.opb.org/article/2023/01/09/oregon-measure-110-drug-addiction-treatment-recovery/.

85 E.g., Jennifer R. Wolch and Stuart A. Gabriel, "Dismantling the Community-Based Human Service System," *Journal of the American Planning Association* 51, no. 1 (March 31, 1985): 53–62, doi:10.1080/01944368508976800; Lois M. Takahashi and Michael J. Dear, "The Changing Dynamics of Community Opposition to Human Service Facilities," *Journal of the American Planning Association* 63, no. 1 (March 31, 1997): 79–93, doi:10.1080/01944369708975725.

86 "Latinxs in the Kansas City Metro Area: Policing and Criminalization in Ethnic Enclaves," *Journal of Planning Education and Research* 40, no. 2 (2020): 151–68, doi:10.1177/0739456x19882749.

87 See Blankenship and Yanarella, "Prison Recruitment as a Policy Tool" for potential criteria.

88 For more discussion, see Courtney Knapp, "Local Planning in the Age of Mass Decarceration," *Journal of Planning Education and Research* 40, no. 2 (June 1, 2020): 169–85, doi:10.1177/0739456X20911704.

PART IV

Governance

The preceding chapters in this book look at specific public policy areas. This section considers the state government more broadly, examining two parts of the political system: the state budget (chap. 13) and voting and representation (chap. 14). The authors assess how well the political system is generally functioning, including producing tax and spending policies that are effective and fair and in equitably representing the diverse interests in the state. If community leaders and policymakers are serious about planning for a better Oregon in 2050, these are essential concerns that need to be considered.

These chapters praise aspects of Oregon government and politics for their efforts to be equitable and inclusive. Oregon's revenue system is strongly dependent on a progressive income tax, one that requires those who earn more to pay a higher tax rate. Thanks to automatic voter registration and vote by mail, Oregon's election system has made it easy for Oregonians to register to vote and cast a ballot.

But these chapters also reveal something important about the current state of Oregon politics. Despite its reputation for innovative policies, the state's political system has severe problems, some of which have lingered for years without being addressed. Among the most challenging is the state's troubled revenue system, which has made it difficult to adequately fund programs and which has witnessed disturbing volatility from year to year. There is also a strong feeling among many Oregonians that their voices are not being well heard in Salem and that there are not adequate choices on the ballot.

In looking at how to improve Oregon's government by 2050, policymakers and the public have to consider and make decisions about how to solve these two critical problems. Potential solutions offered by the authors in this section include new types of taxes and some form of proportional representation. But there are no perfect solutions to these types of problems, and these solutions bring their own concerns. Other forms of taxes are often less equitable than the income tax, requiring poorer Oregonians to pay an increased share of taxes. While proportional representation would improve the opportunity for more diverse voices to be heard in the capitol, a cacophony of diverse voices can make it more difficult for the government to act. The job of policymakers and those who want to work to make Oregon better by 2050 is to weigh the benefits and drawbacks of these and other approaches to the issues raised in these chapters, and then push forward in trying to get a preferred remedy enacted into law.

13
State Revenue and Spending
PETER HULSEMAN AND JENNY H. LIU

In this chapter, we turn our attention to how Oregon's government obtains and spends revenue. How Oregon collects and spends money is a big deal for many reasons, including that the budget is an expression of the state's values, there are both short- and long-term impacts to budget decisions on people and the environment, and it is politically contentious. This is a broad topic, intertwined with many issues addressed in other chapters. This chapter does not delve into the specifics of revenue and spending in any individual topic area. Instead, the focus is on the challenges and implications from government funding and distribution mechanisms. There are some significant problems in the current state of revenue and spending, and there is no panacea for addressing these problems. In addition, almost all tax-and-spend policies generate some winners and some losers. Thus a key to planning for a better 2050 is to understand the trade-offs between different policy approaches, and to recognize who wins and who loses.

Government Revenue

The structure of Oregon's tax system is different from most states, though the ultimate amount of revenue raised by the Oregon government (i.e., own-fund revenue) is average for its population and income. In 2020, Oregon ranked fourteenth highest among states in terms of state and local revenue per capita, or what the average Oregonian pays in state and local taxes. Forty-three percent of revenues was from taxes, while the remainder was from the federal government, program fees, government enterprises (such as earnings from liquor sales), insurance trust revenue (including earnings on public employee retirement funds), and miscellaneous sources. In planning for the future, taxes will

Table 13.1. Oregon Tax Revenue per Capita and as a Percentage of Income

	Amount per Person	State Ranking	Percentage of Personal Income	State Ranking[a]
Total taxes	$5,388	21	10.30	19
Personal income tax	$2,336	7	4.50	2
Corporate income tax	$239	15	0.50	12
General sales tax	$0	48	0.00	48
Selective sales taxes	$596	26	1.10	25
Property tax	$1,671	24	3.20	17
Other taxes	$546	12	1.00	11

[a] The lower the number, the higher the tax is relative to other states. Oregon is ranked 48th for general sales tax, tied with three other states.

Source: Oregon Legislative Revenue Office, *2022 Oregon Public Finance: Basic Facts*, #1-22 (Salem: State of Oregon Legislative Revenue Office, 2022), https://www.oregonlegislature.gov/lro/Documents/Basic%20Facts%202022.pdf (uses 2019 data).

continue to be the most important part of the revenue structure, both because they are the main source of revenue for general public spending and because of their impacts on taxpayers. Most other funding sources are directly tied to specific programs.

The *Basic Facts* report, the Legislative Revenue Office's (LRO) yearly guide to the state's revenue system, puts Oregon's tax revenue into context in two ways: by looking at per capita tax revenue and tax revenue as a percentage of income. Table 13.1 examines both. Instead of total revenue, this table focuses specifically on tax revenue (and does not include fees, etc.). At $5,202 per capita, Oregon ranked twenty-fifth highest in the country in 2020. Per capita is a common measure used for comparison purposes and does not imply this is what a typical person would pay.

Overall, around 72 percent of taxes the average Oregonian pays are personal income and property taxes. Unlike most other states, Oregon does not have a statewide general sales tax. It is one of only five states without one. Oregon does have selective sales taxes (e.g., gasoline or tobacco taxes), but these taxes accounted for about the same as the average state in 2020. Property taxes in Oregon, which primarily provide funds for local education and local governments, have restrictive regulations (Measures 5 and 50; see below) that cap how much revenue can be raised from a given taxpayer. These regulations increase the complexity of legislative efforts to use the property tax system to raise funds. The Corporate Income Tax category in table 13.1 includes the recently implemented Corporate Activity Tax, which functions similarly to a sales tax.

Evaluating Tax Policy

Oregon's current tax structure has benefits and drawbacks. For example, consider the lack of a sales tax. Sales taxes provide stable sources of revenue for government budgets. The state's lack of a sales tax increases the likelihood of revenue shortfalls during recessions. If one were introduced, it would help provide some protection from the state's continued cycle of building up programs only to tear them down in hard times. In contrast, sales taxes tend to be regressive, meaning that individuals with less income pay a higher percentage of their incomes.

The main question for policymakers is to determine the right amount of revenue for Oregon to succeed at its policy goals, and what mixture of taxes is the most effective or equitable way for revenue to be collected. Evaluating tax policies always comes down to evaluating the trade-offs between efficiency, equity, and effectiveness—known colloquially as the "Three E's." These are explained below and help to frame the discussion of the current system.

- *Efficiency*. The most common economic criteria, efficiency signifies the relationship between costs and outputs. An efficient policy would produce the most output (e.g., government services) for the least cost (e.g., tax dollars) compared to feasible alternatives. This is typically considered on the spending side of polices.
- *Equity*. Equity captures the concept of fairness and is typically used with regard to the distribution of resources across a population. An inequitable policy would distribute goods "unfairly" across income groups, race, or other category. In public finance, the notion of vertical equity captures the idea that those with more ability to pay taxes should pay more, called the "ability to pay principle." This is considered both on the taxing and spending side of a potential policy.

- *Effectiveness.* Effectiveness refers to how well the policy objectives are met. Often confused with efficiency, effectiveness is about doing "the right thing," while efficiency is about "doing the thing, right."

Since efficiency is concerned about the relationship between costs and outputs, and this section focuses solely on tax revenue, equity and effectiveness are given the most attention. One example of effectiveness is a 100 percent income tax rate. This tax rate would be highly ineffective at raising revenue. Since there is no incentive to work, no revenue would be collected. An example of inequity would be a new tax on low-cost grocery stores, which would be disproportionately borne by the low-income population. These are extreme examples. Ultimately, there are no perfect tax policies; trade-offs are involved regardless of which ones are adopted.

Who Pays?

Income Taxes Paid by Quintile

To evaluate Oregon's current tax structure, especially regarding equity, it is important to understand the characteristics of who pays taxes. Oregon has a progressive tax system; as shown in figure 13.1, the effective rate of taxes—taxes paid divided by income—rises with income. The vertical bars show the total amount of taxable income (darker gray) and net taxes

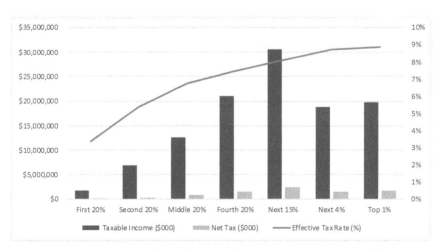

Figure 13.1. Oregon income quintiles and taxes paid. *Source*: Legislative Revenue Office, 2020 Oregon Public Finance: Basic Facts, Research Report #1-20 (Salem, OR: Legislative Revenue Office, 2020), https://www.oregonlegislature.gov/lro/Documents/Basic%20Facts%202022.pdf

(gross taxes minus tax credits, shown in lighter gray) by income quintile; the left-hand axis shows the dollar amount for these bars. The gray line shows the effective tax rate, with the right axis providing the percentage. Generally, the figure shows that the tax rate is higher at higher income levels—which is the definition of a progressive tax system. The exception to this rule is that those reporting the lowest 20 percent of income pay a slightly higher rate than the subsequent group. This is because a number of filers in that group had negative incomes. The first four quintiles of taxpayers pay approximately 31.5 percent of the total income taxes with 36.9 percent of total taxable income, while the top 20 percent of earners pay close to 70 percent. Put succinctly, these statistics reveal that the state has a fairly progressive tax structure.

The Relationship between Income and Race/Ethnicity

One beneficial aspect of the progressive income tax system is that disadvantaged minorities, including Black, Indigenous, and other people of color, tend to pay less, both in terms of their effective tax rate and their net payment, in taxes. This is because the median income of many of these households—with the exception of Asian Americans—is significantly less than the median white household in Oregon, as further discussed in chapter 10. This also illustrates a key point about taxing policy—regressive taxing policies tend to negatively affect racial and ethnic minorities disproportionately, while progressive policies tend to follow the ability to pay principle. Therefore more regressive taxing policies—such as Oregon's property tax system or a general sales tax, which most states other than Oregon have—place a disproportionately high burden on these groups.

Publicly available tax records are not directly tied to demographic variables, and the total taxes paid by race or ethnicity are not available. But this fact does not undermine the larger takeaway that more regressive policies tend to disproportionately affect racial and ethnic minorities, who tend to have lower incomes.

Income Tax by County

To better understand how much Oregonians across the state pay in taxes, we can examine the effective tax rate (i.e., taxes owed as a proportion of income) by county (fig. 13.2).[1] This measure, combined with the high

Figure 13.2. Oregon's effective income tax rate by county, 2020. *Source*: Mark Beilby, Oregon Personal Income Tax Statistics: Characteristics of Filers, 2022 Edition, Tax Year 2020 (Salem: Oregon Department of Revenue, 2022), https://www.oregon.gov/dor/programs/gov-research/Documents/TYpercent202020percent20Oregonpercent20Personalpercent20Incomepercent20Taxpercent20Statisticspercent20Reportpercent202022percent20Edpercent20150-101-406.pdf

variation in average tax liabilities (from $2,210 to $6,350), highlights that differences in income tax liability are directly correlated with differences in incomes between counties. Counties with higher incomes—such as Multnomah—have higher average tax liabilities and effective tax rates. This is consistent with a progressive tax structure.

These statistics reinforce an important lesson about the state's current tax system: the state currently has a more progressive tax structure than if it introduced a sales tax. This is just one of the types of trade-offs to consider in modifying the existing tax structure. The more recent developments in Oregon's tax structure, including the implementation of the corporate activity tax, vehicle privilege tax, and higher tobacco taxes, underscore the structural trend toward broadening its underlying tax base and diversifying tax revenue streams. The state has also attempted to counteract the volatility of the current tax system by requiring ten-year revenue and spending forecasts to attempt to account for the business cycle. Since the government determines its budget based on the revenue forecasts, they have helped reduce budget "surprises" that lead to volatile funding (and budget cuts), though the surprises have not been eliminated entirely.

Government Spending

In looking at the state's sources of revenue, the previous section focused primarily on equity and efficiency, rather than effectiveness. Assessing government spending, however, requires a different focus, one that is more complicated and challenging. In particular, government spending programs include a wide array of policy objectives beyond those in raising revenue, and thus analyzing their success takes detailed knowledge of the subject matter. Another complicating factor in assessing effectiveness is that there is not always agreement on the values tied to government spending. As one example, in transportation spending, some proponents may value higher driving speeds and reduced driving times, while others may value mobility and accessibility by communities unable to drive and lower rates of car crashes.

Another challenge in assessing government spending programs is determining who benefits from them. This is difficult because—unless the program is a direct transfer—it is hard to determine a monetary benefit, especially since most programs provide public goods that have widespread and opaque benefits. For example, it is not just students who benefit from school spending, but so do employers and the community at large. It is not just drivers who benefit from road maintenance; roads are central to the distribution of goods and services, so most Oregonians derive some benefits from having roads maintained. Even more difficult to assess are topics like environmental protections, where everyone receives some benefit—such as cleaner air and water— from a well-executed program.

Because of these complexities and challenges, this section focuses on government spending in the broadest sense, and the challenges to maintaining or increasing current spending levels, rather than focusing on specific policy details. Discussions of specific programs and who they benefit, or how they could be more effectively executed, can be found in the other chapters of this book. Here we provide some food for thought on the budgeting challenges when considering the policy proposals put forward in other chapters.

Spending Breakdown

The state budget is composed of four broad categories. To understand how state budgeting works and the challenges confronting budget writers, it is necessary to understand the uses of and restrictions on each of these categories. Similar to how the Legislative Revenue Office regularly publishes a *Basic Facts* report, the Legislative Fiscal Office publishes a *Budget Highlights* report. To explain the different categories, this chapter relies heavily on the most recent of these reports, which focuses on the 2021-23 Legislatively Adopted Budget.[2] The section focuses solely on state spending and not local spending, which means it does not include a good portion of the spending on schools, police, firefighters, and other local government services.

The total budget adopted for the 2021-23 budget cycle was $121.165 billion, the largest adopted budget in state history and reflecting a trend of increasing budgets for the past two decades. Of that, about 33 percent, $40.44 billion, was from the federal government, and earmarked for specific programs such as for the Oregon Health Authority (44.2 percent of federal funds) and Department of Human Services (28.1 percent of federal funds). These departments deal with administering programs such as Medicaid and the Supplemental Nutrition Assistance Program. Since these funds are provided by the federal government for specific programs, there is little flexibility in terms of what they may be spent on.

About 42.4 percent ($51.42 billion) of the budget is for a category called "Other Funds." Other Funds are everything outside of the categories of Federal Funds, Lottery Funds, and General Funds, and include sources of revenue such as licenses, fees, charges for service, interest, donations, and loan repayments. Other Funds are typically earmarked for specific programs based on their revenue source, and thus there is little flexibility in how they may be spent. The largest share of these funds is dedicated to the Public Employees Retirement System (PERS), 25.4 percent. The share spent on PERS fluctuates with the portfolio's investment return, which may lead to further budget constraints. Human services and transportation spending make up another quarter of spending, while the rest is split between a slew of other programs. Other Funds make up the largest share of total state government spending but are not discussed in this chapter because those funds have little flexibility in terms of how they are spent.[3]

The categories of Lottery Funds and General Funds are where the state government, via the legislature, has the most flexibility in spending, yet these together make up just 24.2 percent of state government spending ($29.31 billion) and are primarily budgeted to pay for education, human services, and public safety. Approximately 29.1 percent of the General and Lottery Funds were directed to K–12 education, 29.5 percent toward human services, and 13.9 percent toward other education (such as higher education). Lottery Funds make up 1.2 percent of the total funds, about $1.45 billion. About 35 percent of Lottery Funds have constitutional dedications, including 18 percent going toward the Education Stability Fund (ESF); 15 percent toward the Parks and Natural Resources Fund; 1.5 percent toward the Veterans' Services Fund; and the remainder toward schools, gambling addition programs, and county fairs. The rest mostly goes to schools and to debt service (lottery bonds are a huge source of local economic development projects throughout the state). The remainder of lottery revenues, which are minor, are spent on things such as gambling addiction treatment programs, county fairs, and the like.

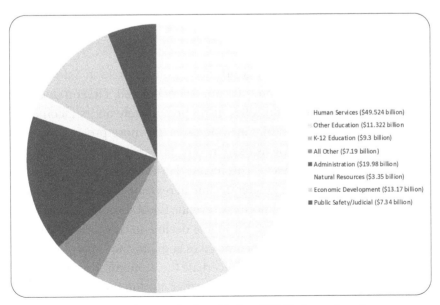

Figure 13.3. Snapshot of the legislatively adopted budget, 2021-23. *Source*: Amanda Beitel, Paul Siebert, and Tom MacDonald, "2021-23 Budget Highlights Update," Oregon Legislative Assembly, Legislative Fiscal Office, 2022. https://www.oregonlegislature.gov/lfo/Documents/2021-23BudgetHighlightsUpdate.pdf

Figure 13.3 provides a more detailed snapshot of state spending, showing the allocations of funds by program area (subcategories). The largest share (42 percent) of state spending is directed toward human services, which performs a number of government services but are primarily known as the state source of health care and social safety net programs. Education makes up 18 percent of total spending, with $9.0 billion going to K–12 education and $6.9 billion going to other education, while administration makes up 17 percent.

Wicked Problems in Revenue and Spending

Oregon's revenue levels are generally on par with most states given its population and income. The state's budget is also similar to that found elsewhere; the two biggest categories of expenditures across the states are routinely education and human services. Yet Oregon faces some unusual, and in some cases unique, challenges that create severe problems in its ability to raise taxes and adequately fund state programs. These are "wicked problems" in that they do not always have solutions, or the solutions come at the expense of another goal, be it equity, efficiency, or effectiveness. While this list is not comprehensive, it does highlight many of the challenges facing policymakers looking forward to 2050.

Volatility and Recessions

One of the biggest challenges confronting policymakers in Salem is the volatility of the state's revenue stream. As mentioned, Oregon does not have a general sales tax and relies disproportionately on its income tax relative to other states. While income taxes are more progressive than general sales taxes, one downside of income taxes is that they are less stable than other forms of taxes.[4] This means that when the state goes into a recession, it experiences a greater decline in revenue than states that also have a sales tax. Put simply, more tax revenue is lost through business closures and lost jobs than is lost through a decline in consumer spending. Yet the problem of relying on income taxes goes beyond simply lost taxes. This decline in revenue can then exacerbate the economic downturn even more as the government is forced to further cut funding, which in turn results in a further decrease in income and economic activity.

Oregon has recently made some changes to its tax system that have dampened this downward cycle. First, the creation of the ESF and the

Oregon Rainy Day Fund (RDF) have provided a type of automatic stabilizer for the state budget. Established in 2002 and 2007, respectively, these reserve funds act as a savings account during expansions and can only be withdrawn under specific conditions normally indicative of a recession.[5] While not a total solution for revenue stability, the reserve funds have been effective in counterbalancing revenue shortfalls. As such, the legislature approved a $400 million withdrawal from the ESF during the COVID-19 global pandemic (in the 2019-21 biennium) to prevent a disruption to public education funding. At the end of the 2021-23 biennium, the ESF and RDF are forecasted to have balances of approximately $695.6 million and $1.288 billion, respectively.

In addition, even though Oregon has not adopted a general sales tax, it has introduced other taxes that act like specific sales taxes. These include taxes on gasoline and marijuana, and even the corporate activity tax, which is discussed below. These taxes appear to be less volatile revenue sources than the income tax.

While these steps have been taken to ease the volatility in revenue, the challenges confronting the state when the nation goes into recession continue to be a significant problem. The volatility is one of the main reasons why several thousand Oregon teachers, parents, and others have been descending on the state capitol every two years to urge legislators to find a stable and adequate source of revenue for funding education. In planning for a better future, policymakers should be aware that the current mix of revenue sources is not only more volatile than other sources, but it also has the potential to exacerbate economic downturns. The most common solution—a general sales tax—generally provides greater stability, but it has its own problems. The most significant is that it is regressive and therefore less equitable than Oregon's current income tax system. In addition, Oregon voters have repeatedly rejected policy proposals to enact a state sales tax, keeping it off the political agenda and allowing volatility to remain a wicked problem.

The Kicker

One law unique to Oregon is what is known as the "kicker," established by the state legislature in 1979. The kicker is a tax credit law that dictates that when actual state revenues exceed forecasted revenues by 2 percent or more over a biennium, the entirety of the excess revenue (including the first 2 percent) is credited to Oregon taxpayers based on their taxes paid.[6] The kicker law applies to both corporate taxes and personal income taxes. The personal tax kicker acts as a catch-all for non-income tax programs and includes sources such as estate taxes and liquor fees. It is possible to have a corporate tax credit without a personal income tax credit, and vice versa, as the credit is triggered for each type of tax independently.

The kicker law is popular in Oregon, but it can be perceived as inequitable or unfair. Because the kicker credits are calculated proportionally to personal income tax liabilities, those with the largest incomes and pay the most taxes receive the largest credits. This law leads to some unique difficulties. For one, the presence of the kicker increases the likelihood of revenue shortfalls during downturns. The last four recessions (not counting the COVID-19 recession) have each come shortly after a kicker was triggered.[7] But while the kicker exacerbates revenue shortfalls during recessions, it does provide direct stimulus to Oregon taxpayers during the recession as well. Unfortunately, this stimulus is based on taxes paid and therefore provides larger (dollar amount) benefits the highest-earning Oregonians, which is not an effective stimulus target (in economist terms, the marginal propensity to consume is very low).

The kicker also affects Oregon's income tax (see table 13.1 above), which prior to the kicker is the most progressive component of the state's tax structure. The credit is based on taxes paid, and thus it is essentially an across-the-board reduction of personal income tax when it is triggered, meaning greater returns for higher-income earners and less for lower-income earners. The personal kicker has been triggered in each of the past four biennia, equaling just over 17 percent of personal income tax liabilities in each of the last two biennia. As income tax is the most progressive component of Oregon's tax revenue structure, whenever the kicker is triggered and that revenue stream is reduced, the state must rely more heavily on other less progressive (or even regressive) revenue streams, creating a more regressive tax system.

Given the fiscal and economic problems created by the kicker, along with its inequities, it is understandable why some reformers would like to rescind the law creating it. Advocates have been actively seeking to get rid of or reform the kicker for more than a dozen years, though with little success owing to both its popularity with voters and the high barriers required for a state constitutional amendment. In 2012, state residents passed Measure 85 to redirect corporate kicker money to the public schools, but the personal kicker has remained unchanged. The inability of the government to get rid of the kicker after all these years, despite strong lobbying do so, may mean that the personal kicker is untouchable, creating another wicked problem.[8]

Measures 5 and 50

Property taxes are fundamental to Oregon's revenue system. They account for over a third of the taxes Oregonians pay within the state and help fund schools, firefighters, the police, and local governments. There are aspects of Oregon's property tax system that are uniquely regressive, however.

In 1990, the passage of Ballot Measure 5 limited the property tax rate that counties could levy to $15 per $1,000 assessed value in Oregon. In 1997, voters approved Measure 50, which prevents the assessed value of all individual properties from increasing more than 3 percent per year beginning with the 1995-96 tax year (unique among all states for pinning home values to a single year). Both measures are embedded in the state constitution, meaning a voter-approved amendment would be necessary to significantly change the property tax system.[9]

The most onerous aspect of Measure 5 and 50 is that they have contributed to the routine shortfalls in state revenue, which have made it difficult for the state to adequate fund state programs year after year. These two measures restrict the amount local governments can contribute to K–12 education and require the state to make up the difference—creating funding challenges for other programs. This is another one of the factors that has spurred the repeated rallies over school funding at the state capitol.

Yet Measure 50 creates other problems beyond just budgeting. Among the most significant is a growing disparity between true market values and taxable assessments, and an unequal tax treatment of taxpayers with similarly valued property.[10]

A 2018 Center on Budget and Policy Priorities report identifies Oregon as one of four states where property tax structures exacerbate economic inequities.[11] As shown in two previous Northwest Economic

Research Center (NERC) studies, one consequence of these tax limitations is inequitable tax burdens for those in the Portland.[12] High-demand areas—for example, inner East Portland—have experienced low property taxes relative to their property value because of the limitations from Measure 50, while slower-growing or lower-demand areas pay taxes on a much higher proportion of their homes' value. Since higher-income individuals currently live in the high-demand areas, the property tax rate is inversely related to income on average—meaning there is a further incentive for higher income property buyers and owners toward gentrification. Figure 13.4 shows the mean assessed value (the average of the assessed value for the given area) as a proportion of real market value. The inequities of this system are most directly related to how fast an area has appreciated and therefore is mostly applicable to areas that have appreciated the most since the mid-1990s.

From the taxpayer perspective, the benefits of the current system are the more predictable year-to-year property tax payments and the limit to the amount that can be levied. Government bonds also affect property tax payments, however, and they are not subject to the caps.

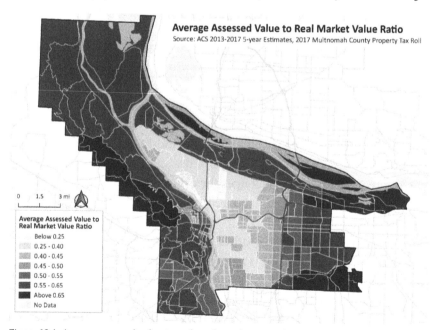

Figure 13.4. Average assessed value to real market value ratio. *Source*: Jenny Liu and Minji Cho, Final Report for the Property Tax Equity Analysis, in Funding and Financial Impact Analysis: Portland Parks and Recreation Services 2022 (Portland, OR: Portland Parks and Recreation, 2022)

As a consequence, payments can still be volatile, and the formula for calculating one's property taxes has grown increasingly complicated owing to the multiple rates and valuation methods.

Based on its location in various taxing districts, each property will have a number of government tax rates and a number of education tax rates. The sum of these rates is then multiplied with the property's assessed value (AV), which is the lower of the property's maximum assessed value (MAV) and real market value (RMV), to calculate the base tax. MAV is equal to the greater of either 103 percent of prior year's AV or 100 percent of prior year's MAV.

Measure 5 caps general government taxes at 1.0 percent of the current RMV and education taxes at 0.5 percent of the current RMV. If the calculated government or education base taxes exceed the corresponding Measure 5 cap, any temporary voter-approved property tax measure for services within that category (such as increased funding for public safety, libraries, or schools) is reduced first, all the way to zero dollars if necessary. If the taxes still exceed Measure 5 caps, each permanent tax rate component within the base tax is then compressed proportionally such that the base tax will equal the Measure 5 cap.

To calculate final taxes, the bonded general government and bonded education rates, which fund capital construction projects such as new buildings or equipment, are multiplied by the AV and added to the base tax. These bonded rates are not subject to the property tax caps.

Ultimately, it is difficult to determine whether the current property tax system is effective—if it is functioning as it is designed to function. Ostensibly, the intention of these ballot measures was to protect lower-income households from displacement by tax; however, the unintended consequences of the measures have proven to do the opposite in densely populated areas: they incentivize gentrification and exacerbate inequities. At the same time, these measures have added to the state's budgeting woes.

Tax Competitiveness

One aspect of tax policy that should be considered in thinking about the future is how specific taxes affect the competitiveness of Oregon businesses and labor on the national and international markets. On the surface, this concern about taxes seems to deal primarily with their efficiency—whether the benefits from the taxes come at the least costs to the taxpayers compared with other alternatives. But many of the taxes that reduce the competitiveness of Oregon businesses in external markets can also be seen as inequitable. Often, the businesses that are able to reroute their supply chains or relocate may do so because of economic advantages, leaving businesses that are not in that same position forced to pay the tax.

The concern over tax competitiveness goes beyond its effect on businesses, to government revenue. State governments often see themselves in a sense competing to retain and attract businesses. As a consequence, policymakers are frequently concerned that businesses will relocate to places with lower taxes. This sets governments up for a "race to the bottom," where governments are incentivized to have the lowest corporate taxes in order to draw in the most businesses.

The state's corporate activity tax (CAT) and its recent efforts to reduce carbon emission through tax policies provide two examples of how the issue of tax competitiveness creates a challenging trade-off between policy goals, equity, and effectiveness. The recently implemented CAT was signed into law as part of the Student Success Act (HB 3427) in May 2019 and was implemented in January 2020. It established the Fund for Student Success, which will pay for new programs, including increased investment in early education and more support for low-income families.[13] In short, all entities with taxable commercial activity (receipts) within the state in excess of $1 million are taxed a flat $250, with a 0.57 percent rate applied to all receipts past the first $1 million. The tax does not apply solely to corporate entities, but rather to any business that generates revenue within the state, aside from some specifically exempt commercial activities, industries, and entities.

There are advantages to taxes such as these for the policymaker. First, because these taxes are applied throughout the supply chain, they can be largely invisible to the end consumer, creating less resistance to them. Second, they have a broader base when compared to a retail sales tax or corporate income tax, thereby allowing relatively low statutory tax rates to raise a considerable amount of revenue. Furthermore, the raised revenue is much more stable because it encompasses economic activity rather than profits. Also, it is difficult for companies to outright avoid, as occurs with corporate income taxes.

Nevertheless, these taxes have their own drawbacks. Perhaps the most significant one is that, like other sales taxes, they can be markedly regressive in that the tax is passed through to those with the lowest incomes.

Another commonly cited disadvantage is "tax pyramiding," which is when a tax is levied on top of another tax, resulting in a larger tax rate on the final product. Because of tax pyramiding, revenue taxes may not affect industries uniformly and thus can distort market competition. While the structure of the CAT limits regressivity to a certain degree, there are few controls for pyramiding.[14] The greatest unintended consequence of tax pyramiding is that it indirectly punishes businesses that have a greater proportion of their supply chain within Oregon; since each Oregon business is assessed the tax, the cost of doing business increases for companies that rely extensively on other Oregon businesses for supplies. Furthermore, since Oregon firms now have increased costs relative to a given business from out of the state, sales by Oregon businesses to those outside of the state may fall, which in turn could negatively affect the revenue collected by those firms, and hence by the tax itself.

According to a study by Ernst and Young for Oregon Business and Industry, Oregon's effective business tax rate went from 2.0 percent to 2.8 percent from 2017 to 2019 as a result of policies such as the CAT (although they assume the full burden of the CAT falls on businesses—a simplifying assumption that likely overstates the tax's effect).[15] The US average effective business tax rate is 2.4 percent, and so by this estimate, Oregon went from a relatively competitive tax environment to one of the higher rates in the country over the past few years. This is one measure of the effective tax rate facing businesses and will undoubtedly be more accurate when more data are available on what proportion of the tax burden businesses face under the CAT. This was part of the trade-off for improved school funding.

Oregon has implemented various carbon-related programs—such as the Clean Fuels Program—and is currently considering other policies to combat carbon emissions within the state. These include cap-and-trade programs, which have also been implemented in places such as California; Vancouver, British Columbia; and across Western Europe. While not every program is the same, most attempt to disincentivize carbon emissions by requiring emitting entities to purchase credits for their emissions, which increases the costs of the emissions. In addition, the revenues from credit sales are then used to invest in clean energy programs.[16]

It is easy to understand why many policymakers and voters are supportive of these programs. For one, carbon emissions are reduced, a necessary step to help slow global climate change (see chap. 3). Furthermore, the air within Oregon becomes less polluted, leading to fewer deaths and better health outcomes for its populace, a goal discussed in detail in chapter 4. Additionally, environmental economists have long supported utilizing market mechanisms such as a carbon tax or carbon cap-and-trade program to help internalize the societal costs of carbon emissions. Previous studies by NERC illustrated that designing these programs in a revenue-neutral way can produce a "double dividend" where the state taxes undesirable goods (carbon in this case) and reduces other types of taxes, such as the personal income tax.[17]

There are arguments against such policies, however. Opponents of these programs often point out that Oregon's emissions are miniscule relative to the world's (and climate change is a global phenomenon). Therefore reducing emissions within the state likely will not do much to prevent global catastrophe. The argument put forward by these opponents is that carbon programs are important but would best be carried out nationally (or even internationally). There are counterarguments to this perspective—Oregon could lead by example, and carbon mitigation can be considered a moral imperative. But it is important to understand that there is not a political consensus across the state on this issue.

More important for budget-makers, there are concerns about how such environmental policies may affect the state's economy, and ultimately the state's tax base. One of the concerns raised about these programs is that local efforts can be costly and will ultimately affect Oregon's economy in the near term. Regardless of how the funds are used, Oregon products could cost more as the tax is passed through to consumers, and some businesses may choose to move out of Oregon. A carbon tax could be designed to be revenue-neutral, though there are not many great models for that. In reviewing programs such as the CAT, or those attempting to reduce the state's carbon footprint, policymakers need to estimate the effectiveness of the program versus the impact on the economy and tax revenue.

Public Employees Retirement System

One of the most daunting challenges in state policymaking is constrained government spending. There are two major types of constraints. First, the bulk of state spending is routinely committed to specific ongoing programs, such as K–12 education, and thus the legislature has little flexibility in redirecting funds. This is not necessarily a negative, as consistent funding is needed for important programs. Second, some sources of revenue are tied to specific expenditures; for example, fees for entering state parks are directed back toward these parks. Certainly, it makes sense to create these ties to ensure that there is not a mismatch between service and funding. Even though the state may understandably continue to fund the same programs year after year, with that specific revenue tied to specific programs, these decisions lock in spending and make it difficult for the government to address other problems, for example, deferred maintenance on infrastructure, enhancing resilience in terms of climate change, or adequately funding programs to reduce homelessness, as discussed in the relevant chapters in this book.

One of the best examples of government constraint is PERS. In recent years, an increasingly large share of government funds has become dedicated to this program. While Oregon is not unique in facing the challenges of funding its public employee retirement program, the demands created by PERS funding have implications for future spending on other programs. The amount of funds the state needs to meet this obligation are dependent on future returns, which may not be as strong as recent decades.[18] If future returns are inadequate, it has the potential to limit the flexibility in government spending.

The current unfunded liability of PERS is more than $12 billion. The PERS governing board estimates that the rate of in the fund's investments will be 7.2 percent over the long haul. If the investments bring this return, the portfolio is expected to be 93 percent funded by 2037.[19] The 7.2 percent anticipated return is higher than projected by some investment professionals and actuarial estimates, however, with the implication that the state may have to come up with more money over a longer period of time.[20] The challenge for budget writers is that the state's budget depends in part on what is owed to PERS recipients, and therefore Oregon's budget is dependent on investment performance. If the growth of the PERS portfolio comes in below the assumed growth rate, then this will be a larger-than-anticipated constraint on public spending. Oregon is doing relatively well in terms of funding its public pension. In 2017, PERS was 83.1 percent funded, compared to the national average of 69.1 percent. While this is positive news, Oregon's ongoing PERS obligations will continue to be a constraint on government spending and even worsen in the next decade. But by the 2030s and later, the PERS obligations will lighten.

Other Budgeting Challenges

There are a number of other challenges to state budgeting that demand greater attention than we give them here, but they are worth noting because they can also shape government revenue and expenditures. Thus these budgeting challenges deserve to be included in the conversation in planning for a better future. Four key ones are border effects, trade exposure, layering taxes, and tax compression.

Since Oregon relies heavily on income taxes to fund its government, some high-income households may be incentivized to move their residence or business to reduce their tax payments. One example of this occurs in the Portland metropolitan area, which is close to communities just across the border in Washington. Since Washington lacks an income tax and is instead primarily funded through a sales tax, there is an incentive for Oregonians to relocate across the border if their income is relatively higher than their consumption. That said, Washington recently implemented a capital gains tax, which may reduce the border effect. The border effect is also evident in in so-called sin taxes, like liquor, tobacco, lottery, and to a lesser extent marijuana.

Oregon relies economically on a number of heavily trade-dependent industries, including manufacturing and agriculture. Not only does this affect the volatility of revenue collection, but it also exacerbates the economic effects of some taxes by potentially creating a competitive disadvantage for trade-heavy industries. The impact of the corporate activity tax on businesses that have a greater proportion of their supply chain within Oregon, rather than from abroad, is an example of trade exposure.

One complicating factor of Oregon's tax system is the interaction of various taxes between different levels of government. For example, a person living in Portland may expect to pay similar taxes at the city, county, Metro, and the state level. Determining the effects and incentives of these many layers of taxation is a complex task, and this high level of complexity likely leads to inefficiencies.

Tax compression is an important characteristic of Oregon's property tax system that affects how local governments are funded. Oregon Ballot Measure 5 requires that total property taxes dedicated to general government are limited to $10 for every $1,000 real market value of a property, while school funding is capped at $5 for every $1,000. When that limit is exceeded, the total tax rate must remain the same, which means there must be decreases in the revenue raised from other property taxes. This decrease in revenue is termed compression. Temporary local options and permanent special district taxes are subject to the compression, while general bond obligations are exempt from it. The order in which other property taxes are decreased is determined by an ordering system created by state policy.

Tax compression has numerous implications. First, an increase in the tax rate does not necessarily coincide with a proportional rise in government revenue since the total tax rate must remain the same. Second, there can be problems when making adjustments to other taxes when a cap is exceeded. The aggregate data used to address tax compression are often inadequate, creating inaccurate estimates of how to adjust the tax rate to meet the revised revenue targets. Third, because of the proportionate compression mechanism, raising revenue for one city or county department will necessarily result in lower revenues for some other departments. In addition, the determination as to which department will experience a reduction depends on what type of property tax funds it. Those that come earlier in the ordering system will be the first to see a reduction. To date, most of the compression in the state has been occurring in Multnomah County and other areas where property values have risen significantly, but this could become a bigger issue in other areas in future tax years.

Looking to 2050

The State of Oregon's financial system reveals something important about the current state of Oregon politics: despite the state's reputation for innovative policies, the state's financial system has severe problems, some of which have lingered for years without being addressed. Among the most challenging is the state's troubled revenue system, which has made it difficult to adequately fund programs and which has witnessed disturbing volatility from year to year.

To be sure, there are many praiseworthy aspects of Oregon's revenue system. For one, it is strongly dependent on a progressive income tax, one that requires those who earn more to pay a higher tax rate. Yet in looking at how to improve Oregon's government by 2050, policymakers and the public must have a serious conversation on what can be done to adequately fund programs and reduce the deep swings in revenue from year to year. Not only are overall revenues seemingly inadequate to fund programs or solve problems that are important for Oregonians—such as climate change, homelessness, health care, or education—but also, as this chapter makes clear, lawmakers have limited capability to reallocate existing funds to achieve these goals. As a result, they may want to consider new types of taxes. The reluctance of Oregonians to give up the personal income tax kicker or to institute a general sales tax may be accounted for on some level by historical inertia. That means that creating new revenue sources such as some form of congestion pricing (discussed briefly in chap. 8), road user charges, or a carbon tax, or reforming existing revenue sources such as the complex property tax system to a simpler and potentially more equitable land value tax system, may be necessary to align Oregon's budgets with its values and priorities.

The idea of a land value tax (LVT) has been long discussed by Oregon leaders, including in early discussions of the statewide land use planning program, thought it has not yet been implemented. The idea keeps reemerging, in no small part owing to its significant potential. The NERC at Portland State University studied the impact of a land value tax in Multnomah County in 2019[21] and determined that indeed a shift to a LVT would "provide a more equitable tax structure, incentivize upgrading and developing properties, and discourage 'holding' land for speculative purposes. Furthermore, the potential downsides of the tax policy—such as increasing taxes on low-income homeowners—can be mitigated with carefully crafted legislation. In short, many of the inequities created by Measure 5 and 50 would likely be reversed if a LVT were implemented in the Portland region."

If the legislature considers revenue alternatives such as LVT, they need to make sure they examine all the different considerations involved. But there are no perfect solutions to these types of problems. The introduction of new taxes brings its own baggage. Other forms of taxes are often less equitable than the income tax, requiring poorer Oregonians to pay an increased share of taxes. For example, a general sales tax typically places a higher burden on lower-income households who spend a larger portion of their income on consumption, even with exemptions on food, groceries, and other necessities. A split-rate land value tax system that taxes land and improvements at different rates may provide a remedy for current property tax system, but it may also lead to rapid, and perhaps undesirable levels of, development, as in the case of Hawaii in the 1970s.[22] Yet another reform of the property tax system to shift some of the burden from residential properties (currently 56.0 percent of total property taxes imposed in fiscal year 2021-22) to commercial and industrial properties (16.6 percent) may relieve some pressure on Oregon residents and potentially generate additional revenues, but such a reform may run into the aforementioned problem of tax competitiveness.

Policymakers and those who want to make Oregon better by 2050 must weigh the benefits and drawbacks of these and other approaches against the issues raised in this chapter, and then push forward in trying to get a preferred remedy enacted into law. Unfortunately, though, such efforts may be in vain, especially in addressing the major problems we have identified. Oregon voters have shown so little support for measures raising revenue, and in addressing the problems created by the kicker and Measures 5 and 50, that finding acceptable solutions may be difficult. While these budgetary challenges may appear daunting and changes that affect people's pocketbooks may be painful, mobilizing Oregonians to help identify and align the state's shared values and priorities looking forward to 2050 and beyond may be an effective framework to think about how to reform, or even revolutionize, Oregon's state and local public finance system. As this book notes in various places, Oregon has been a revolutionary in a lot of ways in the past, such as being the state that first came up with the gas tax, urban growth boundaries, and bottle bill, and thus may be well positioned to advance a unique tax reform effort like a land value tax.

Notes

The authors thank Scott Bruun (Oregon Business and Industry), Michael Paruszkiewicz (adjunct faculty with Portland State University), and Josh Lehner (Oregon Office of Economic Analysis) for constructive feedback on drafts.

1. Mark Beilby, *Oregon Personal Income Tax Statistics: Characteristics of Filers, 2022 Edition, Tax Year 2020* (Salem: Oregon Department of Revenue, 2022), https://www.oregon.gov/dor/programs/gov-research/Documents/TYpercent2020 20percent20Oregonpercent20Personalpercent20Incomepercent20Taxpercent 20Statisticspercent20Reportpercent202022percent20Edpercent20150-101-406.pdf.
2. Amanda Beitel, Paul Siebert, and Tom MacDonald, "2021-23 Budget Highlights Update," Oregon Legislative Assembly, Legislative Fiscal Office, 2022, https://www.oregonlegislature.gov/lfo/Documents/2021-23BudgetHighlightsUpdate.pdf.
3. For additional insight into the other revenue funds, see "Other Funds Revenue Report May 2021," Oregon Department of Administrative Services, accessed January 5, 2024, https://www.oregon.gov/das/OEA/Pages/Other-Funds-Revenue-Report.aspx.
4. Jared Walczak, "Income Taxes Are More Volatile Than Sales Taxes during an Economic Contraction," *Tax Foundation* (blog), March 17, 2020, https://taxfoundation.org/income-taxes-are-more-volatile-than-sales-taxes-during-recession/.
5. "Government Finance—State Government," Oregon Blue Book, accessed January 5, 2024, https://sos.oregon.gov/blue-book/Pages/facts/finance-state.aspx.
6. "2019 Kicker Credit Fact Sheet," Oregon Department of Revenue, 2020, https://www.oregon.gov/dor/press/Documents/kicker_fact_sheet.pdf.
7. Legislative Revenue Office, *2020 Oregon Public Finance: Basic Facts*, Research Report #1-20 (Salem, OR: Legislative Revenue Office, 2020); "Business Cycle Dating," National Bureau of Economic Research, accessed January 5, 2024, https://www.nber.org/research/business-cycle-dating.
8. Ted Kulongoski, "The Oregon Kicker Law," *1859 Magazine*, April 1, 2010; Josh Goodman, "Oregon to Vote on Changing Unique Tax Refund," *Stateline*, September 17, 2012; Josh Lehner, "Economy Is Strong, But Will It Last?" *East Oregonian*, October 12, 2018.
9. There are various ways to amend the Oregon constitution; however, each way takes significant political support from the constituency and legislature.
10. Frank P. McNamara, "Public School Finance Programs of the United States and Canada: 1998-99—Oregon," National Center for Education Statistics, accessed January 5, 2024, https://nces.ed.gov/edfin/pdf/StFinance/Oregon.pdf.
11. Iris J. Lav and Michael Leachman, "State Limits on Property Taxes Hamstring Local Services and Should Be Relaxed or Repealed," Center on Budget and Policy Priorities, July 18, 2018, https://www.cbpp.org/research/state-budget-and-tax/state-limits-on-property-taxes-hamstring-local-services-and-should-be.
12. Jenny H. Liu and Jeff Renfro, *Oregon Property Tax Capitalization: Evidence from Portland*, Northwest Economic Research Center Report (Portland, OR: Northwest Economic Research Center, 2014); Peter Hulseman, Adam Rovang, Devin Bales, and Hoang The Nguyen, *Land Value Tax Analysis: Simulating the Tax in Multnomah County*, Northwest Economic Research Center Publications and Reports 36 (Portland, OR: Northwest Economic Research Center, 2019), https://pdxscholar.library.pdx.edu/nerc_pub/36/.
13. "Student Success Act," *Oregon Early Learning Division* (blog), accessed November 17, 2020, https://oregonearlylearning.com/student-success-act/.

14 Some industries have exemptions from portions of the tax to help avoid pyramiding.
15 Ernst and Young, *Oregon State and Local Tax Burdens* (Portland, OR: Ernst and Young, October 2020), https://www.oregonbusinessindustry.com/clientuploads/OBI_Information/Ernst percent20Young percent20Tax/Oregon_State_and_Local_Business_Tax_Burdens_2020_STRI_final_report.pdf.
16 Sometimes known as a Pigouvian tax.
17 Jenny H. Liu and Jeff Renfro, *Carbon Tax and Shift: How to Make It Work for Oregon's Economy* (Portland, OR: Northwest Economic Research Center, 2013), https://pdxscholar.library.pdx.edu/nerc_pub/20/; Jenny H. Liu, Jeff Renfro, Christopher Butenhoff, Mike Paruszkiewicz, and Andrew Rice, *Economic and Emissions Impacts of a Clean Air Tax or Fee in Oregon (SB306)* (Portland, OR: Northwest Economic Research Center, 2014), https://pdxscholar.library.pdx.edu/nerc_pub/11/.
18 "The State Pension Funding Gap: 2017," Pew Charitable Trusts, June 27, 2019, https://pew.org/2KFZWFl.
19 Oregon Public Employees Retirement System, *PERS by the Numbers* (Salem: Oregon Public Employees Retirement System, 2019), https://www.oregon.gov/pers/Documents/General-Information/PERS-by-the-Numbers.pdf.
20 Chris Butera, "Oregon PERS Keeping Assumed Rate at 7.2 Percent," *Chief Investment Officer*, July 30, 2019, https://www.ai-cio.com/news/oregon-pers-keeping-assumed-rate-7-2/.
21 Hulseman et al., *Land Value Tax Analysis*.
22 Hulseman et al., *Land Value Tax Analysis*.

14
Voting and Representation
RICHARD A. CLUCAS

Other book chapters look at the role and challenges of the state government in specific public policy areas. This chapter looks at the structure of the state government itself, or to be more precise, the state's election system. Elections are not the only aspect of state government that reformers should reevaluate in planning for a better future. The resignation of three state legislators in 2022 over the low salary that legislators are paid, for example, raises questions about the desirability of the legislature's amateur character. Keeping salaries low, as the three legislators argue, restrains who is in a position to serve.[1] The limited number of staff members provided to legislators and the state's restrictions on the number of days the legislature can meet, especially the thirty-five-day cap in even-numbered years, raise questions as to the ability of the legislature to plan for the future.[2] Looking at the executive branch, the state's heavy dependence on independent boards and commissions, rather than a more traditional centralized structure, means that these agencies are less directly accountable to the public, while making it more difficult for governors to lead the state into a better tomorrow.[3]

Even if elections are not the only potential focus for reform, they are an essential starting point given their impact on policy outcomes and the growing importance placed in the state and nation today on equity and inclusiveness. Elections are of fundamental importance for ensuring that the diverse voices in society are reflected in the legislature and public policy. Moreover, the heightened interest across the state in alternative election systems means that election reform is a topic of significant importance to Oregonians. If community leaders and policymakers are serious about planning for a better Oregon in 2050, they need to ensure that the election system produces fair and equitable results and that all the distinct voices across the state are being heard.

Rewriting election rules is not a typical concern in state planning efforts, but it is consistent with the state's planning program. Those involved in planning Oregon's future have long recognized the importance of broad public involvement in making planning decisions. The importance that Oregon has placed on citizen involvement is perhaps most clearly articulated in Oregon's Statewide Land Use Planning Goals, where it is listed first among the nineteen goals. Planning Goal 1 calls unequivocally for citizen involvement in "all phases of the planning process."[4] Ensuring that there is broad and equitable citizen input in the policymaking process is equally, if not more, important as including citizens in the implementation of those policies. Thus it makes sense to include election reform in a discussion about planning Oregon's future.

This chapter is divided into three parts. The first part focuses on aspects of the state's political history and culture that may affect its willingness to revise its election system to improve representation by 2050. The second part focuses on the election system and the extent to which it provides Oregonians with a voice in government. The third part offers a proposal for reform based on election research across the globe.

The Political Context

The primary goal of the Oregon 2050 project is to encourage the public, community leaders, and policymakers to envision a better future for the state in 2050. Pursuing changes in state politics, however, is not simply a matter of identifying where changes need to be made and enacting new laws to achieve the desired goals. The state government operates within a context that both provides opportunities for turning a vision into reality and places restrictions on the ability to do so.

Before assessing how well the election system is functioning and offering proposals for the future, this section examines some of the central contextual factors that shape how politics is played in Oregon today and will likely affect the ability to plan for the future. Several of these factors provide reasons to be optimistic that the state will address the challenges identified in this and other chapters; others provide less reason to be hopeful.

The one factor above all else that provides a reason to be optimistic about the state's ability to plan for a more promising future, including a healthier election system, is the state's strong progressive heritage. The term "progressive" carries many different meanings. I use the term here to refer to the championing of innovative policies and an open political system, which were central characteristics of the Progressive Movement that swept through the state in the late 1800s and continue to resonate in Oregon today. The early leaders of the Progressive Movement wanted to reform the political system, remove the corruption out of state politics (which had persisted since before statehood), and expand popular control over the government. They also wanted to use the government in a more active role in addressing the problems confronting the state.[5]

Progressive leaders pursued these changes by pushing forward a variety of innovative policies. By "innovative" I do not mean liberal, but rather new and untried. Oregon was a leader in the nation during the Progressive Era in adopting innovative policies. These policies include the introduction of the initiative and referendum process, direct primary elections, the nonpartisan election of judges, women's suffrage, child labor laws, the eight-hour workday, and public ownership of state beaches. After a period of dimming, this progressive heritage reemerged in recent decades, when the state enacted numerous innovative policies such as protection of farmlands, expanded health care coverage, physician-assisted suicide, the legalization of marijuana, vote by mail, and automatic voter registration.

The perception that Oregon is willing to pursue innovative policy is part of the state's self-image, a lingering aspect of its heritage captured in Oregon's official motto, "She flies with her own wings." Yet the perception is not just a matter of self-image. The state has been recognized as a policy innovator both in nationwide political analyses and scholarly studies. The *Almanac of American Politics* describes Oregon as "an experimental commonwealth, a laboratory of reform, a maker of national trends."[6] One scholarly study identified Oregon as being the third in the nation in policy innovation; a second listed it as fifth most innovative.[7] By innovative, these studies mean that the Oregon has been an early adoptee of a wide range of different policies across the political spectrum, which were then adopted by other states.

This progressive heritage is not just about innovation, however. The Progressive Movement sought to remove corruption from state politics and expand popular control over the government. There was a strong streak of what is called "populism" in the Progressive Movement, one that remains important in the state's political culture today. Populism is not a political ideology. Rather, it is a concern about the distribution of political power. Populists believe that the general public—"the people"— have the right to determine the direction of government and politics, but they are often denied that right by powerful and corrupt elites.[8]

During the first two decades of the twentieth century, the Progressive Movement put Oregon at the forefront of efforts nationwide in trying to remove corruption from politics and to expand the power of the people over government. It did this through many of the innovative policies mentioned above, as well others. Among these reforms to increase popular control, Oregon was the first state in the nation to introduce preferential primary elections for choosing presidential nominees (1907), to allow voters to recall elected officials (1907), and to require the popular election of US Senators (1907).[9] It was the first state to adopt a corrupt practices act (1908), placing limits on candidate spending and banning corporate contributions to campaigns.[10] It was one of the first two states to introduce direct primaries for state offices and members of Congress (1901), and the third state to introduce the initiative and referendum (1902).[11] Oregon was among the first nine states granting women the right to vote (1912), expanding the franchise eight years before the 19th Amendment was enacted.[12] Oregon was the sixth state to introduce municipal home rule (1906), giving cities greater power to act on their own rather than just following the dictates of the state legislatures, and in so doing, giving local residents greater control over public services.[13] The state also allowed Indigenous residents to vote as early as 1896, almost three decades before the 1924 Indian Citizenship Act was enacted by Congress.[14] After the passage of the 15th Amendment, the Oregon Supreme Court upheld the rights of African Americans to vote in Oregon in 1870.[15]

To be sure, many Oregonians have long had a constricted view of who constitutes "the people," denying the same rights and privileges to minorities and women that are granted to white males. Discrimination has been a significant problem in Oregon dating back to the writing of the state constitution, which included a clause banning Blacks from the state, to more recent policies that have harmed minority communities in housing, education, employment, and elsewhere.[16]

Despite this discrimination, the underlying belief in broad popular rule remains a defining characteristic of the state. Perhaps the best indicators of the influence of populism in the state in recent decades have been the efforts to expand the franchise through the adoption of vote by mail and automatic voter registration. But the populism is also reflected in myriad other ways. It can be seen in a variety of public policies. The first goal listed in the state's innovative land use planning program, for example, requires "the opportunity for citizens to be involved in all phases of the planning process."[17] It can be seen in the continued popularity of the initiative process in the state; Oregon has voted on far more ballot initiatives than any other state in the nation, with California being the only state that comes near.[18] It can similarly be seen in the public's willingness to take its demands to the streets, as have been seen in the protests in downtown Portland after the death of George Floyd.

Combined, this openness to innovation and broad support for populism provide reasons to be hopeful that the state can adopt reforms to improve elections and representation by 2050. In essence, many Oregonians tend to be open to change, and they support a political system that reflects the public's will.

Even though there are reasons to be optimistic, there are other contextual factors that do not bode as well for future planning. These include other aspects of the state's heritage, the state's deep-rooted political divide, and individual self-interest.

Oregon's progressive and populist heritages are not the only legacy from the past that shape current state politics. Despite the state's history of adopting innovative policies, Oregon residents have been unwilling to consider change in some policy areas. In some cases, long-existing policy has become closely wrapped up in the state's self-image, making change difficult. This can be seen in some less consequential policy areas. The state's resistance to self-serve gas stations, for example, is a case in point. The state banned self-service stations in 1951. For more than seventy years, the ban remained in place as the public resisted change. In the past few years, the state began to relax the ban to provide greater availability of gas in rural areas at night. But the ban otherwise remained in effect until the coronavirus pandemic, and the labor shortage it created compelled the legislature to drop the restriction in 2023.[19] But the fact of difficulty in making change can also be seen in some more significant policies. In particular, Oregon voters have rejected the introduction of a sales tax nine times since 1933, despite repeatedly confronting profound fiscal challenges.[20] More recently, resistance to change can be seen in the unsuccessful effort in 2022 to defeat the proposed reform of Portland's city charter. Rather than focusing on the merits of the reforms, the opponents focused their attention primarily on arguing the proposal was too experimental, bringing too much change at once.[21] Thus the state's openness to change is not guaranteed.

A second political challenge for bringing about positive change is the deep divide between urban and rural Oregon.[22] Oregon is not the only state confronting an urban-rural divide, but it has become one of the defining characteristics of the state's politics over the past four decades. The divide is especially apparent in voting on candidates and ballot measures. The urban areas routinely support liberal Democratic candidates and ballot initiatives, while rural areas support conservative Republicans and initiatives. But the divide goes beyond just voting. There are significant economic, demographic, geographical, and ideological differences between the urban and rural areas, which reinforce the political divide. Combined, the divide has created significant regional differences in policy and political concerns, which may stymie change, whether on election or other governmental reforms, or the policy proposals laid out in other chapters.[23]

For many years, this divide made governing difficult in Salem.[24] Throughout the 1990s and into the new millennium, the Republican Party generally retained control of both chambers of the state legislature, providing a voice to the more conservative rural parts of the state. At the same time, the Democratic Party retained control over the governor's office by building support from the more liberal urban regions. The result was conflict and stalemate. Perhaps the worst year of conflict was 2003, when the battles between the two sides kept the legislature in session for a record of 227 days.[25] It was also this conflict that led Governor John Kitzhaber to describe the state as "ungovernable" just before leaving office in 2002.[26]

The divide has become less consequential more recently, but it has not disappeared. Rather, what has happened is the more urban regions of the state have seen a growth in population and stronger support for the Democratic Party, which has boosted its advantage and allowed the legislature to function with less gridlock than it did twenty years ago. This change can be observed in the central part of the Portland metropolitan area, as well as in the broader metropolitan region. In 2002, the Democratic Party held about 67 percent of the two-party registration in Multnomah County.[27] By 2020, the Democrats held 82 percent of the two-party registration. Moreover, the number of registered voters had increased by almost 60 percent, sizably increasing the Democratic Party's advantage. Historically, the suburbs have provided a political middle ground between the urban and rural areas, with the voters split between conservatives and liberals. But in recent years, these regions have become grown closer politically to the urban center. In 2002, for example, the Republican Party held a slight edge over the Democratic Party in voter registration in both Clackamas and Washington Counties, holding about 52 percent of the two-party registration. By 2020, however, the Republican Party's share of the two-party registration in these two counties had plummeted, falling to 40 percent. These regions have also seen a similar total growth in registered voters as Multnomah County, further strengthening the Democratic Party vote.

The growing advantage of the Democratic Party has not, however, brought an end to the conflict between urban and rural Oregon. The 2019 legislative session was described by many observers as the most contentious in recent memory, as urban Democrats faced off against rural Republicans.[28] The session was capped by the walkout of Republican senators in the waning days of the session, which caused the senate to stop working because of the lack of a quorum.[29] The 2021 session was less contentious, but not without conflict.[30] The 2023 session recorded the longest walkout in the state's history, with ten Republican lawmakers refusing to participate in the senate for six weeks, stopping the legislature from conducting its work.[31]

If urban regions continue to grow, it will mean a continued strengthening of liberal politics. This will continue to help make the legislature function more smoothly and bring about more policy change, but it will only increase the feeling among rural voters that their voices are not being heard. More importantly for reformers, the ability to bring about meaningful change may be stifled by the fact that both parties have the ability to stifle it. The passage of Measure 113 in November 2022 will likely reduce the effectiveness of walkouts, as it bans legislators from running for reelection if they have failed to attend ten or more floor sessions without permission. But the election also narrowed the Democratic Party's advantage in both chambers. Prior to the election, the Democrats maintained a supermajority in both chambers, which allowed it to pass the state budget—the legislature's most important bill—without any Republican support. Democratic losses in the election ended the supermajority.[32]

Finally, it is impossible to discount individual self-interest in stifling change. Public policies rarely share benefits evenly across society. There are routinely winners and losers. When changes are proposed, those who benefit from existing policies are frequently averse to change. In some cases, the opposition comes from a sense that the proposed changes represent a direct threat. In others, it is uncertainty about change that brings opposition. For those who seek political reform, whether in elections or elsewhere, current elected officials may quash change, fearing that it may affect their own interests, including retaining their positions within the government.[33] Certainly, there appeared to be some self-interest involved among many of the prominent actors who opposed the reforms to Portland's charter in 2022.[34]

The legislative process has a circumspect character to it, which self-interested actors can use to stifle reform. To get enacted into law, a bill must go through multiple hurdles during the short period in which the legislature is in session, including being voted on by legislative committees, gaining approval by the members in both chambers, and going to the governor for her signature. To stop a bill, however, opponents just need to find one place in that process to defeat it. The presence of these hurdles means that legislative politics tends to favor those who want to protect the status quo versus those championing an expansive new vision. To pass a constitutional amendment, which would be needed for changing the election system, the governor's signature is not needed, but the proposal would still have to go through the multistep policymaking process in both chambers and then be approved by voters, making passage difficult. Oregon has one advantage over many states in amending its constitution, and that is the existence of the initiative process, which may be the only way in which election reform can be enacted.

In sum, the ability of the state to enact the legislation necessary to build a better future for Oregon in 2050 is uncertain. There are good reasons to be optimistic that it can do so. The state has a political heritage that has been supportive of innovative policy and popular rule. If there is broad support for innovative policies to improve the state, there is reason to expect them to be enacted. Yet the state confronts several political realities that may make it difficult to adopt policies to bring about change. This includes an unwillingness to allow some policy proposals to be put on the political agenda, the state's deeply embedded urban-rural divide, and self-interest. These reasons to be optimistic and to also harbor some doubt apply to the challenges confronting Oregon's election system, as well as for all the proposals being laid out elsewhere in the book.

The Election System

The ability of different voices to be heard in the political system must be a central consideration in building a better Oregon, because broad public participation is a fundamental component of democratic government. It is also a significant component of the state's planning rules. The first of the state's nineteen official planning goals begins by explaining the importance of meaningful public involvement in shaping public plans and projects, writing: "A great public involvement program gives participants assurance that they will be heard, and gives elected leaders confidence that decisions will be balanced and positioned for the public good." Despite the importance of participation in democratic ideals and in state planning rules, many Oregonians have routinely been excluded from the political system. For racial and ethnic minorities, racism has often been a central factor in denying participation. A better future has to include ensuring that such barriers do not exist, and that participation is open to all.

Social movements, interest group representation, lobbying, and political organizing all represent ways in which different voices can be raised in politics. But being heard means more than having access to a platform from which to speak. It means that all the different diverse groups within the state must have meaningful and equitable input into the policymaking process and, ultimately, to have their concerns be addressed in policy decisions. The difficulty in ensuring that all groups have meaningful and equitable input is that there are a wide range of factors that may distort whose voices are heard, even when the voices are being raised loudly through social movements and other platforms. Distortions come from such factors as partisan gerrymandering of legislative districts, differences in campaign funding, and the ways in which political organization decide to recruit candidates—all of which affect whose runs for office, who gets elected, and whose voices are shaping policy decisions.

It is beyond the scope of this chapter to look at all the myriad factors that can affect meaningful input into the political system. Instead, I have decided to focus specifically on the ability of the public to have meaningful input through the electoral process, because elections provide the formal mechanism through which diverse voices are represented in government decision-making. If the political system does not provide an election system in which the broad and diverse segments of society are allowed to participate freely and to elect individuals who represent these diverse interests, it limits the ability of different voices to have meaningful and equitable input, and to shape policy outcomes. Thus elections are a critical component of a healthy political system, one that is responsive to Oregonians. I also look at elections because election reform has become of growing interest in the state and because the structure of elections is one aspect of the political system in which the state government actually has the power to reform successfully.

There are several steps involved in making sure that the public has meaningful input through the election system. These steps include being able to register to vote and cast a ballot, being offered meaningful choice on the ballot, being able to affect election results, and seeing the election results influence policy decisions. In this section, I look specifically at the first four of these steps—being able to register, cast a ballot, having a choice on the ballot, and the effect on election results.

Political scientists have long found that the biggest impediments to voting tend to be government regulations.[35] For example, when registration rules are more restrictive, it means that a larger share of a state's residents will be unable to vote on election day because their names will not appear on polling records. When severe limits are placed on when and where a state's residents can cast a ballot, it makes it harder to vote and reduces turnout. Oregon has made an effort over the past two decades to expand the electorate by automatically registering Oregonians to vote through motor vehicle records and to make it easier to cast a ballot by conducting all elections through the mail. The introduction of automatic voter registration and vote by mail are considered so important for improving voting that a national study recently ranked Oregon as being the easiest state in the nation in which to vote.[36]

This top ranking certainly makes a strong statement that Oregon's election system provides a premier opportunity for the public to heard. But ease of voting is not the same thing as actual voting itself. I looked at two different measures to assess whether the election system is open to as many voices as possible. First, I examined the extent to which the voting age population in Oregon is registered to vote. Second, I examined turnout. For both measures, I looked at trends in the state overall and then at differences between urban and rural counties and among different racial and ethnic groups. I focused on urban and rural counties because of the historic importance of the urban-rural divide in Oregon politics. I focused on racial and ethnic groups because of the discrimination they have historically confronted in being able to vote.[37] In both analyses, I looked at the 2020 election because it is the most recent statewide vote for which the data are complete. Since voting turnout is routinely stronger in presidential election years, our findings are likely higher than what would be found in off-year elections.

Figure 14.1A shows the percentage of the voting age population that was registered to vote in November 2020. I focus on voting age population (VAP), rather than voting eligible population (VEP) as used in some studies, because of a lack of availability of VEP data at the county level. Overall, more than 87 percent of Oregon's voting age population was registered to vote based on census estimates of the state population at that time and official registration records. The number registered is high by nationwide standards. The Census Bureau found that approximately 67 percent of the voting age population in the United States was registered to vote.[38]

While there may be an important urban-rural divide in Oregon on political issues, I did not see such a divide in voter registration. In the

VOTING AND REPRESENTATION

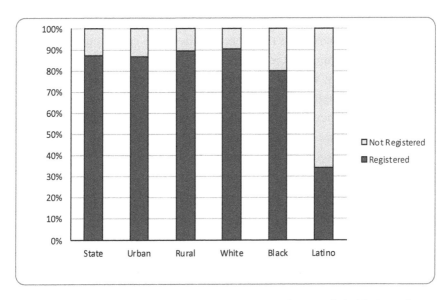

Figure 14.1 (*above*) A. Oregon's voting age population registered to vote. (*below*) B, Oregon's turnout of registered voters. *Sources*: Prepared by the author from US Census Bureau, Reported Voting and Registration, by Sex, Race and Hispanic Origin, for States (Washington, DC: US Census Bureau, November 2020), https://www2.census.gov/programs-surveys/cps/tables/p20/585/table04b.xlsx; "Statistical Summary: November 3, 2020, General Election," Oregon Secretary of State, accessed March 5, 2024, https://sos.oregon.gov/elections/Documents/statistics/november-2020-statistical-summary-participation.pdf; "Citizen Voting Age by Race and Ethnicity 2016-2020," US Census Bureau, March 17, 2022, https://www.census.gov/programs-surveys/decennial-census/about/voting-rights/cvap/2016-2020-CVAP.html

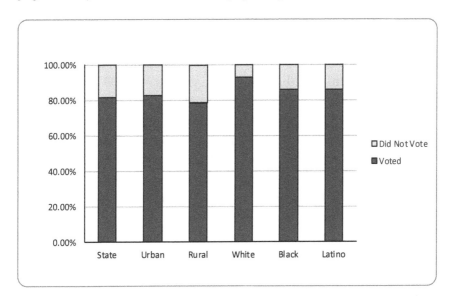

urban counties, almost 87 percent of the population is registered to vote. Almost 90 percent is registered in the more rural counties.

I did find important differences in voter registration based on race and ethnicity, however. More than 90 percent of white residents reported being registered to vote. The number of Black voters was below this, at 80 percent, but the percentage of Latino voters reporting being registered was just 34 percent. The low registration rate for Latinos undoubtedly reflects, in part, the large number of adult-age Latinos residing in the state who are not eligible to vote, but the number is still disconcerting. It means that a large segment of our state has no voice on how the state operates. One factor to keep in mind when comparing registration by race and ethnicity is that the numbers used in figure 14.1 were based on surveys; thus the rates shown are likely lower than the actual rates because some Oregon voters were unaware that they had become registered under the automatic voting registration law, which was just a few years old at the time.

Figure 14.1*B* presents the turnout rate among those who were registered to vote. The overall turnout rate for the 2020 election was almost 82 percent, one of the highest turnout rates in the nation.[39] Looking below this general turnout rate, the urban areas had slightly better turnout than the more rural ones. As for race and ethnicity, the percentage of registered Blacks and Latinos who voted was high, though below the turnout among white-only voters. Not included in the figure is the turnout rate for the Asian American community, which was the lowest among ethnic and racial groups, with 83 percent of the registered voters reporting that they voted in the election.

Combined, these figures and the studies cited suggest that Oregon has created an election system that generally provides an opportunity for Oregonian voices to be heard, though not all voices are being expressed equally. The one group of voters that is not having its voice well heard in elections, and that needs attention in looking toward 2050, are Latino residents. The low participation rate is particularly troubling because the Latino population has been growing at a much faster rate than the state's population overall. According to the 2020 Census, the Latino population grew by 30.8 percent from 2010 to 2020, compared with the state's overall population grow of 10.6 percent. Overall, Latinos constitute almost 14 percent of the state's population.

Moreover, the growth is occurring across the state. The largest growth has occurred in urban counties, but several of the rural counties have the highest concentration of Latinos in the state, led by Morrow County, which is 40.9 percent Latino. Hood River, Malheur, and Umatilla follow close behind.[40] The result is that this increasingly important segment of Oregon's population is not being included in the electoral process, a segment that is beginning to redefine both urban and rural Oregon.

Providing Different Voices in the Legislature

Elections are essential to a democratic system of government. But there is more to having voices being heard than simply pulling a lever in the voting booth or mailing in a ballot. A healthy democracy requires that voters have the opportunity to vote for and elect candidates who share their political perspectives. Choice at the ballot box is just as central to a democracy as having the franchise. If a voter is routinely unable to find candidates on the ballot who support their positions, then the casting of a ballot is a hollow exercise. If groups of voters are routinely unable to get their preferred candidates elected, then the elections are just as hollow to them. In this part of the chapter, I look at election results to assess the extent to which voters are able to elect candidates who represent their perspectives.

The first way that I assess these questions is by examining partisan registration among voters and the party affiliation of state legislators. Political parties represent the preeminent way in politics in which individual interests are aggregated, providing a means for likeminded individuals to work together to have their preferred policies enacted into law. Interest groups also provide a means for interest aggregation, but parties have a more direct and consequential role in politics, providing the opportunity for likeminded individuals to have someone represent their perspective in the actual voting on public policy. Thus having parties that reflect the diversity of interests in society is essential to making sure that those diverse voices are being heard as laws are being made.

Figures 14.2A–C show the party registration in Oregon in November 2020 and the partisan distribution of seats in the subsequent legislative session. The party registration figures suggest that Oregon voters are not particularly enamored with the two major political parties. Overall, a little more than 61 percent of the voters were registered with the two major parties, with 35.7 percent of the voters registered as Democrats and 25.6 percent as Republican. At 6.6 percent, the number of voters registered with third parties was not nearly as large. The more significant number is the large number of voters who were registered as nonaffiliated (32.1 percent). As of November 2020, there were more nonaffiliated voters in the state than there were Republicans, and almost as many as Democrats. Combined, almost 39 percent of voters are registered as nonaffiliated or with a third party. (As of March 2022, the number of nonaffiliated voters also surpassed the number registered as Democrats, reaching 34.5 percent to the Democrats' 34.4 percent.)[41]

Despite the lack of enthusiasm for the two major political parties in the electorate, the two major parties controlled all the seats in the legislature. In the house, Democrats held 61.7 percent of the seats in the 2021 session even though Democratic Party registration was almost half that. Republicans held 38.3 percent of the seats. The story was similar in the senate, with the Democrats holding 60 percent of the seats and the Republicans 40.0 percent.[42]

The question is what to make of these disparities. To some experts on American politics, these disparities need to be taken with a grain of salt. Political science research has found that most individuals who register as or say that they are independent are not truly so. Rather, the actual number of true independents is small. Most of these nonaffiliated voters are hidden partisans with beliefs and actions that are consistent with the two major parties.[43]

Even so, the high number of nonaffiliated and third-party voters raises concerns about the health of the political system and whether the current two-party system is working. There is a large body of research that has found the type of election system used in Oregon provides poor representation of the diverse interests in society. Oregon uses what is called the "first-past-the-post" system, in which the elected officials are chosen separately in single-member districts and require only a plurality of votes to win office. This system is also known as single-member

---

Opposite page: Figure 14.2 (*top*) A: Party registration in Oregon, November 2020. (*middle*) B: Party distribution in the Oregon House, 2021. (*bottom*) C: Party distribution in the Oregon Senate, 2021. *Source*: Compiled by the author from Oregon Secretary of State, "Statistical Summary November 3, 2020, General Election," Oregon Legislative Assembly website, accessed February 28, 2024, https://sos.oregon.gov/elections/Pages/electionsstatistics.aspx

VOTING AND REPRESENTATION

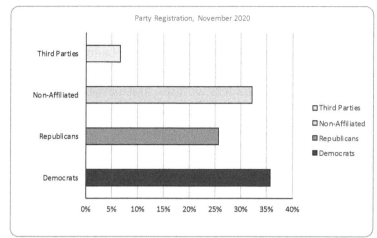

A.

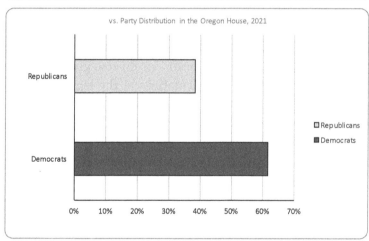

B.

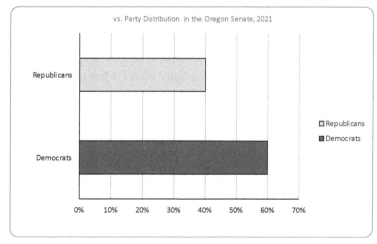

C.

district with plurality voting. One of the problems with this type of election system is that it almost always leads to the creation of just two competitive parties, reducing the choice on the ballot to only two real options.[44] If reformers want additional parties, it is not a good election system to use. Another problem with the first-past-the-post system is that it opens the door to gerrymandering and underrepresenting the diversity among voters, which is a topic I take up next.

A second important way in which voices need to be heard within the legislature is through what is called descriptive representation. Descriptive representation refers to having elected officials who are of the same race, ethnicity, and gender of voters. Descriptive representation is considered important in democratic government because it is thought to produce public policy that is more reflective of and responsive to the diversity among voters.[45] Put succinctly, who serves matters. While social movements, interest group representation, lobbying, and political organizing provide means for diverse groups to speak, it is important that there are representatives in the legislature who are listening to their constituents. In looking toward 2050, then, one of the questions that needs to be considered is how well the election system is doing in providing descriptive representation. The goal of reformers should be to ensure that the election system is open to women and minorities. It is also important to consider representation of urban and rural areas since the conflict between those areas has been so central to Oregon politics.

Figure 14.3 shows the population of different groups within the state and the percentage of seats held in the legislature by representatives from those groups. Figure 14.3A shows the percentage of the population that lives in urban and rural counties and the percentage of senators and representatives who were elected from the two regions in November 2020 and then served in the 2021 legislative session.

Opposite page: Figure 14.3 (*top*) A: Percentage of Oregon's population from urban and rural counties and the corresponding percentage of senators and representatives from those areas; (*middle*) B: Percentage of Oregon's white and nonwhite population, senators, and representatives; (*bottom*) C: Percentage of Oregon's female and male population, senators, and representatives. Source: Prepared by the author from "QuickFacts: Oregon," US Census Bureau, accessed March 5, 2024, https://www.census.gov/quickfacts/fact/table/OR/PST040223; "County Populations," Oregon Blue Book, accessed March 5, 2024, https://sos.oregon.gov/blue-book/Pages/local/county-population.aspx; legislative biographies and news reports available at the website of the Oregon House of Representatives, accessed March 5, 2024, https://www.oregonlegislature.gov/house/Pages/RepresentativesAll.aspx

VOTING AND REPRESENTATION

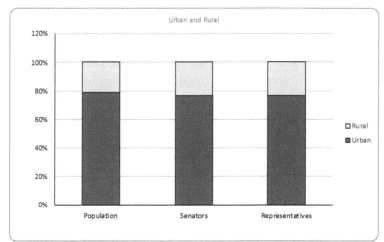

A.

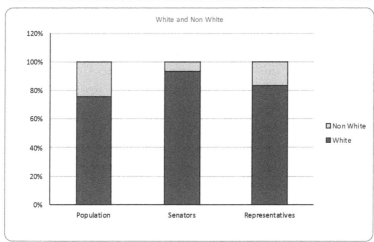

B.

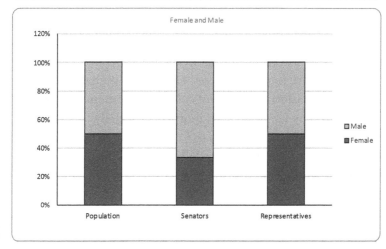

C.

Despite concerns that rural areas are not being heard in the legislature, the figure suggests that the rural areas are receiving representation that is consistent with their population. To be sure, this is not a perfect measure. There are some rural areas in urban counties, and some cities in rural counties. Given the concentration of voters in the few counties stretching primarily down the Willamette Valley, however, the figures capture a reasonable picture of urban and rural representation.

Figures 14.3*B* and *C* show the population and representation based on race and gender, respectively. Rather than providing individual figures for each racial and ethnic group, figure 14.3*B* shows the percentage of white population and legislators in comparison with all people of color, indicating that people of color are underrepresented within the legislature. Some 75 percent of the public is identified as white alone in 2020 Census data, whereas 93 percent of the senate and 83 percent of the house are white. In total, there were seven Latinos, three African Americans, one Asian American, and one American Indian in the Legislative Assembly at the start of the 2021 session.[46] It is worth noting that Latino representation in the 2021 session was a record high, but all those elected were from the Willamette Valley. In other words, even though some rural counties are becoming increasing Latino, their representatives are not.

As for gender, the Oregon Legislature has generated considerable attention in the past few sessions because of the growing number of female legislators and the increased importance of these legislators in positions of power. In the 2019 session, the house speaker, house majority leader, and senate majority leader were all women. Despite these gains, as of the 2021 session, female legislators had not yet attained their fair share of the seats, at least in the senate, where only ten of the thirty senators were female. Figures 14.3*B* and *C* reveal that while there is some representation of people of color and women, the legislature is overrepresented by white male legislators, especially in the senate.

There are two caveats to keep in mind in interpreting these figures, however. The first is that the numbers reported in figure 14.3 do not capture the story leading up to the 2021 session. The state has seen a significant increase in the number of people of color in the legislature in recent years, but this is a new trend. During the first two decades of this century, there was only one session in which more than four minorities were serving in the legislature, and that was in 2001. It was not until 2017 that these numbers rose significantly. In 2017, the numbers of people of color more than doubled, bringing the total number of minority legislators to nine. The total reached twelve in 2021 and nineteen in 2023. The story for women is better, but they still have been underrepresented historically. Before the turn of the century, the number of seats held by female legislators in both chambers combined never surpassed 30 percent and only went slightly above that figure until 2019, when 42.2 percent of the legislators were women. In the 2021 session, the number reached 45.6 percent.[47]

The second caveat is that the legislature sees approximately one-quarter of its members leave office every election, so these positive gains may disappear quickly, which is what happened in the 1990s. At that time, the legislature saw the election of four African Americans and one Asian American in different sessions, but then it went back to having no members of color. While the 2023 session included a record number of people of color, it also saw a decline in the number of Latino and female legislators. The total number of Latinos fell to just five members, which constituted 5.56 percent of those in office. Given that Latinos constitute 14 percent of the population, their voices are considerably underrepresented. The big gain in 2023 was the election of five Vietnamese lawmakers.[48] The number of women also fell in 2023, dropping to 44.4 percent. Thus, while the representation of people of color has improved since 2017, this was a change from the past and it is not assured in the future. As a consequence, ensuring equitable racial, ethnic, and gender representation is an issue—along with Latino voting and partisan representation—that should be of concern in thinking about Oregon's political system in 2050.

Reimagining the Election System

What can be done to reimagine Oregon's electoral system so it can do a better job in getting residents to participate and in generating election results that ensure the diverse voices from across the state are equitably and consistently represented?

A variety of reform proposals have been circulating in Oregon over the past few decades to change the way the state holds elections and address some of these concerns. In the early 2000s, political reformers were championing three main proposals: a top-two primary system, nonpartisan elections, and fusion voting.[49] Underlying the call for these reforms was a sense that the current party system is not doing a good job of representing Oregonians and that it produces undesirable conflict. In 2009, the legislature passed a bill permitting fusion voting, which allows more than one political party to nominate the same candidate for office. In 2014, supporters of the top-two primary were able to get the state to vote on this reform through the initiative process. The reform proposal (Measure 90) was overwhelmingly defeated, however, with more than two-thirds of the vote cast against it. If adopted, the measure would have allowed all the candidates running for office to compete in the same primary election, regardless of their party affiliation. The top two vote-getters would then go on to compete against each other in the general election, even if they were from the same political party.

While all three of these proposals have generated public attention, none of them are ideal solutions.[50] Nonpartisan elections tend to produce a less informed electorate, one in which the voters are less able to identify candidates who agree with their policy preferences and to know where elected officials stand on issues. The result is worse representation. The top-two primary can lead to the least preferred candidates being nominated; plus it retains many of the problems associated with first-past-the-post systems. The problem with fusion voting is that while it tries to provide greater choice in elections, it does not go far enough in offering a diversity of alternatives to voters and creating successful third parties. Moreover, none of these reforms are specifically concerned with ensuring equitable representation of women and minorities.

More recently, many reformers and "good government" organizations have begun to look more seriously at the use of some form of proportional representation to improve the diversity of voices heard within Oregon politics both at the state and local level. The use of proportional representation got its biggest boost in November 2022, when Portland voters approved a new city charter that includes the use of single-transferable vote, a form of proportional representation.

The Portland commission that proposed the new charter is just one of many groups in the state that have been advocating for some form of proportional representation. One of the most prominent advocates in recent years has been the Sightline Institute, a nonprofit organization that conducts research on a variety of social issues, including sustainability, housing, and transportation. In 2017, a coalition of Oregon civic groups published a report advocating for a more racially just democracy, which included a call for the use of proportional representation. Among the leaders putting together the report were representatives of the NAACP Portland Chapter, the Asian Pacific American Network of Oregon, and Common Cause. Some of the political parties in the state have begun to use or support proportional representation. The Libertarian Party of Oregon, for example, uses single-transferable vote when multiple positions in the party are being filled, while the Green Party's platform calls for the introduction of proportional representation in state elections. Prior to the 2022 election, the Portland City Club released a report on rethinking the city's commission form of government, which recommended that the city adopt multimember districts with proportional representation as a means to achieve greater diversity on the council than is produced by the first-past-the-post system.[51] While not advocating for a specific form of proportional representation, the Oregon League of Women Voters has produced two reports on different types of elections system, including proportional representation, in response to the growing interest in election reform in the state.[52]

There are, as this listing of organizations suggests, several different types of proportional systems. It is beyond the scope of this chapter to review all the different forms of proportional representation and how they work, but there are few systems that are frequently proposed for replacing the traditional first-past-the-post system and are worth describing briefly.

One of them is single transferable vote (STV), which is the type of voting adopted in Portland in 2022. Under STV, a state or country is divided into districts, with each district electing several representatives using multimember districts. Voters are given a list of all the candidates running for election in their district. On their ballots, voters rank their preferences among the candidates, marking their first choice, second choice, and so on. Candidates need a specific number of first-place votes to be elected. If a candidate receives more than the required number of first-place votes, the candidate's extra votes are transferred proportionally to other candidates on the basis of the percentage of

INSTRUCTIONS TO VOTERS	Candidates for City Council from District One	Only one vote per candidate
Mark Your Choices by Filling in the Numbered Boxes Only.	(Three to be elected)	Only one vote per column
Fill in the number one [1] box next to your first choice; fill in the number two [2] box next to your second choice; fill in the number three box [3] next to your third choice, and so on. You may fill in as many choices as you please.	Greg Odom (Dem.)	1 2 3 4 5 6 7 8 9
	Brandon Roy (Rep.)	1 2 3 4 5 6 7 8 9
	Joel Pryzbilla (Reform)	1 2 3 4 5 6 7 8 9
	Travis Outlaw (Dem.)	1 2 3 4 5 6 7 8 9
	LaMarcus Aldridge (Ind.)	1 2 3 4 5 6 7 8 9
	Sergio Rodriguez (Rep.)	1 2 3 4 5 6 7 8 9
Fill in no more than one box per candidate.	Write-In	1 2 3 4 5 6 7 8 9
	Write-In	1 2 3 4 5 6 7 8 9
Fill in no more than one box per column.	Write-In	1 2 3 4 5 6 7 8 9

Figure 14.4. Sample single transferable vote ballot. *Source*: League of Women Voters of Oregon, "Multiple Seat Election Methods—Detailed Discussion," in Election Methods: Review of Alternatives and Oregon Proposals (Salem: League of Women Voters of Oregon, 2008), https://www.lwvor.org/_files/ugd/54a310_9e4a927ebcae41d381d5840c6ef5ea78.pdf

second-place votes cast by all that candidate's supporters. Transferring occurs until all the seats are filled. Figure 14.4 displays an illustration developed by the Oregon League of Women Voters to explain how an STV ballot would look.

A second type is the party list system, which is the most common form of proportional system found across the globe. In this system, each political party puts together a ranked list of candidates in each legislative district (see fig. 14.5). In the simplest form, voters select the party they prefer, and then legislative seats are distributed proportionally

District One				
Voting Instructions: 1. You only have ONE vote. 2. Place an X in the box UNDER the party for whom you wish to vote.				
Democrats	Republicans	Reform	Libertarian	Green
☐	☐	☐	☐	☐
1. Benjamin Foster	1. Wendy Berg	1. Steven Wong	1. Tom Wartenberg	1. Rachel Folson
2. Sam Rosen-Amy	2. Steve Grolnic	2. Deborah Gorlin	2. Damon Washington	2. Robert Moll
3. Colin Volz	3. Sarah McClurg	3. Bran Crenshaw	3. Beata Panagopoules	3. Juan Hernandez
4. Benjamin Pike	4. Gerald Epstein	4. Naomi Gerstel	4. Alice Morey	4. Meryl Fingrutd
5. Megan Gentzler	5. Fran Deutsch	5. Robert Zussman	5. Sarah Pringle	5. Daniel Czitrom

Figure 14.5. Sample party list system ballot. *Source*: League of Women Voters of Oregon, "Multiple Seat Election Methods—Detailed Discussion," in Election Methods: Review of Alternatives and Oregon Proposals (Salem: League of Women Voters of Oregon, 2008), https://www.lwvor.org/_files/ugd/54a310_9e4a927ebcae41d381d5840c6ef5ea78.pdf

among the parties on the basis of the votes each party received. The actual legislators selected to serve depend on how high they are ranked on the party's list. Countries vary in their rules on how the names on the list are ordered. Party organizations create the ranking in some countries; elsewhere, voters have a say.

Some countries have a mixed member system of elections, using both first-past-the-post and party list systems. Voters cast two votes on the ballot. The first vote is to choose the candidate to represent the district. In the second, voters vote on their preferred party. The election brings two groups of candidates into the legislature. First, the candidates receiving the most votes in each individual district are elected. The vote on preferred parties brings in a second group; the seats in this second group are distributed proportionally to ensure that the overall partisan composition of the legislature reflects the total percentage of votes each party received. The benefit of this system is that it allows voters to determine the specific individual to represent their district, as is done in Oregon currently, while also ensuring that the actual composition of the legislature is consistent with the amount of support the parties enjoy in the electorate.

The reason reform groups and civic organizations have begun to push proportional representation is that these types of systems have been found to do a better job in allowing diverse voices to be heard in legislative politics and to produce policies that better reflect citizen preferences. These reformers and organizations are advocating for proportional representation because it is considered by election experts to provide diverse groups and interests with more meaningful and equitable input into policymaking.[53]

In studies from around the globe, the use of first-past-the-post election systems has been found consistently to produce two-party systems. The only way to ensure that more than two parties are represented in legislative politics is by using some type of proportional system, such as the party list system or single transferable vote. Without the adoption of a proportional system, efforts to create third parties are going to fail.[54] Oregon currently has six official minor parties: Constitution, Independent, Libertarian, Progressive, Pacific Green, and Working Families. None of these parties can reasonably expect to see any of their candidates ever elected to the legislature—except if also nominated by one of the two major parties under fusion voting—without the introduction of some type of proportional system.

Representation is also improved by giving a voice to Democrats and Republicans who live in regions of the state dominated by the other party. In Oregon, as elsewhere in the nation, the rural parts of the state are dominated by the Republican Party, while the urban regions elect Democrats. As a consequence, Democratic voters in rural Oregon and Republican voters in the urban areas do not have someone representing their political values. To use the terminology from election studies, the votes of these Oregonians are "wasted." The introduction of proportional representation will better allow these unrepresented Oregonians to have their voices heard.

By allowing multiple parties to flourish and reducing wasted votes, one of the great benefits of proportional systems is that it causes a larger share of the public to feel that there is someone representing their interest in government. With just two parties, many voters do not feel that way, which is clearly a problem in Oregon.[55]

Yet the benefit of proportional representation is not just in providing greater choice of parties on the ballot; it can also help improve diversity in the legislature. Political science studies have consistently found that proportional representative systems elect far more women to office than first-past-the-post systems.[56] Moreover, there is evidence that proportional systems can benefit racial and ethnic minorities. A recent study by the Sightline Institute of sixty local governments in Oregon found that all but two of them had underrepresented minorities on their governing councils, which the study linked to the use of the first-past-the-post system.[57] In addition, the Portland City Club study on rethinking Portland's government reported that the use of single-member districts would not increase diversity because minority voters are not concentrated enough geographically to affect election outcomes. After reviewing prior research on election systems, the report concluded "that traditional, single-member districts are not the best option" for advancing representation and equity.[58] By using multimember districts and some form of proportional system, the results would be a more diverse city council.

Proportional systems have also been found to generate greater turnout for elections than first-past-the-post systems. The reason for the greater turnout, studies have found, is that voters view their participation as being more effective in expressing their political preferences in proportional systems than they do in first-past-the-post systems.[59]

Lastly, researchers have found that some forms of proportional representation, most notably ranked choice voting, may reduce political conflict, which is an important consideration in our highly polarized political world. The reason for this is that candidates in ranked choice voting systems may need the extra votes from winning candidates in order to get elected. Rather than attacking opponents, which would alienate their opponents' supporters, candidates work to build a good image among their opponents' base in order to obtain transferred votes.[60]

In looking forward to a better state by 2050, reformers need to consider the possible introduction of some type of proportional system, as voters in Portland did in 2022. As of today, many Oregonians clearly do not support the two-party system, while state election results have routinely failed to provide consistent equitable representation of women and minorities, despite recent gains. The most effective way for state policymakers to address these problems is through proportional representation.

Addressing the Challenges of Voting and Representation in 2050

There are many aspects of Oregon's election system that deserve praise for opening the door to greater participation and a more inclusive political system. The introduction of vote by mail and the creation of automatic voter registration in particular have made it easy for Oregonians to be registered and cast a ballot.

Yet in looking at how to improve Oregon's government by 2050, policymakers and the public must hold a serious conversation on how to make Oregonians feel that their voices are being heard and that there are adequate choices on the ballot. The senate walkouts, the frequent protests in Portland, the limited public support for the two major partie, and the growing calls for election reform from a litany of groups reveal that many Oregonians do not feel that the current system serves the state well. To ensure that the election system is inclusive and that the diversity of voices is heard in an equitable way—to make certain that every vote is meaningful in 2050—the state needs to consider making changes in the election system. Among reformers and those who study electoral systems, the best form of elections for ensuring fair, equitable, and broad representation is some type of proportional system.

If policymakers and others do look at some form of proportional representation, however, they need to recognize the limitations of this reform. It is important to understand that proportional representation is not a cure-all for Oregon government. Scholars who study political reform have not found a single answer or political structure that solves all governing ills. Different political reforms, including different types of election systems, bring their own baggage. For example, while proportional representation would definitely improve the opportunity for more diverse voices to be heard in the capitol, a cacophony of diverse voices can make it more difficult for the government to act.

On a more pragmatic level, elections are only one aspect of state government that Oregon leaders should reevaluate in planning for a better future. While proportional representation offers a better election system, poor pay may still limit those who are willing to serve. Limited staff support and restrictions on session length place unnecessary constraints on the ability of the legislature to address state problems, while the decentralized executive branch reduces effective gubernatorial leadership. Finally, other criticisms can be raised about the state's political system beyond these structural concerns, including inadequate campaign finance rules, poor media literacy, and the lack of strong civic education in the schools. All of these issues deserve attention.

Electoral reform, including proportional representation, is a good place to start for planning a better Oregon government in 2050. Studies from across the globe have found that there are considerable benefits to proportional representation, including allowing more diverse voices to be heard in the policymaking process, giving voters a greater sense that their opinions are being considered, increasing turnout, and moderating some of the political conflict. Moreover, Oregon has the power to introduce proportional systems if it chooses. In 1908, Oregon voters approved an amendment to the state constitution (Measure 15; Article 2, Section 16) that allows the state legislature and local governments to adopt proportional representation.

If such a reform is not adopted, then many Oregonians will remain disillusioned with the current political system, seeing it as unrepresentative of their concerns, while poor representation and lack of diversity will remain severe problems.

Notes

1. Ethan Hauck, "Oregon Legislators Resign, Citing Poor Pay," *Corvallis Advocate* 4 (March 2022).
2. Each legislator is provided an allowance to cover personal staff, services and supplies, and other expenditures. If stretched, the staff allowance may allow an individual legislator to hire two staff members at most, though not all hire two. To understand the importance of adequate session time and staff support, see Citizens Conference on State Legislatures, *The Sometime Governments: A Critical Study of the 50 American Legislatures* (New York: Bantam Books, 1973).
3. Douglas Morgan, Jeanine Beatrice, and Sajjad Haider, "The Role of Bureaucracy in Oregon State and Local Government," in *Governing Oregon: Continuity and Change*, ed. Richard A. Clucas, Mark Henkels, Priscilla L. Southwell, and Edward P. Webber (Corvallis: Oregon State University Press, 2018), 115-33.
4. "Goal 1: Citizen Involvement," Oregon's Statewide Planning Goals and Guidelines, accessed January 6, 2024, https://www.oregon.gov/lcd/OP/Pages/Goal-1.aspx.
5. Richard A. Clucas, Mark Henkels, and Brent S. Steel, *Oregon Politics and Government: Progressive versus Conservative Populists* (Lincoln: University of Nebraska Press, 2005).
6. Richard Cohen, James Barnes, Charlie Cook, Michael Barone, Louis Jacobson, and Louis F. Peck, *Almanac of American Politics 2018* (Bethesda, MD: Columbia Books and Information Services, 2017).
7. Frederick J. Boehmke and Paul Skinner, "State Policy Innovativeness Revisited," *State Politics and Policy Quarterly* 12 (2012): 303-29.
8. Clucas et al., *Oregon Politics*, 1-6.
9. James D. Barnett, "The Presidential Primary in Oregon," *Academy of Political Science* 31 (1916): 81-104; Elizabeth E. Mack, "The Use and Abuse of Recall: A Proposal for Legislative Recall Reform," *Nebraska Law Review* 67 (1988): 624; William B. Murphy, "The National Progressive Republican League and the Elusive Quest for Progressive Unity," *Journal of the Gilded Age and Progressive Era* 8 (2009): 515-43.
10. Jeff Wiltse, "The Origins of Montana's Corrupt Practices Act: A More Complete History," *Montana Law Review* 73 (2012): 299-337.
11. Jamie L. Carson and Ryan D. Williamson, "Candidate Emergence in the Era of Direct Primaries," in *Routledge Handbook of Primary Elections*, ed. Robert C. Boatright (Abingdon: Routledge, 2018); Margaret A. Schaffner, "The Initiative, The Referendum, and the Recall: Recent Legislation in the United States," *American Political Science Review* 2 (1907): 32-42
12. "Women's Suffrage in the US by State," Center for American Women and Politics, Rutgers University, accessed January 6, 2024, https://tag.rutgers.edu/wp-content/uploads/2014/05/suffrage-by-state.pdf.
13. Richard Briffault, Nestor M. Davidson, Paul A. Diller, Sarah Fox, Laurie Reynolds, Erin A. Scharff, Richard Schragger, and Rick Su, "Principles of Home Rule for the Twenty-First Century," National League of Cities, February 12, 2020, https://scholarship.law.columbia.edu/faculty_scholarship/2609.

14 "Indigenous Voting Rights in Oregon," Oregon Secretary of State, accessed January 6, 2024, https://sos.oregon.gov/archives/exhibits/suffrage/Pages/context/indigenous-oregon.aspx.
15 David Peterson del Mar, "15th Amendment," *Oregon Encyclopedia*, January 21, 2021, https://www.oregonencyclopedia.org/articles/15th_amendment/#.YDgciOhKhEY.
16 Urban League of Portland, *The State of Black Oregon* (Portland: Urban League of Portland, 2015; Portland Bureau of Planning, *The History of Oregon's African American Community* (Portland: Bureau of Planning, 1993).
17 "Oregon's Statewide Land Use Planning Goals," Oregon Department of Land Conservation and Development, accessed January 6, 2024, https://www.oregon.gov/lcd/op/pages/goals.aspx.
18 Alana S. Jeydel and Brent S. Steel, "Public Attitudes toward the Initiative Process in Oregon," *State and Local Government Review* 34 (2002): 173-82; "Overview of Initiative Use, 1900-2019," Initiative and Referendum Institute, accessed January 6, 2024, http://www.iandrinstitute.org/docs/IRI-Initiative-Use-(2019-2).pdf.
19 Bill Poehler, "Oregon Lifts Ban on Self-Serve Gas Stations for Two Weeks to Stem Covid-19 Spread," *Statesman Journal*, March 28, 2020; Samantha Raphelson, "Oregonians Aren't Pumped about New Law Allowing Self-Service Gas Stations," Oregon Public Broadcasting, January 5, 2018; Andrew Selsky, " 'It's about Time': You Can Now Pump Your Own Gas in Oregon for the First Time in 72 Years," *Fortune*, August 5, 2023.
20 Jeff Mapes, "New Oregon Tax Aims to Succeed after Long History of Sales Tax Failures," Oregon Public Broadcasting, June 10, 2019; Reid Wilson, "Oregon Likely to Try on Sales Tax," *Washington Post*, October 8, 2013.
21 Alex Zielinski, "Why Are Portland's Leaders Opposing Proposed Charter Reforms? Hint: It Might Be Because the Reforms Dilute Their Power," *Portland Mercury*, September 7, 2022.
22 There are numerous ways in which scholars have defined urban and rural. In this chapter, we identified urban and rural counties based on the criteria developed by the US Office of Management and Budget. Under this definition, eleven counties in Oregon are considered urban: Benton, Clackamas, Columbia, Deschutes, Jackson, Lane, Marion, Multnomah, Polk, Washington, and Yamhill. The rest are categorized as rural.
23 See Michael Hibbard, Ethan Seltzer, Bruce Weber, and Beth Emshoff, eds., *Toward One Oregon: Rural-Urban Interdependence and the Evolution of a State* (Corvallis: Oregon State University Press, 2011).
24 Clucas et al., *Oregon Politics*.
25 Richard A. Clucas and Mark Henkels, "Continuity and Change in Oregon Politics," in *Governing Oregon: Continuity and Change*, ed. Richard A. Clucas, Mark Henkels, Priscilla L. Southwell, and Edward B. Weber (Corvallis: Oregon State University Press, 2018), 3-6.
26 Rick Attig, "John Kitzhaber: After a Bitter Goodbye, Another Hello," *The Oregonian*, May 29, 2009.
27 The analysis in this paragraph is based on 2002 and 2020 data available at "Voter Registration by County," Oregon Secretary of State, Elections Division, accessed February 12, 2024, https://sos.oregon.gov/elections/Pages/electionsstatistics.aspx.
28 Clucas and Henkels, "Continuity and Change," 3-18.
29 Dirk VanderHart and Lauren Dake, "Triumphs and Bruising Battles Made Oregon's 2019 Legislative Session One for the Books," Oregon Public Broadcasting, July 1, 2019; Dirk VanderHart, "Oregon Legislature Adjourns in

Tense Final Day after Senate GOP Walkout," Northwest Public Broadcasting, July 1, 2019; Connor Radnovich and Whitney Woodworth, "Oregon Legislature Finally Adjourns but Not without Political Fireworks," *Statesman Journal*, June 30, 2019.

30 Dirk VanderHart and Sam Stites, "Oregon Lawmakers Conclude 2021 Session in a Crush of Bills," Oregon Public Broadcasting, June 26, 2021.

31 Dirk VanderHart and Lauren Dake, "After Record-Breaking Legislative Walkout, Oregon 2023 Legislative Session Ends in Crush of Bills," Oregon Public Broadcasting, June 25, 2023.

32 Mike Mcinally, "Oregon GOP Hailed End to Democrats' 'Supermajority' but Will That Matter Much?," *Oregon Capital Chronicle*, December 16, 2022.

33 Shaun Bowler, Todd Donovan, and Jeffrey A. Karp, "Why Politicians Like Electoral Institutions: Self-Interest, Values, or Ideology?," *Journal of Politics* 68 (2006): 434-46.

34 Zielinski, "Why Are Portland's Leaders Opposing Proposed Charter Reforms?"

35 Richard G. Niemi and Herbert F. Weisberg, eds., *Classics in Voting Behavior* (Washington, DC: Congressional Quarterly Press, 1993), 13-23.

36 Quan Li, Michael J. PomanteII, and Scot Schraufnagel, "Cost of Voting in the American States," *Election Law Journal: Rules, Politics, and Policy* 17, No. 3 (2018): 234-47.

37 Chandler Davidson, ed., *Minority Vote Dilution* (Washington, DC: Howard University Press, 1989).

38 US Census Bureau, "Voting and Registration in the Election of November 2020" (press release), April 2001, https://www.census.gov/data/tables/time-series/demo/voting-and-registration/p20-585.html.

39 "Voter Turnout Rate in the Presidential Election in the United States as of December 7, 2020, by State," Statista, accessed January 6, 2024, https://www.statista.com/statistics/1184621/presidential-election-voter-turnout-rate-state/.

40 American Counts Staff, "Oregon Population 4.2 Million in 2020, up 10.6 Percent from 2010," August 25, 2021, US Census Bureau, accessed January 6, 2024, https://www.census.gov/library/stories/state-by-state/oregon-population-change-between-census-decade.html);

41 Nigel Jaquiss, "Nonaffiliated Oregon Voters Now Outnumber Democrats and Republicans for the First Time," *Willamette Week*, March 31, 2022.

42 State Senator Brian Boquist was elected as a Republican in the 2020 election but switched to being an independent in early January 2021. Since Boquist was elected as a Republican, I have categorized him in fig. 14.2 as such. See Northwest Spotlight, "Senator Brian Boquist Has Left GOP, Is Now a Member of the Independent Party of Oregon," *Oregon Catalyst*, January 15, 2021.

43 Bruce E. Keith, David B. Magleby, Candice J. Nelson, Elizabeth Orr, Mark C. Westlye, and Raymond E. Wolfinger, *The Myth of the Independent Voter* (Berkeley: University of California Press, 1992); David B. Magleby, Candice J. Nelson, and Mark C. Westlye, "The Myth of the Independent Voter Revisited," in *Facing the Challenge of Democracy: Explorations in the Analysis of Public Opinion and Political Participation*, ed. Paul M. Sniderman, Benjamin Highton, and Paul M. M. Sniderman (Princeton, NJ: Princeton University Press, 2015).

44 Richard A. Clucas and Melody Ellis Valdini, *The Character of Democracy* (New York: Oxford University Press, 2015), 55-85.

45 Clucas and Valdini, *Character of Democracy*, 112-14.

46 A fourth African American, Kayse Jama, was appointed to the senate in January 2021 to replace Shemia Fagan.

47 "Oregon: State Legislature—Numbers and Percentage of Officeholders by Year," Center for American Women and Politics, accessed January 6, 2024, https://cawp.rutgers.edu/facts/state-state-information/oregon.
48 Julia Shumway, "Oregon Legislature's Racial Diversity Continues to Grow after 2022 Election," *Oregon Capital Chronicle*, November 28, 2022.
49 Richard A. Clucas, "The Oregon Constitution and the Quest for Party Reform," *Oregon Law Journal* 87 (2008): 1061-100.
50 Clucas, "Oregon Constitution."
51 "New Government for Today's Portland: Part II Rethinking How We Vote Amendment," City Club of Portland, accessed February 12, 2024, https://www.pdxcityclub.org/new-government/.
52 Women Voters of Oregon Education Fund, *Election Methods: Review of Alternatives and Oregon Proposals* (Salem: League of Women Voters of Oregon Education Fund, 2008); Women Voters of Oregon Education Fund, *Election Methods Study Update Proposals* (Salem: League of Women Voters of Oregon, 2016).
53 Clucas and Valdini, *Character of Democracy*, 55-85.
54 Clucas and Valdini, *Character of Democracy*, 55-85.
55 Clucas and Valdini, *Character of Democracy*, 55-85.
56 Clucas and Valdini, *Character of Democracy*, 73.
57 Kristin Eberhard, "Of 60 Oregon Councils, School Boards, All but Two Underrepresent People of Color," Sightline Institute, December 17, 2018, https://www.sightline.org/2018/12/17/58-of-60-oregon-councils-school-boards-underrepresented-people-of-color/.
58 City Club of Portland, "New Government for Today's Portland: Rethinking 100 Years of the Commission System," *City Club of Portland Bulletin*, February 10, 2019, 19.
59 Clucas and Valdini, *Character of Democracy*, 75.
60 Benjamin Reilly, "Centripetalism and Electoral Moderation in Established Democracies," *Nationalism and Ethnic Politics* 24 (2018): 201-21; Todd Donovan, "Don't Believe These 5 Common Myths about Ranked-Choice Voting," *Seattle Times*, October 13, 2022.

Conclusion
MEGAN HORST

Our goal in this book is to think as futurists about our home state. We aim to influence Oregon's future in ways that capitalize on our state's existing strengths, respond to concerning trends, and advance progress toward a strong social foundation and ecological balance. The topics focused on in this book include planning and planning-adjacent topics in the areas of natural, built, and social environment. We also reflected on two key areas of state governance: revenue and voting/representation.

For the past fifty years, the foundation for Oregon's planning approach, the state land use planning program, has been about encouraging relatively dense urban and regional population centers while protecting resource lands and areas like forestland and farmland. That vision, while challenged over the years, has endured both here in Oregon and as a guidepost for planners and leaders in other cities, regions, states, and countries. Some important questions for further consideration are: Is the vision for Oregon land use planning still a meaningful and viable idea? Is it producing the kind of Oregon we want to live in and leave for future generations? Is this the way we want to continue for the next thirty years or more? A secondary question is (since good planning always examines alternatives), If not, then what are the alternatives?

This book makes a strong case that, yes, the vision for Oregon land use planning remains a meaningful and viable idea as we look ahead to 2050. There have been many positive environmental, social, and economic impacts of the program and other good leadership and policy innovation. In terms of the natural environment, Oregonians emit less greenhouse gas emissions than their counterparts in many other states.

Many Oregon communities are already acting to mitigate the impacts of climate change. Many water and air pollutants have been declining across the state. Our forests are in moderately (though variable) decent health and quality, and Oregon is producing more renewable energy than many other states, and more than ever before. In terms of the built environment, Oregon has protected forest- and farmland relative to other states. The state has less sprawl and more multimodal transportation options than many comparable states, as well as many vibrant urban neighborhoods and town centers. Oregon also has more diverse housing types of various sizes and types (e.g., duplexes, apartments) than many other states, especially in both urban and rural cities and regions where population has been growing. In terms of the social environment, of which the state planning program has less direct influence, Oregonians are active in arts and cultural organizations and activities. The state and local governments are innovative in responding to issues like homelessness and attempting some alternatives to incarceration. Oregonians participate in voting at higher rates than in most other states, and they enjoy a somewhat progressive tax system.

With all these impacts, it continues to make sense, for the public interest and for better environmental and social outcomes, to steer population growth into already built-up areas and to protect resource areas and working lands. It continues to make sense to work toward energy efficiency, diverse housing types, and multimodal forms of transportation. Oregon's approach to planning is significantly and importantly better than an alternative of not having a statewide planning program. And yet the program can be strengthened. It also on its own is not comprehensive and should be complemented by other changes in state policy to promote a more sustainable and equitable Oregon.

While there are good trends, all is not well in our state. Each of the chapters in this book identifies some concerning patterns and trends, demonstrating that we are far from being balanced in the middle of the sustainable development doughnut model discussed in chapter 1. We have areas of ecological "overshoot" and lack of social foundations. In the natural environmental realm, Oregon is already experiencing a more volatile climate, including more extreme summer heat waves and forest fires, as well as changing precipitation patterns, less reliable snowpack, and more intense storms. The state is underprepared to address the accompanying predicted sea level rise or other hazards like earthquakes. Some communities—notably where there are high percentages of low-income Native American and/or Hispanic/Latino residents—contend with poor air and water quality. Oregon's forests face many threats like fragmentation, pests, and increasing fires. Across the state, there are concerns over water misuse and scarcity.

In terms of the built environment, we are contending with the limitations and negative impacts of expensive automobile-oriented infrastructure and land use patterns. While farms and forestland have been well protected, not all lands are stewarded responsibly, and the benefits of that protection are often accruing to nonlocal owners, corporate interests, and investors, not local communities. Among the most extreme concerns statewide is the lack of sufficient available and affordable housing, especially for lower-income households—a problem that seems likely to greatly worsen by 2050 unless we take significant action.

In terms of the social environment, there are ongoing and in some cases increasing economic inequities; a lack of affordable health care, which particularly affects working single parents; and visible crises in homelessness, substance abuse, and mental health problems. Local and state governments do not have sufficient capacity to address these problems. While Oregon is renowned for its arts and culture, many artists and cultural organizations are struggling financially.

In terms of governance, many residents express dissatisfaction with their voting options. There is ongoing political stalemate on many issues, including the role of the state in regulating business and private property owners regarding public health and environmental impacts, service delivery to more vulnerable Oregonians, the threats of climate change, and persistent and worsening issues like homelessness. Meanwhile, the state's ability to initiate any major new changes in programming or service delivery is constrained by the dedication of existing revenue streams, the long list of so-called unfunded mandates, and the lack of appetite by voters or elected officials for serious tax reform.

If these trends are not addressed, the future of Oregon in 2050 is not very bright, and even less so for Oregonians who are poor; are renters rather than homeowners; are Black, Indigenous, or people of color; or are otherwise less resourced or powerful. Meanwhile, the richest

10 percent of the state residents, alongside corporations, continue to gobble up the state's housing stock and resource lands. Another wicked problem related to all of this is the irresponsible exploitation of natural resources, one impact of which is climate change. For Oregon to correct course, it will take tackling the root causes of these problems. At the same time, there is no one silver bullet, and it will take interconnected efforts across a range of fronts. The roots of these inequities and exploitations are deep and complex, often residing way upstream of land use planning. Therefore we do not imply that the land use planning program causes them. In fact, in many cases, the land use planning program may mitigate the worst of these problems.

That said, authors identified a range of ways to strengthen the program, and other related reforms and policies, to change course in advance of 2050. To better address our current and future ecological and social challenges, Oregon must expand the approach from the original planning program beyond simple land protection into a more comprehensive and deeper sustainable development framework, such as the one discussed in chapter 1 with ecological ceilings and social foundations, with an orientation toward stewarding for future generations, not just current powerful residents.

The chapter authors discuss some big, bold goals and ideas, such as getting to 100 percent renewable energy, making sure Oregonians of all income levels have clean air and drinking water, decarbonizing our transportation system, and expanding access to non-driving transportation options, ensuring community benefits of resource lands, enacting various land reforms, ending homelessness (or at least dramatically reducing it), lowering poverty, ensuring access to culturally relevant mental health and substance abuse services, and expanding access to arts and culture to everyone. All of these are part of the sustainable development doughnut model (see fig. 1.1). But achieving those goals will take resources, commitment, and a change in practices. Many of the chapters argue for a more proactive role for state government, both within and outside of the land use planning system. Recognizing that it will take new streams of funding to advance some of the big ideas, one common theme in this book is that Oregon can rethink its taxing policies, including higher taxes to support environmental stewardship and social equity rather than for the wealth accumulation of a minority of residents, business owners, and corporate interests. Many of the authors offered creative and more equitable revenue-generating ideas (e.g., a land value tax, carbon tax, and higher taxes on corporations, polluters, and wealthy residents). Some of the ideas are focused on making our current taxation systems more progressive. Some of the big ideas proposed may result in cost savings for the state.

Chapter authors also call for doing away with outdated models and tools, such as old ways of using population models, to get away from the limits of path dependency. They also advise developing new models that are more suitable for today's understandings and context, one in which the impacts of climate change are already being felt and in which class, racial, and other inequalities are seen across a wide range of issues. Given the interconnected nature of these topics, policymakers must get at the root causes of wicked problems and pursue deep change and both/and solutions rather than quick or easy fixes.

It will not be easy to implement the big ideas. For one, there are political barriers. The slow but certain impacts from climate change are occurring at a pace that challenges elected leaders, and their voters, given the limited terms of office and the urgency of other economic and social issues. Meanwhile, although the larger concerns of state residents and voters overlap, there is divergence—often by social identity and political party—about what the appropriate role for the state is in resolving those issues. Many residents are unhappy with the current political system and are not optimistic about its ability to address big problems. A third barrier is that many of the commonly used tools and practices in planning, development, management, and public administration are outdated or too narrow to address the root causes of problems, to fully consider structural inequalities like colonialism and racism, or to think through the impacts to future generations. A fourth challenge comes from the wealthy and powerful, who benefit financially from current systems and may contest any deep changes that threaten their wealth or power. While we must acknowledge these challenges, they cannot be used as justification for inaction. Not taking on the big ideas means letting Oregon get worse in a lot of environmental and social areas. It would mean not leaving our state better for future generations. The authors in this book do not see that as a good choice.

Collectively, the big ideas presented here offer a new and more equitable, sustainable direction for Oregon by 2050. The path toward implementation of these big ideas is not necessarily clear or easy, and there will likely be opposition, especially when the big ideas confront historical powerful structures or require funding from actors that do not want to pay. But they set us down a path of leaving our state better for future generations. These big ideas carry on the legacy of Tom McCall, cofounder of 1000 Friends of Oregon and Oregon's thirtieth governor, who signed SB 100 into law:

> You and I shouldn't claim we love Oregon more than anyone else, but that we love Oregon as much as anyone. Our thoughts today, and our deliberations to come, must spring from our determination to keep Oregon lovable and to make it even more livable.

We, too, love Oregon, and this book is our love letter to this state. We hope this book provides a platform for common knowledge of patterns, trends, projections, and foresight across a range of issues important to Oregonians and our shared future. We also hope the big ideas raised here contribute to deep discussions and, ultimately, to advancing policy and other changes at the state and other levels.

Contributors

SY ADLER is professor emeritus of urban studies and planning at Portland State University. He also served as director of the Toulan School of Urban Studies and Planning and associate dean and interim dean of PSU's College of Urban and Public Affairs. He taught history and theory of planning in the Toulan School starting in 1982. His publications about the Oregon statewide land use planning program include: co-editing *Planning the Oregon Way* (1994); co-authoring *Planning a New West: The Columbia River Gorge National Scenic Area* (1997); and authoring *Oregon Plans: The Making of an Unquiet Land-Use Revolution* (2012) and *Planning the Portland Urban Growth Boundary: The Struggle to Transform Trend City* (2022), all published by Oregon State University Press. He earned a PhD in city and regional planning from University of California, Berkeley, in 1980.

CARLOS ANDRÉS ARIAS holds a BA in anthropology from the University of Alaska, Anchorage; an MA in applied anthropology from California State University, Long Beach; and an MPP from Portland State University. He is currently pursuing a PhD in public affairs and policy at Portland State University, focused on sustainable development initiatives in cases of civil disorder in the Global South. Professionally, he has worked as a design researcher and strategist for organizations like the Beeck Center for Social Impact and Innovation at Georgetown University and Nike.

EMMA BROPHY worked as a research economist at Portland State University for six years, where she also taught introductory economics following the completion of her BS and MS in 2017, both in economics. Her areas of specialty are regional and impact analysis, and credited reports with the Northwest Economic Research Center include topics such as media production, the accessory dwelling unit market, clean fuels, homelessness, and prosperity metrics.

MELIA CHASE graduated with a Masters of Urban Studies degree from Portland State University in 2021. She assisted with some of the data collection, writing, and fact-checking for this book.

RICHARD A. CLUCAS is a professor of political science in the Department of Politics and Global Affairs at Portland State University and the executive director of the Western Political Science Association, the nation's second largest regional political science association. His expertise includes legislative politics, state government, and democratic reform. Among other works, he is co-editor of *Governing Oregon*, co-author of *The Character of Democracy*, editor of *Readings and Cases in State and Local Politics*, and author of *Encyclopedia of American Political Reform*. He was also the set editor for the encyclopedia series, *About State Government*.

SHANE DAY is an associate professor of public administration in the Mark O. Hatfield School of Government at Portland State University, and an affiliated faculty member of the Ostrom Workshop at Indiana University – Bloomington. His research and teaching interests are in natural resource management, environmental policy, Native American and comparative indigenous group governance, economic development, international relations, public policy theory, policy analysis, and program evaluation.

MATTHEW GEBHARDT is an Associate Professor at Portland State University. He teaches classes in the Real Estate Program and in Urban Studies and Planning. His research focuses on how institutions, financing tools, regulations, and other factors can either impede or ease plan implementation. He is interested in how the public and private sector can work together to promote sustainability and social justice. Prior to joining academia, Dr. Gebhardt worked as a senior associate for an interdisciplinary consulting firm in Chicago.

CONTRIBUTORS

JACEN GREENE is the co-founder and assistant director of Portland State University's Homelessness Research & Action Collaborative, a multidisciplinary research center dedicated to addressing homelessness through a racial equity lens. He previously designed and managed social innovation programs at Portland State University, and is an instructor, speaker, and author on social entrepreneurship. Jacen holds an MBA in sustainability from Portland State University.

DANA HELLMAN is an environmental social scientist and climate adaptation consultant. She conducts assessments to help cities and communities understand the human impacts of climate change and identify appropriate solutions. Her work emphasizes themes including resilience, disproportionate hazard exposure, collaborative approaches, and (sense of) place. Her research has been published in outlets including *International Journal of Environmental Research & Public Health* and *Natural Hazards*. She holds a PhD in earth, environment & society from Portland State University.

MEGAN HORST is associate professor in the Toulan School of Urban Studies and Planning at Portland State University. Her research and practice focuses include climate action, food justice, and land use planning. Her work has appeared in publications such as the *Journal of the American Planning Association, Journal of Planning Theory and Practice*, and in books by the Planners' Press. She is currently the Director of the Masters of Urban and Regional Planning (MURP) program. She has a PhD in urban design and planning from the University of Washington.

PETER HULSEMAN is the city economist for the City of Portland. Prior to 2021, he held the role of senior economist at Portland State University's Northwest Economic Research Center, where he conducted economic policy and macroeconomic analysis, forecasting, and demographic modeling for clients from across the Portland metro region. Peter has also served as an adjunct faculty member teaching economics courses at Portland State University, and has served on the Bureau of Development Services Finance Committee for the past six years. Peter received his BA in mathematics from the University of Portland and his MS in economics from Portland State University.

JENNY H. LIU is associate professor of urban studies and planning at Portland State University, assistant director of the Northwest Economic Research Center (NERC), and director of the Center for Urban Studies. She is an applied environmental and transportation economist with a focus on public policy, sustainability, economic development, and social equity. She has served on the Oregon Governor's Council of Economic Advisors since 2020. She holds a PhD in agricultural and resource economics from University of California, Berkeley.

JOHN MACARTHUR is the sustainable transportation program manager at TREC at Portland State University. He is active in research related to sustainable and equitable transportation, particularly in the areas of emerging technologies, e-bikes, bike share, transit, and the relationship between transportation and public health. He also co-founded the Light Electric Vehicle Education and Research (LEVER) Institute. John holds a MS in environmental health sciences from the School of Public Health at the University of Michigan and a BS in Civil Engineering from Lehigh University.

MORIAH MCSHARRY MCGRATH is a teaching assistant professor in the School of Urban Studies and Planning at Portland State University (PSU). Her work centers on the interplay between public health and urban planning, including topics such as housing, environmental justice, and infectious disease. She holds a PhD in urban studies from PSU, master's degrees in urban planning and public health from Columbia University, and a BA in reminist and gender studies from Haverford College.

ARTHUR C. NELSON was a Portland State University student intern on the joint legislative land use committee that wrote SB 100 in 1972, which was adopted in 1973. He later served in various planning capacities including county planning director and planning consultant. Nelson earned his PhD in urban studies at PSU in 1984 and proceeded to serve at numerous universities including: Georgia Tech where he cofounded the nation's only dual planning and law degree (between Georgia Tech and Georgia State); Virginia Tech where he founded the graduate planning and urban affairs program serving the national capital region;

the University of Utah where he founded the Metropolitan Research Center, the master of real estate development degree, and the doctoral degree in metropolitan planning, policy, and design; and the University of Arizona where he was inaugural associate dean for research in the College of Architecture, Planning and Landscape Architecture and designed the nation's largest and top-rated online master of real estate development program, which has a unique focus on responsible and sustainable real estate development. He has written more than twenty books, has more than four hundred other publications, and has been principal investigator or co-PI on more than $50 million in grants. Nelson is University of Utah emeritus presidential professor of city and metropolitan planning and University of Arizona emeritus professor of urban planning and real estate development.

CONNIE P. OZAWA is professor emerita of urban studies and planning at Portland State University where she taught environmental policy since 1994, served as school director (2009-2015), and chaired the national Planning Accreditation Board (2018-2020). She has published on the application of negotiation theory to promote collaborative planning in several journals and edited books, is author of *Recasting Science*, and editor and co-editor of *The Portland Edge* and *Planning the Pacific Northwest*. Her PhD was awarded from the Massachusetts Institute of Technology.

VIVEK SHANDAS is a professor of climate adaptation and founding director of the Sustaining Urban Places Research Lab at Portland State University. He studies the effects of urban development patterns and processes on environmental health and social justice. He serves on the National Urban and Community Forestry Advisory Council, Oregon State Climate Rules Advisory Committee, Portland Metro's Regional Bond Oversight Committee, and is the former chair of the City of Portland's Urban Forestry Commission. He received his PhD in urban design and planning from the University of Washington.

ETHAN SHARYGIN is director of the Population Research Center and a research professor at Portland State University. His recent work concerns statistical adjustments to improve census data and new race and ethnicity classifications. He also researches demographic consequences of disasters such as famine and wildfire, data development for environmental justice assessments, and methodology for small area estimation. He holds a PhD in demography from the University of Pennsylvania.

TYLER WOLFE is a 2023 graduate of the Public Affairs and Policy PhD program in the Mark O. Hatfield School of Government at Portland State University. Prior to doctoral work he received his MPA degree from the Evergreen State College and a BA in behavioral health from Southwestern College.

MARISA A. ZAPATA is an Associate Professor of Land-Use Planning at Portland State University and Director of PSU's Homelessness Research & Action Collaborative. As an educator, scholar, and planner, Dr. Zapata is committed to achieving spatially based social justice by preparing planners to act in the face of the uncertain and inequitable futures we face. She believes how we use land reflects our social and cultural values.

Index

#
100-Year Water Vision for Oregon, 19
2015 Climate Action Plan (Portland), 71
2020 Biennial Energy Report, 124

A
Abbott, Carl, 11, 16
accessory dwelling units (ADUs), 47, 145, 154
Adler, Sy, 1–28, 435
Affordable HOME (Housing Opportunities Made Equitable) Act, 168
African Americans. *See* Black Oregonians
agriculture
   agricultural labor, 15, 279, 296
   climate change and, 64, 131
   water and, 131, 133, 181
   See also farmland
air quality, 93–99, 107, 222–223
Akinjiola, Oluyinka, 260
Albany, 254
Albina (Portland), 15, 149, 209
alcohol-related deaths, 41
Almanac of American Politics, 400
American Community Survey (ACS), 275, 282–284, 286, 288, 290–291
American Farmland Trust, 176, 179–181
American Institute of Architects, 3
American Institute of Certified Planners, vii–ix
American Planning Association, 3–4
American Public Health Association (APHA), 89
American Rescue Plan Act (2021), 82, 329
American Society of Civil Engineers, 187, 194
American Society of Landscape Architects, 3
Americans for the Arts (AFTA), 254–255
Amtrak, 230
Angelou, Maya, 260
Arias, Carlos, 115–136, 435
Arkin, Lisa, 110
Armenian blackberry, 130
Art in the High Desert, 243, 258
Art-Collecting.com, 255
arts and culture, 243–270
ArtsCare Program, 248
Ashland, 64, 183, 191, 195, 243
Asian Oregonians, 43, 52–53, 90, 283–286
   elections and, 410, 416–417
   housing and, 150, 311–312
   incarceration and, 341, 360
Asian Pacific American Network of Oregon (APANO), 249, 419
asthma, 64, 89, 93, 96–99, 223
Astoria, 183
Atiyeh, Victor, 17
autonomous vehicles, 234–236

B
baby boomers, 33, 44–45, 213
Baker City, 177, 183, 189, 282
Baker County, 281
bald eagles, 129
"ballot box zoning," 196
ballot initiatives, 401, 405–406
   See also specific ballot measures
Ballot Measure 5 (1990), 374, 385–387, 393, 395

Ballot Measure 11 (1994), 342, 357
Ballot Measure 17 (1994), 341
Ballot Measure 37 (2004), 12–13, 17–18, 178–179
Ballot Measure 49 (2007), 12–13, 18, 178–179, 202
Ballot Measure 50 (1997), 374, 385–386, 395
Ballot Measure 57 (2008), 360
Ballot Measure 85 (2012), 385
Ballot Measure 90 (2014), 418
Ballot Measure 110 (2020), 362
Ballot Measure 113 (2022), 405
Basic Facts (Legislative Revenue Office), 374
battery electric vehicles (BEVs), 218–219
Beach Bill (1967), 5
Beaverton, 195, 349
Been Ready, 260
Behavioral Health Justice Reinvestment Initiative, 359
Behavioral Health Resource Network (BHRN), 362–363
Bend
    the arts and, 243, 248
    climate change and, 67, 71
    housing and, 169, 188, 195
    transportation and, 221
    urban growth boundary of, 184
Benton County, 354
Beyond Toxics, 97–99, 110
Big Look Task Force, 17
birth rates, 40–45
Black exclusion, 14, 317
Black Lives Matter (BLM), 359
Black Oregonians, 14–16, 43, 52
    the arts and, 260
    economic inequities and, 277, 283–286, 377
    elections and, 409–410, 416–417
    environmental justice and, 71, 90, 102
    health inequities and, 223
    housing and, 146–147, 149–150, 164, 308, 310–312, 319, 323, 327
    incarceration and, 339–341, 357, 359
    mental health and, 346, 361
    SUD treatment programs and, 353–354
    voting and, 401, 409–410
Blumenauer, Earl, 168
Bottle Bill (1971), 5

Bracero Program, 15
Brendale v. Confederated Yakima Indian Nation (1989), 187–188
Brookings Institution, 248
Brophy, Emma, 275–302, 435–436
Brown, Kate, viii, 18–19, 69, 174, 217
Bruun, Scott, 396
Budget Highlights (Legislative Revenue Office), 380
budget of Oregon, 373–395
Business Oregon, 250–251, 267, 281, 297
Bybee Lakes Hope Center, 360

C

California State University, 311
Campbell, Brian, vii–ix, 205
Canada, 194
cancer, 89, 93, 96, 109–110, 223, 247
Cannon Beach, 77
Carney, Sadie, 28
Cascadia Health, 350
Cascadia Subduction Zone, 65, 73–74, 210, 220, 224
cash bail, 358
cash transfers, 326
Cedar Mills Hospital, 349
Center on Budget and Policy Priorities, 385
Centers for Disease Control and Prevention (CDC), 89, 92–93
Central City Concern, 328
Centro Latino Americano, 97–98
Challenges and Costs of Rapid Population Growth, 10
CHAMP, 252
Chase, Melia, 175–205, 339–364, 436
Child Care Aware of America, 288
childcare, 277, 287–289, 300–301
China, People's Republic of, 294
Chinese Exclusion Acts, 15
City Observatory, 227
Clackamas County, 11, 282, 323, 345, 354, 358, 404
Clatsop County, 355
Clean Air Act (1963), 92, 96
Clean Electricity and Coal Transition Act, 124
Clean Water Act (1972), 92, 96, 131
climate change, 59, 62–65, 68–72
    housing and, 187, 319

INDEX 443

infrastructure and, 195, 220, 228
water and, 131–132
Climate Change Adaptation Framework, 69
Climate Emergency Workplan (Portland), 71, 183
Climate Friendly Equitable Communities, 83
Clucas, Richard A., 243–270, 398–425, 436
Coalition of Communities of Color, 359–360
Columbia County, 183, 344, 355
Columbia River Intertribal Fisheries Commission, 120
Commission of Environmental Quality, 70
committees for citizen involvement (CCI), 7
Common Cause, 419
community development financial institutions (CDFIs), 169–170
Community Emergency Response Team (CERT), 72, 76–77
compact neighborhoods, 181–183, 186–187
Confederated Tribes of Grand Ronde, 176, 205, 350
Confederated Tribes of the Umatilla Indian Reservation (CTUIR), 10, 119–120, 187–188, 260
Confederated Tribes of Warm Springs (CTWS), 99–100, 110, 119–120
Congo, Democratic Republic of, 301
Continuums of Care (CoCs), 310, 321
cooperatives and community land trusts (CLTs), 168–169
Coos County, 342, 355, 360–361
Corbett, 91
corporate activity tax (CAT), 388–390
Cortright, Joe, 227–228
Corvallis, 183, 248
Council for Aging, 248
COVID-19 pandemic
the arts and, 258, 265–266
economic inequities and, 295
Education Stability Fund (ESF) and, 383
housing and, 158, 308, 310, 327
life expectancy and, 40

Crisis Assistance Helping Out On The Streets (CAHOOTS), 328–329, 358
Crook County, 185
Crow's Shadow Institute of the Arts, 260
culture and the arts, 243–270

D

Dalles, The, 184
Dammasch State Hospital, 348
Daniels, Katherine, 205
Dawes Act (1887), 176
Day, Shane, 115–136, 436
Death and Life of Great American Cities, 11
Decent, Affordable, Safe Housing (DASH) for All Act, 168
deinstitutionalization, 346–348
Democratic Party, 403–404, 412–413
Deschutes County, 156, 185, 254, 282
descriptive representation, 414
diabetes, 222–223
disabilities and people with disabilities
the arts and, 248, 260–261, 265
economic inequities and, 290–292
environmental hazards and, 60–61
homelessness and, 314–315, 318, 322
incarceration and, 339–340, 342, 359
transportation and, 211, 229, 235
Donation Land Claim Act (1850), 13–14, 176
doubled-up homelessness, 310–313
Douglas County, 181, 183, 191
drought, 62–67, 107, 130, 132

E

earned income tax credit (EITC), 299
earthquakes, 59, 65–66, 73–80, 187, 210, 220, 224
Eastern Oregon Opioid Solutions, 362
economic development districts (EDDs), 280–281
Education Stability Fund (ESF), 381–383
elderly people. *See* older adults
Emergency Volunteer Corp, 77
Endangered Species Act (1973), 118, 127–129, 132
energy efficiency, 72, 124–127, 133, 158
Engaging the Future, 5
Environ Utah, 19

environmental hazards. *See* drought; earthquakes; flooding; wildfires
environmental justice, 78, 90–92, 96–104
Environmental Protection Agency (EPA), 92, 133
environmental quality, 88–110, 115
See also air quality; water quality
Ernst & Young, 389
Eugene
  the arts and, 254
  CAHOOTS and, 328–329, 358
  climate change and, 71, 231
  economy of, 186
  environmental justice issues and, 91, 96–98
  housing and, 149, 164
  transportation and, 216, 229–231, 233
Evans, Taren, 205
evictions and eviction prevention, 326–327
exclusive farm use (EFU) zones, 18, 178–180, 195
Executive Order 20-04, 18, 69, 174

F

Fair Housing Act (1968), 149
Falls City, 181
Family Sentencing Alternative Pilot Program (FSAPP), 358
farmland, 6–7, 12, 18, 34, 178–181, 191, 193–195, 429–430
  renewable energy and, 117, 125
Federal Emergency Management Agency (FEMA), 70, 72, 79, 296
Federal Highway Act (1956), 177
Federal Reserve, 157, 162–163, 277, 295
fertility rates, 44–45
flooding, 7, 63, 73, 103, 107, 199–200, 220, 319
Florida 2070, 19
Floyd, George, 401
food stamps, 301, 380
Foote, Hilary, 205
Foresight As a Strategic Long-Term Planning Tool for Developing Countries, 4
Forest Practices Act, 10, 122
forestlands, 7, 12, 18, 57, 116–124, 176, 178–181, 185, 190–196, 203, 429–430
  water quality and, 77, 122, 181

forestry, 115–124, 181, 185–186, 193, 203, 281, 296
fossil fuels, 214–215, 219, 231–232
  taxation on, 383

G

Gailey, Matthew, 261
Garcia-Hallett, Janet, 363
gas taxes, 231–232
Gebhardt, Matthew, 436
gender pay gap, 287–288, 298
geothermal energy, 126–127
Gilliam County, 96, 343
Gini coefficient, 275
GivingUSA, 258–259
goals. *See* Oregon's Statewide Planning Goals
Gold Beach, 76
Grants Pass, 191
gray wolves, 129
Great Recession, 276–277, 293
Green Party, 419
Greene, Jacen, 307–332, 437
greenhouse gas (GHG) emissions, 69–70, 147, 209, 214–218, 227–228, 296, 389–390, 429
Gresham, 168, 229
gross domestic product (GDP) of Oregon, 276
Growing Smart Legislative Guidebook, 19

H

haloacetic acids five (HAA5), 93–95, 99
Halprin, Lawrence, vii
Handy, Susan, 219
Harney County, 282
Hatfield, Mark, 250
Hatfield Marine Science Center, 75
HazVu, 67, 74
Health Share of Oregon, 322
Hellman, Dana, 88–110, 437
High Desert Collaborative, 81
high-rise development, 160–162
Hillsboro, 183, 229
Hispanic Oregonians. *See* Latino Oregonians
Historical Context of Racist Planning, 177

INDEX

homelessness, 64, 152, 156–157, 289, 307–332, 356, 363
Homelessness Management Information System (HMIS), 321
Homelessness Research and Action Collaborative (HRAC), 165, 311, 313–315, 323, 329
Hood River, 195, 243
Hood River County, 254, 343, 354, 411
Hopkins, Lewis D., 5
Horning, Tom, 110
Horst, Megan, viii, 1–28, 175–205, 437
House Bill 2001 (2019), 154
House Bill 2001 (2020), 18, 201, 217
House Bill 2003 (2019), 154
House Bill 2017 (2017), 187, 232
House Bill 2086 (2021), 361
House Bill 2186 (2009), 217
House Bill 2949 (2021), 361
House Bill 3078 (2017), 342
House Bill 3115 (2021), 317, 328
House Bill 3194 (2013), 342, 357
House Bill 3427 (2019), 388
House Bill 3503 (2015), 358
housing, 44–48, 53–54, 145–172, 323–326, 363
"housing first" model, 321–323
housing needs analyses (HNAs), 33, 150, 154–157
Howe, Deborah, 16
Hulseman, Peter, 373–395, 437
Human Rights Campaign, 290
hydropower, 127

I

I Love Lucy, 45
Imarisha, Walidah, 13
incarceration, 339–364
income inequality, 275, 283–292
 tax kicker and, 385
 See also poverty
income taxes, 299, 376–378, 381, 392
Independent Venue Coalition, 255
Indian Citizenship Act (1924), 401
Indigenous peoples. *See* Native Americans
infill development, 159–160, 183–184, 195, 197–203
Inflation Reduction Act (2022), 70, 193–194

in-migrations, 41–43
Intercity Bus, 230
International Panel on Climate Change (IPCC), 62, 68, 71
international trade, 294–296
invasive species, 129–130

J

Jackson County, 71, 158, 185, 254, 344
Jacksonville, 177
Jacobs, Jane, 11
Jefferson County, 99
Jordan Schnitzer Museum, 269
Josephine County, 344–345
Junction City, 349
Justice Reinvestment Initiative, 357

K

Kaiser, Henry, 15
Keller Auditorium, 269
Kelley, Gil, vii–ix
"kicker," 383–385, 395
Kitzhaber, John, 250–251, 403
Klamath County, 344
Klamath Falls, 67, 126
Klamath Restoration Act (1986), 120
Klamath Termination Act (1953), 119–120
Klamath Tribes of Southern Oregon, 119–120
Klamath Water Project, 132–133
Kulongoski, Ted, 17, 252

L

La Grande, 84, 157, 183, 189
labor force participation rate, 277, 282–283, 287
Lake County, 96, 126, 282, 342, 360–361
Lake Oswego, 152
Lakeview, 126
Land Conservation and Development Commission (LCDC), 9, 34–35, 70, 279–280
 See also Oregon Department of Land Conservation and Development (DLCD)
land reform, 204–205
Land Use Board of Appeals (LUBA), 6, 9
land value taxes (LVT), 203–204, 394

Latino Oregonians, 15–16, 52–53, 189, 213
   the arts and, 259–260
   economic inequities and, 283–286
   elections and, 409–411, 416–417
   environmental justice and, 97–98
   homelessness and, 311–312, 323, 327
   mental health and, 346
   SUD treatment programs and, 353
Lavadour, James, 260
lead poisoning, 96
Lead-Safe Housing Rule, 96
League of Women Voters of Oregon, 419–420
Legislative Revenue Office's (LRO), 374, 380
Lehner, Joshua, 28, 302, 396
Lewis and Clark College, 268
Leymon, Mark, 364
LGBTQ+ Oregonians, 289–290, 298, 319, 340, 359
Libertarian Party, 419
libraries, 186, 244, 387
life expectancy, 40
Lincoln City, 75
Lincoln County, 185–186, 190, 355
Lincoln Institute of Land Policy, 19
Lindblom, Charles, 77
Linn County, 6, 185, 355
Liu, Jenny H., 275–302, 373–395, 438
Local Initiatives Fast Track (LIFT), 153, 163
Lottery Funds, 380–381
low-income housing tax credits (LIHTCs), 155, 163

M

MacArthur, John, 209–236, 438
Malheur County, 96, 189, 282, 355, 411
manufacturing, 277–278, 283, 292–294
Manzanita, 77
marbled murrelets, 128
Marion County, 192, 345, 360–361
Martin v. Boise, 317
Martinez, Dan, 110
Marylhurst University, 268
McCall, Tom, vii, 6, 434
McCurdy, Mary Kyle, 205
McGrath, Moriah McSharry, 339–364, 438

McMinnville, 177
McPherson, Hector, 6
Medford, 40, 67, 168, 184, 191, 248
Medicaid, 322, 329, 348, 350, 353–354, 359, 380
Medication Assisted Treatment-Prescription Drug and Opioid Addiction Project, 362
medication-assisted treatment (MAT), 354–356, 360, 362
mental health, 318, 345–352, 359, 361
Mental Health and Addiction Certification Board of Oregon, 361
Merkley, Jeff, 82, 168
Metro (regional government), 11–12, 193
   economy of, 293
   housing and, 153, 163, 325, 327
   sprawl and, 190–191
   transportation and, 225–230, 234–235
metropolitan planning organizations (MPOs), 193, 212
micromobility, 229, 234
Milagro Theater, 259
minimum wage, 293, 299–300
mixed-income neighborhoods, 185
mixed-use neighborhoods, 181–183, 190
Moloch, Harvey, 77
Morrow County, 181, 411
mountain pine beetles, 129–130
Move-In Multnomah, 326
Multnomah County, 11, 254, 282, 301, 323, 345, 350, 354–355, 358, 404
Mumford, Lewis, 2

N

National Assembly of State Arts Agencies (NASAA), 253, 258
National Association for the Advancement of Colored People (NAACP), 419
National Association of Realtors, 47
National Drought Mitigation Center, 67
National Endowment for the Arts (NEA), 243, 245, 250, 255, 261
National Endowment for the Humanities (NEH), 250
National Energy Policy Act (1969), 133
National Flood Insurance Program (NFIP), 73, 175

INDEX

National Foundation on the Arts and Humanities Act (1965), 250
National Renewable Energy Laboratory (NREL), 125
Native American Rehabilitation Association of the Northwest (NARA), 354
Native Americans, 10, 13–14, 176–177, 204–205
   elections and, 401, 416
   environmental hazards and, 77
   health inequities and, 223
   housing and, 148–150, 308–312
   incarceration and, 339, 341, 357, 359–360
   mental health and, 350, 361
   SUD treatment programs and, 353–354, 362
   See also specific peoples, tribes, and organizations
Natural Hazards Mitigation Plan, 69
Nature Conservancy, The, 132
negative income tax, 299
Nehalem, 77
Neighborhood Emergency Teams (NETs), 76
Nelson, Arthur C., 1–28, 31–54, 438–439
Netusil, Noelwah, 279–280, 296, 302
Network for Oregon Affordable Housing (NOAH), 170
New Leaf Project (Vancouver, BC), 326
"New Majority," 32, 35–39, 51–53
New Yorker, 65
Nez Perce Tribe, 120
Nicholson, Dan, 110
Ninth Circuit Court of Appeals, 317, 328
nonaffiliated voters, 412–413
North Bethany County Service District for Roads (NBCSDR), 196
North Coast Land Conservancy, 77
Northeast Oregon Area Health Education Center, 360–361
Northeast Oregon Economic Development District, 281
Northern Oregon Corrections (NORCOR), 343–344
northern spotted owls, 128
Northwest Economic Research Center (NERC), 313–315, 385–386, 390, 394, 438

Northwest Forest Plan, 121, 123
Nyssa, 184

O

"O&C lands," 121
obesity, 69, 182, 223, 248
Oil Pollution Act (1990), 92
older adults, 48–51, 282
   the arts and, 265
   climate change and, 64–65, 100–101
   community-based services and, 248, 350, 355
   housing and, 45, 314
   transportation and, 211, 213, 229, 235
"One Strike, You're Out," 357
Ontario, 189
Oregon 2000 Commission, 10–11
Oregon Arts Commission (OAC), 250–251, 261, 264
Oregon Board of Forestry, 122–123
Oregon Business and Industry, 389
Oregon Cares, 298
Oregon Center on Behavioral Health and Justice Integration, 362
Oregon Climate Change Research Institute (OCCRI), 68
Oregon College of Art and Craft, 268
Oregon Community Foundation, 258, 264
Oregon Constitution, 14, 341, 358, 385, 396, 405–406
Oregon Criminal Justice Commission, 357
Oregon Cultural Trust (OCT), 251, 255–259, 261, 266–269
Oregon Department of Agriculture, 118, 130
Oregon Department of Corrections, 318, 341–343, 359–360
Oregon Department of Education, 262–264
Oregon Department of Energy, 127, 217
Oregon Department of Environmental Quality (DEQ), 70, 90, 92, 103, 109, 217, 234
Oregon Department of Fish and Wildlife, 118–119
Oregon Department of Forestry, 119, 122, 129

Oregon Department of Geology and Mineral Industry (DOGAMI), 74, 118
Oregon Department of Human Services, 321, 380
Oregon Department of Land Conservation and Development (DLCD), 9–10, 69–71, 73, 90–92, 103, 117, 175, 189, 196, 201–202, 211, 279–280
See also Land Conservation and Development Commission (LCDC)
Oregon Department of State Lands, 119
Oregon Department of Transportation (ODOT), 178, 211, 217, 220–221, 223, 232, 360
Oregon Environmental Quality Commission, 217
Oregon Global Warming Commission (OGWC), 62–65, 68, 217
Oregon Health Authority (OHA)
environmental quality and, 90–104, 107, 109–110
funding of, 380
mental health and, 349–350, 359, 361
substance use disorders (SUDs) and, 359, 361–362
transportation and, 223
Oregon Health Plan, 359
Oregon Heritage Commission, 251–252
Oregon Historic Preservation Office, 251
Oregon Historical Society, 251–252
Oregon Household Activity Survey (OHAS), 210–211
Oregon Housing and Community Services (OHCS), 152–155, 161, 167, 321, 331
Oregon Humanities, 251–252, 261
Oregon Office of Film and Video, 252
Oregon Older Adult Behavioral Health Initiative, 350
Oregon Parks and Recreation Department, 118–119, 252
Oregon Public Broadcasting, 252
Oregon Rainy Day Fund (RDF), 383
Oregon Resilience Plan, 65
Oregon Seismic Safety Policy Advisory Commission (OSSPAC), 65, 73–74
Oregon Shakespeare Festival, 64, 243, 258
Oregon Shines State Strategic Plan, 18–19

Oregon State Hospital, 348–349
Oregon State University, 252
Oregon Sustainable Transportation Initiative (OSTI), 217
Oregon Trail, 13–14
Oregon Transportation Commission (OTC), 217, 232
Oregon Values and Beliefs Center, 2, 12, 178–179
Oregon Water Trust, 58, 132, 134–135
Oregon Watershed Councils, 136
Oregon Watershed Enhancement Board, 118
Oregonian, 250
Oregon's Statewide Planning Goals, 6–9
Goal 1, 7, 75, 297, 399, 406
Goal 2, 7, 178
Goal 3, 7, 178–179
Goal 4, 7, 116, 178–179
Goal 5, 7, 116, 279
Goal 6, 7, 91–92
Goal 7, 7, 68, 72–75, 82
Goal 9, 8, 33, 279–281, 296–297
Goal 10, 8, 33, 150–151, 154
Goal 11, 8, 33, 178
Goal 12, 8, 33, 212, 221
Goal 13, 8, 116–117
Goal 14, 8, 33, 151, 178, 184
Goal 18, 9, 189
Ozawa, Connie P., 59–85, 439

P

Pacific City, 195
Paisley, 126
parking, 159–161, 174, 201–202, 204, 221–222, 231–232
party list system, 420–421
Paruszkiewicz, Michael, 396
Pendleton, 189
PHAME Academy, 260
Phenomenally, 260
phylloxera, 130
Planning for States and Nation States, 19
Planning the Oregon Way, 16
"-plex" housing, 47, 54, 151, 154
plug-in hybrid electric vehicles (PHEVs), 218–219
Poet's Shadow, The, 261
point in time (PIT) counts, 310–311, 313–314, 326

Point Source Youth, 326
Polk County, 181, 183, 186
population growth, 31–54
  elections and, 404, 411
  housing and, 145, 147, 157
  natural resources and, 131–133
  transportation and, 212–216, 224–225, 229–230
Population Research Center (PRC), 32–34, 41, 48, 52–53, 225, 439
populism, 401–402
Portland, 11–12
  the arts and, 243, 249, 254–255, 259–260
  economy of, 276, 295
  environmental hazards and, 67, 71, 76, 91, 100–102
  housing and, 149, 153, 156, 158–159, 163, 166, 168–169
  infill development and, 201
  life expectancy in, 40
  population growth in, 35–39
  proportional representation and, 418–419
  redlining and, 149, 177
  "resilience hubs" and, 84
  sprawl and, 178, 183, 190–191
  transportation and, 83, 216, 221, 232
  urban growth boundary of, 159, 183–184, 195
  See also Metro (regional government)
Portland Bureau of Emergency Management (PBEM), 76
Portland City Club, 2, 11, 419, 422
Portland Clean Energy Community Benefits Fund (PCEF), 71
Portland Police Bureau, 328
Portland State University, viii, 1, 20–21, 435–440
  the arts and, 268–269
  Homelessness Research and Action Collaborative (HRAC), 165, 311, 313–315, 323, 329
  Northwest Economic Research Center (NERC), 313–315, 385–386, 390, 394, 438
  Population Research Center (PRC), 31–34, 41, 48, 52–53, 225, 439
Portland Street Response Program, 329, 358

poverty
  environmental justice and, 60, 97, 101
  policy and, 291, 326
  social inequities and, 286, 289–291, 340, 356
Prineville, 188
Progressive Movement, 400–401
Project ECHO, 362
Project Foresight, 6
property taxes, 170–171, 178, 185–186, 193–194, 203–204, 385–387
proportional representation, 418–425
Prosper Portland, 281
Protect, To, 260
Public Employees Retirement System (PERS), 380, 391–392
public transportation, 82, 147, 227–228

R
racial diversity, 15–16, 31–32, 49–50, 52–53, 213, 282–286, 298
  the Oregon Legislature and, 415–417
racial exclusion, 14–15
  See also redlining
Randolph, Anita, 364
Rawls, John, 80
Raworth, Kate, 22
Razi-Robertson, Nadejda, 364
Reagan, Ronald, 348
Red Lodge Transition Services, 360
redlining, 90, 102, 109, 148–150, 177
Redmond, 188
regional housing needs analyses, 150, 154–157, 171
Regional Supportive Housing Impact Fund (RSHIF), 322
regional transportation plans (RTPs), 212, 225, 227
Rejoice! Diaspora Dance Theater, 260
renewable resources, 116–117, 124–127
rent assistance, 325–326
rental housing, 146, 148, 152, 155, 157, 163–165
Republican Party, 403–404, 412–413
"resilience hubs," 84
Resource Conservation and Recovery Act (1976), 92
restorative justice, 356–357

retirement, 49–51
  See also Public Employees Retirement System (PERS)
ridesharing, 234
road usage fees, 231–232
rush skeletonweed, 130

S

Safe Routes to School Program (SRTS), 224
Safe Water Drinking Act (1974), 131
Sahaptin peoples, 176
Salem, 71, 216, 221
sales taxes, 178, 375, 382–383, 403
Salish peoples, 176
salmon, 128
Sanchagrin, Ken, 364
Sandoval, Gerard, 28
Save Portland Buildings, 76
Schuster, Mark, 246
Scotch broom, 130
seafood industry, 64
Seaside, 77
Seattle, Washington, 231, 300, 326–327
Seismic Rehabilitation Grant Program, 74
self-serve gas stations, 402–403
Seltzer, Ethan, 28
Senate Bill 8 (2021), 155
Senate Bill 96 (1991), 73
Senate Bill 100 (1973), vii, 5–6, 31–40, 43, 53, 211, 244
  See also Oregon's Statewide Planning Goals
Senate Bill 145 (1967), 250
Senate Bill 608 (2019), 154
Senate Bill 762 (2021), 73, 79
Senate Bill 1008 (2018), 357
Senate Bill 1051 (2017), 154
seniors. *See* older adults
seventh-generation thinking, 2
severance taxes, 186
Shakespeare Company, The, 64
Shandas, Vivek, 88–110, 439
shared-equity housing, 168–169
Sharygin, Ethan, 31–54, 439–440
Sherman County, 343
Siegel, Dave, vii–ix, 205
Sierra Club, 132

Sifuentes, Julie, 110
Sightline Institute, 422
single transferable vote (STV), 419–420
single-family homes, 47–48, 54, 149, 179, 183, 197–200, 204
single-person households, 44, 46–47, 53
Sisters, 157, 188
smart growth, 19, 197–201, 224–225
Smith, Brenda, 110
social determinants of health, 103–105, 222
solar energy, 84–85, 116–117, 125, 133–134, 192
species diversity, 127–130
Sperling, Daniel, 234
sprawl, 177–178, 181–183, 194–195, 197–200
Springfield, 329
Statewide Housing Plan (SHP), 152–153
Statewide Transportation Strategy (STS), 217
strategic foresight, 4
Straub, Robert W., 10–11
Studio at Living Opportunities, 248
substance use disorders (SUDs), 41, 318, 353–355, 357–363
suicide, 40–41
Sullivan, Edward, 279–280, 296, 302
Superfund, 92
Supplemental Nutrition Assistance Program (SNAP), 301, 380
syringe services programs, 362
systems development charges (SDCs), 194–195

T

Targeted Response to the Opinion Crisis Program, 362
taxes, 302, 374–379
  tax base sharing, 204
  See also corporate activity tax (CAT); earned income tax credit (EITC); income taxes; "kicker"; land value taxes (LVT); property taxes; sales taxes; severance taxes
tenant opportunity to purchase (TOP), 170
Three Revolutions, 234
Tillett, Paddy, vii–ix

tourism
  the arts and, 252, 255, 265
  COVID-19 pandemic and, 295
  environmental hazards and, 63–64, 77, 191
Tovey, J. D., 205
transgender Oregonians, 289–290
  See also LGBTQ+ Oregonians
transportation, 82, 147, 186, 193, 209–236
Transportation and Growth Management Program (TGM), 212
Travel Oregon, 252
Treatment Advocacy Center, 346
Tribal Health System, 350
trihalomethanes (TTHM), 93–95, 99
TriMet, 193, 227–228, 230
Troutdale, 297

U

Umatilla County, 185, 344, 411
unemployment insurance, 301
Union County, 281
United Nations Development Programme, 4
United States Bureau of Economic Analysis (BEA), 243, 253–254, 276
United States Bureau of Labor Statistics (BLS), 243, 254, 278, 288
United States Bureau of Land Management (BLM), 117–118, 121–122
United States Bureau of Reclamation, 132–133
United States Census Bureau, 39, 255, 266, 282–283, 290–291, 408–409
United States Department of Agriculture, 60, 279
United States Department of Defense, 121
United States Department of Education, 310
United States Department of Housing and Urban Development, 156, 310–313, 331
United States Department of Justice, 328, 349
United States Federal Housing Administration (FHA), 149
United States Fish and Wildlife Service (FWS), 117–118, 121–122, 127
United States Forest Service (USFS), 117–118, 121–122
United States Immigration and Customs Enforcement (ICE), 344–345
United States Internal Revenue Service, 256–257
United States National Guard, 349
United States National Marine Fisheries Service (NMFS), 127
United States National Park Service (NPS), 117–118
Unity Behavioral Health Center, 349
universal basic income, 298–299, 326
Universal Health Services, 349
University of Arizona, 327
University of Nebraska-Lincoln, 67
University of Oregon, 268
University of Oxford, 22
University of Washington, 300
unreinforced masonry buildings (URMs), 76, 79
unsheltered people, 307–308
  See also homelessness
urban and rural divide, 13, 21, 282, 403–410
urban growth boundaries (UGBs), 6, 9, 33, 159–161, 181–184, 195–196, 201–202
urban growth management areas (UGMAs), 201
urban heat island effect, 100–102, 182, 185, 239
Urban Indian Health Care Program, 354
Utah, 19

V

Vancouver, British Columbia, 230–231, 326
Vanport, 15
vehicle miles traveled (VMT), 215–217, 219–220, 222, 225, 227–231
voting, 398–425

W

Walla Walla Tribe, 260
Wallowa County, 189, 281
Wasco County, 99, 189, 343
Washington, DC, 322

Washington County, 11, 181, 183, 194, 282, 323, 345, 404
water quality, 93–96, 99–100, 131–134, 181
Weyerhaeuser, 75, 185
Wheeler, 77
Wheeler County, 189, 282, 354
White Bird Clinic, 328–329
wildfires, 59–64, 67, 73, 79–81, 124, 181, 187–188
   housing and, 158, 319
wildland urban interface (WUI), 181, 187
Willamette Valley Choices for the Future, The, vii
Willamette Valley Environmental Protection Plan, 6
Wilson, Jay, 110
Wilsonville, 229, 348–349
wind-generated energy, 116–117, 125–126, 133–134
Wolfe, Tyler, 115–136, 440

women Oregonians
   gender pay gap, 287–289
   homelessness and, 318
   incarceration and, 342–343
   the Oregon Legislature and, 414–423
   women's suffrage, 400–401
World Health Organization, 247
Wuschke, Katie, 364
Wyden, Ron, 82, 168

Y

Yakama Nation, 120
Yamhill County, 181, 183, 185, 192
Yaquina Bay, 75
Your Utah, Your Future, 19

Z

Zapata, Marisa A., 5, 307–332, 440
zero-emission vehicles (ZEVs), 217–219, 227, 233–236